COMMONALITIES

To my wife Sharla,
and my children, Ricky and Annika.
May our family be together forever.

COMMONALITIES

A Positive Look at Latter-day Saints from a Bahá'í Perspective

Serge van Neck

GEORGE RONALD · OXFORD

George Ronald, Publisher Ltd.
www.grbooks.com

ISBN 978-0-85398-537-2

*A catalogue record for this book is available
from the British Library*

Cover design: Steiner Graphics

CONTENTS

Prayer for America

O Thou kind Lord! This gathering is turning to Thee. These hearts are radiant with Thy love. These minds and spirits are exhilarated by the message of Thy glad-tidings.

O God! Let this American democracy become glorious in spiritual degrees even as it has aspired to material degrees, and render this just government victorious.

Confirm this revered nation to upraise the standard of the oneness of humanity, to promulgate the Most Great Peace, to become thereby most glorious and praiseworthy among all the nations of the world.

O God! This American nation is worthy of Thy favors and is deserving of Thy mercy. Make it precious and near to Thee through Thy bounty and bestowal.

'Abdu'l-Bahá

PREFACE

This book is written primarily for a Bahá'í audience. As such, it assumes a certain basic familiarity with the principles, teachings and Central Figures of the Bahá'í Faith. Unfamiliar readers are urged to read *Bahá'u'lláh and the New Era* by J. E. Esslemont, an excellent introduction to the Bahá'í Faith and its rich history. There are also many resources available on the Internet; a good starting point is the official web site of the Bahá'ís at *www.bahai.org,* as well as the official web site of the Bahá'ís of the United States at *www.bahai.us.* A comprehensive collection of the Bahá'í Sacred Writings can be found at *reference.bahai.org.*

To the Mormon reader

Mormon readers should be forewarned that while this book paints a positive picture of the Church of Jesus Christ of Latter-day Saints overall, it nevertheless contains characterizations and observations that may come across as critical. To those who feel they may take offense I offer my sincere apologies in advance, with my assurance that no offense whatever is intended.

As an eager student of the Mormon faith, I set out to read the LDS scriptures – including the Book of Mormon – with an open mind and a soft heart, and I feel that I have remained true to that goal. Yet in keeping with the principle of independent investigation of truth, I did not hesitate to put the various scriptural and doctrinal claims to the test of reason, recognizing that while faith is required to accept the Word of God, it must also appeal to man's intelligence. The Bahá'í Writings state that God 'has endowed [man] with mind or the faculty of reasoning by the exercise of which he is to investigate and discover the truth; and that which he finds real and true, he must accept. He must not be an imitator or blind follower of any soul. He must not rely implicitly upon the opinion of any man without investigation; nay, each soul must seek intelligently and independently, arriving at a real conclusion and bound only by that reality.'[1] Likewise, in the words revealed by Joseph Smith, 'you must study it out in your mind; then you must ask me if it be right, and if it is right I will cause that your bosom shall burn within you; therefore, you shall feel that it is right.'[2]

During my investigation, a number of observations forced themselves upon my mind, many of which I felt constrained to report in this book. The fact that studying the Mormon scriptures did not bring about my unconditional acceptance should not be misconstrued as a lack of appreciation for the many truths they convey. What follows is an honest, frank and – insofar as this is possible – objective report on my findings.

A note about the author

I should clarify here that unlike most commentators on the Mormon faith, I have never been a member of the Church of Jesus Christ of Latter-day Saints. While this no doubt handicaps me in terms of my knowledge of Mormon doctrine, it also relieves me of a certain stigma attached to ex-Mormons who all too often (and sometimes with justification) are dismissed as 'Mormon antagonists' – disgruntled former church members with an axe to grind, and therefore not to be taken seriously.

In fact, I had never been seriously confronted with the Mormon faith until I met my wife Sharla in 1995. Even so, it was not until after I accepted the Bahá'í Faith three years later that I started – reluctantly at first – to attend church with her to show my support. Slowly but surely, my reluctance ebbed as I began to recognize that this was in fact a great bounty from God, an opportunity for me to 'walk the talk,' as 'Abdu'l-Bahá exhorted us:

> All must abandon prejudices and must even go to each other's churches and mosques, for, in all of these worshipping places, the Name of God is mentioned. Since all gather to worship God, what difference is there? None of them worship Satan. The Muhammadans must go to the churches of the Christians and the Synagogues of the Jews, and vice versa, the others must go to the Muhammadan Mosques. They hold aloof from one another merely because of unfounded prejudices and dogmas.[3]

As time progressed, I started looking forward to church, recognizing that I had been given a unique opportunity to learn as much as I wanted about another faith, while quietly making others aware of mine. My subsequent research into the Mormon faith was driven not only by an innate curiosity, but also by a deep desire to better understand my wife's spiritual motivation.

Although both of our children have been baptized into the LDS Church, they have been taught to love both Jesus *and* Bahá'u'lláh, according to the counsel of 'Abdu'l-Bahá:

The infant, while yet a suckling, must receive Bahá'í training, and the loving spirit of Christ and Bahá'u'lláh must be breathed into him, that he may be reared in accord with the verities of the Gospel and the Most Holy Book.[4]

Personal interpretations

I've taken great pains to represent as accurately as possible the official interpretation of both Mormon and Bahá'í scripture where noted. However, this book could not have been conceived without some unconventional interpretations, particularly of the Mormon scriptures. Suffice it to say that all such interpretations, and any perceived links between the two faiths, reflect my personal opinion and are not to be taken as necessarily representing either Mormon or Bahá'í belief. Should the reader have questions concerning any issue mentioned in this book, he should research the matter independently.

Sources for this book

In starting to write this book, I decided that although it was to be geared to a Bahá'í readership, it would have to be suitable for a Mormon audience as well. Recognizing that the majority of Mormons would almost certainly take exception to my unorthodox treatment of their scriptures, I was prepared to defend my position on the basis that the Word of God is given to all of humanity and not just to a select group, and that I am entitled to my own personal interpretations as much as anyone else – Mormon or not. However, I was adamant that this book would not be criticized on the grounds that it relied upon dubious sources. While it was necessary to locate independent source materials about Mormon doctrine and history – so as not to rely solely on official church publications which might be accused of 'toeing the company line' – finding unbiased information proved to be somewhat of a challenge.

The Internet offers a profusion of information about the Church of Jesus Christ of Latter-day Saints from both official and independent sources. However, it became clear early on in my research that a number of 'independent' web sites were little more than outlets for open criticism of and hatred toward the Church. Some of these sites are operated by ex-Mormons angry and disillusioned with the church leadership and doing their best to get their story out to the world, while others are run by evangelical Christian groups hoping to convince the Mormon faithful of the error of their ways. Some notable exceptions deserve mention:

- *The Utah State Historical Society* (history.utah.org). Operated as a state agency by the State of Utah, it was founded on the 50th anniversary of the first settlement in the Salt Lake Valley by the Mormon Pioneers, and its web site contains a rich collection of Mormon historical information.

- *The Mormon History Association* (mhahome.org). The MHA is 'an independent non-profit organization dedicated to the study and understanding of all aspects of Mormon history.' Membership includes scholars from both Mormon and non-Mormon backgrounds, and the organization emphasizes scholarly and objective research. While the MHA appears to give much deference to Mormon 'loyalist' positions, it regularly publishes articles by such universally recognized dissidents as D. Michael Quinn, the respected Latter-day Saint scholar and former Brigham Young University historian who was excommunicated in 1993 over his authorship of some controversial books and articles.

Historical collections such as *History of the Church* and *Journal of Discourses*, while official church publications, are uniquely valuable to the researcher desiring to place historical events in context and to track the evolution of church practices and doctrine over time. The *Journal of Discourses* presents the spoken or written opinions of early church leaders with minimal editorialization, while the *History of the Church* provides an essentially uncensored record of the daily events that shaped the fledgling Church of Jesus Christ of Latter-day Saints. In fact, the many personal diary entries by Joseph Smith himself – including his commentaries on world events, experiences of the day, and newspaper clippings he deemed of interest – seem to transport the reader directly into the life of Smith and his close associates, making for an almost voyeuristic experience.

A great deal of valuable independent information was found in *Mormon America: The Power and The Promise* by Richard N. Ostling and Joan K. Ostling. The authors, neither of whom have ever been members of the Church of Jesus Christ of Latter-day Saints, describe their work as 'a candid but nonpolemical overview written for non-Mormons and Mormons alike.'

I am truly indebted to William P. Collins, the Bahá'í scholar and author of, among other publications, a two-part comparative article in *World Order* magazine. His insights contributed greatly to my own understanding and to this book, in which he is quoted extensively.

Finally, much credit for inspiring me to write this book goes to Kenneth D. Stephens, author of *So Great A Cause*, in which he chronicles his own spiritual journey from devout Mormon to dedicated Bahá'í, and in the process provides an excellent introduction to the Bahá'í Faith from a Latter-day Saint perspective.

These and other independent sources notwithstanding, the preponderance of quotations in this book have been taken from officially recognized scriptures and publications on both the Mormon and the Bahá'í side of the equation.

Quotations

The majority of quotations cited in this book may be placed in one of three categories: *scriptural, authoritative* and *supplemental.* While quotations are not grouped or identified in any way based on these categories, it may help the reader to be aware of this distinction so no misunderstandings arise. The kinds of sources that fall into each category differ between Mormon and Bahá'í quotations, reflecting the level of authority they enjoy within their respective religions.

Scriptural quotations

For the purposes of this book, Bahá'í scriptural references are limited to the Writings of the Báb, Bahá'u'lláh, and 'Abdu'l-Bahá, as well as the Old and New Testaments of the Bible and the Qur'án.

Mormon quotations are considered scriptural if they are taken from the officially recognized canon of scriptures: the King James Version of the Bible, *The Book of Mormon, The Doctrine and Covenants,* and *The Pearl of Great Price.*

Authoritative quotations

For the purpose of referencing Mormon sources, this category is very broad, encompassing not just the written statements of past and current church presidents, but also those of 'general authorities' and other prominent church elders; educational materials from official church curricula; and most articles of a doctrinal nature published in official church magazines. Mormons themselves consider all of these sources authoritative. The inclusion of the First Presidency and general authorities requires little explanation, since their authority is regarded by Mormons as second only to scripture – in fact, some of the writings of early church presidents are incorporated into the Doctrine and Covenants. As for church magazine publications, these are the primary means by which new doctrines revealed by the First Presidency are disseminated to the body of believers, and can therefore be considered authoritative as of the date of publication. Furthermore, each of these publications is vetted for confusing or contradictory content prior to printing, and may be relied upon to reflect, at least in essence, the official position of the Church.

Bahá'í authoritative texts consist of writings by (or on behalf of) Shoghi Effendi and the Universal House of Justice in addition to authorized translations of the works of Bahá'u'lláh, the Báb, and 'Abdu'l-Bahá.

Supplemental quotations

This category represents those sources that are not, following the criteria set forth above, either scriptural or authoritative. On the Mormon side, this may include church magazine articles that are not doctrinal in nature (such as those involving personal observations and experiences); transcripts of talks by people not considered to have doctrinal authority; and well-researched publications by third parties. On the Bahá'í side, supplemental sources may include pilgrims' notes, Bahá'í articles published in magazines such as *Star of the West* and *World Order*; non-authoritative Bahá'í books (e.g. those written by J. E. Esslemont, George Townshend and William Sears); and any well-researched publications by third parties.

Purpose

This is not a book on how to 'teach' Mormons the Bahá'í Faith. Rather, it seeks merely to break down any perceived barriers on the part of the Bahá'í audience by highlighting the many things Mormons and Bahá'ís have in common, and by providing an in-depth look at the very core of Mormon belief. This increased understanding, it is hoped, will motivate Bahá'ís to reach out to their Mormon family, friends and neighbors in a spirit of true friendship.

In addition to the many commonalities between the Mormon and Bahá'í faiths, naturally there are a number of differences as well. It's important to recognize where these points of disagreement may arise in our conversations, and to have a basic understanding of the specific beliefs held by Latter-day Saints. In this book, the differences are highlighted where appropriate to provide a context for the many similarities. Addressing theological differences in an atmosphere of loving consultation and detachment is a necessary part of interreligious dialogue, and should not be shunned, as Bahá'u'lláh called upon the peoples of the world to 'root out whatever is the source of contention amongst you.'[5]

That fact notwithstanding, this remains a book on how to better understand and appreciate our Mormon friends, and should not be viewed as a tool to sharpen our skills in debating the various abstruse and esoteric elements of either Mormon or Bahá'í theology. No matter how intriguing such debates might be, they serve absolutely no purpose in our objective to associate more closely with Mormons, since we will not be debating them on their faith – at least not if we're truly interested in being their friends rather than proving them wrong. Furthermore, 'Abdu'l-Bahá has stated that if 'two souls quarrel and contend about a question of the divine questions, differing and disputing, both are wrong.'[6]

Scope

This book is not intended to be an exhaustive treatise on the Church of Jesus Christ of Latter-day Saints, whether scientific, theological, or historical. A number of well-respected scholars, including devout Mormon apologists, highly critical polemicists and disinterested non-Mormon commentators, have already published many such books. Rather, its primary purpose is to find and expose commonalities between Mormons and Bahá'ís, an explicit bias which rules it out as an impartial analysis. However, as its secondary purpose is to present Bahá'ís with as complete and honest a portrayal of Mormon doctrine and history as possible, it is the author's duty to maintain an appropriate level of objectivity and healthy skepticism.

Furthermore, an attempt will be made to demystify some of the more difficult to accept elements of Mormon doctrine. By casting these in a different light – sometimes by offering observations and hypotheses that depart from the official church view – we can try to move beyond these issues so we can appreciate the underlying beauty of the Mormon faith.

INTRODUCTION

Most Bahá'ís are familiar with Bahá'u'lláh's exhortation to 'consort with the followers of all religions in a spirit of friendliness and fellowship.'[1] While this is a high standard to meet, 'Abdu'l-Bahá has raised the bar several more notches:

> Love ye all religions and all races with a love that is true and sincere and show that love through deeds and not through the tongue; for the latter hath no importance, as the majority of men are, in speech, well-wishers, while action is the best.[2]

It is not enough, 'Abdu'l-Bahá tells us, to merely consort or associate with people of other faiths. No, Bahá'ís must learn to love the faith of others, to respect it, and to show their love and respect through actions and not merely by paying lip service to it! As Bahá'ís, we are the standard-bearers of the oneness of God, of religion, and of mankind. It is therefore our sacred duty to do everything in our power to find commonalities and points of agreement between the various religions and sects, and to lead receptive souls to the recognition of the oneness of all religions.

In order to point out similarities between two specific faiths, we must be familiar with the basic tenets, and conversant in the sacred scriptures, of both. By learning about other faiths, we also become better teachers of our own. If we are familiar only with the Bahá'í Writings, we can only present our case from our own point of view, not from that of our audience. 'Abdu'l-Bahá explained the necessity of learning about other religions:

> If for example a spiritually learned Muslim is conducting a debate with a Christian and he knows nothing of the glorious melodies of the Gospel, he will, no matter how much he imparts of the Qur'án and its truths, be unable to convince the Christian, and his words will fall on deaf ears. Should, however, the Christian observe that the Muslim is better versed in the fundamentals of Christianity than the Christian priests themselves, and understands the purport of the Scriptures even better than they, he

will gladly accept the Muslim's arguments, and he would indeed have no other recourse.[3]

By way of analogy, if we desire to teach English to the inhabitants of a South American country, we will be much more effective if we are conversant in the Spanish and Portuguese languages. Likewise, if we live in a predominantly Christian society, it is logical that we should acquaint ourselves with the Christian Bible, and become familiar with both its various Christian interpretations and its spiritual meanings as revealed by Bahá'u'lláh.

Why should Bahá'ís actively seek to associate with Mormons? The Church of Jesus Christ of Latter-day Saints is growing at a record pace, and has millions of followers in the United States alone. It is no longer confined to its traditional stronghold states of Utah, Oregon, Idaho and Arizona, and is starting to gain significant ground in previously unfamiliar quarters such as New York and the 'Bible Belt' states. And even if the projections of non-Mormon sociologist Rodney Stark – predicting that the world will be home to some 265 million Mormons by the year 2080 – are off the mark, we are certain to come in contact with Latter-day Saints with ever greater frequency. Using our language analogy, we should strive to familiarize ourselves with LDS doctrine and scriptures.

Use of the term 'Mormon'

What's in a name? As anyone knows who's ever had his name mispronounced, misspelled, or plain forgotten, names are extremely important because they reflect our very identity. Therefore, if we are to effectively communicate with our Mormon friends, we must be aware of their sensitivities in this regard. As it turns out, there are several issues surrounding the term 'Mormon' of which we should be aware.

Origin

The term *Mormon* (or *Mormonite*) was first used as a pejorative referring to followers of Joseph Smith, after Smith's first publication, *The Book of Mormon*, which is itself named after one of the chroniclers appearing in that book. Over time, *Mormon* – while technically a misnomer – has become a mainstream and acceptable appellation.

Mormon Church (the institution)

In recent years, the Church has re-emphasized that the term *Mormon*, while acceptable when referring to an individual member, is to be avoided in reference to the institution, as in 'The Mormon Church.' Its official name is 'The Church of Jesus Christ of Latter-day Saints,' and if an abbreviation is to be used, it prefers simply 'The Church of Jesus Christ,' although this latter designation is obviously shared with a number of unrelated sects of Christianity. The Church thus seeks to clarify that Christ is at the center of its theology, and to dispel lingering misconceptions that it is not a Christian church.

Indeed the very question as to whether Mormons are Christians is offensive in the extreme. Mormons in fact see themselves as the only 'true' Christians, and consider all other Christian sects and non-Christian religions to be 'born of religious syncretism.' This, in turn, offends many mainstream Christians, who counter with a syncretism charge of their own and point out that a number of Mormon doctrines depart significantly from traditional Christian beliefs and appear to have been influenced by both Paganism and Freemasonry.

Another informal abbreviation for the Church used by Mormons is 'The LDS Church.' For the sake of brevity, I will primarily use that term to refer to the institution. However, various sources quoted in this book – including some by Mormon publications – still use the more common term *Mormon Church*.

Mormon church (the building)

It is acceptable to use the term 'Mormon church' when referring to the church *building*, as in 'we go to the Mormon church every Sunday.' As a matter of interest, the LDS Church divides its membership into geographic districts or *stakes*, and stakes are again divided into neighborhoods or *wards*. Each stake has a large church building called a *stake center*, and in most cases several smaller satellite churches, each of which is shared by up to three wards.

Mormon vs. Latter-day Saint

When referring to an individual believer, the terms *Mormon* and *Latter-day Saint* may be used interchangeably. Although *Latter-day Saint* is technically more correct, it can be awkward in everyday speech. Since the term *Mormon* is commonly used by Mormons themselves, this book will use the same convention. Incidentally, Mormons are quick to point out that the term *Saint* in no way implies that they consider themselves saintly, or in any way superior to people of other faiths. Rather, it is (among other things) a reference to this prophecy from the Bible:

And the graves were opened; and many bodies of the saints which slept arose, And came out of the graves after his resurrection, and went into the holy city, and appeared unto many.[4]

Mormonism

The term *Mormonism*, while accepted as a valid reference to the faith and doctrine of the Church of Jesus Christ of Latter-day Saints, should probably be avoided in everyday use. Even though the term appears in many articles written by Mormon scholars, it is rarely used in conversation. Within the LDS community, the term *Mormonism* is sometimes used to describe an attitude of judgmental self-righteousness exhibited by some of its members, as opposed to the spirit of tolerance that is exemplified by the life of Christ and the official teachings of the Church.

Some statistics

Membership distribution

The membership of the Church of Jesus Christ of Latter-day Saints is heavily concentrated in the United States, which is home to 45% of its roughly 12.5 million members (the state of Utah alone accounts for 1.7 million members). North and South America together represent fully 84% of the total, with the remaining 16% being distributed as follows: Asia (including Russia and Turkey), 7.2%; Europe, 3.4%; Africa, 1.9%; and the Pacific countries, 3.4%. There are 330 missions established in 120 countries. The church curriculum is available in 157 languages.[5]

Not included in these figures are the roughly 250,000 members of the *Reorganized Church of Jesus Christ of Latter Day Saints* (RLDS),[6] which was established in the mid-19th century by a group of dissident Mormons and later headed by Joseph Smith's son, Joseph III. The RLDS Church is discussed in greater detail later on in this book.

There are approximately 6 million Bahá'ís in the world (with independent estimates ranging from 5.5 to 7.5 million), spread over 188 independent countries and 45 territories.[7] Although exact population statistics are not readily available, the roughly 127,000 localities in which the Faith is established are distributed as follows: Asia, 47%; Africa, 24%; the Americas, 19%; Australasia, 5%; and Europe, 5%. The Bahá'í Writings have been translated into 802 different languages.[8]

Active vs. inactive membership

Differences in membership accounting between the two faiths could mean that they are even closer in size than the numbers suggest. The 12 million figure used to describe worldwide LDS membership refers to the number of baptized members on the rolls, including those who may have fallen away from the Church over time. According to one study, this causes the membership figures to be particularly skewed in countries like Brazil, where an estimated 40 to 55 per cent of the membership has little or no contact with the church.[9]

To its credit, the LDS Church warns against direct comparisons based on reported membership:

> According to the National Council of Churches, The Church of Jesus Christ of Latter-day Saints is the second-fastest-growing church in the United States. However, despite its increasing numbers, the Church cautions against overemphasis on growth statistics. The Church makes no statistical comparisons with other churches and makes no claim to be the fastest-growing Christian denomination despite frequent news media comments to that effect. Such comparisons rarely take account of a multiplicity of complex factors, including activity rates and death rates, the methodology used in registering or counting members and what factors constitute membership. Growth rates also vary significantly across the world. Additionally, many other factors contribute to the strength of the Church, most especially the devotion and commitment of its members.[10]

Of course, no one suggests that every person who has ever signed a Bahá'í declaration card is still an active member, or for that matter even considers himself a Bahá'í. It is exactly for this reason that the Bahá'í World Centre has consistently published the most conservative numbers to describe worldwide membership in the Bahá'í Faith. While there has been healthy growth in the number of active Bahá'ís – according to the World Christian Encyclopedia, it is the world's fastest-growing independent religion with over 7 million members – the official estimate has remained unchanged at 'over 5 million' since the mid-1980s.[11] Coincidentally, the LDS Church marked its 5 million mark in May 1982.

Contrasting patterns of growth

According to the statistics, there are approximately twice as many Mormons in the world as there are Bahá'ís, but they are not nearly as spread out across the globe. Any combination of factors could be responsible for this disparity, but two stand out most predominantly. One possible factor is the role of diversity in each religion. While diversity is a distinguishing feature of the Bahá'í Faith, it is something Mormons have had to adapt to over time. Even today, the Church of Jesus Christ of Latter-day Saints is perceived by the outside world not only as a distinctly American, but also as a largely 'white' religion. This may be an impediment to the Church's expansion in non-Western countries. It is perhaps telling that, until very recently, the only Mormon temple on the African continent was located in Johannesburg, South Africa, serving a mostly white membership. Two new African temples were dedicated in Ghana and Nigeria in January 2004 and August 2005, respectively.

A more compelling reason for the difference in global spread between the Bahá'í Faith and the Church of Jesus Christ of Latter-day Saints may be their contrasting approaches to growth. In the early 19th century, the epicenter of the LDS Church was Nauvoo, Illinois, where the focus was on building up the ranks locally through conversion and immigration. Later, the Church relocated to Salt Lake City, Utah, which became the new Mormon home-land. From there, concentrations of believers sprouted up in adjacent Idaho and Arizona, again with the focus on increasing local membership. What resulted was a relatively small cluster of Mormon communities in the western United States and Canada, each comprising many believers who could pool their resources to build up temples and church houses – a task nevertheless requiring great sacrifices on the part of these fledgling agrarian communities, evidenced by the fact that the Salt Lake temple took forty years to complete.

The LDS Church's expansion to the rest of the world is a relatively recent phenomenon, fueled not only by committed missionaries, but also by the Church's now considerable temporal wealth resulting from member tithes as well as lucrative business enterprises such as the Zions Cooperative Mercantile Institution (ZCMI). Furthermore, both missionary activity and the construction of buildings are highly centralized, with all aspects of growth controlled from (and largely financed by) church headquarters in Salt Lake.[12]

The Bahá'í pattern of growth is much more organic. The Bahá'í principle of the oneness of mankind, together with the emphasis on pioneering – both abroad and in one's own country – for the last sixty years of the 20th century, along with Bahá'u'lláh's commandment 'that in every city a House of Justice be established'[13] necessarily resulted in many small communities spread far and wide across the globe. The Local Spiritual Assembly (the governing council of the Bahá'ís in each local community) is an embryonic form of this House of Justice, and can be formed whenever a Bahá'í community has at least nine members.

Whereas Mormons seeking to relocate generally prefer areas with a strong LDS presence, Bahá'ís have historically been encouraged to settle in communities in which the Faith was not yet represented, or where the membership was close to the minimum number required to establish a Local Spiritual Assembly. This trend appears to be changing somewhat now that an increasing number of communities are experiencing accelerated growth and are actively attracting human resources to help sustain that growth; yet what remains unchanged is the idea of the Bahá'í as not merely a congregant, but as an active participant in bringing the message of Bahá'u'lláh to mankind.

The Bahá'í Administrative Order is itself decentralized. Unlike the LDS Church, where most activities around the world are directed from Salt Lake City, the Bahá'í administrative structure gives a certain autonomy to the National Spiritual Assemblies directing the affairs of the Faith in each country. At the local level, a large metropolitan area may be home to a dozen or more individual Bahá'í communities, each with its own Spiritual Assembly. And the four 'core activities' that are increasingly dominating Bahá'í life – devotional gatherings, children's classes, junior youth groups and study circles – are conducted at the neighborhood level, often at a park or in a home as well as in local Bahá'í centers.

Many similarities

At first glance, it would seem that Mormons and Bahá'ís have little in common other than high morals, a belief in Christ and the proscription of alcohol. However, a closer examination yields an astonishing number of similarities between these two faiths, on many different levels. Shoghi Effendi, the Guardian of the Bahá'í Faith, has pointed out that Mormons and Bahá'ís share a number of common principles, and hinted that these similarities could be a starting point for dialogue:

> The Guardian would advise you to teach the Mormons, like everyone else, the Faith, when you find them receptive. They have many great principles and their teachings regarding charity, not drinking or smoking, etc., are quite similar to ours and should form a point of common interest.[14]

As we continue our investigation into these similarities, we will discover that many aspects of Mormon doctrine appear to be more closely aligned with the Bahá'í teachings than with traditional Christian views. For example, it is the Mormons' belief in what they call *continuing revelation* that at once alienates them from traditional Christendom and links them to the Bahá'í Faith. While this concept is not as closely related to the Bahá'í concept of *progressive revelation* as the name suggests, both have at the root of their argument the understanding that revelation is not final. We will delve deeper into this subject later on in this book.

In addition, a surprising number of Mormon prophecies (separately from Christian prophecies, with most of which we are already familiar) appear to be fulfilled by the Báb and Bahá'u'lláh.

A special bond

Beyond these similarities of conduct and belief, there are further indications that Mormons and Bahá'ís share a special bond and a common purpose:

(a) Both faiths were born in the first half of the 19th century, in an environment of unprecedented millennial zeal, when the Day of the Lord was expected to arrive at any time.

(b) Both faiths originally came out in protest at the hypocrisy and corruption of the religious establishment in their respective birth nations.

(c) Both are directly concerned with the establishment of the Kingdom of God on earth; Mormons in a preparatory mode, and Bahá'ís in active implementation. Mormons believe their church to be the Kingdom of God on earth, organized so that Jesus Christ may come to be its head and hold the reins of theocratic government for a thousand years. Bahá'ís understand their administrative order to be both the embryonic manifestation of, and the blueprint for, the World Order to be established during the Dispensation of Bahá'u'lláh (at least a thousand years) and through which the rule of God will extend over all mankind for at least five hundred thousand years to come.

(d) Both share a history of persecution and exile, albeit in different parts of the world and on vastly different scales.

(e) Mormons and Bahá'ís are acutely aware that they are ambassadors of their respective faiths, and potentially subject to the scrutiny of a wary populace. This, along with their shared sense of duty to attract new believers into their communities, provides an incentive to act at all times in accordance with what each group holds to be divinely ordained principles.

(f) Both religions are extremely effective in spreading their message throughout the world.

(g)   Their current memberships are comparable in size relative to the world population.

History of religious persecution

I will not attempt to recount the religious persecutions that have beset the Báb, Bahá'u'lláh and their followers, and which are still suffered by Bahá'ís in many countries today. The voluminous early narrative by Nabíl, *The Dawn-Breakers*, is but one account of the unspeakable atrocities committed against Bábís and Bahá'ís, tens of thousands of whom laid down their lives in the path of God.

In terms of sheer scope, the persecutions suffered by Mormons cannot be compared to those endured by the Bahá'ís. However, they have left deep impressions in the Mormon collective consciousness, and have shaped the Mormon ethos nearly as much as the Bahá'í persecutions have defined that community's identity.

In 1844, Joseph Smith and his brother Hyrum were both shot to death while in prison on trumped-up charges. Soon after, an all-out campaign against the Mormons was launched, making life difficult if not unbearable for the large body of Smith's followers. One historical account paints the following picture:

> In September 1845 the anti-Mormons under Colonel Levi Williams began burning Mormon homes, first at Morley's in southwestern Hancock County, then in other settlements. One after another, unprotected families were forced from their log farm homes to watch the vigilantes set the torch. In all, more than two hundred homes and farm buildings, plus many mills and grain stacks, were destroyed.[15]

At last the Mormons – under the new leadership of Brigham Young – decided to migrate westward, embarking on a grueling trek in covered wagons (and later in hand-drawn carts, to conserve precious resources) across the west, and finally settling in Utah. The total number of casualties from the Mormon persecutions in Illinois is estimated around forty, and several hundred men, women and children succumbed to illness, freezing temperatures or exhaustion on their way to Utah.[16] The numerous stories of sacrifice, privation and death play an important role in Mormon history and heritage.

As Bahá'ís, we should not minimize the persecutions of the early Mormons against the backdrop of our own history. Rather, we can build an instant bond by conveying the truth that there are few religious groups in the world today more sympathetic to the early Mormons' suffering than the Bahá'ís.

Learning from each other

Despite its relatively small membership, the Church of Jesus Christ of Latter-day Saints is one of the best-organized Christian churches in the world. Certainly its social structure is worthy of admiration and study. On a local level, the firm spiritual and social bonds within the community, and the strong emphasis on family and service, can serve as a real-life example for other kinds of local communities as they grow in size and complexity. On a global level, the zeal and detachment with which young adults embark on their missions, and the support they receive from their communities at home, is nothing short of inspiring. The Church has also been quick to embrace technology and has fostered innovation in this field to aid in its various teaching efforts.

A spiritual people

As a group, Mormons are a highly spiritual people brimming with the love of God. Our interaction with them will enable them to recognize that same love of God within us, and establish lasting friendships and cooperation between our two faith communities.

There are additional reasons why friendships with members of other religions ought to be pursued. On March 11, 1936, Shoghi Effendi wrote these ominous words:

> Time alone can reveal the nature of the role which the institutions directly associated with the Christian Faith are destined to assume in this, the Formative Period of the Bahá'í Era, this dark age of transition through which humanity as a whole is passing. Such events as have already transpired, however, are of such a nature as can indicate the direction in which these institutions are moving ...
>
> That these institutions are becoming increasingly restive, that a few among them are already dimly aware of the pervasive influence of the Cause of Bahá'u'lláh, that they will, as their inherent strength deteriorates and their discipline relaxes, regard with deepening dismay the rise of His New World Order, and will gradually determine to assail it, that such an opposition will in turn accelerate their decline, few, if any, among those who are attentively watching the progress of His Faith would be inclined to question.[17]

It has been repeatedly stated by Bahá'u'lláh and 'Abdu'l-Bahá, and expounded upon by the Guardian and the Universal House of Justice, that the emerging from obscurity of the Bahá'í Faith will be accompanied by a number of religious institutions, with whom we may currently enjoy friendly cooperation and mutual respect, coming out in fierce opposition to the Faith. No one can venture to guess how the LDS Church will position itself in the future with respect to the Bahá'í Faith. However, by associating *now* with the individual members of other religions – including Mormons – and by showing forth such humility, love, and fellowship as never before expressed by any member of another faith, we will gain permanent friends who may well come to our defense in a future climate of hostility. Of course, the purpose of this is not to ease our own suffering, just as Bahá'u'lláh did not seek to ease His suffering:

> It is not Our purpose in addressing to thee these words to lighten the burden of Our woe, or to induce thee to intercede for Us with any one. No, by Him Who is the Lord of all worlds! We have set forth the whole matter before thee, that perchance thou might realize what thou hast done, might desist from inflicting on others the hurt thou hast inflicted on Us, and might be of them that have truly repented to God, Who created thee and created all things, and might act with discernment in the future. Better is this for thee than all thou dost possess, than thy ministry whose days are numbered.[18]

Rather, the result may well be to speed the process of entry by troops. The more vicious the accusations the world's religious leaders level against us, the more alienated our friends will become from that leadership. The Báb reminded us of the responsibility of detached souls to find their own salvation, even though their leaders may be left behind:

> Thus on the Day of Resurrection God will ask everyone of his understanding and not of his following in the footsteps of others. How often a person, having inclined his ears to the holy verses, would bow down in humility and would embrace the Truth, while his leader would not do so. Thus every individual must bear his own responsibility, rather than someone else bearing it for him. At the time of the appearance of Him Whom God will make manifest the most distinguished among the learned and the lowliest of men shall both be judged alike. How often the most insignificant of men have acknowledged the truth, while the most learned have remained wrapt in veils. Thus in every Dispensation a number of souls enter the fire by reason of their following in the footsteps of others.[19]

CHAPTER 1

ORIGINS: WHO WAS JOSEPH SMITH?

While it is beyond the scope of this book to offer an in-depth history of the life of Joseph Smith, Jr., any study of Mormon belief must necessarily include a brief discussion of the founder of the Mormon faith, the man behind the Church of Jesus Christ of Latter-day Saints, and what he claims led him to start this new religious movement. We can then attempt to place some of these experiences in a Bahá'í context.

The darkness before the dawn

The story of Joseph Smith, as he tells it, begins with his confusion about the many conflicting sects of Christianity, and his desire to know which one he should join. The part of upstate New York in which he resided had been seized by an unprecedented religious fervor. Movements of every kind were sprouting up, with doctrines too exotic and diverse to enumerate. Smith, intensely interested in all things religious from a very early age, investigated and briefly participated in some of these movements, including Methodism and Freemasonry. In fact, Smith's continued active involvement in the latter is often credited for the deeply ritualistic nature of the Mormon religion.[1]

Mormons acknowledge the existence of revivalist movements in the area where Joseph Smith grew up, although they are keen to separate their prophet from the crowd:

> Were there local revivals in the early spring of 1820? This is a loaded question because it narrows geography as well as the Prophet's own time limits. His 1832 record says his religious investigations began 'at about the age of twelve years,' describing his scriptural searching and 'intimate acquaintance with those of different denominations' up to the time of the First Vision. In this period he 'pondered' the surrounding 'contentions and divisions,' which certainly included public disputations. He turned twelve on 23 December 1817, and that year a major revival was reported in

Palmyra, with 150 people displaying 'the triumphs of grace.' So religious awakenings in the vicinity reached scores in 1817 and hundreds in 1824, as indicated above. These dates show major religious interest on either side of 1820, and local society undoubtedly did not fall into spiritual stupor in the intervening years . . . Joseph gave this Methodist fervor an early time frame: the Smiths had moved to their farm home, on the boundary of Wayne and Ontario Counties, and conversion fever was already intense while he was in his 'fifteenth year' . . .[2]

According to this account, Joseph Smith's religious investigations began shortly after Bahá'u'lláh's birth in 1817.

Joseph Smith's First Vision

The official genesis of the LDS Church was Joseph Smith's 'First Vision,' which occurred some time 'early in the spring of eighteen hundred and twenty,' although the precise date is not given. Actually, Joseph Smith gave various differing accounts of his First Vision, two of which were committed to writing in 1832 and 1838, respectively. The 1838 version, canonized as the 'Joseph Smith History' in *Pearl of Great Price*, is considered most significant by Mormons, many of whom are unaware of the earlier accounts.

In this First Vision account, Joseph Smith began by describing the contentions that ensued among the many competing sects, and his inability to know which of them was right:

Some time in the second year after our removal to Manchester, there was in the place where we lived an unusual excitement on the subject of religion. It commenced with the Methodists, but soon became general among all the sects in that region of country. Indeed, the whole district of the country seemed affected by it, and great multitudes united themselves to the different religious parties, which created no small stir and division amongst the people, some crying, 'Lo, here!' and others, 'Lo, there!' Some were contending for the Methodist faith, some for the Presbyterian, and some for the Baptist . . .

During this time of great excitement my mind was called up to serious reflection and great uneasiness; but though my feelings were deep and often poignant, still I kept myself aloof from all these parties, though I attended their several meetings as often as occasion would permit. In process of time my mind became somewhat partial to the Methodist sect, and I felt some desire to be united with them; but so great were the confusion and strife among the different denominations, that it was impossible for a person young as I was, and so unacquainted with men and things, to come to any certain conclusion who was right and who was wrong.[3]

Joseph Smith was 14 years old. Inspired by a verse from the Bible,[4] he decided to go into the woods near his hometown of Palmyra to seek an answer from God through prayer. There he received a vision in which he was visited by two beings, whom he presumed to be God the Father and Jesus Christ:

> I saw a pillar of light exactly over my head, above the brightness of the sun, which descended gradually until it fell upon me.
>
> It no sooner appeared than I found myself delivered from the enemy which held me bound. When the light rested upon me I saw two Personages, whose brightness and glory defy all description, standing above me in the air. One of them spake unto me, calling me by name and said, pointing to the other – *This is My Beloved Son. Hear Him!* [5]

This description bears a striking similarity to Bahá'u'lláh's account of a vision He received while imprisoned in a dungeon underneath Tehran, a vision Bahá'ís understand to mark the official inauguration of His Mission. Bahá'u'lláh wrote:

> While engulfed in tribulations I heard a most wondrous, a most sweet voice, calling above My head. Turning My face, I beheld a Maiden – the embodiment of the remembrance of the name of My Lord – suspended in the air before Me. So rejoiced was she in her very soul that her countenance shone with the ornament of the good pleasure of God, and her cheeks glowed with the brightness of the All-Merciful. Betwixt earth and heaven she was raising a call which captivated the hearts and minds of men. She was imparting to both My inward and outer being tidings which rejoiced My soul, and the souls of God's honoured servants.
>
> Pointing with her finger unto My head, she addressed all who are in heaven and all who are on earth, saying: By God! This is the Best-Beloved of the worlds, and yet ye comprehend not. This is the Beauty of God amongst you, and the power of His sovereignty within you, could ye but understand. This is the Mystery of God and His Treasure, the Cause of God and His glory unto all who are in the kingdoms of Revelation and of creation, if ye be of them that perceive. This is He Whose Presence is the ardent desire of the denizens of the Realm of eternity, and of them that dwell within the Tabernacle of glory, and yet from His Beauty do ye turn aside.[6]

All the sects are wrong

Joseph Smith continued the account of his First Vision:

> My object in going to inquire of the Lord was to know which of all the
> sects was right, that I might know which to join. No sooner, therefore,
> did I get possession of myself, so as to be able to speak, than I asked the
> Personages who stood above me in the light, which of all the sects was right
> . . . and which I should join. I was answered that I must join none of them,
> for they were all wrong; and the Personage who addressed me said that all
> their creeds were an abomination in his sight; that those professors were
> all corrupt; that: 'they draw near to me with their lips, but their hearts are
> far from me, they teach for doctrines the commandments of men, having
> a form of godliness, but they deny the power thereof.'[7]

The same corruption of religion – and the resulting bewilderment of the people
– is described in the following passage from the Writings of Baháʾuʾlláh, in
which He expounds the meaning of 'the oppression of those days' that is the
precursor to every new Revelation:

> What 'oppression' is more grievous than that a soul seeking the truth, and
> wishing to attain unto the knowledge of God, should know not where to
> go for it and from whom to seek it? For opinions have sorely differed, and
> the ways unto the attainment of God have multiplied . . .
>
> Whereas, by 'oppression' is meant the want of capacity to acquire spir-
> itual knowledge and apprehend the Word of God. By it is meant that
> when the Day-star of Truth hath set, and the mirrors that reflect His light
> have departed, mankind will become afflicted with 'oppression' and hard-
> ship, knowing not whither to turn for guidance.[8]

ʾAbduʾl-Bahá confirmed the religious corruption of this period in time:

> Darkness and ignorant fanaticism were widespread; no trace of fellow-
> ship or brotherhood existed amongst the races. On the contrary, human
> hearts were filled with rage and hatred; darkness and gloom were manifest
> in human lives and conditions everywhere. At such a time as this His
> Holiness Baháʾuʾlláh appeared upon the divine horizon, even as the glory
> of the sun, and in that gross darkness and hopelessness of the human world
> there shone a great light. He founded the oneness of the world of human-
> ity, declaring that all mankind are as sheep and that God is the real and
> true Shepherd. The Shepherd is one, and all people are of his flock.[9]

And Thomas Carlyle, referring to the close of the 18th century, offered a
secular viewpoint:

> . . . a Century which has no History and can have little or none. A Century
> so opulent in accumulated falsities . . . as never Century before was! Which
> had no longer the consciousness of being false, so false had it grown; and
> was so steeped in falsity, and impregnated with it to the very bone, that
> – in fact the measure of the thing was full, and a French Revolution had
> to end it . . .
>   . . . A very fit termination, as I thankfully feel, for such a Century . . .
> For there was need once more of a Divine Revelation to the torpid
> frivolous children of men, if they were not to sink altogether into the ape
> condition.[10]

The gradual corruption of religion and the concept of dispensations

The Bahá'í Faith teaches that each of God's religions, having been established
by a Divine Messenger, gradually became corrupted by man and reached its
lowest state of abasement just before the dawn of a new dispensation, a state
characterized by an apparent lack of spiritual guidance on earth:

> The beginnings of all great religions were pure; but priests, taking posses-
> sion of the minds of the people, filled them with dogmas and superstitions,
> so that religion became gradually corrupt.[11]

Mormon doctrine supports the concept of dispensations in much the same
way as the Bahá'í Faith. A church magazine article comparing Islam and
Mormonism states:

> Most fundamental are certain doctrinal traditions that, while found in
> the Koran, have been rejected by conventional Christianity and Judaism
> but have always been a part of Mormonism. Great emphasis is placed, for
> example, on the concept of dispensations, i.e., the restoration of prophetic
> gifts and divine authority after long periods of apostasy and darkness
> through the sending of a great prophet.[12]

In fact, Mormons believe that the current age will bring about the fulfillment
of all previous dispensations:

> The Lord has established gospel dispensations several times among people

on the earth; sometimes a dispensation endured for a while and then ceased to function on earth because of wickedness and unbelief. The gospel dispensation given to us is appropriately called the fulness of times because it will bring the culmination of all previous dispensations, plus the fruition of some unique things never before accomplished on the earth.[13]

The mission of Joseph Smith

On September 21, 1823 – three and a half years after his 'First Vision' – Joseph Smith received another vision while preparing for bed. According to Smith's autobiographical account, an angel by the name of Moroni appeared and revealed to him his mission and destiny:

> While I was thus in the act of calling upon God, I discovered a light appearing in my room, which continued to increase until the room was lighter than at noonday, when immediately a personage appeared at my bedside, standing in the air, for his feet did not touch the floor . . .
>
> Not only was his robe exceedingly white, but his whole person was glorious beyond description, and his countenance truly like lightning. The room was exceedingly light, but not so very bright as immediately around his person. When I first looked upon him, I was afraid; but the fear soon left me.
>
> He called me by name, and said unto me that he was a messenger sent from the presence of God to me, and that his name was Moroni; that God had a work for me to do; and that my name should be had for good and evil among all nations, kindreds, and tongues, or that it should be both good and evil spoken of among all people.
>
> He said there was a book deposited, written upon gold plates, giving an account of the former inhabitants of this continent, and the source from whence they sprang. He also said that the fulness of the everlasting Gospel was contained in it, as delivered by the Savior to the ancient inhabitants;
>
> Also, that there were two stones in silver bows – and these stones, fastened to a breastplate, constituted what is called the Urim and Thummim – deposited with the plates; and the possession and use of these stones were what constituted 'seers' in ancient or former times; and that God had prepared them for the purpose of translating the book . . .
>
> Again, he told me, that when I got those plates of which he had spoken – for the time that they should be obtained was not yet fulfilled – I should not show them to any person; neither the breastplate with the Urim and Thummim; only to those to whom I should be commanded to show them;

if I did I should be destroyed. While he was conversing with me about the plates, the vision was opened to my mind that I could see the place where the plates were deposited, and that so clearly and distinctly that I knew the place again when I visited it.[14]

The angel reappeared twice more that same night, each time repeating the entire revelation 'without the least variation,' except for a warning to Joseph not to seek personal gain from what he was about to uncover.[15] The next day, guided by his recollections, Smith located the place shown to him by the angel and discovered a box containing the items exactly as described in his vision. Moroni however, had warned him not to remove anything yet. For the next four years, Joseph Smith returned to the same site – dubbed the Hill Cumorah – and met the angel Moroni to receive additional information and instructions 'respecting what the Lord was going to do, and how and in what manner his kingdom was to be conducted in the last days.'[16] Finally in the fall of 1827 he was allowed to take the golden plates and the other items into his possession.

Another eighteen months passed before Joseph Smith began his translation of the Book of Mormon, a process involving not a literal interpretation of the words engraved on the golden plates, but rather the spiritual divination of their content using nothing but the Urim and Thummim, or seer stones, that had accompanied them. Joseph Smith spoke the words as they came to his mind, and dictated them to his associate and scribe, Oliver Cowdery.[17]

The Aaronic priesthood

According to Joseph Smith's account, it was while this translation was in progress that he and Oliver Cowdery went into the woods to ask God through prayer about baptism – a principle they encountered while working on the Book of Mormon. While in prayer, they both had a vision of John the Baptist conferring upon them the 'Priesthood of Aaron' by which they would have the power of baptism for the remission of sins. Smith and Cowdery promptly went to the river to baptize each other:

> Immediately on our coming up out of the water after we had been baptized, we experienced great and glorious blessings from our Heavenly Father. No sooner had I baptized Oliver Cowdery, than the Holy Ghost fell upon him, and he stood up and prophesied many things which should shortly come to pass. And again, so soon as I had been baptized by him, I also had the spirit of prophecy, when, standing up, I prophesied concerning the rise of

this Church, and many other things connected with the Church, and this generation of the children of men. We were filled with the Holy Ghost, and rejoiced in the God of our salvation.

Our minds being now enlightened, we began to have the scriptures laid open to our understandings, and the true meaning and intention of their more mysterious passages revealed unto us in a manner which we never could attain to previously, nor ever before had thought of. In the meantime we were forced to keep secret the circumstances of having received the Priesthood and our having been baptized, owing to a spirit of persecution which had already manifested itself in the neighborhood.[18]

The gospel restored

In March 1830, the Book of Mormon was completed and published. Subtitled 'Another Testament of Jesus Christ,' it claimed to represent no less than the 'restoration' and 'fulness' of the gospel of Jesus Christ, a gospel which in the eyes of Joseph Smith had been stripped of most of its spiritual potency even before the end of the first century. The Book of Mormon inspired confidence and hope; if its claims were true, then the waywardness and splintering of Christendom was not a failure of Jesus' mission, but rather the natural outcome of apostasy, corruption and the excision of many 'plain and most precious' teachings. Best of all, these teachings were not truly lost, but had only been lying dormant, hidden in a box under an unassuming hill in Ontario County, New York, waiting to be unearthed by an adolescent farm boy prone to remarkable visions.

The Book of Mormon thus became the preeminent missionary tool of Joseph Smith's followers (and it remains so today). No longer dependent on the personal charisma of their leader or their own oratory skills, they now had a tangible work of scripture written in the style of, and nearly as voluminous as, the Old Testament. The Book of Mormon extolled the American continent as the promised land, and promoted social justice based on religious principles. It was clear that receptive souls would be found, and it was not long before Joseph Smith's followers set out to spread the newly restored gospel beyond the borders of their local communities.

The rise and spread of the Church

Surprisingly, the earliest targets of concerted missionary activity were American Indians. Mormons believe that the indigenous populations of America are descendant from the Lamanite people mentioned in the Book of Mormon, and by extension, from the Israelites who came to America at the beginning of its narrative. Although the Book of Mormon states that the Lamanites were cursed with a dark skin because of their transgression, it also prophesies that in the latter days this same Lamanite people would assist in building the New Jerusalem.[19] According to the Book of Mormon, then, the Israelite lineage of the American Indian is noble, and his future glorious.[20]

In October 1830, four Mormon missionaries set out on an expedition to preach to the Indians west of the Missouri river, convinced that their message of hope would be well received. Along the way, they converted and baptized over a hundred people (all of them white) and organized them into church branches. One of these branches, located in Kirtland, Ohio, would eventually be home to the first LDS temple. Continuing on their 'Lamanite Mission,' the four missionaries then traveled to Jackson County, Missouri – a place later to be named the new promised land by Joseph Smith. Upon entering a small Indian village, the missionaries initially met with distrust but were in the end allowed to preach to receptive members of that community. However, efforts to establish a permanent mission were scuttled by the federal Indian agent in charge, who ordered the missionaries off Indian lands under threat of arrest. Although the Lamanite Mission had failed in its primary objective of converting American Indians, it proved extremely successful in laying the administrative foundation of the Church of Jesus Christ of Latter-day Saints.[21]

Ohio and Missouri

Although it had been operating since August 1829, the LDS Church was not officially organized until April 6, 1830, less than a month after the Book of Mormon was published. At the organizing meeting in Fayette, New York, Joseph Smith and Oliver Cowdery were named church leaders.

By 1831 Mormons were increasingly persecuted by those who saw the new religion as a threat. Eager to leave this hostile environment, and encouraged by the missionaries' success in Ohio, Joseph Smith moved his family to Kirtland and called on the members of his newly organized church in New York to follow him there. He then traveled to Independence in Jackson County, Missouri and identified it as the central gathering place for the Mormons – the New Jerusalem (or Zion) of the latter days. Consequently many of the Ohio and New York converts migrated to Jackson County, although Smith remained in Kirtland to consolidate the Church's headquarters there.

It was not long before the growing Latter-day Saint presence in Missouri gave rise to tensions with the established settlers. The Mormons' northeastern extraction and foreign religious beliefs, not to mention their amicable relations with the Indians, were seen as a social, economic and political threat, and the resulting clash of cultures soon came to a head. In 1833, violent mobs drove more than a thousand Mormons into neighboring Clay County where they were offered temporary refuge. However, after three years of failed attempts to return to Jackson County, the burgeoning Mormon population had worn out its welcome. Loath to use force, the Clay County government held meetings on an appropriate course of action, and in June 1836, the Mormons were officially asked to leave. The Church negotiated with the state legislature to create a political safe haven for the Mormon community in the as yet unsettled northwestern part of Missouri. In December, two new counties – Daviess and Caldwell – were created, with the understanding that the latter would be a Mormon sanctuary.

While Joseph Smith made several visits to the Missouri church branches over the years, he spent the majority of his time in Kirtland overseeing the construction of the first Mormon temple, the completion of which had become his most pressing priority. As soon as the Kirtland Temple was finished in 1836, he produced a number of revelations that represented a significant evolutionary jump in the Church's doctine and administration. Mormons consider their temples to be the holiest places on earth, divine portals within whose walls the sacred rituals and ordinances required for the salvation of mankind must be carried out. Although most of the temple rituals known to Mormons today were not yet in place, there was a sense that the spiritual work of the Church could now begin in earnest. On the temporal side, membership growth required changes in its organizational structure, and a number of new church positions were created.

The following year, Latter-day Saints became the majority population in Kirtland, and Mormons were elected to several important town offices. This created a political backlash from non-Mormon residents. To make matters worse, the Church had set up an unchartered bank, of which Joseph Smith was treasurer. When the economy collapsed in 1838, it took the bank, which had never been on sound footing, down with it. Joseph Smith became the focal point of criticism and hatred, boiling over into mob violence and death threats, forcing him and most of his followers to flee Ohio for Missouri. Although Caldwell County, Missouri was the unofficial Mormon homeland, the collapse of Kirtland caused a Mormon migration that spilled over into neighboring Daviess County. There, non-Mormon Missourians feared that church members would dominate economic and political life as they had done elsewhere. After a number of violent confrontations between pro- and anti-Mormon militias, the governor of Missouri accused the Mormons of instigating hostilities and ordered his state militia to expel them. In 1839, about 10,000 Mormons fled across the Mississippi River into Illinois, while Joseph Smith and other church leaders were arrested and charged with treason. Smith was imprisoned in Liberty Jail, from where he produced a number of influential letters and revelations.

The Nauvoo years

After six months, Joseph Smith escaped from jail and met his followers in Illinois, where he immediately began to establish a new community. The beleaguered Mormons, having lost most of their property in Missouri, were able to purchase some swampy land on the banks of the Mississippi, which they drained and turned into the city of Nauvoo. Despite some initial struggles, the LDS community began to thrive again. In the early 1840s construction began on a second temple, and a successful mission to the British Isles resulted in thousands of new converts, many of whom migrated to Nauvoo over the ensuing years. The city eventually became the second largest in Illinois (after Chicago) with about 12,000 inhabitants.

Since Nauvoo was almost entirely Mormon, it became an unusual experiment in American theocracy. The Church had negotiated a unique city charter that rendered it nearly immune from outside control. Joseph Smith, founder and prophet of the Church of Jesus Christ of Latter-day Saints, now also wielded considerable political power in his various roles as city councilman, mayor, and editor of the local newspaper. He even served as commanding general of the Nauvoo Legion, which at the time was the largest militia in Illinois, and the only one not beholden to the state. Nearly every position of influence or authority was held by a loyal church member who considered Joseph Smith to be an infallible prophet of God.

Inevitably, questions arose about Nauvoo's autocratic style of government, and the apparent impunity with which church leaders were able to operate. Smith's continued involvement with Freemasonry led to the creation of secret councils and doctrines (some of which later evolved into LDS temple rituals), adding to the atmosphere of suspicion. In 1844, egged on by antagonists from neighboring communities worried about Nauvoo's growing economic strength and powerful militia, a group of dissident Mormons published a newspaper titled *The Nauvoo Expositor*, specifically to expose perceived wrongdoings by the church leadership. The Nauvoo city council's terse response was to outlaw the paper and to have its press destroyed. This act of reprisal served only to deepen resentment, with disastrous consequences.

Joseph Smith as the herald

Although the urgency of his original message seems to have gotten lost over time, Joseph Smith had devoted much of his energy to preaching the imminent return of Jesus Christ, and calling on all to purify themselves in preparation for this great event. In many ways, his station of herald is reminiscent of that occupied by John the Baptist.

Return of Christ the predominant theme

Joseph Smith made repeated warnings regarding the Return of Christ, echoing those of John the Baptist 1,800 years earlier. Furthermore, Joseph Smith made mention of not one, but two Manifestations to come after him.

Whatever the source of his inspiration, Smith seems to have been convinced that the Second Coming was close at hand. If there is any single theme that dominates his writings, it is that the Day of the Lord is fast approaching, and that everyone had better look out for it and be prepared. He issued numerous warnings to the body of his followers that many of them would not recognize Christ, exhorting all to 'seek me [Christ] diligently and ye shall find me'[22] and to 'seek . . . out of the best books words of wisdom; seek learning even by study and also by faith.'[23] He promised that Christ would 'reason as with men in days of old, and I will show unto you my strong reasoning.'[24] He even indicated that the Lord was 'in your midst and ye cannot see me.'[25] Bahá'ís might interpret this last statement, revealed in 1831, as an allusion to Christ's physical presence on earth before making himself known. Both the Báb and Bahá'u'lláh were living at the time, but had yet to declare their respective missions.

It is also worth noting that, according to his 1832 'First Vision' account, Joseph Smith's religious investigations began 'at about the age of twelve years.' Smith turned twelve on December 23, 1817, shortly after the birth of Bahá'u'lláh.

The Great Disappointment of 1844

In the days of John the Baptist, there were many others who were convinced that the Christ, or Messiah, was near. Ben Witherington's *New Testament History* (cited later in this book) describes numerous messianic movements sprouting up in the Holy Land around the time of Jesus' mission, although many of these had radical political agendas. Earlier still, the three Magi who came to visit Jesus recognized the signs of His appearance, based on the prophecies of their faith. It is widely believed, both in Mormon and Bahá'í circles, that these Magi were followers of Zoroaster.

In the years leading up to the opening of the Bahá'í Era, messianic fervor was even more widespread; and since this latest revelation was to be the culmination of all those that came before it, it is logical that the precursors should also be more plentiful. In fact, almost every religion on earth experienced a revival around the same time, spawning countless offshoots predicting the imminent return of their Promised One.

Joseph Smith appeared to be part of a wave of Christian millennial zeal that produced the Campbellite and Millerite sects, among others. One biographer of Joseph Smith described this period as follows:

> Beginning around 1800 and extending through this period, the country was aflame with the peculiar religious revivalism referred to as 'the Second Great Awakening.' Religious enthusiasms swept back and forth across upper New York, centered around Palmyra, until the area was called 'the Burned-over District.' The revivalism reached its zenith during the period of our interest, 1820–30, and continued to 1850.[26]

While many of these groups' attentions focused on or around the year 1844, William Miller went out on a limb by setting a definite time frame for the Second Coming. Although his first prediction had Christ returning between 1843 and 1845 – based on calculations he and other Bible scholars made from prophecies in the Book of Daniel and the Revelation of St John – he later pinpointed the exact date to March 21, 1844. Astonishingly, this coincides with the first day of the first year of the Bahá'í Era (1 Bahá, 1 BE), even though it predates the Declaration of the Báb on May 23.

The disillusionment and despair that followed the apparent no-show is known to history as 'The Great Disappointment.' Eventually, the Millerites split off into different groups, one of which became the Seventh-Day Adventists.

Signs in the heavens

Joseph Smith himself was aware of William Miller's predictions concerning the time of Christ's advent. A note in *History of the Church* dated February 12, 1843 recounts a visit Smith received from a group of young Millerites:

> Seven or eight young men came to see me, part of them from the city of New York. They treated me with the greatest respect. I showed them the fallacy of Mr. Miller's *data* concerning the coming of Christ and the end of the world, or as it is commonly called, Millerism, and preached them quite a sermon; that error was in the Bible, or the translation of the Bible;

24

that Miller was in want of correct information upon the subject, and that he was not so much to blame as the translators. I told them the prophecies must all be fulfilled; the sun must be darkened and the moon turned into blood, and many more things take place before Christ would come.[27]

William Sears, in his ground-breaking book *Thief in the Night*, contends that these physical events did in fact come to pass:

Many biblical scholars pointed to the exact fulfilment, and in the proper order of the prophecies concerning the heavens and the signs of the coming of Christ as given in the sixth chapter of *Revelation*

First: The appearance of the great earthquake in 1755.

Second: The sun darkened and the moon turned into blood on the Dark Day of 1780.

Third: The stars falling from the heavens in 1833 . . .

The millennial scholars pointed to the great convergence of prophecies on the year 1844. Now that the three signs in the heavens, promised as a prelude in *Revelation*, had been fulfilled, it further strengthened their belief that the hour of the *return of Christ* was at hand.[28]

While Joseph Smith appeared to have been unaware of the 1755 and 1780 events, he was in fact an eyewitness to the third occurrence in that prophetic sequence. On November 13, 1833 he observed:

About 4 o'clock a.m. I was awakened by Brother Davis knocking at my door, and calling on me to arise and behold the signs in the heavens. I arose, and to my great joy, beheld the stars fall from heaven like a shower of hailstones; a literal fulfilment of the word of God, as recorded in the holy Scriptures, and a sure sign that the coming of Christ is close at hand. In the midst of this shower of fire, I was led to exclaim, 'How marvelous are Thy works, O Lord! I thank Thee for Thy mercy unto Thy servant; save me in Thy kingdom for Christ's sake. Amen.'

The appearance of these signs varied in different sections of the country: in Zion, all heaven seemed enwrapped in splendid fireworks, as if every star in the broad expanse had been suddenly hurled from its course, and sent lawless through the wilds of ether. Some at times appeared like bright shooting meteors, with long trains of light following in their course, and in numbers resembled large drops of rain in sunshine. These seemed to vanish when they fell behind the trees, or came near the ground. Some of the long trains of light following the meteoric stars, were visible for some seconds; these streaks would curl and twist up like serpents writhing. The appearance was beautiful, grand, and sublime beyond description; and it seemed as if the artillery and fireworks of eternity were set in motion to enchant and entertain the Saints, and terrify and awe the sinners of the earth. Beautiful and terrific as was the scenery, it will not fully compare with the time when the sun shall become black like sack-cloth of hair, the moon like blood, and the stars fall to the earth.[29]

Smith's reference to a future falling of the stars is a bit puzzling, however, considering that he had just witnessed this very sign and referred to it as 'a literal fulfilment of the word of God . . . and a sure sign that the coming of Christ is close at hand.' In any case – judging by his meticulous recording of natural disasters, political upheavals and other world events – it is clear that Joseph Smith never gave up his search for outward signs of Christ's return. The following note, recorded on March 10, 1843, is representative:

With Willard Richards, Wilford Woodruff and many others, about seven p.m., I discovered a stream of light in the southwest quarter of the heavens. Its pencil rays were in the form of a broad sword, with the hilt downward, the blade raised, pointing from the west, southwest, raised to an angle of forty-five degrees from the horizon, and extending nearly, or within two or three degrees to the zenith of the degree where the sign appeared. This sign gradually disappeared from half-past seven o'clock, and at nine had entirely disappeared. As sure as there is a God who sits enthroned in the heavens, and as sure as He ever spoke by me, so sure will there be a speedy and bloody war;[30] and the broad sword seen this evening is the sure sign thereof . . .

A shock of an earthquake felt in Lancashire, England, and on the Isle of Guernsey, produced considerable alarm.

The papers teem with accounts of singular phenomena. Fearful sights are seen in all parts of the world.[31]

On the 19th of the same month, a scientific explanation was found for the 'sword' in the sky. Joseph Smith reported:

Sir James South, Sir John Hershel, and other astronomers in Europe have published notices of the sword seen in the heavens on the eve of the 10th and several successive evenings. They represent it as the stray tail of a comet, as no nucleus could be discovered with the most powerful instruments. At Paris, M. Arago communicated to the Academy of Sciences, on the subject of the comet, that the observations of the astronomers were not complete, the nucleus not being discovered.[32]

The phenomenon Joseph Smith witnessed is now known as 'the Great Comet of 1843' or 'the Great March Comet,' and was visible throughout the world from early February until mid April. The nucleus of that comet was very faint, and its tail holds the record for actual extent. Its appearance fueled expectations of Judgment Day in many religious communities.

A few days later on March 23rd, Smith reported seeing another phenomenon that received worldwide attention, 'a splendid appearance of circles, accompanied by mock suns.'[33] A visual representation of this event appears on page 190 of *Thief in the Night*.

The martyrdom of Joseph Smith

The writings of Joseph Smith intimate that he might have had an opportunity to 'see the face of the Son of Man.' Smith recalls:

> I was once praying very earnestly to know the time of the coming of the Son of Man, when I heard a voice repeat the following: Joseph, my son, if thou livest until thou art eighty-five years old, thou shalt see the face of the Son of Man . . .[34]

As Smith was born in 1805, this prophecy points to 1890, the year in which the first Westerners were allowed access to the Holy Presence of Bahá'u'lláh. However, this chance was lost when on June 27, 1844 – a mere 35 days after the Declaration of the Báb – Joseph Smith's life was abruptly put to an end.

As a lamb to the slaughter

Joseph Smith and his elder brother Hyrum both met their demise on June 27, 1844 while they were imprisoned in Carthage, Illinois on charges stemming from the destruction of a Nauvoo newspaper's printing press. Larry Porter, director of Church History at Brigham Young University's Religious Studies Center, describes the event as follows:

> As we know, a double murder was committed on the hot Thursday afternoon of 27 June 1844 at Carthage, Illinois. The Prophet Joseph Smith and his brother Hyrum were slain in a violent outburst by an armed mob of one-hundred to two-hundred men. The attackers were primarily members of

the Warsaw (Illinois) militia, aided and abetted by certain of the Carthage Greys who had been posted to guard the prisoners.[35]

Mormons portray the martyrdom of Joseph Smith in a similar light to Jesus' crucifixion. As Jesus knowingly went to Jerusalem to be judged before the people, so Smith likened himself to one taken 'like a lamb to the slaughter.' This comparison is quite limited, however. While in jail, Smith had been slipped a gun by his friend Cyrus H. Wheelock, which he fired in self-defense.[36] Before his imprisonment, Joseph Smith had prepared to escape arrest by fleeing to the Rocky Mountains with some companions, including his brother Hyrum. He was finally persuaded by Hyrum to give himself up, but warned: 'If you go back I will go with you, but we shall be butchered.'[37]

John Taylor, then a member of the Council of the Twelve (and a later church president), gave the following eyewitness account of Smith's last moments:

> When Joseph went to Carthage to deliver himself up to the pretended requirements of the law, two or three days previous to his assassination, he said: 'I am going like a lamb to the slaughter; but I am calm as a summer's morning; I have a conscience void of offense towards God, and towards all men. I SHALL DIE INNOCENT, AND IT SHALL YET BE SAID OF ME – HE WAS MURDERED IN COLD BLOOD.' . . .
>
> Hyrum Smith was forty-four years old in February, 1844, and Joseph Smith was thirty-eight in December, 1843; and henceforward their names will be classed among the martyrs of religion; and the reader in every nation will be reminded that the Book of Mormon, and this book of Doctrine and Covenants of the church, cost the best blood of the nineteenth century to bring them forth for the salvation of a ruined world; and that if the fire can scathe a green tree for the glory of God, how easy it will burn up the dry trees to purify the vineyard of corruption. They lived for glory; they died for glory; and glory is their eternal reward. From age to age shall their names go down to posterity as gems for the sanctified.[38]

The following independent account completes the picture:

> Smith surrendered on June 24 and was taken to the Carthage Jail, where he was imprisoned along with Hyrum and apostles John Taylor and Willard Richards. The jailer treated the prisoners kindly, but [Illinois Governor Thomas] Ford had left the anti-Mormon Carthage Grays guarding the jail. Inside, the prisoners passed the time in prayer and talk and wrote brave

notes to their families. Joseph asked Taylor to sing a popular song that he liked, 'A Poor Wayfaring Man of Grief.'

Late in the afternoon of June 27, a mob of men disguised with blackened faces approached the jail. The Grays fired weapons preloaded with blanks. One gang bounded up the stairs and fired through the door where Smith's party was held. The bullet that passed through the door struck Hyrum Smith in the face, killing him instantly, but the mob kept firing. As attackers burst into the room, Joseph Smith discharged his gun all six times with three misfires and wounded three. While the assailants continued to fire away, Smith leaped or fell through the window, beginning the Masonic cry for help, 'Oh, Lord, my God,' but not living to complete the words: 'Is there no help for the widow's son?' Some of the attackers pumped more bullets into Joseph's body by the well before the crowd dispersed. Richards was uninjured; Taylor was wounded seriously but survived to become the church's president decades later in Utah. Hyrum and Joseph Smith lay bloodied and dead.[39]

Shift of priorities

Referring to the events following Joseph Smith's tragic death, Kenneth D. Stephens in his book *So Great A Cause* asks the question: 'Why did the [Latter-day] Saints not go out in search of the Promised One foretold in their beloved leader's prophecies? Why did they not search their scripture diligently in order to know where the Lord was to be found?' He answers himself: 'Instead, just as Christ's disciples had fled at the time of the crucifixion of their Lord, so did the followers of Joseph Smith look to the protection of their own lives.'[40] Indeed, following the martyrdom of Joseph Smith, the Mormon persecutions rose to unprecedented levels.

To make matters worse, the rumblings of schism could clearly be discerned. Shortly before his death, Joseph Smith was reported to have called a meeting at which several of his apostles and some bishops were present, as well as his brother Hyrum and his 11-year-old son, Joseph Smith III. At this meeting, Smith allegedly named his son as his successor, saying 'Brothers and sisters, I am no longer your prophet – this is your prophet. I have finished my work, and am going to rest.'[41] However, in March 1844, Joseph Smith is also said to have called a council meeting in which he appointed the Quorum of the Twelve Apostles as temporary custodians in case of his death:

Brethren, the Lord bids me hasten the work in which we are engaged. Some important scene is near to take place. It may be that my enemies will kill me. And in case they should, and the keys and power which rest on me not be imparted to you, they will be lost from the earth. But if I can only succeed in placing them upon your heads, then let me fall a victim to murderous hands if God will suffer it, and I can go with all pleasure and satisfaction, knowing that my work is done, and the foundation laid on which the kingdom of God is to be reared in this dispensation of the fulness of times. Upon the shoulders of the Twelve must the responsibility of leading this church henceforth rest until you shall appoint others to succeed you.[42]

Immediately following the murders of Joseph and Hyrum Smith, there was great confusion about the future leadership of the Church. The Quorum of the Twelve Apostles quickly assumed temporary control. Many expected that Joseph Smith's elder brother Samuel would succeed Hyrum as patriarch and lead the Church until Joseph III came of age. Tragically, Samuel died a month later on July 30th,[43] and on August 8th – after an unsuccessful attempt by Sidney Rigdon to be named 'guardian'[44] – the Quorum of the Twelve Apostles convened a special meeting at which it was decided that the Twelve should permanently preside over the Church.[45] Under the leadership of Brigham Young, who presided over that body, the Saints eventually made their way westward to Utah. This may have been inspired by Joseph Smith's thoughts, originally expressed in February 1844, of establishing a Mormon homeland in California or Oregon.[46]

However, several small groups of Mormons broke away from the Church and remained behind, citing disagreement with Brigham Young's successorship and with some of the new 'values' he promoted, not the least of which was polygamy. Significant among those who remained were the prophet's wife, Emma Hale Smith, and their son, Joseph III. Emma remarried a few years later and became known as Emma Smith Bidamon. In 1860, many of these splinter groups were united in the Reorganized Church of Jesus Christ of Latter Day Saints (RLDS), under the leadership of Joseph Smith III.

For both of these two groups – but especially for the Utah contingent – the temporal administration of the Church became the paramount issue. Many new ordinances were established and existing ones expanded. Leadership of the Church, initially given to the Quorum of the Twelve Apostles collectively, over time devolved to a single person who was considered not only its new president, but also its prophet, seer and revelator.[47] For lack of a better explanation, Mormons had all but forgotten the urgency of their beloved prophet's warnings about the impending Day of the Lord, and turned their focus instead to the consolidation and expansion of the Church itself.

By the turn of the century, it had become clear that Joseph Smith's predictions concerning the time of the Second Coming were not going to be fulfilled, at least not according to the prevalent expectations. The fire of millennialism that had so dominated the early Mormon movement had waned to a flickering candle.

How can Bahá'ís view Joseph Smith?

A number of religious leaders and commentators – most notably from other Christian denominations – have dismissed Joseph Smith either as an impostor or as one suffering from delusion. In stark contrast, Shoghi Effendi appears to have called him a 'seer,' the same term used by Mormons.

A seer shall the Lord raise up

Latter-day Saints describe Joseph Smith both as a *prophet* and a *seer*. The Book of Mormon contains the following prophecy, which is believed to refer to Joseph Smith in the latter days:

> For Joseph truly testified, saying: A seer shall the Lord my God raise up, who shall be a choice seer unto the fruit of my loins . . .[48]

Merriam-Webster's *Dictionary* defines the term *seer* as a 'person credited with extraordinary moral and spiritual insight.'[49] According to a Bahá'í pilgrim's note,[50] Shoghi Effendi applied this same definition to Joseph Smith:

> The Guardian was asked about the Mormons. He said that Joseph Smith was a Seer, not a Prophet, neither major nor minor; that he had high standards – but we have the power that comes from the Word of God for this age, which they do not have until they turn to Bahá'u'lláh.[51]

It is important to note here that the LDS Church makes no such distinction between the terms *seer* and *prophet*; in fact, some Mormon scriptures even suggest that a seer is greater than a prophet.[52] This lack of distinction is related to the nature of prophecy as it is understood and experienced by Mormons.

Prophethood understood differently

Shoghi Effendi has stressed that Joseph Smith was not a prophet, whereas Mormons are convinced that he was. However, this may in part be a disagreement over semantics. The definition of the word *Prophet* in the Bahá'í Faith includes Jesus Christ Himself, yet no Mormon would place Joseph Smith on the same level as Christ (although they do equate his prophethood to that of Moses). This suggests that at least part of the disagreement lies in the different stations associated with the title of prophethood.[53]

Underscoring that assertion is the fact that Mormons consider *all* presidents of their Church to have been prophets, who were infallible and whose interpretations are authoritative. Bahá'ís, on the other hand, do not even consider their primary exemplar – 'Abdu'l-Bahá – to have been a Prophet, notwithstanding the fact that they see Him as infallible and take His utterances to be authoritative.

This kind of 'amplification of terms' is characteristic of Mormon nomenclature, as the following examples illustrate:

   (a) *Bishop*. In other Christian churches, this term refers to a position highly elevated in rank. In the LDS Church each local congregation has its own bishop, who is at once the head clergyman and guidance counselor for his congregation, comparable to a pastor.
   (b) *Priest*. In the Catholic Church, this term is reserved for those who have completed seminary and taken a vow of celibacy, whereas in the LDS Church every male member is expected to obtain the lay 'priesthood.'
   (c) *Saint*. This title is usually bestowed posthumously upon those rare individuals who have lived a life of extraordinary piety, service and courage. In the LDS Church it refers to any faithful member of the church, and carries with it no special status or privilege.
   (d) *Personal revelation*. In LDS terminology, this generally refers to the following of one's inner spiritual guidance, and does not imply that each individual is capable of revealing scripture.

Joseph Smith influenced by Bahá'í Revelation

In an unequivocal statement about the influence of the Bahá'í spirit on the development of the Mormon faith, the Universal House of Justice wrote:

> As for the status of Joseph Smith, founder of the Mormon Faith, he is not considered by Bahá'ís to be a prophet, minor or otherwise. But of course he was a religious teacher sensitive to the spiritual currents flowing in the early 19th century directly from the appearance of the Báb and Bahá'u'lláh and the Revelation of Their Messages of hope and divine Guidance.[54]

William P. Collins, in an article comparing the Bahá'í Faith and Mormonism, concludes that 'Bahá'ís may regard Joseph Smith not as a prophet, but as a seer – one endowed with extraordinary powers of insight' and that he was one of several 'religious prodigies,' who 'enunciated a number of ideas that had formed in the collective unconscious of mankind over a long period of incubation, finally to emerge in the early nineteenth century.'[55]

It is generally accepted by Bahá'ís that Joseph Smith was at the very least a visionary moved by the spiritual winds of the time. However, notwithstanding his apparent inspiration and clairvoyance, he was still a man capable of error. The Mormon scriptures acknowledge that Smith was not perfect:

> Your eyes have been upon my servant Joseph Smith, Jun., and his language you have known, and his imperfections you have known; and you have sought in your hearts knowledge that you might express beyond his language; this you also know.[56]

> And now, verily I say unto Joseph Smith, Jun. – You have not kept the commandments, and must needs stand rebuked before the Lord . . .[57]

The human fallibility of Joseph Smith should not be perceived as a disparagement of the Mormon faith, but rather as an inevitability that enables us to appreciate the many gems of wisdom and truth in his writings without being unduly distracted by those things we are unable to accept.

This characterization is shared by members of the Community of Christ, formerly known as the Reorganized Church of Jesus Christ of Latter Day Saints (RLDS). Its web site offers the following statement in connection with evidence that Joseph Smith engaged in polygamy:

> The Community of Christ, in its ongoing quest for truth, remains open to a more complete understanding of its history. Through careful study and the ongoing guidance of the Holy Spirit, the church is learning how to own and responsibly interpret all of its history. This process includes putting new information and changing understandings into proper perspective while emphasizing those parts that continue to play a vital role in guiding and shaping the church's identity and mission today. In this way, we can genuinely affirm the prophetic vision of Joseph Smith Jr., while acknowledging the fallibility present in his life and in the lives of all prophetic leaders.[58]

My own research into the life and teachings of Joseph Smith has left me convinced that, despite being subject to the usual human frailties, he genuinely believed what he professed; that, regardless of what one believes about the validity of the Book of Mormon and Smith's many revelations, he never set out to deliberately deceive any human being. When it came to his religion, he was a man of principles, and was prepared to die for them.

Whatever the actual station of Joseph Smith, it behooves us to think of him as a brilliant man who rebelled against the waywardness and apathy of the Christian churches of the time, and led his followers to a renewed love for God and the person of Jesus Christ, much as John the Baptist called his followers to repentance. In the words of William P. Collins, 'Joseph Smith, in founding a highly successful missionary movement and in tapping and channeling the spiritual current of a new age, showed himself to be a religious genius of a most profound kind.'[59]

CHAPTER 2

THE MORMON SCRIPTURES

A distinguishing feature of the Church of Jesus Christ of Latter-day Saints is its wealth and variety of primary scriptural materials beyond the standard biblical canon. This is not surprising considering that the LDS Church, while at its root a Christian denomination, claims its founder was a prophet. However, not all of the fruits of Joseph Smith's labor are considered revelation. Mormons distinguish between works of 'translation' such as the Book of Mormon, and the direct revelation that is found in the Doctrine and Covenants. This distinction between translated and revealed texts is somewhat blurred owing to Smith's manner of translation being essentially a spiritual process with a strong revelatory aspect, as is the case with the Joseph Smith Translation of the Bible, discussed later in this chapter.

In the following sections I briefly describe each of the seminal scriptural works that, in addition to the Bible, are recognized and revered by Mormons.

The Book of Mormon

The Book of Mormon is without doubt the principal scriptural work of the Mormon faith. When it was first published in 1830, it caused a considerable stir in the American religious community, and its authenticity has been debated by theologians, historians, archaeologists, anthropologists, and etymologists ever since. Epitomizing this controversy is Alexander Campbell's characterization of the Book of Mormon as gathering 'every error and almost every truth discussed in New York for the last ten years.'[1] In 1831, Campbell – a contemporary of Joseph Smith and leader of a popular Protestant movement of the time that later transformed into the Disciples of Christ – published a sardonic commentary on the Book of Mormon in his periodical *The Millennial Harbinger*, in which he presented numerous anachronisms and other 'internal evidences' of its inauthenticity.

It is far beyond the scope of this book to provide anything more than a cursory glance at this 'other testament of Jesus Christ' which is guiding the lives of some 12 million Mormon faithful, and which has kept so many bright minds occupied in either proving or disproving its truth. Therefore, we will confine ourselves to a brief introduction, followed by some Bahá'í perspectives.

The Golden Plates

The Book of Mormon was, according to its introduction, 'translated by the gift and power of God' from 'golden plates' – the ancient brass plates which Joseph Smith uncovered based on information he received in his second vision, and which are believed to have originated in South or Central America. The title page further states that the original plates were

> Written and sealed up, and hid up unto the Lord, that they might not be destroyed – To come forth by the gift and power of God unto the interpretation thereof – Sealed by the hand of Moroni, and hid up unto the Lord, to come forth in due time by way of the Gentile – The interpretation thereof by the gift of God.[2]

Latter-day Saints believe that soon after Christ's death and resurrection, He reappeared on the American continent to a people who had long been expecting His Coming. The history of this civilization, culminating in Jesus' appearance, was considered lost until Joseph Smith discovered the golden plates from which he translated the Book of Mormon. Smith later produced additional writings which he attributed to Abraham and Moses, and also altered portions of the King James Version of the Bible to bring them into literal conformity with what he considered to be their original, true meaning.

Mormon scholars are in agreement – in fact, it is readily admitted by the LDS Church – that Smith's process of translating the Book of Mormon was spiritual, not scientific, in nature. Its English translation, therefore, came about without Joseph Smith actually reading the original plates, which he claimed were written in 'reformed Egyptian' hieroglyphics. This fact alone makes it difficult for many to accept the Book of Mormon as wholly authentic, and it does not help that the only evidence of the plates' existence is the collective testimony of eight of Smith's companions, some of whom later admitted that they saw these plates only with a 'spiritual eye.'[3]

Yet the mention of golden plates should not in and of itself cause us to doubt the truth of Smith's assertions. In *So Great a Cause*, Kenneth Stephens notes that 'Gold and silver plates were common in ancient times both in the Old and New Worlds . . . Such plates have also been found in southern Mexico, clearly establishing their use in ancient times.' Stephens, who wrote his landmark book shortly after leaving the LDS Church to embrace the Bahá'í Faith, appears at that time not to have abandoned his belief in the Book of Mormon, and in fact dedicates much of his introductory chapter to its defense. This is good news, because it suggests that Latter-day Saints should not feel they need to reject their most precious scriptures in order to accept the Bahá'í Revelation.

Historicity of the Book of Mormon

The Book of Mormon tells the story of a group of Israelites who migrate westward to the American continent circa 600 BC, sailing the Atlantic Ocean in what bears a striking resemblance to Noah's Ark, aided by a mysterious compass-like device called a *Liahona.* Not long after their arrival they become divided into two main warring factions, the Nephites and the Lamanites. Mormons believe these Lamanites to be the forefathers of today's Native American cultures, and do not accept scientific evidence that these cultures migrated from Asia some 15,000 to 30,000 years ago.

Kenneth Stephens, who wrote his book *So Great a Cause* as an introduction to the Bahá'í Faith from a Mormon perspective, declares:

> The Lamanite faction of the original Israelite people in America does not appear to have possessed a pure written account of their religious history and teachings . . . Nevertheless, they did preserve a knowledge of some of the most important events in their history, as well as some of the high moral teachings of Christ and the Nephite prophets. These were written down by some of the Maya and Aztec scholars who learned to write in Spanish, as well as by some of the Catholic priests and missionaries who lived among them, and bear a remarkable resemblance to historical accounts given in the pages of the Book of Mormon.[4]

Stephens appears to take the claims of the Book of Mormon at face value, deducing that some of the events it portrays were retained in the collective consciousness of the native people, and reflected in their more recent writings. Of course, the 'high moral teachings' of which he speaks could have easily been brought by the missionaries themselves, and do not prove their existence in pre-Columbian times. For that matter, they could have been established by indigenous prophets long since forgotten, considering that all religions teach the same basic spiritual laws. But Stephens, armed with thorough research, defends the authenticity of the Book of Mormon on the grounds that Joseph

Smith could not have known of the history and religious teachings of those cultures through ordinary means:

> There are three highly valid writings of the early Catholic fathers, reliable because of the objectivity of their writers and their long acquaintance with the native peoples. These are the writings of Diago de Landa, the first Catholic bishop of Yucatan, 1524–1579; Bernardino de Sahagun, a Catholic padre who lived in Mexico from 1529 to 1590, and Juan the Torquemada, who lived in sixteenth century Mexico for many years.
>
> The first translation of any of these writings into English appeared in Antiquities of Mexico, written by Lord Edward King Kingsborough, in nine volumes, between 1831 and 1848, the ninth volume, containing the writings of Ixlilxochitl, appearing in the latter year. This nine volume set was published by Henry G. Bohn in London, England and is available in most university libraries. The first edition of the *Book of Mormon* was in 1830. It is thus easily provable that Joseph Smith had no access to any of these earlier accounts concerning the history and religious teachings of the early Indian civilizations in Middle America at the time of the translation of the gold plates into what is now known as the *Book of Mormon*.[5]

Lack of physical evidence

Notwithstanding numerous efforts to discover physical evidence that might corroborate some of the events recounted in the Book of Mormon, so far such evidence has eluded even the most diligent of Mormon researchers. For example, while the book describes a great storm and flood, in which 'many great and notable cities were sunk, and many were burned,'[6] there is no indication of any major floods on this continent during the time frame in which they are said to have taken place. The Book of Mormon also states that the 'whole face of the land had become covered with buildings, and the people were as numerous almost, as it were the sand of the sea.'[7] Although there have been several archaeological finds of Incan and Mayan cities, these did not reach nearly the size described in the Book of Mormon, and in any case were not built until centuries after the end of that book's narrative.

Historians, archaeologists and anthropologists, Mormon and non-Mormon alike, have long argued over this issue of historical and physical evidence, or lack thereof. Yet many biblical scholars have similarly disputed the authenticity of the Bible on the grounds that it contradicts archaeological and scientific fact. William P. Collins, in his two-part article comparing the Bahá'í Faith and Mormonism, illustrates the folly of debating the historicity of scriptural works:

It is quite unmistakable that Shoghi Effendi regarded the Bible, the Qur'án, and the Bahá'í Scriptures as the only Holy Books that can be accepted as authentic; and since Bahá'ís do not look upon Joseph Smith as a prophet, the Book of Mormon cannot also be regarded as a divinely revealed scripture in the same category as those he lists.

There is not, however, a simple choice of becoming a total believer in, or a total skeptic about, the Book of Mormon and the gifts of Joseph Smith. This is particularly the case if one turns to the Book of Mormon as an historical document. A number of scholars well-known in Mormon circles, including members of the Reorganized Church of Jesus Christ of Latter Day Saints who believe in the divine inspiration of the Book of Mormon, have questioned whether the Book of Mormon can be viewed as a reporting of historical fact . . . All of the conclusions point to the Book of Mormon's being not the annals of a lost pre-Columbian civilization but rather the product of the mind of a nineteenth-century New Yorker with a fervent religious imagination. Moreover, there is lack of independent evidence from the archaeological record to confirm the events or places described in the Book of Mormon.

One would be unwarranted, however, in dismissing Joseph Smith as pure fraud and the Book of Mormon as falsehood simply on the basis of these findings. When one speaks of truth, he is liable to equate it with historical fact. One is dealing, however, with two different levels or strata of truth. The recounting of what has actually happened in a given circumstance may leave one unaffected, whereas a fictitious construction may cause him to be deeply moved . . . The question of historicity or pure historical fact is out of place in dealing with many aspects of writings claimed as sacred scripture, because the question of what is historically true or false is inadequate in the face of the power and influence exercised by the spiritual and relevant truths embodied in those scriptures.[8]

Latter-day Saints consider the Book of Mormon to be 'the most correct of any book on earth,'[9] and even if it were proven beyond a shadow of a doubt to be an elaborate hoax, the vast majority of Mormons would not be swayed in the least. We are better served, then, to examine the theological content of this truly remarkable book – no matter its origin – rather than debate the accuracy of the historical events it portrays. Indeed, when asked about the Book of Mormon, Shoghi Effendi was careful not to undermine its authenticity:

As there is nothing specific about Joseph Smith in the teachings, the Guardian has no statement to make on his position or about the accuracy of any statement in the Book of Mormon regarding American history or its peoples. This is a matter for historians to pass upon.[10]

As William P. Collins observed concerning the above quote, this 'leaves Bahá'ís free to base their judgment of the accuracy of *The Book of Mormon* on the available historical evidence.'[11]

How can Bahá'ís view the Book of Mormon?

To non-Mormons, the Book of Mormon can appear to be the epitome of self-fulfilling prophecy: once a person accepts it and its claims to historicity, that person is then continually amazed at how accurately it predicts 'future' events, forgetting that these events were historical relative to the time of Joseph Smith. On the other hand, we cannot be sure that some of the history depicted in the Book of Mormon, particularly that pertaining to early Indian cultures, is completely ungrounded in fact. Moreover, Kenneth Stephens, the author of *So Great a Cause*, was able to eloquently explain the truth of the Bahá'í Faith without ever casting doubt on the authenticity of the Book of Mormon.

We should not let an apparent lack of historicity prevent us from appreciating the spiritual truths enshrined in the Book of Mormon. As Bahá'ís, we already accept those portions of it that are direct quotations from the Bible. Many of the events recounted in the Book of Mormon, while purportedly describing the First Coming of Christ, may in fact be referring to His Second Coming, a conclusion that is quickly drawn from the copious quotations from Isaiah and Daniel concerning 'the last days.' This fact alone testifies to the major thrust of the message of Joseph Smith, which is to prepare spiritually for the Return of Christ. The story itself, when taken allegorically, provides valuable moral lessons and is well worth the read. Thus the Book of Mormon may, in the most banal sense, be considered an effective narrative device for conveying some intriguing spiritual observations; and in a more favorable light, it can be seen as a work touched by a degree of inspiration. According to William P. Collins:

> When one turns to an examination of relevant truth in the Book of Mormon, his reading reveals that, even if the stories are not historical fact, they embody powerful, eternal, spiritual meaning that is capable of changing and guiding the lives of men. The Book of Mormon is a parable of the struggle between good and evil, between those who heed the commands of their Creator and those who turn from His precepts and sink to the level of the animal. It is not an abstract statement, for it breathes with the

excitement of the cosmic confrontation of light and darkness, mirrored in the archetypal personalities and characters who people the book. Thus it is at this level of relevant truth that a Bahá'í may find a method of approach to the Book of Mormon that is at once sympathetic and yet in conformity with the statements of Shoghi Effendi on the subject.[12]

Most importantly, the Book of Mormon is sacred to our Mormon brothers and sisters, and we can have a constructive dialogue about religion without undermining its authority. In conclusion, writes Collins, '[e]ven if one does not accept the Book of Mormon as a translation from literal golden plates, the book can, nevertheless, be viewed as the product of Joseph Smith's genuine religious experience.'[13]

An excerpt from the Book of Mormon

Before leaving the topic of the Book of Mormon, I would like to present the reader with a short excerpt of particular beauty. Much of the book appears to emulate the rhythm and flow of the Old Testament, and is quite repetitive – some would say monotonous – in nature. Phrases such as 'and behold . . .' and 'it came to pass . . .' occur so frequently in the Book of Mormon that Mark Twain wryly dismissed it as 'chloroform in print.' However, Joseph Smith (or the ancient prophets whose writings he is purported to translate) also had the ability to wax poetic. The mystical mood conveyed by the following stirring words of Nephi is reminiscent not only of the Psalms of the Old Testament, but also of the Long Obligatory Prayer, the Fire Tablet and other Bahá'í Writings, and is powerful evidence that Joseph Smith possessed a spiritual awareness rivaled by few:

> Behold, my soul delighteth in the things of the Lord; and my heart pondereth continually upon the things which I have seen and heard. Nevertheless, notwithstanding the great goodness of the Lord, in showing me his great and marvelous works, my heart exclaimeth: O wretched man that I am! Yea, my heart sorroweth because of my flesh; my soul grieveth because of mine iniquities. I am encompassed about, because of the temptations and the sins which do so easily beset me. And when I desire to rejoice, my heart groaneth because of my sins; nevertheless, I know in whom I have trusted. My God hath been my support; he hath led me through mine afflictions in the wilderness; and he hath preserved me upon the waters of the great deep. He hath filled me with his love, even unto the consuming of my flesh. He hath confounded mine enemies, unto the

causing of them to quake before me. Behold, he hath heard my cry by day, and he hath given me knowledge by visions in the night-time. And by day have I waxed bold in mighty prayer before him; yea, my voice have I sent up on high; and angels came down and ministered unto me. And upon the wings of his Spirit hath my body been carried away upon exceedingly high mountains. And mine eyes have beheld great things, yea, even too great for man; therefore I was bidden that I should not write them. O then, if I have seen so great things, if the Lord in his condescension unto the children of men hath visited men in so much mercy, why should my heart weep and my soul linger in the valley of sorrow, and my flesh waste away, and my strength slacken, because of mine afflictions? And why should I yield to sin, because of my flesh? Yea, why should I give way to temptations, that the evil one have place in my heart to destroy my peace and afflict my soul? Why am I angry because of mine enemy? Awake, my soul! No longer droop in sin. Rejoice, O my heart, and give place no more for the enemy of my soul. Do not anger again because of mine enemies. Do not slacken my strength because of mine afflictions. Rejoice, O my heart, and cry unto the Lord, and say: O Lord, I will praise thee forever; yea, my soul will rejoice in thee, my God, and the rock of my salvation. O Lord, wilt thou redeem my soul? Wilt thou deliver me out of the hands of mine enemies? Wilt thou make me that I may shake at the appearance of sin? May the gates of hell be shut continually before me, because that my heart is broken and my spirit is contrite! O Lord, wilt thou not shut the gates of thy righteousness before me, that I may walk in the path of the low valley, that I may be strict in the plain road! O Lord, wilt thou encircle me around in the robe of thy righteousness! O Lord, wilt thou make a way for mine escape before mine enemies! Wilt thou make my path straight before me! Wilt thou not place a stumbling block in my way – but that thou wouldst clear my way before me, and hedge not up my way, but the ways of mine enemy. O Lord, I have trusted in thee, and I will trust in thee forever. I will not put my trust in the arm of flesh; for I know that cursed is he that putteth his trust in the arm of flesh. Yea, cursed is he that putteth his trust in man or maketh flesh his arm. Yea, I know that God will give liberally to him that asketh. Yea, my God will give me, if I ask not amiss; therefore I will lift up my voice unto thee; yea, I will cry unto thee, my God, the rock of my righteousness. Behold, my voice shall forever ascend up unto thee, my rock and mine everlasting God. Amen.[14]

The Doctrine and Covenants

The second most important body of LDS scripture, *The Doctrine and Covenants*, represents a radical departure from the biblical style of storytelling found in the Book of Mormon. Instead it is a roughly chronological collection of revelations by Joseph Smith, some rendered in the voice of God or Jesus and some in his own voice, touching on a wide range of topics as lofty as the nature of God and the qualities of a true believer, or as mundane as the proper location of the printing press for publishing the Mormon scriptures. Many of these revelations are dedicated to, in praise of or in condemnation of specific individuals; others provide unambiguous spiritual guidance to the generality of mankind. Some concern themselves with ancient history, while others prophesy future events. There are a number of threads connecting all of these revelations, however, and the language in which they are rendered evinces power and authority.

The 'explanatory introduction' to the Doctrine and Covenants states that

> The Doctrine and Covenants is a collection of divine revelations and inspired declarations given for the establishment and regulation of the kingdom of God on the earth in the last days. Although most of the sections are directed to members of The Church of Jesus Christ of Latter-day Saints, the messages, warnings, and exhortations are for the benefit of all mankind, and contain an invitation to all people everywhere to hear the voice of the Lord Jesus Christ, speaking to them for their temporal well-being and their everlasting salvation.[15]

Portions of what now constitutes the Doctrine and Covenants were originally published in 1831 in a collection titled *A Book of Commandments, for the Government of the Church of Christ*. Brief excerpts were also printed in the church periodical *The Evening and the Morning Star* between 1832 and 1833. In 1834, a committee was appointed 'to arrange the items of the doctrine of Jesus Christ for the government of the church of Latter-Day Saints . . . to be taken from the Bible, book of mormon, and the revelations which have been given to the church up to this date or shall be, until such arrangement is made.'[16] The committee was populated by Joseph Smith and his brother Samuel H. Smith, as well as high-ranking church officials Oliver Cowdery, Sidney Rigdon, and Frederic G. Williams. Revelations by Joseph Smith recorded up to that time were carefully selected for canonization in the new book, and in some cases updated to reflect new developments in the Church.[17] In 1835, the first official edition of *The Doctrine and Covenants* was published.

In its current form, the Doctrine and Covenants (D&C) comprises 138 sections of varying length, plus two 'Official Declarations': the first an 1890 statement from the First Presidency affirming the discontinuance of the practice of plural marriage,* and the second a 1978 letter extending the Mormon priesthood to members of African descent.† Of the 138 main sections, all but three were revealed by Joseph Smith himself.

Among the most popular revelations in the book is D&C 89, better known as the Word of Wisdom, in which Joseph Smith condemns the use of alcohol and tobacco and gives general advice on health and nutrition.

The Pearl of Great Price

The third and smallest volume in the LDS Church's 'triple combination' of standard scriptures is *The Pearl of Great Price*, a collection of mostly unrelated texts that include revelations, translations and narrations by Joseph Smith, as well as a brief summary of church tenets. Originally compiled in 1851, the content of this book has changed over the years, with some of the original material later moved to the Doctrine and Covenants, and other items (including a poem not written by Joseph Smith) removed. The current version of *The Pearl of Great Price* is dated 1981.

Selections from the Book of Moses

The first and most substantial section of *The Pearl of Great Price* is what the LDS Church describes as an 'extract from the translation of the Bible as revealed to Joseph Smith the Prophet,' eight chapters believed to contain original revelations by Moses, including prophecies of the prophet Enoch pointing to the establishment of the LDS Church in the latter days. The Book of Moses tracks closely to the King James Version of Genesis (verses 1:1–6:13), employing similar or identical language but enlarging upon and interpreting the original Bible text. One notable difference is that the Book of Moses is written in the first person of God conversing directly with Moses, whereas Genesis refers to God in the third person.

Joseph Smith's interpretations dominate this creative translation. His purpose was no doubt to clarify the meaning of the verses as he understood them, but in doing so he also removed the possibility of a spiritual interpretation of the words. For example, Genesis 1:16 states:

---

* See Appendix 1 for a discussion of the role of polygamy in the LDS Church.
† See Appendix 2 for more information.

44

And God made two great lights; the greater light to rule the day, and the lesser light to rule the night: he made the stars also.[18]

Verse 2:16 of the Book of Moses reads:

And I, God, made two great lights; the greater light to rule the day, and the lesser light to rule the night, and the greater light was the sun, and the lesser light was the moon; and the stars also were made even according to my word.[19]

The first chapter of Genesis never mentions the sun and moon, and allows for various hidden meanings beyond the physical orbs in the sky. Joseph Smith's alterations effectively force a literal interpretation.

Many of the LDS Church's unique doctrines – including those concerning the Creation and the existence of multiple worlds – find their origin in the Book of Moses. For example, Mormons believe that Jesus Christ was not only present at the Creation, but was co-creator with God. This is reflected in the Book of Moses:

And I, God, said unto mine Only Begotten, which was with me from the beginning: Let us make man in our image, after our likeness; and it was so. And I, God, said: Let them have dominion over the fishes of the sea, and over the fowl of the air, and over the cattle, and over all the earth, and over every creeping thing that creepeth upon the earth.[20]

The corresponding verse in Genesis portrays God as the sole agent of the Creation:[21]

And God said, Let us make man in our image, after our likeness: and let them have dominion over the fish of the sea, and over the fowl of the air, and over the cattle, and over all the earth, and over every creeping thing that creepeth upon the earth.[22]

The Book of Abraham

Probably the most controversial work of LDS scripture outside of the Book of Mormon itself, the Book of Abraham is described in its summary as 'A Translation of some ancient Records, that have fallen into our hands from the catacombs of Egypt. – The writings of Abraham while he was in Egypt, called the Book of Abraham, written by his own hand, upon papyrus.'[23]

In 1835, Joseph Smith claimed to have found a set of ancient Egyptian papyri penned by Abraham himself. Though unlettered in Egyptian hieroglyphics, Smith produced a translation of these papyri under the title *The Book of Abraham*. Unlike the Book of Mormon, whose original brass plates have never been seen except by a handful of 'witnesses,' the Book of Abraham's source documents – or at least three rather inadequately reproduced facsimiles thereof – were published along with it to prove their authenticity. No serious analysis of these documents was undertaken until 1851, when an Egyptologist at the Louvre, M. Theodule Deveria, was asked to decipher them. The poor quality of the reproduction prevented a full translation of the text, but it was clear to Deveria, and countless Egyptologists since, that at least one of the facsimiles (no. 3) was a funeral illustration for a man named Horus, and thus had nothing to do with the Abraham of the Old Testament. In 1967, the original of facsimile no. 1, which had once been in Joseph Smith's possession, was discovered among a number of papyri held by the Metropolitan Museum of Art in New York. The first person to produce a translation was Dr Klaus Baer, who identified it as an illustration in connection with a deceased person named Hor(us), son of Tikhebyt. Facsimile no. 2 was first translated by Mormon scholar Michael Dennis Rhodes, revealing that it belonged to another deceased person named Sheshonk, and not, apparently, to Abraham.[24] Over the ensuing decades, Egyptologists and Mormon apologists have traded barbs and fired verbal salvos at each other over the issue of authenticity and whether Joseph Smith's interpretation of the papyri has any merit.

Whatever its provenance, the Book of Abraham is significant in that it, like the Book of Moses, reveals the origin of a number of uniquely Mormon beliefs. Its five chapters are roughly divided into three themes: Chapters 1 and 2 describe Abraham's persecution and his ultimate migration from Ur to Canaan. Chapter 3 covers a wide range of metaphysical concepts; in just the last seven verses of that chapter we learn of pre-existence and that the world was not created so much as organized from existing materials, and are introduced to the concepts of 'first estate' and 'second estate' in relation to different kingdoms of glory.* We also get a glimpse of Satan and his fall from grace:

> Now the Lord had shown unto me, Abraham, the intelligences that were organized before the world was; and among all these there were many of the noble and great ones; And God saw these souls that they were good, and he stood in the midst of them, and he said: These I will make my

---

* See Chapter 5, 'The Nature of the Soul and the Afterlife'.

rulers; for he stood among those that were spirits, and he saw that they were good; and he said unto me: Abraham, thou art one of them; thou wast chosen before thou wast born. And there stood one among them that was like unto God, and he said unto those who were with him: We will go down, for there is space there, and we will take of these materials, and we will make an earth whereon these may dwell; And we will prove them herewith, to see if they will do all things whatsoever the Lord their God shall command them; And they who keep their first estate shall be added upon; and they who keep not their first estate shall not have glory in the same kingdom with those who keep their first estate; and they who keep their second estate shall have glory added upon their heads for ever and ever. And the Lord said: Whom shall I send? And one answered like unto the Son of Man: Here am I, send me. And another answered and said: Here am I, send me. And the Lord said: I will send the first. And the second was angry, and kept not his first estate; and, at that day, many followed after him.[25]

The last two chapters support the Mormon belief in a multiplicity of Gods, and provide yet another recitation of the first two chapters of Genesis (up to Gen. 2:20), albeit with some distinct modifications:

And then the Lord said: Let us go down. And they went down at the beginning, and they, that is the Gods, organized and formed the heavens and the earth. And the earth, after it was formed, was empty and desolate, because they had not formed anything but the earth; and darkness reigned upon the face of the deep, and the Spirit of the Gods was brooding upon the face of the waters. And they (the Gods) said: Let there be light; and there was light. And they (the Gods) comprehended the light, for it was bright; and they divided the light, or caused it to be divided, from the darkness. And the Gods called the light Day, and the darkness they called Night. And it came to pass that from the evening until morning they called night; and from the morning until the evening they called day; and this was the first, or the beginning, of that which they called day and night . . .[26]

Joseph Smith–Matthew

During his study of the Bible, Joseph Smith found himself at odds with a number of statements in it. He believed that while the origin of the Bible was divine, faulty translation was the cause of a number of textual errors through which many 'plain and precious things' had been taken away. He thus began an 'inspired translation' of various parts of both the Old and New Testaments in order to restore what he felt was the original meaning of the texts.

Joseph Smith–Matthew is one such translation, and consists of a single chapter which more or less corresponds to the King James Version of Matthew, verse 23:39 and Chapter 24. Most of the verses remain unaltered, or use a slightly different word or spelling. A few are expanded to clarify Joseph Smith's understanding of their meaning, and throughout the chapter the order of the verses is mixed up somewhat, with several being repeated even though they appear only once in the original.

Except for the handful of expanded verses, the changes in *Joseph Smith– Matthew* at first glance do not seem to warrant special inclusion in *The Pearl of Great Price*, especially in light of the more substantial emendations found in the Joseph Smith Translation of the Bible (see below). However, a careful examination of this translation will no doubt shed additional light on the mind of Joseph Smith.

The Joseph Smith Translation of the Bible

Although they are not included in *The Pearl of Great Price* nor considered part of the LDS standard scriptural canon, Joseph Smith made many more 'inspired interpretations' of the Bible, collectively known as the *Joseph Smith Translation*. Most of these alterations apply to the books of Genesis and Matthew, but very little of the Bible escaped his critical pen; in the Old Testament, he reinterpreted one or more verses in Genesis, Exodus, Deuteronomy, 1 and 2 Samuel, 1 and 2 Chronicles, Psalms, Isaiah, Jeremiah, and Amos; in the New Testament, he modified parts of Matthew, Mark, Luke, John, Acts, Romans, 1 Corinthians, Galatians, Ephesians, Colossians, 1 and 2 Thessalonians, 1 Timothy, Hebrews, James, 1 and 2 Peter, 1 John and Revelation.

An official guide explains that the Joseph Smith Translation is

A revision or translation of the King James Version of the Bible in English, which the Prophet Joseph Smith began in June 1830. He was commanded by God to make the translation and regarded it as part of his calling as a prophet.

Although Joseph completed most of the translation by July 1833, he continued until his death in 1844 to make modifications while preparing a manuscript for publication. Though he published some parts of the translation during his lifetime, it is possible that he would have made additional changes had he lived to publish the entire work. The Reorganized Church of Jesus Christ of Latter Day Saints published the first edition of Joseph

Smith's inspired translation in 1867. They have published several editions
since that time . . . Although it is not the official Bible of the Church,
this translation does offer many interesting insights and is very valuable
in understanding the Bible. It is also a witness for the divine calling and
ministry of the Prophet Joseph Smith.[27]

While Mormons accept these translations as inspired, the official Bible of the
LDS canon is the original King James Version. The Joseph Smith Translation
is discussed in more detail later on in this book.[28]

The Joseph Smith History

The Joseph Smith History is a short (75 verses) autobiographical work which
was written, according to its author, in response to 'the many reports which
have been put in circulation by evil-disposed and designing persons, in relation to the rise and progress of the Church of Jesus Christ of Latter-day Saints,
all of which have been designed by the authors thereof to militate against its
character as a Church and its progress in the world.' Having thus been established as an apologetic work, it serves its purpose by providing a background
of the social and religious milieu in which the Church – and the prophet who
founded it – arose, and giving an account of the visions and experiences in
Joseph's life which impelled him to start this new religious movement.

Arguably the most significant of the events portrayed in this document
is the 'First Vision,' in which a 14-year-old Joseph withdraws to a quiet spot
in the woods to supplicate the Lord in prayer. It is here that he is visited by
two personages whom he understands to be God the Father and Jesus Christ.
When he recounts his experience to a preacher, he is ridiculed and then persecuted.

The next event concerns the vision Joseph received a few years later, in
which he is visited by the angel Moroni who tells him of a book written on
golden plates, and shows him where it is hidden. He resolves to find the spot
and indeed finds the plates of the Book of Mormon along with the Urim and
Thummim, or stone spectacles, that enable the wearer to spiritually divine its
meaning. He is however prevented from taking the treasure from its hiding
place until four years later, after his marriage to Emma Hale.

Joseph next describes the circumstances surrounding the translation of the
Book of Mormon, which he dictated first to Martin Harris and later to Oliver
Cowdery.

The final eight verses describe how Joseph Smith and Oliver Cowdery,
inspired by their translation work on the Book of Mormon, 'went into the

woods to pray and inquire of the Lord respecting baptism for the remission of sins.' According to this account, they both receive a vision in which they are visited by a messenger from heaven who confers upon them the *Aaronic Priesthood* and instructs the two men to baptize each other, after which they receive the Holy Ghost and the spirit of prophecy. The messenger then declares that he is John the Baptist.

The Articles of Faith

The final section in *The Pearl of Great Price* is a summary listing of the thirteen principal tenets of the Mormon faith, written by Joseph Smith. They are:

1. We believe in God, the Eternal Father, and in His Son, Jesus Christ, and in the Holy Ghost.
2. We believe that men will be punished for their own sins, and not for Adam's transgression.
3. We believe that through the Atonement of Christ, all mankind may be saved, by obedience to the laws and ordinances of the Gospel.
4. We believe that the first principles and ordinances of the Gospel are: first, Faith in the Lord Jesus Christ; second, Repentance; third, Baptism by immersion for the remission of sins; fourth, Laying on of hands for the gift of the Holy Ghost.
5. We believe that a man must be called of God, by prophecy, and by the laying on of hands by those who are in authority, to preach the Gospel and administer in the ordinances thereof.
6. We believe in the same organization that existed in the Primitive Church, namely, apostles, prophets, pastors, teachers, evangelists, and so forth.
7. We believe in the gift of tongues, prophecy, revelation, visions, healing, interpretation of tongues, and so forth.
8. We believe the Bible to be the word of God as far as it is translated correctly; we also believe the Book of Mormon to be the word of God.
9. We believe all that God has revealed, all that He does now reveal, and we believe that He will yet reveal many great and important things pertaining to the Kingdom of God.
10. We believe in the literal gathering of Israel and in the restoration of the Ten Tribes; that Zion (the New Jerusalem) will be built upon the American continent; that Christ will reign personally upon the earth; and, that the earth will be renewed and receive its paradisiacal glory.
11. We claim the privilege of worshiping Almighty God according to the

dictates of our own conscience, and allow all men the same privilege, let them worship how, where, or what they may.

12. We believe in being subject to kings, presidents, rulers, and magistrates, in obeying, honoring, and sustaining the law.

13. We believe in being honest, true, chaste, benevolent, virtuous, and in doing good to all men; indeed, we may say that we follow the admonition of Paul – We believe all things, we hope all things, we have endured many things, and hope to be able to endure all things. If there is anything virtuous, lovely, or of good report or praiseworthy, we seek after these things.

Although they are the words of Joseph Smith, the Articles of Faith are not considered scripture on the same level as the Book of Mormon or the Doctrine and Covenants. Nevertheless, they are an essential part of the LDS canon.

The following chapter will examine each of these Articles and how they can be understood from a Bahá'í perspective.

CHAPTER 3

THE ARTICLES OF FAITH

Most Mormons can recite by heart all thirteen Articles of Faith, which collectively form a synopsis of the most important beliefs held by members of the Church of Jesus Christ of Latter-day Saints. Naturally, this should be the first stop in our search for commonalities between the Mormon and Bahá'í faiths.

What follows is a sequential listing of the LDS Articles of Faith. The reader should keep in mind that since we are traversing the list of doctrines that are important to Mormons, there is not always a basis for comparison with Bahá'í principles. Nevertheless, I have attempted to make such comparisons wherever possible, and to identify agreements as well as disagreements between the two faiths. Due to the abbreviated nature of these Articles, I have included background information where appropriate.

The First Article of Faith

> *We believe in God, the Eternal Father, and in His Son, Jesus Christ, and in the Holy Ghost.*

It is no coincidence that the first (and presumably the principal) Article of Faith involves a declaration of faith in the Father, the Son and the 'Holy Ghost,' or Holy Spirit. There are several observations to be made about the particular wording of this Article:

- The explicit mention of Jesus Christ is an important reminder of the centrality of the Person of Christ to the LDS Church, and appears to be directed both to the faithful and at detractors who claim that it is not a truly Christian church.
- The three entities mentioned are collectively known to Christendom as the Holy Trinity, the belief in which is a basic tenet of the overwhelming majority of Christian churches. The indirect reference to the Trinity is

another sign that this is very much a Christian church.

- The fact that the three Persons of the Trinity are listed separately – without mention of the Trinity itself – is telling. In contrast to the traditional Christian concept of the Trinity, Mormon doctrine holds each of these three Persons to be a separate and distinct god, an idea that appears, at least on the surface, at variance with the entire notion of monotheism. According to this principle, God the Father, God the Son (Jesus) and God the Holy Ghost each have physical attributes, including location. God and Jesus are both believed to have a body of flesh and bones, and although God can physically be in only one place at a time, spiritually he can be everywhere. The Holy Ghost's body is not physical but is nonetheless in the 'form and likeness of a man,'[1] and can only be in one place at a time. Like God, however, his influence can be felt everywhere at the same time, just the like sun's rays are felt by everyone on earth.[2]

Thus, Mormons do not subscribe to the traditional Christian model of the Trinity, and prefer instead to use the term *Godhead* to refer to the tripartite entity. The following excerpt from an article in the church periodical *Ensign* provides a good illustration of how Mormons view the Trinity:

> The Church's first Article of Faith is 'We believe in God, the Eternal Father, and in His Son, Jesus Christ, and in the Holy Ghost.' This is a straight-forward statement of belief that there are three members in the Godhead. However, Latter-day Saints do reject the doctrines of the Trinity as taught by most Christian churches today. For the most part, these creeds – the most famous of which is the Nicene Creed – were canonized in the fourth and fifth centuries A.D. following centuries of debate about the nature of the Godhead. Consequently, it is highly questionable whether these creeds reflect the thinking or beliefs of the New Testament church.[3]

And in Bruce R. McConkie's *Mormon Doctrine* we read:

> Three separate personages – Father, Son, and Holy Ghost – comprise the Godhead. As each of these persons is a God, it is evident, from this stand-point alone, that a plurality of Gods exists.[4]

Interestingly, this doctrine of multiple gods is unsupported by the Book of Mormon, which states quite unambiguously that there is but one God:

> Now Zeezrom said: Is there more than one God? And he answered, No.[5]

... verily I say unto you, that the Father, and the Son, and the Holy Ghost are one; and I am in the Father, and the Father in me, and the Father and I are one.[6]

And now, behold, this is the doctrine of Christ, and the only and true doctrine of the Father, and of the Son, and of the Holy Ghost, which is one God, without end.[7]

A Baháʼí explanation of the Trinity

The Baháʼí teachings are in agreement with the first Article of Faith *as it is written*, i.e. the belief in God, Jesus Christ (including His Sonship) and the Holy Spirit. However, the Baháʼí Writings shed new light on the concept of the Trinity, which is considered by most Christian churches to be one of God's great mysteries. According to mainstream Christian doctrine, in one way the Father, the Son and the Holy Spirit are separate parts of the whole, working together in one accord. In another way, all three are one and indivisible.

For over fifteen centuries – starting with its official adoption as a Christian doctrine at the Nicene Council – no one has been successful in reconciling these two conflicting conceptions of the Trinity. Yet in *Some Answered Questions*, ʻAbduʼl-Bahá unraveled its secrets in a few short paragraphs:

> God is pure perfection, and creatures are but imperfections. For God to descend into the conditions of existence would be the greatest of imperfections; on the contrary, His manifestation, His appearance, His rising are like the reflection of the sun in a clear, pure, polished mirror ... So the Reality of Christ was a clear and polished mirror of the greatest purity and fineness. The Sun of Reality, the Essence of Divinity, reflected itself in this mirror and manifested its light and heat in it; but from the exaltation of its holiness, and the heaven of its sanctity, the Sun did not descend to dwell and abide in the mirror. No, it continues to subsist in its exaltation and sublimity, while appearing and becoming manifest in the mirror in beauty and perfection.
>
> Now if we say that we have seen the Sun in two mirrors – one the Christ and one the Holy Spirit – that is to say, that we have seen three Suns, one in heaven and the two others on the earth, we speak truly. And if we say that there is one Sun, and it is pure singleness, and has no partner and equal, we again speak truly.
>
> The epitome of the discourse is that the Reality of Christ was a clear mirror, and the Sun of Reality – that is to say, the Essence of Oneness, with

its infinite perfections and attributes – became visible in the mirror. The meaning is not that the Sun, which is the Essence of the Divinity, became divided and multiplied – for the Sun is one – but it appeared in the mirror. This is why Christ said, 'The Father is in the Son,' meaning that the Sun is visible and manifest in this mirror . . .

It has now become clear, from this explanation, what is the meaning of the Three Persons of the Trinity. The Oneness of God is also proved.[8]

'Abdu'l-Bahá also explained the Trinity in another way:

> But as to the question of the Trinity, know, O advancer unto God, that in each one of the cycles wherein the Lights have shone forth upon the horizons . . . there are necessarily three things: The Giver of the Grace, and the Grace, and the Recipient of the Grace; the Source of the Effulgence, and the Effulgence, and the Recipient of the Effulgence; the Illuminator, and the Illumination, and the Illuminated . . . Look at the sun and its rays and the heat which results from its rays; the rays and the heat are but two effects of the sun, but inseparable from it; yet the sun is one in its essence, unique in its real identity, single in its attributes, neither is it possible that anything should resemble it. Such is the essence of the Truth concerning the Unity, the real doctrine of the Singularity, the undiluted reality as to the (Divine) Sanctity.[9]

In summary, we can compare the 'Father' (God) to a bright sun radiating the light of truth, and the 'Son' (the Christ spirit that dwells in every Manifestation) to a mirror reflecting this light and shedding it upon all mankind. The Holy Spirit can be likened to the rays emanating from that sun and manifesting themselves in the mirror, from where they illumine the entire world.

The Second Article of Faith

> *We believe that men will be punished for their own sins, and not for Adam's transgression.*

This is in agreement with the Bahá'í principle of the nobility of the human soul, and in direct opposition to the traditional Christian belief in original sin. However, Mormons do believe in the literal story of Adam and Eve as it is related in the book of Genesis. They also maintain that there was no physical death on earth before the Fall of Adam.

'Abdu'l-Bahá dismissed the concept of original sin as both illogical and contrary to God's justice:

> . . . the mass of the Christians believe that, as Adam ate of the forbidden tree, He sinned in that He disobeyed, and that the disastrous consequences of this disobedience have been transmitted as a heritage and have remained among His descendants. Hence Adam became the cause of the death of humanity. This explanation is unreasonable and evidently wrong, for it means that all men, even the Prophets and the Messengers of God, without committing any sin or fault, but simply because they are the posterity of Adam, have become without reason guilty sinners, and until the day of the sacrifice of Christ were held captive in hell in painful torment. This is far from the justice of God.[10]

The Bahá'í Writings also affirm that every man is accountable for his own deeds:

> Justice hath a mighty force at its command. It is none other than reward and punishment for the deeds of men. By the power of this force the tabernacle of order is established throughout the world, causing the wicked to restrain their natures for fear of punishment.[11]

> O Son of Being! Bring thyself to account each day ere thou art summoned to a reckoning; for death, unheralded, shall come upon thee and thou shalt be called to give account for thy deeds.[12]

Nobility of the soul

Both the Mormon and the Bahá'í scriptures uphold the nobility of the human soul. In the Doctrine and Covenants we read:

> Every spirit of man was innocent in the beginning; and God having redeemed man from the fall, men became again, in their infant state, innocent before God.[13]

While Bahá'u'lláh addresses human beings thus:

> O Son of Spirit! Noble have I created thee, yet thou hast abased thyself. Rise then unto that for which thou wast created.[14]

The Book of Mormon denounces the baptism of infants on the grounds that they are already pure and need no cleansing:

> Listen to the words of Christ, your Redeemer, your Lord and your God. Behold, I came into the world not to call the righteous but sinners to repentance; the whole need no physician, but they that are sick; wherefore, little children are whole, for they are not capable of committing sin; wherefore the curse of Adam is taken from them in me, that it hath no power over them; and the law of circumcision is done away in me. And after this manner did the Holy Ghost manifest the word of God unto me; wherefore, my beloved son, I know that it is solemn mockery before God, that ye should baptize little children.[15]

While this verse from the Book of Mormon (anachronistically) speaks out against the Catholic practice of baptizing infants, Mormon children are baptized as soon as they turn eight years old, this being the 'age of accountability' at which they are expected to know the difference between right and wrong.

Similar sentiments regarding the spiritual purity of children are found in the Bahá'í Writings. When asked about the condition of 'children who die before attaining the age of discretion or before the appointed time of birth,' 'Abdu'l-Bahá replied:

> These infants are under the shadow of the favor of God; and as they have not committed any sin and are not soiled with the impurities of the world of nature, they are the centers of the manifestation of bounty, and the Eye of Compassion will be turned upon them.[16]

The Third Article of Faith

> *We believe that through the Atonement of Christ, all mankind may be saved, by obedience to the laws and ordinances of the Gospel.*

This agrees with the Bahá'í view as it pertains to the Christian dispensation. Of course, Bahá'ís believe the same about other Manifestations in their day and age, including the Báb and Bahá'u'lláh:

> As to the souls who are born into this world radiant entities and who through excessive difficulty are deprived of great benefits and thus leave

the world – they are worthy of all sympathy, for in reality this is worthy of regret. It is for this purpose (that is, it is with regard to this wisdom) that the great Manifestations (of God) unveil themselves in this world, bear every difficulty and ordeal – to make these ready souls dawnings of light and confer upon them eternal life. This is the real atonement that His Holiness Christ made – He sacrificed Himself for the life of the world.[17]

The Ancient Beauty hath consented to be bound with chains that mankind may be released from its bondage, and hath accepted to be made a prisoner within this most mighty Stronghold that the whole world may attain unto true liberty. He hath drained to its dregs the cup of sorrow, that all the peoples of the earth may attain unto abiding joy, and be filled with gladness. This is of the mercy of your Lord, the Compassionate, the Most Merciful. We have accepted to be abased, O believers in the Unity of God, that ye may be exalted, and have suffered manifold afflictions, that ye might prosper and flourish. He Who hath come to build anew the whole world, behold, how they that have joined partners with God have forced Him to dwell within the most desolate of cities![18]

Say: From My laws the sweet-smelling savour of My garment can be smelled, and by their aid the standards of Victory will be planted upon the highest peaks. The Tongue of My power hath, from the heaven of My omnipotent glory, addressed to My creation these words: 'Observe My commandments, for the love of My beauty.' Happy is the lover that hath inhaled the divine fragrance of his Best-Beloved from these words, laden with the perfume of a grace which no tongue can describe. By My life! He who hath drunk the choice wine of fairness from the hands of My bountiful favour will circle around My commandments that shine above the Dayspring of My creation.[19]

The Fourth Article of Faith

We believe that the first principles and ordinances of the Gospel are: first, Faith in the Lord Jesus Christ; second, Repentance; third, Baptism by immersion for the remission of sins; fourth, Laying on of hands for the gift of the Holy Ghost.

The first two principles mentioned in this Article, faith and repentance, are clearly emphasized in the Bahá'í teachings:

Ask a Bahá'í to deny any of the great Prophets, to deny his faith or to deny Moses, Muhammad or Christ, and he will say: I would rather die. So a Muhammadan Bahá'í is a better Christian than many so called Christians.[20]

Wherefore, hearken ye unto My speech, and return ye to God and repent, that He, through His grace, may have mercy upon you, may wash away your sins, and forgive your trespasses. The greatness of His mercy surpasseth the fury of His wrath, and His grace encompasseth all who have been called into being and been clothed with the robe of life, be they of the past or of the future.[21]

The remaining principles involve two specific rituals which appear to have been based on a verse from the New Testament (Hebr. 6:2), 'baptism by immersion' and the 'laying on of hands.' Since the Bahá'í Faith is devoid of ritual there is no direct basis for comparison, although 'Abdu'l-Bahá did confirm that the 'principle of baptism is purification by repentance.'[22]

However, if such 'first principles and ordinances' were to be defined for the Bahá'í Faith, they might read as follows:

The first duty prescribed by God for His servants is the recognition of Him Who is the Day Spring of His Revelation and the Fountain of His laws, Who representeth the Godhead in both the Kingdom of His Cause and the world of creation. Whoso achieveth this duty hath attained unto all good; and whoso is deprived thereof, hath gone astray, though he be the author of every righteous deed. It behoveth every one who reacheth this most sublime station, this summit of transcendent glory, to observe every ordinance of Him Who is the Desire of the world. These twin duties are inseparable. Neither is acceptable without the other. Thus hath it been decreed by Him Who is the Source of Divine inspiration.[23]

The Fifth Article of Faith

We believe that a man must be called of God, by prophecy, and by the laying on of hands by those who are in authority, to preach the Gospel and administer in the ordinances thereof.

This is a clear affirmation of the authority of clergy in the Mormon faith, declaring that one cannot preach the restored gospel unless brought into the priesthood by 'those who are in authority.'

Since the Bahá'í Faith has no clergy, no direct analogy for the Mormon priesthood exists. However, because the Mormon term 'priesthood' has a very different meaning from what is traditionally thought of as a religious vocation, and because the importance of that priesthood to the spiritual and social life of Mormon individuals and families cannot be overestimated, a brief explanation of this very distinct institution is appropriate here.

The Mormon priesthood is the prerogative of all male members of the LDS Church in good standing, and its ordination occurs in progressive stages, starting as early as age twelve. It is a lay priesthood, with no formal education or special vows. This universality of the Mormon priesthood is vaguely reminiscent of Martin Luther's 'priesthood of all believers.' Yet while Mormons would certainly agree with that doctrine's underlying premise that all believers can have a direct relationship with God – through what the LDS Church calls 'personal revelation' – the same would not be true of Luther's assertion that there was no need for guidance from a religious authority, or that anyone can form his own interpretation of the Bible. Furthermore, the LDS priesthood requires official ordination and is not open to women.*

There are two primary levels of the Mormon priesthood; the *Aaronic priesthood* is available to boys age twelve and up, while the higher *Melchizedek priesthood* is attainable only after age eighteen. Each of these two priesthood levels is further broken down into smaller stages.

The first stage of the Aaronic priesthood is that of *deacon*, by which a young priesthood holder can distribute the sacrament, collect fast offerings and perform other miscellaneous services. Between the ages of fourteen and sixteen a boy can become a *teacher*. In addition to the duties they had as deacons, teachers can also prepare the sacrament, usher, speak at ward meetings, and participate in monthly 'home teaching' visits to individual ward families. The final stage of the Aaronic priesthood is that of *priest*. A priest may conduct home teaching sessions, administer the sacrament, baptize, and ordain other deacons and teachers to the priesthood.

The Melchizedek priesthood is likewise broken down into three stages. An *elder* must be at least eighteen years of age, and in addition to any Aaronic priesthood function he can give blessings and confer the Aaronic or Melchizedek priesthood on others. This level of the priesthood is required for missionary work and to hold ward leadership positions, and is held by the vast majority of adult male church members. Ranking above elders are the

---

* Before 1978 church members of African descent could not be ordained to the priesthood. See Appendix 2.

high priests, to which the higher church authorities belong; each ward counts among its members a dozen or so high priests. The third and highest level of the Melchizedek priesthood, that of *Seventy* or *Apostle*, is held by the general authorities of the Church, although this station is attained only by a select few.

The priesthood is absolutely central to Mormon family life. As priesthood holder, the husband and father is believed to receive divine guidance – known in LDS parlance as *personal revelation* – regarding important family decisions, to which his wife and children must ultimately defer. The LDS family is thus patriarchal in nature, although women are considered equal to men in importance if not in function. The priesthood also allows a father to give *patriarchal blessings* to his children, which are believed to possess limited healing powers, as well as the ability to glimpse the beneficiary's future.

The Sixth Article of Faith

> *We believe in the same organization that existed in the Primitive Church,*
> *namely, apostles, prophets, pastors, teachers, evangelists, and so forth.*

Mormons define the term *Primitive Church* as 'the Church as Jesus organized it when He lived on the earth.'[24] The LDS concept of this organization is based loosely on the New Testament, but much more so on statements in the Book of Mormon. We will digress here for a short while to explore some biblical and extrabiblical information about the organization of the Christian Church in the first century AD, because it will lead us to an important concept in Mormon doctrine, the *great apostasy*.

Organization of the early Christian Church

The New Testament is not particularly clear on the organization of the early church, nor does it mention that Jesus Himself ordained any specific structure. In any case, it would be a mistake to characterize Jesus' ministry as a 'church' while He was living on the earth; in academic circles, it is most often referred to as 'the Jesus movement,' with the first signs of organization occurring only after Jesus' ascension. Some believe, based on Matthew 16:18, that Jesus personally entrusted Peter with the continuation of the work, yet the most prolific and influential of His apostles was not even one of the original twelve: Paul was named an apostle around AD 48, and prior to his conversion in AD 34 he was one of the principal persecutors of Christian Jews.

The first Christian church was based in Jerusalem, led by a group of Jesus' original disciples and some of His family, including Peter and James. There appears to have been a division of labor within that leadership, based on personal strengths and cultural background. For example, Paul – while raised as a Pharisaic Jew in Jerusalem – was also a Roman citizen, making him particularly well suited to proclaiming the Gospel to Jews and Gentiles alike.

In *New Testament History: A Narrative Account*, non-Mormon historian Ben Witherington III offers one view of the first organization of the church:

> According to Acts 1:13-14, after the disappearance of Jesus from the earth several weeks after his resurrection appearances, the Eleven turned to the upper room, where they were joined by some women and Jesus' mother and brothers. Here was the nucleus of the Christian movement at its inception. This was the group that would provide the continuity between the original followers of Jesus (the Jesus movement) and the fledgling Christian movement . . .
>
> Thus, the early leadership of the church in Jerusalem was made up of some of Jesus' followers, such as Peter, and some of Jesus' family, such as James. An early letter of Paul tells us that in the early days, something of a triumvirate led the Jerusalem church, and they were called the 'pillars' (of the new temple?) – Peter, John, and James the brother of Jesus (Gal. 2:9). But Gal. 2:12 makes clear, as does a text like Acts 15, that the administrative head of the Jerusalem church was James, while Peter seems to have been the chief proclaimer, or evangelist.[25]

The various churches that were established by Paul, for example in Corinth and Galatia, were very different from our current notion of a church as a large congregation having its own church building. Rather, small groups of Christians usually met in the homes of individual believers, and there was no discernible administrative structure within these groups until the early part of the second century – when presbyters, and later bishops, were elected as church leaders over a specific city or area. The Bible does mention apostles, prophets, evangelists, pastors and teachers,[26] but these appear to refer to specific functions in the spreading of the Gospel, not official positions in the Church. And where prophets are mentioned, they enjoy no greater stature than teachers or apostles.[27] Non-Mormon theologian Bart D. Ehrman, Chair of the Department of Religious Studies at the University of North Carolina at Chapel Hill, explains:

> In Paul's day the churches that were set up were not set up with hierarchical structures; they did not have church leaders. The church in Corinth, like Paul's other churches, was organized as a charismatic community.

Now the term charismatic comes from the Greek word charisma, which means gift. Paul understands the churches to be organized and run by the Holy Spirit, who gave gifts to the individuals within the church . . .

Paul indicates that anybody who is baptized in Christ receives a spiritual gift, and different people have different gifts. Some people are gifted as teachers. That's not just a natural ability; that's a gift, charisma that the spirit has given to some people for the benefit of the whole congregation. Some people are given the gift of leadership, some people are given the gift of prophecy, some people are given the gift of healing, some people are given the gift of miracles, and some people are given the gift of speaking in tongues . . .[28]

This points to the possibility that Paul's use of the term 'prophet' is quite different from how it is currently understood by Mormons. Of course, if we employ the LDS definition of a prophet as someone who is able to receive divine inspiration through visions, we must of necessity place Paul and Peter in this category, if not the entire company of believers present at the Pentecost.

The great apostasy

Mormons believe that the early Christian church entered a 'great apostasy' during which important teachings of Christ were lost. One of the claims of the Church of Jesus Christ of Latter-day Saints is that it restored the original administrative order of the Christian dispensation, based on teachings found in the Book of Mormon and other latter-day scriptures. It should be noted that Jesus Christ does not actually appear in the Book of Mormon until near the end (3 Nephi chapters 11-26), and His teachings as related in that story are not appreciably different from those given in the Sermon on the Mount – in fact, it contains a near verbatim recital of that famous discourse as it occurs in the King James Version of the New Testament. The most significant additional revelation provided in this 'other testimony of Jesus Christ' appears to be the explicit establishment of the office of the priesthood, through which many additional ordinances and teachings could then be revealed in the future.

The LDS Church teaches that with the death of the last of Jesus' original disciples, the 'keys' to this priesthood – i.e. the authority of the church – were lost also. It explains that self-appointed rulers took over the leadership of the church, which then crumbled into different sects. Because these rulers did not have their authority granted them by Jesus Christ, they strayed from His original teachings and started teaching 'false doctrine.' An article in *Ensign* magazine states:

Supported by scripture and the words of prophets, The Church of Jesus Christ of Latter-day Saints teaches unequivocally that there was an apostasy from the Lord's one and only true church following the deaths of Christ's early Apostles. So thorough was this apostasy that the original Church of Jesus Christ was supplanted by an institution having a form of godliness but devoid of priesthood power and priesthood keys.[29]

This departure from the original teachings of Christ is in large part confirmed by Shoghi Effendi:

None, I feel, will question the fact that the fundamental reason why the unity of the Church of Christ was irretrievably shattered, and its influence was in the course of time undermined, was that the Edifice which the Fathers of the Church reared after the passing of His First Apostle[30] was an Edifice that rested in nowise upon the explicit directions of Christ Himself. The authority and features of their administration were wholly inferred, and indirectly derived, with more or less justification, from certain vague and fragmentary references which they found scattered amongst His utterances as recorded in the Gospel. Not one of the sacraments of the Church; not one of the rites and ceremonies which the Christian Fathers have elaborately devised and ostentatiously observed; not one of the elements of the severe discipline they rigorously imposed upon the primitive Christians; none of these reposed on the direct authority of Christ, or emanated from His specific utterances. Not one of these did Christ conceive, none did He specifically invest with sufficient authority to either interpret His Word, or to add to what He had not specifically enjoined.[31]

Furthermore, the LDS characterization of the post-apostasy church as 'having a form of godliness but devoid of priesthood power' is not all that different from this description given by 'Abdu'l-Bahá:

Thus among the Jews, at the end of the cycle of Moses, which coincides with the Christian manifestation, the Law of God disappeared, only a form without spirit remaining. The Holy of Holies departed from among them, but the outer court of Jerusalem – which is the expression used for the form of the religion – fell into the hands of the Gentiles. In the same way, the fundamental principles of the religion of Christ, which are the greatest virtues of humanity, have disappeared; and its form has remained in the hands of the clergy and the priests.[32]

However, in order to fully understand the Mormon concept of apostasy, one idea must be firmly established in the reader's mind: it is not the loss of the *original teachings* – or adherence to them in spirit – that is so crucial in the story of the apostasy. Rather, it is the loss of *the priesthood authority itself*. Even if churches of the time had reflected all the founding principles of Christianity, still Mormons would not consider those churches valid since they did not have the 'keys to the priesthood,' or the authority to bind on earth as in heaven spoken of in the Bible:

> And I will give unto thee the keys of the kingdom of heaven: and whatsoever thou shalt bind on earth shall be bound in heaven: and whatsoever thou shalt loose on earth shall be loosed in heaven.[33]

These keys were, according to Joseph Smith, the sole means of discernment between false spirits and those that were of God, and represented the authority of Christ by which the church could be guided:

> The Apostles in ancient times held the keys of this Priesthood – of the mysteries of the kingdom of God, and consequently were enabled to unlock and unravel all things pertaining to the government of the Church, the welfare of society, the future destiny of men, and the agency, power and influence of spirits; for they could control them at pleasure, bid them depart in the name of Jesus, and detect their mischievous and mysterious operations when trying to palm themselves upon the Church in a religious garb, and militate against the interest of the Church and spread of truth.[34]

From a Bahá'í perspective, the 'keys of the priesthood' could thus be likened to the Covenant of Bahá'u'lláh, because it is the Covenant which at once establishes the authority, and promises the infallible guidance, of the head of the Faith. The LDS Church contends that these keys were taken away by the Lord because of the waywardness of those who represented the church, so that Joseph Smith might restore them seventeen centuries later.

The process of apostasy

The great apostasy is seen by Mormons not as an event, but as a process during which early Christians – having been deprived of the institution of the priesthood – allowed themselves to be influenced by human learning and become further and further removed from the original meaning of the text of the Gospel. Apostle Dallin H. Oaks provided the following explanation of this process:

> We maintain that the concepts identified by such nonscriptural terms as 'the incomprehensible mystery of God' and 'the mystery of the Holy Trinity' are attributable to the ideas of Greek philosophy. These philosophical concepts transformed Christianity in the first few centuries following the deaths of the Apostles. For example, philosophers then maintained that physical matter was evil and that God was a spirit without feelings or passions. Persons of this persuasion, including learned men who became influential converts to Christianity, had a hard time accepting the simple teachings of early Christianity: an Only Begotten Son who said he was in the express image of his Father in Heaven and who taught his followers to be one as he and his Father were one, and a Messiah who died on a cross and later appeared to his followers as a resurrected being with flesh and bones.
>
> The collision between the speculative world of Greek philosophy and the simple, literal faith and practice of the earliest Christians produced sharp contentions that threatened to widen political divisions in the fragmenting Roman empire. This led Emperor Constantine to convene the first churchwide council in A.D. 325. The action of this council of Nicaea remains the most important single event after the death of the Apostles in formulating the modern Christian concept of deity. The Nicene Creed erased the idea of the separate being of Father and Son by defining God the Son as being of 'one substance with the Father.' . . .
>
> In the process of what we call the Apostasy, the tangible, personal God described in the Old and New Testaments was replaced by the abstract, incomprehensible deity defined by compromise with the speculative principles of Greek philosophy. The received language of the Bible remained, but the so-called 'hidden meanings' of scriptural words were now explained in the vocabulary of a philosophy alien to their origins. In the language of that philosophy, God the Father ceased to be a Father in any but an allegorical sense. He ceased to exist as a comprehensible and compassionate being. And the separate identity of his Only Begotten Son was swallowed up in a philosophical abstraction that attempted to define a common substance and an incomprehensible relationship.[35]

While Apostle Oaks' conclusions about the nature of God and the Holy Trinity differ sharply from the Bahá'í view, Bahá'ís do agree that Christianity was to a certain extent 'polluted' during the time of Constantine through the introduction of pagan doctrines and rituals. However, Bahá'ís disagree that Greek philosophy was to blame. Many of its highly evolved principles were informed by the teachings of Moses, recognized a single divine source, and prescribed no rituals. Oaks' comments also fail to take into account that some of the chroniclers of the New Testament (including Mark and Luke) were thoroughly Hellenized Jews steeped in Greek culture, philosophy, and language. They wrote in Greek, and even consulted a Greek translation of the Old Testament in their quotations.

Remarkably, here are two related yet diametrically opposed accounts of what happened at Nicaea. Mormons claim that the Council erroneously combined the separate gods of Father, Son and Holy Spirit into one tripartite entity. Bahá'ís, on the other hand, maintain that Christ always taught the Oneness of God, and that the Holy Trinity was conceived as a means to reconcile the seemingly conflicting statements in the Gospels concerning the nature of Jesus' humanity and divinity and, to a lesser degree, placate pagan beliefs in multiple gods. Ironically, these pagan beliefs appear to support several of Mormonism's essential doctrines: the exaltation of ordinary human beings to a divine rank, the resulting multiplicity of god-like beings including a 'Heavenly Mother' or Goddess, and the existence of spirit as a form of matter.

Daniel C. Petersen and Stephen D. Ricks, in an *Ensign* article about the Trinity, wrote:

> . . . Latter-day Saints do reject the doctrines of the Trinity as taught by most Christian churches today. For the most part, these creeds – the most famous of which is the Nicene Creed – were canonized in the fourth and fifth centuries A.D. following centuries of debate about the nature of the Godhead. Consequently, it is highly questionable whether these creeds reflect the thinking or beliefs of the New Testament church.
>
> 'The exact theological definition of the doctrine of the Trinity,' notes J. R. Dummelow, 'was the result of a long process of development, which was not complete until the fifth century, or maybe even later.' As Bill Forrest remarks, 'To insist that a belief in the Trinity is requisite to being Christian, is to acknowledge that for centuries after the New Testament was completed thousands of Jesus' followers were in fact not really "Christian." '[36]

Unwittingly, Petersen and Ricks have precisely echoed Bahá'í sentiments concerning the validity of the Nicene concept of the Trinity, and Bill Forrest's remark in the last paragraph is particularly succinct. William Sears noted in his book *The Wine of Astonishment*:

The concept of the Trinity was not a teaching of Christ. It was a doctrine of the Church which received official recognition in AD 325, nearly three hundred years after the Crucifixion.[37]

However, Sears used this to underscore the inability of the early Christ-ians to discern the true meaning of *the Father, the Son and the Holy Spirit*:

> The Writings of the Bahá'í Faith explain that, in one respect, each of the great religions has a Trinity. It is found in Hinduism, Judaism, Zoroastrianism, Buddhism, Christianity, Islám, and the Bahá'í Faith. However, this Trinity is merely the *outward symbol* of an *inward truth*. It should never be interpreted as meaning that God can be defined, divided, or limited in any way.
>
> God is One, single, unknowable, indefinable, indivisible, and infinite, Bahá'u'lláh tells us. There is no exception to this truth.
>
> The Trinity is to be understood in the following manner: In every revealed religion there are three essential actors, (1) *the Giver*, (2) *the Gift*, and (3) *the Receiver of the Gift*.
>
> Almighty God is the Giver. The Messenger of God is the Receiver of the Gift. The Holy Spirit is the Gift.
>
> In the case of *Judaism, God* was the *Giver, Moses* the *Receiver of the Gift*, and the *Holy Spirit* revealed in the symbol of the *Burning Bush* was the *Gift*. In the case of Christianity, God, Christ, and the Holy Spirit in the symbol of the Dove.[38]

The Gospel taken away

The Mormon contention that some of the knowledge concerning Jesus Christ was lost through the ages – including the account of His appearance on the American continent and key prophecies of Abraham and Moses – is somewhat similar to the Muslim claim that the Gospel was corrupted by having references to Muhammad removed. In the Kitáb-i-Íqán, Bahá'u'lláh referred to those Muslims as follows:

> We have also heard a number of the foolish of the earth assert that the genuine text of the heavenly Gospel doth not exist amongst the Christians, that it hath ascended unto heaven. How grievously they have erred! How oblivious of the fact that such a statement imputeth the gravest injustice and tyranny to a gracious and loving Providence! How could God, when once the Day-star of the beauty of Jesus had disappeared from the sight of His people, and ascended unto the fourth heaven, cause His holy Book,

His most great testimony amongst His creatures, to disappear also? What would be left to that people to cling to from the setting of the day-star of Jesus until the rise of the sun of the Muhammadan Dispensation? What law could be their stay and guide? How could such people be made the victims of the avenging wrath of God, the omnipotent Avenger? How could they be afflicted with the scourge of chastisement by the heavenly King? Above all, how could the flow of the grace of the All-Bountiful be stayed? How could the ocean of His tender mercies be stilled? We take refuge with God, from that which His creatures have fancied about Him! Exalted is He above their comprehension![39]

Yet there are important differences between the Mormon teachings concerning the great apostasy and the claims so decisively dismissed by Bahá'u'lláh. Certainly, the above passage requires one to reflect on the illogicality of the assertion that the Gospel, or any part thereof, had been withheld from the faithful. However, Mormons do not say that the genuine text of the Gospel has 'ascended unto heaven.' Rather, they maintain that the keys to the priesthood – and thereby the authority and successorship of the church – were lost. Furthermore, they blame 'the great and abominable church' of Satan for taking away key scriptures containing 'many parts which are plain and most precious':

And after they go forth by the hand of the twelve apostles of the Lamb, from the Jews unto the Gentiles, thou seest the formation of that great and abominable church, which is most abominable above all other churches; for behold, they have taken away from the gospel of the Lamb many parts which are plain and most precious; and also many covenants of the Lord have they taken away . . . And after these plain and precious things were taken away it goeth forth unto all the nations of the Gentiles; and after it goeth forth unto all the nations of the Gentiles, yea, even across the many waters which thou hast seen with the Gentiles which have gone forth out of captivity, thou seest – because of the many plain and precious things which have been taken out of the book, which were plain unto the understanding of the children of men, according to the plainness which is in the Lamb of God – because of these things which are taken away out of the gospel of the Lamb, an exceedingly great many do stumble, yea, insomuch that Satan hath great power over them.[40]

These verses from the Book of Mormon challenge the commonly held view that Jesus primarily spoke in parables, alleging that He in fact spoke plainly about many things but that these utterances had been lost. This not only suggests that those who followed that same Gospel were deprived of the truth concerning these 'plain' things, but also excuses others for never having recognized the Gospel at all! The Bible attributes the following sayings to Jesus:

> Therefore speak I to them in parables: because they seeing see not; and hearing they hear not, neither do they understand.[41]

> I have yet many things to say unto you, but ye cannot bear them now.[42]

> These things have I spoken unto you in proverbs: but the time cometh, when I shall no more speak unto you in proverbs, but I shall shew you plainly of the Father.[43]

While Bahá'ís understand this last prophecy to refer to Bahá'u'lláh, Mormons say it was fulfilled by Jesus Christ revealing Himself on the American continent shortly after His resurrection, exactly as described in the Book of Mormon, and by the restoration of this additional Gospel through Joseph Smith.

The great and abominable church

The Mormon phrase 'great and abominable church' may lead one to think of the Christian church during its darkest period in history, but this is not what is meant. It is understood by Mormons to refer not to any specific church, but collectively to all those who stand against God and follow in the ways of Satan:

> And he said unto me: Behold there are save two churches only; the one is the church of the Lamb of God, and the other is the church of the devil; wherefore, whoso belongeth not to the church of the Lamb of God belongeth to that great church, which is the mother of abominations; and she is the whore of all the earth.[44]

Of course, it could be argued that at some point in history the Christian church did take away the most precious parts of the Gospel – without altering a single letter in the book – by keeping it firmly in control of the clergy and out of the hands of ordinary believers. Few laymen were able to read Latin or Greek, let alone afford a hand-copied Bible. As a result, those who had authority in the church were able to teach whatever would suit their interests, all in the name of Jesus Christ. Referring to Muslim divines who were engaged in this same practice, Bahá'u'lláh said:

Verily by 'perverting' the text is not meant that which these foolish and abject souls have fancied, even as some maintain that Jewish and Christian divines have effaced from the Book such verses as extol and magnify the countenance of Muhammad, and instead thereof have inserted the contrary . . . Nay, rather, by corruption of the text is meant that in which all Muslim divines are engaged today, that is the interpretation of God's holy Book in accordance with their idle imaginings and vain desires . . . In yet another instance, He saith: 'A part of them heard the Word of God, and then, after they had understood it, distorted it, and knew that they did so.' This verse, too, doth indicate that the meaning of the Word of God hath been perverted, not that the actual words have been effaced. To the truth of this testify they that are sound of mind.[45]

Mormon doctrine mentions the 'great apostasy' in the same breath as the 'restoration of the gospel,' the latter being considered the long-promised reversal of the former. Like the apostasy, the restoration of the gospel is also considered a process, beginning with the various inspirations, visions and revelations received by Joseph Smith and continuing today through the current president and 'prophet' of the Church of Jesus Christ of Latter-day Saints.

Organization of the LDS Church

The Church of Jesus Christ of Latter-day Saints claims to have no clergy, at least not in a professional sense as is the case with the Catholic Church. However, it does have a highly centralized hierarchy, which in its authoritarian government and system of succession is not appreciably different from the Vatican. At the top of the hierarchy is the 'president, prophet, seer, and revelator,' who is considered the infallible mouthpiece of God, and roughly analogous to the Pope in terms of his position, influence and lifetime appointment. A first and second counselor complete the threesome that is known as the *First Presidency*. In fact, most offices in the church hierarchy are composed of three members, one at the head of the office and the other two serving as counselors. This arrangement is no coincidence, as it is modeled after the LDS view of the *Godhead*, with the president or bishop representing the Father and the two counselors mirroring the Son and the Holy Ghost.

Reporting directly to the First Presidency is the *Quorum of the Twelve Apostles*, who are appointed in order of seniority and enjoy a lifetime position (to maintain our analogy to the Vatican, this group could be compared to the Curia). Whenever a new church president is to be chosen, the Quorum of the Twelve forms the pool of eligible candidates, although virtually without fail it is the most senior Apostle who is given the honor of succession. Each of the members of the First Presidency and the Quorum of the Twelve are also known as *general authorities*, presumably because their opinions about church doctrine are considered authoritative. These are salaried positions, and each carry additional responsibilities that are delegated through an intricate administrative structure.

Next in line are the *Quorums of Seventies*.[46] Somewhat confusingly, *Seventy* is a title referring to a single person, not a quantity. The number seventy is also a recurring theme. Supervising all Quorums of the Seventy is a group of seven men collectively known as the *Presidency of the Seventy*. It is believed that in the future, each Quorum of the Seventy will comprise seventy members, or 'Seventies.' The Presidency of the Seventy is also referred to as the First Quorum, and its members are full-time salaried executives with a retirement age of seventy. Starting with the Second Quorum, members do not receive salaries, and the Third Quorum and beyond are considered *Area Seventies*, each quorum being assigned a specific geographic region in the world. While the Quorums of the Seventies are generally concerned with the expansion and consolidation of the Church throughout the world, there is a parallel entity which handles administrative and financial, or 'temporal,' matters related to the Church as a whole: the *First* or *Presiding Bishopric*, answerable to the Twelve and the First Presidency, is at the head of the administrative structure to which the individual ward bishops belong. As with most callings, the bishop has at his side a first and second counselor, the three making up the bishopric. All tithings collected by the local ward bishops are forwarded directly to the Presiding Bishopric.

There are various other administrative posts at the regional and local levels, with at the bottom the ward bishoprics in each stake. Finally, within each ward there are several administrative bodies, or *presidencies* (each made up of a president and two counselors), which report either to the ward bishop or the stake president. For example, each ward has its own Missionary president, Elder's Quorum president, and Relief Society president, among others.

Clergy or no clergy?

Unlike some other Christian denominations, the LDS Church has no divinity school; in fact no theological training whatsoever is required to occupy even the highest positions within the church hierarchy. Also, except for the highest ranks of leadership, those individuals called upon to serve in the Church do not receive any financial remuneration. However, it would be inaccurate to conclude that there is no Mormon clergy. A local ward bishop, though not trained by anything but experience, is the unquestioned leader of the congregation. As such he exercises full authority over his flock, is looked to for spiritual guidance, and is believed to receive 'personal revelation' regarding the direction of the ward. Furthermore, all those occupying a position of leadership (including youth) are seated at the front of the chapel or meeting room, set apart from – and usually elevated above – the rest of the congregation. And finally, all leadership positions are filled by direct appointment (referred to as a 'calling') by someone further up in the church hierarchy.

Of course, the Bahá'í Faith has its own uniquely elaborate Administrative Order which is expected to be obeyed by its followers. However, it differs from the LDS Church in significant ways. All the governing bodies of the Faith – Local Spiritual Assemblies, Regional Bahá'í Councils, National Spiritual Assemblies as well as the head of the Faith, the Universal House of Justice – are democratically elected by the believers in an atmosphere of prayer and unity, without any nominations or campaigning; furthermore, every institution within this elected framework is composed of several people (usually nine), none of whom have any religious or administrative authority outside of an official gathering of the entire group. Running parallel to, and working in close collaboration with, these elected bodies is a group of learned individuals collectively known as the Institution of the Counsellors. At the highest level, the Counsellor members of the International Teaching Centre have a global mandate and work in close proximity to the Universal House of Justice. Reporting to the International Teaching Centre are five Continental Boards of Counsellors (for Africa, the Americas, Asia, Australasia and Europe). All Counsellors at the international and continental levels are appointed by the Universal House of Justice. Each Continental Board additionally appoints Auxiliary Boards, whose members are assigned to a smaller region within the continent. The Institution of the Counsellors has the special function in the Bahá'í Administrative Order of providing guidance and encouragement to the elected bodies at each level, and sharing with them the twin duties of propagating and protecting the Faith. However, neither the Counsellors nor their Auxiliary Board members have any administrative function or decisionmaking authority in the Faith.[47] More significantly still, every Bahá'í is responsible for his own salvation and spiritual growth, and for playing his own unique role in the establishment of the Kingdom on Earth. Bahá'ís are encouraged to use individual initiative in aiding their Cause, although the Universal House of Justice periodically formulates worldwide plans to be implemented by National and Local Assemblies, communities and individuals.

The Seventh Article of Faith

We believe in the gift of tongues, prophecy, revelation, visions, healing, interpretation of tongues, and so forth.

Mormons believe that every person is capable of prophecy and revelation, a belief that is not shared by Bahá'ís in those same terms. However, this kind of 'personal revelation' primarily manifests itself as listening to one's inner guidance. Bahá'ís continually pray for guidance and are told to be receptive to an answer.

The Mormon concept of revelation

The following is an explanation of the term *revelation* as defined in the LDS *Bible Dictionary*:

> Divine revelation is one of the grandest concepts and principles of the gospel of Jesus Christ, for without it, man could not know of the things of God and could not be saved with any degree of salvation in the eternities. Continuous revelation from God to his saints, through the Holy Ghost or by other means, such as vision, dreams, or visitations, makes possible daily guidance along true paths and leads the faithful soul to complete and eternal salvation in the celestial kingdom . . . It also consists of individual guidance for every person who seeks for it and follows the prescribed course of faith, repentance, and obedience to the gospel of Jesus Christ. 'The Holy Ghost is a revelator,' said Joseph Smith, and 'no man can receive the Holy Ghost without receiving revelations.' Without revelation, all would be guesswork, darkness, and confusion.[48]

Individual Mormons often claim to have received personal revelation when they feel they have been inspired to do something by God. This could be something as simple as driving home by a different route in order to prevent a possible accident, or as serious as a decision about family planning or a new career.

To Latter-day Saints, there is no significant distinction between the kind of revelation experienced by their prophets – be they Joseph Smith or any of the presidents of the Church – and that claimed by individual believers. Across the board, these subjective experiences are considered to be direct promptings of the Holy Spirit, and provided the recipient is subject to the blessings of the priesthood and lives in accordance with the principles of the restored gospel, they are assumed to be correct and uncorrupted by selfish promptings. The only real difference between the revelations of a rank-and-file member and that of a church president is in their relative sphere of influence: whereas the former are limited mainly to the family, the latter apply to the Church as a whole.

Visions

When Mormons experience particularly strong or recurring feelings, dreams or thoughts, these are sometimes recounted as *visions*. These visions are seen as a clear message from the Holy Spirit to take some specific action.

Nabíl's narrative of the early days of the Bahá'í Faith *The Dawn-Breakers* contains a number of accounts of ordinary people being visited by a Manifestation (such as Muhammad, the Báb or Bahá'u'lláh) in a vision or dream. And in his delightful book, *God Loves Laughter*, Hand of the Cause of God William Sears recounts a vivid recurring dream he had as a small child in which he saw a 'shiny man,' a figure whom he would later recognize as 'Abdu'l-Bahá. However, we should keep in mind the following warning issued on behalf of Shoghi Effendi regarding the validity of visions:

> There is a fundamental difference between Divine Revelation as vouch-safed by God to His Prophets, and the spiritual experiences and visions which individuals may have. The latter should, under no circumstances, be construed as constituting an infallible source of guidance, even for the person experiencing them.[49]

The collection *History of the Church* contains a similar warning by Joseph Smith:

> We may look for angels and receive their ministrations, but we are to try the spirits and prove them, for it is often the case that men make a mistake in regard to these things . . . Lying spirits are going forth in the earth. There will be great manifestations of spirits, both false and true.[50]

The Eighth Article of Faith

> *We believe the Bible to be the word of God as far as it is translated correctly; we also believe the Book of Mormon to be the word of God.*

This agrees with the Bahá'í view as it pertains to the Bible, except that no point is made of the accuracy of its translation. Bahá'ís consider the Bible a spiritual book first and foremost, and while certain literal descriptions may have been altered through translation, the spiritual truths have essentially remained unchanged.

Authenticity of the Bible

Shoghi Effendi did make one qualification in this regard, when he stated that 'the Bible is not wholly authentic, and in this respect not to be compared with the Qur'án, and should be wholly subordinated to the authentic Sayings of Bahá'u'lláh.'[51] However, this should not be taken as a wholesale dismissal of the authenticity of the Bible, but rather as a clarification of its relative degree of literal accuracy.[52] Most of the Qur'án was committed to writing during the life of Muhammad, and is unlikely to contain many literal errors. The Writings of the Báb and Bahá'u'lláh were either dictated or penned directly by the Manifestation Himself – something that simply cannot be said of the Bible, in which the words of the Manifestation were not fixed in scripture until decades (in the case of Jesus) or even centuries (in the case of Moses and other prophets) after their passing from this world. Furthermore, the Bahá'í Writings have never been truncated or abridged through canonization, as is the case with both the Old and the New Testament.[53]

The eighth Article of Faith's statement that the Bible is 'the word of God as far as it is translated correctly' is curious, considering that the Book of Mormon contains lengthy quotations from the King James Version of the Bible – including the New Testament – notwithstanding the claim that it was written down in ancient hieroglyphics centuries before Christ and independently translated into English. It has also left the door open for some Mormons to dismiss portions of the Bible they do not understand or agree with, citing faulty translation. Bahá'ís, on the other hand, accept the entire Bible as the Word of God, and ascribe any lack of understanding to their own limitations.

The Joseph Smith Translation of the Bible

The phrase 'as far as it is translated correctly' has yet another significance. In addition to Joseph Smith's translation of the Book of Mormon from ancient golden plates, and his many revelations collectively known as the Doctrine and Covenants, he also added to and revised the Bible itself in an effort to bring it into conformity with his own doctrines. He made numerous textual alterations to various books in both the Old and the New Testament, particularly Genesis and Matthew. An article in *Ensign* magazine explains:

> The Prophet Joseph Smith loved the Bible. He regularly read it, revered its teachings, and found divine truths in its writings. His preaching and writings are full of biblical allusions and interpretations. He relied upon the Bible for comfort . . .
>
> Yet the Prophet's reverence for the Bible was accompanied by his awareness of its incompleteness and of problems with the transmission of its texts. On one occasion he said, 'I believe the Bible as it read when it came from the pen of the original writers. Ignorant translators, careless transcribers, or designing and corrupt priests have committed many errors.'
>
> As early as June 1830, the Prophet responded to divine direction by beginning an inspired revision of the book of Genesis. The section of the Pearl of Great Price known as the book of Moses began to come forth through revelation at this time. Work on the book of Genesis proceeded until 7 March 1831, when the Prophet was instructed by the Lord to pursue a rigorous study and inspired revision of the New Testament . . . The Lord later called the Prophet's efforts a 'new translation' . . . The Prophet took this task very seriously, referring to it as a 'branch' of his prophetic calling. The result of his inspired efforts, known today as the Joseph Smith Translation (JST), is a most remarkable body of work . . .
>
> During the translation of the Book of Mormon, the Prophet learned even more clearly that the Bible was not complete and that the Restoration of the gospel would include the restoration of many 'plain and precious things which had been taken away' . . . from the biblical record.[54]

However, allegations of the Bible's 'incompleteness' and 'problems with the transmission of its texts' are contradicted by historical evidence. In *Mormon America*, Ostling and Ostling maintain that the Bible we know today is quite faithful to the original text:

> The Bible is actually the best-attested body of literature from the ancient world. The Codex Sinaiticus and the Codex Vaticanus (the latter lacking the last books of the New Testament) are full biblical manuscripts dating from circa A.D. 350. But there are thousands of other ancient New Testament texts or fragments and sixty other codices (complete books) . . .
>
> All these ancient texts indicate that the text of the Bible we have has substantially been transmitted through the ages with surprising accuracy. Some of the New Testament fragments represent a shorter time span back to the biblical author than the time span from our day to Joseph Smith. As

evidence for translation, all the ancient texts share in common support for the traditional Bible text; none support any changes introduced by Joseph Smith.[55]

What is perhaps most interesting is not the fact that Joseph Smith amended the Bible, but his precise reason for doing so:

> Early in his life, Joseph recognized the uncertainty of reading the biblical text with limited, mortal understanding; he saw that 'the teachers of religion of the different sects understood the same passages of scripture so differently as to destroy all confidence in settling the question [of which church was right] by an appeal to the Bible' . . . He recalled: 'While I was laboring under the extreme difficulties caused by the contests of these parties of religionists, I was one day reading the Epistle of James, first chapter and fifth verse, which reads: If any of you lack wisdom, let him ask of God, that giveth to all men liberally, and upbraideth not; and it shall be given him' . . . Thus Joseph Smith went to the Sacred Grove to pray for further light and knowledge and received the First Vision in response. From this experience he learned that revelation was needed to understand the doctrines taught in the Bible and that mortals could turn directly to God for enlightenment.[56]

Smith identified the most significant problem that has plagued previous religions, namely that 'the teachers of religion . . . understood the same passages of scripture so differently as to destroy all confidence in settling the question.' Bahá'u'lláh established His Covenant in large part to prevent such divisions and disagreements from arising in the Bahá'í Faith. Furthermore, if the term 'revelation' is to be understood in the traditional LDS context of personal inspiration, Smith's observations are also in accord with the Bahá'í defense of an individual's right to personal interpretation of the Sacred Word, so long as it adds to, and does not diminish or contradict, its authoritative interpretation. However, his remedy – producing a revised translation of the Bible – seems to go against the very spirit of these observations. Rather than encouraging his followers to 'turn directly to God for enlightenment' regarding these abstruse biblical passages, he instead chose to add yet another interpretation to the mix.

The Joseph Smith Translation vs. The King James Version

It is important to understand the process Joseph Smith used to arrive at his alternative translation of the Bible:

The Prophet [Joseph Smith] did not 'translate' the Bible in the traditional sense of the word – that is, go back to the earliest Hebrew and Greek manuscripts to make a new rendering into English. Rather, he went through the biblical text of the King James Version and made inspired corrections, revisions, and additions to the biblical text. Both the Lord and Joseph Smith consistently refer to the process of these inspired revisions and additions as 'translation' . . .

While it is not always possible to determine the exact nature of each of the Prophet's revisions, we accept them as being inspired. From his studies Brother Matthews concludes: 'The translation was not a simple, mechanical recording of divine dictum, but rather a study-and-thought process accompanied and prompted by revelation from the Lord. That it was a revelatory process is evident from statements by the Prophet and others who were personally acquainted with the work.'[57]

While the textual differences between the King James Version (KJV) and the Joseph Smith Translation (JST) are usually minor, the doctrinal consequences can be quite dramatic. For example, in Matt. 4:1 (KJV) we read that after having been baptized and visited by the Holy Spirit, Jesus was 'led up of the spirit into the wilderness *to be tempted of the devil*,' implying that there was a divine purpose to this temptation, and Jesus willingly submitted to it. The JST version of the same verse instead recounts that Jesus was 'led up of the Spirit into the wilderness *to be with God*.' The devil is not introduced until Matt. 4:3, when, unannounced, he tempts Jesus to turn the stones into bread. Instead of Jesus being a willing and knowing participant in the temptation, here the devil suddenly and inexplicably forces himself onto the scene. The original KJV text allows for the spiritual interpretation that Jesus' forty days in the desert were a preparation for His immensely difficult mission ahead. Since Bahá'ís understand the term *Satan* to refer to man's lower nature or ego, the three temptations could be seen as an internal struggle between the human and divine aspects of Jesus, the purpose of which was the eradication of any last remnants of self from His blessed Person. The Joseph Smith Translation effectively pre-empts this kind of interpretation by redefining the very nature of this crucial episode.

In practice, however, the Joseph Smith Translation is not as prevalent in the Mormon consciousness as might be expected. The Old and New Testaments included in the canon of LDS scriptures are the original King James Version (except for annotations), and the amended translations are maintained as a separate entity. Furthermore, the Joseph Smith Translation is rarely consulted except when comparing specific verses to their King James counterparts, or to get a different perspective on a particular doctrinal issue, as illustrated by the above example.

The Ninth Article of Faith

We believe all that God has revealed, all that He does now reveal, and we believe that He will yet reveal many great and important things pertaining to the Kingdom of God.

This is an important affirmation of the nonfinality of revelation. In contrast to the Bahá'í principle of *progressive revelation*, however, the Mormon concept of *continuing revelation* minimizes the significance of revelation as it pertains to Manifestations of God. Rather, these 'many great and important things pertaining to the Kingdom of God' are believed to come through the *living prophet*, i.e. the current president of the LDS Church. Mormons believe that their president is continually guided from above in directing the affairs of the Church, an idea that should be familiar to Bahá'ís, who ascribe a similar infallibility and divine guidance to their supreme institution, the Universal House of Justice.

Incidentally, the Reorganized Church of Latter Day Saints (now known as *Community of Christ*) does not accept the president of the Church of Jesus Christ of Latter-day Saints as its prophet. On its web site, the topic of revelation is addressed as follows: 'As in the past, God continues to reveal divine will and love through scripture, the sacraments, the faith community, prayer, nature, and in human history.' This emphasizes the personal aspect of continuing revelation as opposed to that pertaining to a living prophet.

The very belief that God never ceases to guide humanity should make Mormons more receptive to the idea of progressive revelation than some mainstream Christians. In fact, part of a Mormon missionary's job in bringing his message to other Christians is to convince them that God continues to reveal His Will to mankind, and that He has given us a new revelation for this day. At the same time, the Mormon belief in a 'living prophet' may also be a barrier to the acceptance of other revealed truths. Since their prophet's opinion is considered a reflection of God's opinion, anything that prophet does not deem of value is likely to be judged unworthy of investigation by his followers.

The Tenth Article of Faith

We believe in the literal gathering of Israel and in the restoration of the Ten Tribes; that Zion (the New Jerusalem) will be built upon the American continent; that Christ will reign personally upon the earth; and, that the earth will be renewed and receive its paradisiacal glory.

The first part of this Article of Faith refers to two kinds of gatherings. The 'literal gathering of Israel' appears to speak for itself, yet Mormons do not understand this in the same way most other people do. Secondly, 'the restoration of the Ten Tribes' suggests the spiritual gathering of religions and nations under one banner. Thirdly, the reign of Christ and the establishment of Paradise on earth is an obvious reference to 'Thy kingdom come, Thy will be done in earth, as it is in heaven.'[58] Finally, the centrality of the American continent in bringing this about begs a comparison to the special role of America as expressed in the Writings of the Bahá'í Faith. We shall look at these various aspects individually.

The spiritual gathering

Mormon doctrine teaches that

> . . . the Israelites are to be gathered spiritually first and then physically. They are gathered spiritually when they join The Church of Jesus Christ of Latter-day Saints. This spiritual gathering began during the time of the Prophet Joseph Smith and continues today all over the world. Converts to the Church are Israelites either by blood or adoption. They belong to the family of Abraham and Jacob.[59]

In other words, those who are baptized into the LDS Church automatically become 'Israelites' by adoption, and since they are gathered together in the Church, this is seen as signifying the spiritual 'gathering of Israel.' The Bahá'í Writings describe a spiritual gathering as follows:

> One of the great events which is to occur in the Day of the manifestation of that Incomparable Branch (Bahá'u'lláh) is the hoisting of the Standard of God among all nations. By this is meant that all nations and kindreds will be gathered together under the shadow of this Divine Banner, which is no other than the Lordly Branch itself, and will become a single nation. Religious and sectarian antagonism, the hostility of races and peoples, and differences among nations, will be eliminated. All men will adhere to one

religion, will have one common faith, will be blended into one race, and become a single people. All will dwell in one common fatherland, which is the planet itself.[60]

The physical gathering

Around the year 1844, the government of Turkey – then the administrative center of the Ottoman Empire – either explicitly or implicitly granted religious tolerance within its borders, which included Palestine.[61] For the first time in 1,200 years Jews were able to return to their 'land of inheritance' with reasonable assurances of the right to remain there. Circa 1905, 'Abdu'l-Bahá indicated that this gathering of Israel is the fulfillment of a divine promise as given in the Old Testament:

> Universal peace and concord will be realized between all the nations, and that Incomparable Branch will gather together all Israel, signifying that in this cycle Israel will be gathered in the Holy Land, and that the Jewish people who are scattered to the East and West, South and North, will be assembled together.
>
> Now see: these events did not take place in the Christian cycle, for the nations did not come under the One Standard which is the Divine Branch. But in this cycle of the Lord of Hosts all the nations and peoples will enter under the shadow of this Flag. In the same way, Israel, scattered all over the world, was not reassembled in the Holy Land in the Christian cycle; but in the beginning of the cycle of Bahá'u'lláh this divine promise, as is clearly stated in all the Books of the Prophets, has begun to be manifest.[62]

Surprisingly, the Mormon view of the physical gathering does not actually involve the coming together of different peoples in one place; rather, each of the 'tribes' is thought to have its own promised land. According to Mormon doctrine, 'the physical gathering of Israel means that the Israelites will be 'gathered home to the lands of their inheritance, and shall be established *in all their lands of promise* . . . The tribes of Ephraim and Manasseh will be gathered to the land of America. The tribe of Judah will return to the city of Jerusalem and the area surrounding it. The ten lost tribes will receive from the tribe of Ephraim their promised blessings.'[63] In other words, the interpretation of the word *gathering* was changed to signify that all the tribes, having converted to the Mormon faith, would gather in their own local church houses.

However, this was not the original Mormon interpretation of the gathering. Initially, the promised land of Zion was considered to be located in Jackson

County, Missouri. After being effectively expelled from Missouri, Joseph Smith changed the gathering place to Nauvoo, Illinois, although Jackson County never lost its designation as 'the promised land.' Finally, Zion moved westward, along with the overwhelming majority of Mormons, to Utah. After thousands of European converts had settled in each of these Zions, the meaning of 'gathering' was eventually changed so that the faithful would remain in their respective birth nations to build up the Lord's Zion there.

Ironically, this interpretation may have prevented some Mormons from recognizing the literal fulfillment of the LDS prophecy that Israel will gather 'from the four parts of the earth, *and the leading of the ten tribes from the land of the north.*'[64] In one Sunday school session I attended, participants openly wondered about this verse. Various interpretations were offered, all involving movements of peoples within the American continent. Many of those present were surprised at my suggestion that it might in fact refer to the gathering of Jews in the Holy Land, primarily from eastern European countries situated directly to the north.

America as the Promised Land

Mormons consider America to be the promised land of the latter days, playing a central role in the establishment of the kingdom of God on earth. They also believe the framing of the United States Constitution to have been an 'entering wedge for the introduction of a new era':

> As far as constitutional liberty is concerned, I will say, the God of heaven has raised up our nation, as foretold by his prophets generations ago. He inspired Columbus, and moved upon him to cross the ocean in search of this continent. . . . And what was the object of this? It was to prepare the way for the building up of the kingdom of God in this the last dispensation of the fulness of times; and as long as the principles of constitutional liberty shall be maintained upon this land, blessings will attend the nation.[65]

> It is true that the founders of this nation, as a preliminary step for the introduction of more correct principles and that liberty and the rights of man might be recognized, and that all men might become equal before the law of the land, had that great palladium of liberty, the Constitution of the United States, framed. This was the entering wedge for the introduction of a new era, and in it were introduced principles for the birth and organization of a new world.[66]

Baháís share a unique bond with Mormons in that the centrality of the American continent in the establishment of that promised kingdom, the World Order of Baháu'lláh, is clearly spelled out in 'Abdu'l-Bahás *Tablets of the Divine Plan* and elaborated in Shoghi Effendi's *The Advent of Divine Justice* (1939):

> The one chief remaining citadel, the mighty arm which still raises aloft the standard of an unconquerable Faith, is none other than the blessed community of the followers of the Most Great Name in the North American continent. By its works, and through the unfailing protection vouchsafed to it by an almighty Providence, this distinguished member of the body of the constantly interacting Baháí communities of East and West, bids fair to be universally regarded as the cradle, as well as the stronghold, of that future New World Order, which is at once the promise and the glory of the Dispensation associated with the name of Baháu'lláh.
>
> Let anyone inclined to either belittle the unique station conferred upon this community, or to question the role it will be called upon to play in the days to come, ponder the implication of these pregnant and highly illuminating words uttered by 'Abdu'l-Bahá, and addressed to it at a time when the fortunes of a world groaning beneath the burden of a devastating war had reached their lowest ebb. 'The continent of America,' He so significantly wrote, 'is, in the eyes of the one true God, the land wherein the splendors of His light shall be revealed, where the mysteries of His Faith shall be unveiled, where the righteous will abide, and the free assemble.'[67]

Mormons think of the United States Constitution as a 'heavenly banner' providing a shelter for humanity, and enabling the fulfillment of the central purpose of this dispensation:

> Here is a principle also, which we are bound to be exercised with, that is, in common with all men, such as governments, and laws, and regulations in the civil concerns of life. This principle guarantees to all parties, sects, and denominations, and classes of religion, equal, coherent, and indefeasible rights; they are things that pertain to this life; therefore all alike are interested; they make our responsibilities one towards another in matters of corruptible things, while the former principles do not destroy the latter, but bind us stronger, and make our responsibilities not only one to another, but unto God also. Hence we say, that the Constitution of the United States is a glorious standard; it is founded in the wisdom of God. It is a heavenly banner; it is to all those who are privileged with the sweets of

its liberty, like the cooling shades and refreshing waters of a great rock in a thirsty and weary land. It is like a great tree under whose branches men from every clime can be shielded from the burning rays of the sun.[68]

[God's] plan made it possible for the holy priesthood and the Church to be restored upon the earth – the restoration of the gospel of Jesus Christ – but only in America . . . The purpose of America was to provide a setting wherein that was possible. All else takes its power from that one great, central purpose.[69]

Bahá'ís, similarly, see America as the 'center from which waves of spiritual power will emanate', and the continent that 'will lead all nations spiritually':

O ye friends of God! Exert ye with heart and soul, so that association, love, unity and agreement be obtained between the hearts, all the aims may be merged into one aim, all the songs become one song and the power of the Holy Spirit may become so overwhelmingly victorious as to overcome all the forces of the world of nature. Exert yourselves; your mission is unspeakably glorious. Should success crown your enterprise, America will assuredly evolve into a center from which waves of spiritual power will emanate, and the throne of the Kingdom of God will, in the plenitude of its majesty and glory, be firmly established.[70]

The American continent gives signs and evidences of very great advancement; its future is even more promising, for its influence and illumination are far-reaching, and it will lead all nations spiritually.[71]

However, the Bahá'í Writings also warn that America must undergo a number of purifying tests and trials before it can lay claim to such spiritual leadership.

America as the Garden of Eden

Mormons take the spiritual significance of America to yet another level: they believe that the Garden of Eden in which Adam and Eve lived was actually located on the American continent:

The most sacred of places, then, will always be those locations which God has designated for holy and eternal purposes, locations where he is the 'doer of the deed.' These places are revered forever by his faithful children wherever they may be. America is such a place, but of course it wasn't always called America nor has it always been identified by a distinctive continental shape. Originally it was simply a portion of that large, single land mass which God in his creative process called 'Earth' . . . Whatever its name and geographical configuration, however, it was from the beginning a land of divinity as well as a land of destiny. The choicest part of this earthly creation was a garden 'eastward in Eden' where God placed our first parents, Adam and Eve. This resplendent place filled with paradisiacal glory was located on that part of the land mass where the city Zion, or the New Jerusalem of the earth's last days, would eventually be built. . . . After Adam and Eve were driven out of the Garden, they dwelt at a place called Adam-ondi-Ahman, located in what is now Daviess County, Missouri. In that region this first family lived out their days, tilling the soil, tending the flocks, offering sacrifices, and learning the gospel of Jesus Christ from on high.[72]

Bahá'ís understand the biblical story of Adam and Eve to be spiritual in nature, and do not see the Garden of Eden as having been located on earth.

Paradisiacal glory

With reference to the establishment of Paradise on earth, Bahá'u'lláh has revealed innumerable verses on the regenerating effects of His revelation on the entire planet. For example, He wrote:

The Divine Springtime is come, O Most Exalted Pen, for the Festival of the All-Merciful is fast approaching. Bestir thyself, and magnify, before the entire creation, the name of God, and celebrate His praise, in such wise that all created things may be regenerated and made new.[73]

Through the movement of Our Pen of glory We have, at the bidding of the omnipotent Ordainer, breathed a new life into every human frame, and instilled into every word a fresh potency. All created things proclaim the evidences of this world-wide regeneration.[74]

And in a prayer for Spiritual Assemblies, 'Abdu'l-Bahá revealed this supplication:

O Thou our Provider! Send down Thine aid, that each one gathered here may become a lighted candle, each one a centre of attraction, each one a summoner to Thy heavenly realms, till at last we make this nether world the mirror image of Thy Paradise.[75]

This sentiment is echoed by LDS president John Taylor in his 1852 publication, *The Government of God*:

> Peace is a desirable thing; it is the gift of God, and the greatest gift that God can bestow upon mortals. What is more desirable than peace? Peace in nations, peace in cities, peace in families. Like the soft murmuring zephyr [or west wind], its soothing influence calms the brow of care, dries the eye of sorrow, and chases trouble from the bosom; and let it be universally experienced, and it would drive sorrow from the world, and make this earth a paradise . . .[76]

Lastly, from a Bahá'í perspective the 'personal' presence of Christ on earth as described in the above Article of Faith is to be fulfilled, in the words of Shoghi Effendi, through 'the establishment of the Bahá'í World Commonwealth . . . which will signalize the long-awaited advent of the Christ-promised Kingdom of God on earth.'[77]

Although Bahá'ís see the way American politics are conducted as far from ideal, the Bahá'í Writings have likened a future worldwide commonwealth of nations to this American federation, in which each state maintains a degree of sovereignty and yet regards itself as part of one nation and is subject to a common economy, government and judiciary. However, this cannot come about until there is unanimity of purpose among every nation in the world. In a letter of July 7, 1976 on behalf of the Universal House of Justice, the Secretariat wrote:

> You have asked whether it is possible to have a World Federation when not all countries have attained their independence. The answer is in the negative. Both 'Abdu'l-Bahá and Shoghi Effendi likened the emergence of the American Republic and the unification of the 'diversified and loosely related elements' of its 'divided' community into one national entity, to the unity of the world and the incorporation of its federated units into 'one coherent system.' Just as the American Constitution does not allow one state to be more autonomous than another, so must the nations of the world enjoy equal status in any form of World Federation. Indeed one of the 'candles' of unity anticipated by 'Abdu'l-Bahá is 'unity in freedom.'[78]

The Eleventh Article of Faith

*We claim the privilege of worshiping Almighty God according to the
dictates of our own conscience, and allow all men the same privilege, let
them worship how, where or what they may.*

This Article appears to support free and individual expression of faith, and to
promote tolerance of other religions – very much in line with Bahá'í principles. The LDS Church itself, however, is steeped in conformity; for example,
church dress code and hymnbooks are uniform across the world, and children
are taught to pray a specific way.

Separation of church and state

Mormons are quite tolerant of other religions, and generally do not shun
friendships with people of different faiths. In areas where the Church is a
predominant influence, this commitment to the freedom of worship has
societal ramifications, as well. During the theocratic rule of the Church in
Nauvoo, Illinois, specific allowances were made for Muslims to practice their
faith, although there is no evidence that any resided there. The Mormon
scriptures also affirm the separation of church and state, particularly in limit-
ing the ability of civil society to either promote or restrict specific religious
practices:

> We believe that religion is instituted of God; and that men are amenable to
> him, and to him only, for the exercise of it, unless their religious opinions
> prompt them to infringe upon the rights and liberties of others; but we do
> not believe that human law has a right to interfere in prescribing rules of
> worship to bind the consciences of men, nor dictate forms for public or
> private devotion; that the civil magistrate should restrain crime, but never
> control conscience; should punish guilt, but never suppress the freedom
> of the soul . . .
>
> We believe that rulers, states, and governments have a right, and are
> bound to enact laws for the protection of all citizens in the free exercise of
> their religious belief; but we do not believe that they have a right in justice
> to deprive citizens of this privilege, or proscribe them in their opinions,
> so long as a regard and reverence are shown to the laws and such religious
> opinions do justify sedition nor conspiracy . . .
>
> We do not believe it just to mingle religious influence with civil gov-
> ernment, whereby one religious society is fostered and another proscribed

in its spiritual privileges, and the individual rights of its members, as citizens, denied.[79]

These high-minded ideals notwithstanding, the Church of Jesus Christ of Latter-day Saints has been under occasional criticism for attempting to shape civil law to its religious beliefs. Salt Lake City, Utah – where the Church is headquartered and the majority of elected city officials are also church members – is known for its strict laws on the sale and consumption of alcohol, laws which are seen by many non-Mormon residents as an affront to their freedoms. A short-lived city ordinance closing all public swimming pools on Sundays (when swimming is prohibited to Mormons) was denounced even by some of the faithful as going too far in foisting church doctrine upon civil society. And in 2003, the city came under public scrutiny for allowing the Church to purchase the last remaining section of a historic downtown street near the Mormon temple and turn it into a private plaza. The sale enabled the Church to place certain restrictions on free speech and other behavior, such as smoking, on visitors to the plaza.[80] According to some critics, this also included an apparent monopoly of Mormon missionaries to solicit passersby, to the exclusion of other faith groups.

However, these are isolated incidents, and although Mormon elected officials obviously feel morally compelled to promote those causes which are compatible with their beliefs, most are careful not to impose their faith on their constituents.

The Twelfth Article of Faith

We believe in being subject to kings, presidents, rulers and magistrates, in obeying, honoring, and sustaining the law.

A further elaboration of this principle is found in the Doctrine and Covenants:

We believe that all men are bound to sustain and uphold the respective governments in which they reside, while protected in their inherent and inalienable rights by the laws of such governments; and that sedition and rebellion are unbecoming every citizen thus protected, and should be punished accordingly; and that all governments have a right to enact such laws as in their own judgments are best calculated to secure the public interest; at the same time, however, holding sacred the freedom of conscience.[81]

This is in full agreement with the following words of Bahá'u'lláh:

> What mankind needeth in this day is obedience unto them that are in authority, and a faithful adherence to the cord of wisdom. The instruments which are essential to the immediate protection, the security and assurance of the human race have been entrusted to the hands, and lie in the grasp, of the governors of human society. This is the wish of God and His decree . . .[82]

In addition, both religions warn of the consequences of unchecked freedom without the rule of law. In the Doctrine and Covenants we read:

> We believe that every man should be honored in his station, rulers and magistrates as such, being placed for the protection of the innocent and the punishment of the guilty; and that to the laws all men show respect and deference, as without them peace and harmony would be supplanted by anarchy and terror; human laws being instituted for the express purpose of regulating our interests as individuals and nations, between man and man; and divine laws given of heaven, prescribing rules on spiritual concerns, for faith and worship, both to be answered by man to his Maker.[83]

While Bahá'u'lláh explains in the Kitáb-i-Aqdas:

> Liberty must, in the end, lead to sedition, whose flames none can quench. Thus warneth you He Who is the Reckoner, the All-Knowing. Know ye that the embodiment of liberty and its symbol is the animal. That which beseemeth man is submission unto such restraints as will protect him from his own ignorance, and guard him against the harm of the mischief-maker. Liberty causeth man to overstep the bounds of propriety, and to infringe on the dignity of his station. It debaseth him to the level of extreme depravity and wickedness.
>
> Regard men as a flock of sheep that need a shepherd for their protection. This, verily, is the truth, the certain truth. We approve of liberty in certain circumstances, and refuse to sanction it in others. We, verily, are the All-Knowing.[84]

The Thirteenth Article of Faith

We believe in being honest, true, chaste, benevolent, virtuous, and in doing good to all men; indeed, we may say that we follow the admonition of Paul – We believe all things, we hope all things, we have endured many things, and hope to be able to endure all things. If there is anything virtuous, lovely or of good report or praiseworthy, we seek after these things.

This admonition to 'believe all things' is a paraphrase from Paul's first letter to the Corinthians, specifically his explanation of the nature of charity:

Charity suffereth long, and is kind; charity envieth not; charity vaunteth not itself, is not puffed up, Doth not behave itself unseemly, seeketh not her own, is not easily provoked, thinketh no evil; Rejoiceth not in iniquity, but rejoiceth in the truth; Beareth all things, believeth all things, hopeth all things, endureth all things.[85]

In addition to the high virtues taught by all religions, this Article of Faith affirms the principle of independent investigation of truth, and supports the acceptance of additional revelation. And while many church members look to their leadership to tell them which things are 'virtuous, lovely or of good report,' an increasing number of Mormons reject the narrow focus on officially sanctioned materials, believing instead that to read about other religions and philosophies can only serve to enrich the mind and spirit, and to deepen one's own faith.

The Bahá'í Writings are of course replete with references to the spiritual qualities we must all strive to exhibit. A number of parallels to the above Article of Faith are found in Bahá'u'lláh's Tablet of Wisdom (Lawḥ-i-Ḥikmát):

O peoples of the world! Forsake all evil, hold fast that which is good. Strive to be shining examples unto all mankind, and true reminders of the virtues of God amidst men. He that riseth to serve My Cause should manifest My wisdom, and bend every effort to banish ignorance from the earth. Be united in counsel, be one in thought. Let each morn be better than its eve and each morrow richer than its yesterday. Man's merit lieth in service and virtue and not in the pageantry of wealth and riches. Take heed that your words be purged from idle fancies and worldly desires and your deeds be cleansed from craftiness and suspicion. Dissipate not the wealth of your precious lives in the pursuit of evil and corrupt affection, nor let your endeavours be spent in promoting your personal interest. Be generous in your days of plenty, and be patient in the hour of loss. Adversity is followed by success and rejoicings follow woe. Guard against idleness and sloth, and cling unto that which profiteth mankind, whether young or old, whether high or low. Beware lest ye sow tares of dissension among men or plant thorns of doubt in pure and radiant hearts.

O ye beloved of the Lord! Commit not that which defileth the limpid stream of love or destroyeth the sweet fragrance of friendship. By the righteousness of the Lord! Ye were created to show love one to another and not perversity and rancour. Take pride not in love for yourselves but in love for your fellow-creatures. Glory not in love for your country, but in love for all mankind. Let your eye be chaste, your hand faithful, your tongue truthful and your heart enlightened. Abase not the station of the learned in Bahá and belittle not the rank of such rulers as administer justice amidst you. Set your reliance on the army of justice, put on the armour of wisdom, let your adorning be forgiveness and mercy and that which cheereth the hearts of the well-favoured of God.[86]

CHAPTER 4

REVELATION

We have seen *revelation* referred to many times thus far in this book, in a variety of contexts. In this chapter we discuss how revelation is understood differently by Mormons and Bahá'ís, and how this knowledge can be used to avoid unnecessary misunderstandings.

As we shall see, the meaning of the term *revelation* differs sharply between Mormon and Bahá'í vernacular. In any interreligious dialogue, it is essential to understand that different groups may use the same term to describe different concepts, much as the same literal word can be shared by two languages or dialects without having the slightest equivalence of meaning. For example, in the United Kingdom an attorney is referred to as a solicitor. In the United States, however, a solicitor is someone who knocks on doors or calls during dinnertime trying to sell something. Without an understanding of semantic differences, one can imagine the difficulty a British attorney might encounter in finding gainful employment in the United States!

In light of the many differences that exist between the Mormon and Bahá'í concepts of revelation, the two faiths share some remarkable features on this subject.

Revelation not final

One of the most important links between the Mormon and Bahá'í faiths is the belief that revelation is not final. When engaging mainstream Christians on the nonfinality of revelation, Mormons and Bahá'ís deal with very much the same issues, because the majority of Christians understand the verse 'If any man shall add unto these things, God shall add unto him the plagues that are written in this book'[1] to mean that the Bible is the final Word of God. What most people do not take into account is that what we know as the Holy Bible was not canonized until centuries after this verse was written, so it could not possibly refer to the Bible as a whole. Rather, it appears to warn against the willful corruption of the text by apostates, something that was attempted within the Bahá'í Faith as well. Another common oversight concerns the term 'man.' Certainly it is not for a man to add to any holy text, but a Manifestation of God is no ordinary man. Lastly, Bahá'u'lláh did not claim to add anything to the Bible itself, but like the Báb and Muhammad before Him, He revealed an entirely new book. Mormons, therefore, face a much greater challenge than Bahá'ís, since Joseph Smith added to the Bible itself and made textual alterations to both the Old and New Testaments.

The Mormon scriptures dismiss the notion that the wellspring of revelation has dried up:

> We believe all that God has revealed, all that He does now reveal, and we believe that He will yet reveal many great and important things pertaining to the Kingdom of God.[2]

> Wherefore murmur ye, because that ye shall receive more of my word? Know ye not that the testimony of two nations is a witness unto you that I am God, that I remember one nation like unto another? Wherefore, I speak the same words unto one nation like unto another. And when the two nations shall run together the testimony of the two nations shall run together also. And I do this that I may prove unto many that I am the same yesterday, today, and forever; and that I speak forth my words according to my own pleasure. And because that I have spoken one word ye need not suppose that I cannot speak another; for my work is not yet finished; neither shall it be until the end of man, neither from that time henceforth and forever. Wherefore, because that ye have a Bible ye need not suppose that it contains all my words; neither need ye suppose that I have not caused more to be written.[3]

The above verses bear a close resemblance to these words of Bahá'u'lláh:

> Think ye, O My servants, that the Hand of My all-encompassing, My overshadowing, and transcendent sovereignty is chained up, that the flow of Mine ancient, My ceaseless, and all-pervasive mercy is checked, or that the clouds of My sublime and unsurpassed favors have ceased to rain their gifts upon men? Can ye imagine that the wondrous works that have proclaimed My divine and resistless power are withdrawn, or that the potency of My will and purpose hath been deterred from directing the destinies of mankind? If it be not so, wherefore, then, have ye striven to prevent the deathless Beauty of My sacred and gracious Countenance from being unveiled to men's eyes?[4]

The call of the New Testament to 'despise not prophesyings' is repeated in the LDS scriptures:

> Behold, great and marvelous are the works of the Lord. How unsearchable are the depths of the mysteries of him; and it is impossible that man should find out all his ways. And no man knoweth of his ways save it be revealed unto him; wherefore, brethren, despise not the revelations of God.[5]

And finally, the Book of Mormon offers one of the most cogent reasons why revelation cannot possibly cease if one believes that God is an unchangeable Being; if God revealed in the past, and God has not changed, then God can reveal again:

> And again I speak unto you who deny the revelations of God, and say that they are done away, that there are no revelations, nor prophecies, nor gifts, nor healing, nor speaking with tongues, and the interpretation of tongues; Behold I say unto you, he that denieth these things knoweth not the gospel of Christ; yea, he has not read the scriptures; if so, he does not understand them. For do we not read that God is the same yesterday, today, and forever, and in him there is no variableness neither shadow of changing? And now, if ye have imagined up unto yourselves a god who doth vary, and in whom there is shadow of changing, then have ye imagined up unto yourselves a god who is not a God of miracles. But behold, I will show unto you a God of miracles, even the God of Abraham, and the God of Isaac, and the God of Jacob; and it is that same God who created the heavens and the earth, and all things that in them are . . . And if there were miracles wrought then, why has God ceased to be a God of miracles and yet be an unchangeable Being? And behold, I say unto you he changeth not; if so he would cease to be God; and he ceaseth not to be God, and is a God of miracles.[6]

A similar argument can be found in the Writings of Bahá'u'lláh. Referring to certain respected religious scholars of the day, He wrote:

> Yea, these servants regard the one true God as He Who 'doeth as He willeth' and 'ordaineth as He pleaseth'. Thus they view not as impossible the continued appearance in the contingent world of the Manifestations of His Unity. Should anyone hold otherwise, how would he be different from those who believe the hand of God to be 'chained up'? And if the one true God – glorified be His mention! – be indeed regarded as unconstrained,

then whatever Cause that Ancient King may please to manifest from the wellspring of His Command must be embraced by all. No refuge is there for anyone and no haven to hasten unto save God; no protection is there for any soul and no shelter to seek except in Him.[7]

The phrase 'chained up' in the above verse is a reference to certain Jewish divines at the time of Muhammad who rejected His Message on the grounds that no further revelation was possible.[8]

Nonfinality of revelation understood differently

Despite these marvelous scriptural similarities, we must be careful to distinguish between the Mormon concept of the nonfinality of revelation – known as *continuing revelation* – and the Bahá'í principle of *progressive revelation*. Whereas the latter holds that revelation gradually increases the education of mankind with the appearance of each subsequent Manifestation of God, the former is understood to mean that the current president of the LDS Church is a prophet who continuously reveals the will of God. However, the nature of this continuing revelation as Mormons describe it is far removed from the kind of direct revelation Bahá'ís attribute to a Manifestation of God; rather, it is more accurately described as an inner sense of inspiration. Boyd K. Packer, a member of the Quorum of the Twelve Apostles, explains:

> The Holy Ghost communicates with the spirit through the mind more than through the physical senses. This guidance comes as thoughts, as feelings, and through impressions and promptings. It is not always easy to describe inspiration. The scriptures teach us that we may 'feel' the words of spiritual communication more than hear them, and see with spiritual rather than mortal eyes. The patterns of revelation are not dramatic. The voice of inspiration is a still voice, a small voice. There need be no trance, no sanctimonious declaration. It is quieter and simpler than that. If you have experienced inspiration, you understand.[9]

As such, the role of the president of the Church as 'prophet, seer and revelator' is not very different from that of the Pope to the Catholic Church, who is considered by adherents to be divinely guided in his words and actions. In any case, the similarities of Mormon and Bahá'í thought on the subject of the nonfinality of revelation are remarkable. The following two excerpts are from LDS sources:

What is revelation but the uncovering of new truths, by him who is the fountain of all truth? To say that there is no need of new revelation, is equivalent to saying that we have no need of new truths – a ridiculous assertion. As well, too, might we say that the revelations which Abraham received were sufficient for the prophets; that the revelations given to Enoch were sufficient for Noah, whose mission was to build the ark and preach repentance; or that the words spoken to Moses were sufficient for all time; or that what Abraham received would be ample for his children through all the ages . . . So we moderns stand in need, oh so greatly! of constant revelation, that we individually may fill our missions acceptably to our Father, and that we may the better work out our own salvation; and also that we may know the will of God concerning his Church, his people, and his purposes in regard to the nations. These are a few of the thousand needs that exist for revelation.[10]

The most important prophet, so far as we are concerned, is the one who is living in our day and age. This is the prophet who has today's instructions from God to us today. God's revelation to Adam did not instruct Noah how to build the ark. Every generation has need of the ancient scripture plus the current scripture from the living prophet. Therefore, the most crucial reading and pondering which you should do is of the latest inspired words from the Lord's mouthpiece.[11]

While the preceding statement was made to prove the necessity of a 'living prophet' – the current president of the LDS Church – it is actually a better argument for the Bahá'í concept of progressive revelation (i.e. the renewal of God's message every 500 to 1,000 years), because there was no continuous revelation from a living prophet between Adam and Noah. Yet even in the Bahá'í Faith, a close analogy is found in the institution of the Covenant. In his seminal treatise *The Covenant of Bahá'u'lláh* Adib Taherzadeh echoes the sentiment, expressed above, that 'we moderns stand in need, oh so greatly! of constant revelation,' and gives one of the primary reasons why Bahá'u'lláh ordained the establishment of the Universal House of Justice:

Bahá'u'lláh has envisaged, and this has already become evident, that in His Dispensation man will advance and progress at an unprecedented rate, needing new laws at every stage of his development. Therefore, He has empowered the Universal House of Justice to enact secondary laws that conform with the circumstances of the time, laws which can be changed at a later time as conditions change. It must be noted, however, that the teachings, laws and ordinances which are revealed by Bahá'u'lláh Himself are unalterable until the advent of a future Manifestation of God who has the right to abrogate them.[12]

The following words of 'Abdu'l-Bahá shed additional light on this subject:

Those matters of major importance which constitute the foundation of the Law of God are explicitly recorded in the Text, but subsidiary laws are left to the House of Justice. The wisdom of this is that the times never remain the same, for change is a necessary quality and an essential attribute of this world, and of time and place. Therefore the House of Justice will take action accordingly . . .[13]

Christ to reveal all things upon His return

Surprisingly, Mormons do not generally see the many references to the renewal of revelation as applicable to Christ upon His return. However, the Mormon scriptures do affirm that when Christ returns, He will 'reveal all things':

Yea, verily I say unto you, in that day when the Lord shall come, he shall reveal all things – Things which have passed, and hidden things which no man knew, things of the earth, by which it was made, and the purpose and the end thereof – Things most precious, things that are above, and things that are beneath, things that are in the earth, and upon the earth, and in heaven.[14]

As will be shown in a later chapter, Mormons expect Christ to clear up a number of mysteries upon His return, particularly on issues where LDS doctrine appears to be in conflict with scientific evidence.

Dispensations

Continuous revelation notwithstanding, Mormon doctrine does acknowledge the concept of *dispensations*, in which God's plan is dispensed to mankind at certain intervals through chosen prophets. This view, however, falls short of recognizing that these dispensations occur in progressive stages; rather, each dispensation is said to bring a renewal of the selfsame spiritual principles:

The Lord has a plan, an order, a system for the salvation of the human family. It is an ancient plan – an eternal plan. It was explained to us and implemented in the premortal life and has been introduced – or 'dispensed'

98

– several times to mankind on the earth through chosen prophets, beginning with Adam. Dispensations are those periods or eras wherein the Lord
has called someone to administer or preside over a major assignment or
oversee the flow of gospel blessings. Michael, or Adam, headed the first
gospel dispensation. We could say that he was the Lord's administrator
for dispensing gospel truths and ordinances. The Lord has established
gospel dispensations several times among people on the earth; sometimes
a dispensation endured for a while and then ceased to function on earth
because of wickedness and unbelief.[15]

In each dispensation, from the days of Adam to the days of the Prophet
Joseph Smith, the Lord has revealed anew the principles of the gospel.
So that while the records of past dispensations, insofar as they are uncorrupted, testify to the truths of the gospel, still each dispensation has had
revealed in its day sufficient truth to guide the people of the new dispensation, independent of the records of the past.[16]

This is partially in agreement with the Bahá'í teachings, which say that with
each new dispensation the same *spiritual principles* are renewed. The Bahá'í
Writings clarify that in addition to these spiritual laws, a new set of *social
laws* is revealed, abrogating those of the previous dispensation and preparing
humanity for a new era of spiritual growth. However, the following statement
from an LDS church magazine article about 'the fulness of times' does in fact
suggest that this latest dispensation, in addition to renewing age-old spiritual
principles, establishes new goals for humanity:

The saving principles and ordinances of the gospel are the same in every
dispensation. We do not have any doctrines or ordinances in the Church
today that have not been had at some time in earlier dispensations. There
are, however, some things to be accomplished in this dispensation that
have not been done before, such as the building of the New Jerusalem, the
gathering of Israel, the second coming of the Savior, the beginning of the
Millennium, and the renewing of paradisiacal glory to the earth, restoring
it as it was before the Fall.[17]

Adam considered a prophet

In an interesting parallel to the Bahá'í Faith, Mormon doctrine holds Adam to
be a prophet, the first in a number of dispensations leading up to the fullness
of times:

Adam was the Lord's prophet-leader over the earth for his own day; he also stands as earth's presiding high priest, the man who, under Christ, holds the keys of authority for the blessing of humankind and the perpetuation of righteousness in the earth.[18]

However, Mormon doctrine upholds the traditional belief that Adam was the first man on earth.

The culmination of all previous dispensations

Like Bahá'ís, Mormons recognize the age in which we live as the 'fullness of times' or 'last days' referred to in the Bible, and see the current dispensation as the culmination of all previous ones. Mormons, however, consider the revelation of Joseph Smith to be the fulfillment of that prophecy, even though in their estimation, Christ has not yet returned:

> The gospel dispensation given to us is appropriately called the fulness of times because it will bring the culmination of all previous dispensations, plus the fruition of some unique things never before accomplished on the earth. [19]

> Adam . . . was the first man, who is spoken of in Daniel as being the 'Ancient of Days' . . . Adam holds the keys of the dispensation of the fullness of times; i.e., the dispensation of all the times have been and will be revealed through him from the beginning to Christ, and from Christ to the end of the dispensations that are to be revealed. And again, God purposed in Himself that there should not be an eternal fullness until every dispensation should be fulfilled and gathered together in one . . . therefore He set the ordinances to be the same forever and ever, and set Adam to watch over them, to reveal them from heaven to man, or to send angels to reveal them . . . These angels are under the direction of Michael or Adam, who acts under the direction of the Lord.[20]

In the above quotation, Joseph Smith uses the names *Adam, Michael* and *Ancient of Days* interchangeably, as though they were one and the same person. In contrast, Bahá'ís believe the Biblical titles of *Michael* ('he who looks like God') and *Ancient of Days* to be references to Bahá'u'lláh.

How many dispensations have there been?

Mormons recognize a number of dispensations throughout history, beginning with Adam, and ending with Joseph Smith:

> How many dispensations have there been? We often hear that there are seven: Adam, Enoch, Noah, Abraham, Moses, Jesus, and Joseph Smith. This list is far too shallow, however. The seven are only a few of the dispensations mentioned in the Bible. (What about Melchizedek, Elijah, and John the Baptist?) And the list completely ignores what we know about the gospel being among the Nephites, the Jaredites, and the Lost Tribes. There have been many dispensations. The dispensation of Adam was the first, and the dispensation of the fulness of times is a combination of them all.[21]

It is remarkable that five out of seven dispensations listed above – those of Adam, Noah, Abraham, Moses and Jesus – are also recognized by the Bahá'í Faith. The Bahá'í Writings not only state that Adam was a prophet, but also that there were many other Manifestations that came before the Adam we know from the Bible. And although Noah is not specifically identified by Shoghi Effendi as a Manifestation of God, Bahá'u'lláh referred to him as a major prophet whose dispensation lasted for 950 years,[22] and the Báb identified Noah as a Manifestation in the excerpts from Dalá'il-i-Sab'ih (The Seven Proofs).

However, it should also be noted that from a Bahá'í perspective, there are some misunderstandings within Mormon doctrine concerning the inaugurators of these dispensations. For example, in some Mormon texts Adam is equated to the Archangel Michael, and Noah is identified with Gabriel. Also, it is unclear from the above quotation whether Jesus' Second Coming would be considered a new dispensation in its own right, or a mere extension of Joseph Smith's.

The nature of Joseph Smith's revelatory experience

As noted in the introduction, a certain 'amplification of terms' is found within Mormon terminology. Could this phenomenon be used to explain how the process of revelation experienced by the Manifestations of God (e.g. Jesus and Bahá'u'lláh) differs from that claimed by Joseph Smith? In an article in *World Order* magazine, William P. Collins explained:

> To understand what constitutes the inspiration that Joseph Smith received through the advent of the Báb and Bahá'u'lláh it is necessary to grasp what

Bahá'u'lláh and Joseph Smith describe as revelation and how the two may differ from each other . . . Bahá'u'lláh describes His experience of revelation in a number of ways: (1) God's voice speaks directly to Bahá'u'lláh, as in *The Fire Tablet* in answer to His anguished cry; (2) God speaks to Bahá'u'lláh through an intermediary, such as the Maid of Heaven; (3) God imbues Bahá'u'lláh with His own Spirit in such a way that Bahá'u'lláh's person and deeds *become* the revelation; (4) knowledge is revealed to Bahá'u'lláh in the form of a Tablet which appears before His face. All of these modes of revelation, while appearing to the rest of mankind to be internal to Bahá'u'lláh, are described by Him as objective phenomena arising outside Himself.

Joseph Smith's experiences, as he describes them, are a distinctive form of 'revelation.' In speaking of the experience of 'translating' the Book of Mormon, he writes: 'But behold, I say unto you, that *you must study it out in your mind*; then you must ask me if it is right, and if it is right I will cause that your bosom shall burn within you . . .' And in a telling description of the process of 'revelation' Smith says: 'A person may profit by noticing the first intimation of the spirit of revelation; for instance, when you feel pure intelligence flowing into you, *it may give you sudden strokes of ideas* . . . [T]hus by learning the Spirit of God and understanding it, you may grow into the principle of revelation . . .'

In contrast to the experience of revelation spoken of by Bahá'u'lláh, Joseph Smith described his as a subjective phenomenon – one that arose within Smith's own mind and that required the recipient's own initiative and discovery . . .[23]

This comparison is useful in understanding the differing uses of the term 'revelation.' While Joseph Smith allowed his own 'self' to actively participate in the revelatory process, interpreting and studying out in his mind everything that came to him, Bahá'u'lláh was a pure conduit transmitting the Holy Spirit, the 'hollow reed' of which 'Abdu'l-Bahá wrote:

This reed is a Perfect Man Who is likened to a reed, and the manner of its likeness is this: when the interior of a reed is empty and free from all matter, it will produce beautiful melodies; and as the sound and melodies do not come from the reed, but from the flute player who blows upon it, so the sanctified heart of that blessed Being is free and emptied from all save God, pure and exempt from the attachments of all human conditions, and is the companion of the Divine Spirit. Whatever He utters is not from Himself, but from the real flute player, and it is a divine inspiration.[24]

Bahá'u'lláh described in moving detail the complete state of self-abnegation He found Himself in while revealing the Word of God. Referring to the Manifestations of God, He wrote:

> Were the eye of discernment to be opened, it would recognize that in this very state, they have considered themselves utterly effaced and non-existent in the face of Him Who is the All-Pervading, the Incorruptible. Methinks, they have regarded themselves as utter nothingness, and deemed their mention in that Court an act of blasphemy. For the slightest whispering of self within such a Court is an evidence of self-assertion and independent existence. In the eyes of them that have attained unto that Court, such a suggestion is itself a grievous transgression. How much more grievous would it be, were aught else to be mentioned in that Presence, were man's heart, his tongue, his mind, or his soul, to be busied with any one but the Well-Beloved, were his eyes to behold any countenance other than His beauty, were his ear to be inclined to any melody but His Voice, and were his feet to tread any way but His way . . .[25]

Joseph Smith did not fully understand all of the revelation he received

It is evident from certain statements by Joseph Smith that sometimes, while in the process of receiving revelation, he was unsure of the exact nature of what he was getting. Based on these accounts it appears that Smith, while continually striving to understand the impressions he was receiving, was not altogether successful in his endeavor, and was rather left to himself to figure out their meaning:

> I was once praying very earnestly to know the time of the coming of the Son of Man, when I heard a voice repeat the following: Joseph, my son, if thou livest until thou art eighty-five years old, thou shalt see the face of the Son of Man; therefore let this suffice, and trouble me no more on this matter. I was left thus, without being able to decide whether this coming referred to the beginning of the millennium or to some previous appearing, or whether I should die and thus see his face.[26]

In Smith's defense, a similar situation is recorded in the Book of Daniel:

> And I heard, but I understood not: then said I, O my Lord, what shall be the end of these things? And he said, Go thy way, Daniel: for the words are closed up and sealed till the time of the end.[27]

Personal revelation

Mormons believe that all church members are able to receive *personal revelation*. To a Bahá'í, this may appear to suggest that every member of the Church has claims to prophethood. Actually, personal revelation simply refers to personal guidance from the Holy Spirit, and is described as 'the whisperings of the still small voice of the Spirit of the living God.'[28]

A similar concept is found in the Bahá'í Faith. According to Shoghi Effendi, the 'inspiration received through meditation is of a nature that one cannot measure or determine. God can inspire into our minds things that we had no previous knowledge of, if He desires to do so.'[29] However, he also warned that our personal desires can present themselves to us in the guise of inspiration:

> We cannot clearly distinguish between personal desire and guidance, but if the way opens, when we have sought guidance, then we may presume God is helping us.[30]

'Abdu'l-Bahá offered a similar warning about the inherent fallibility of human judgment, particularly when it comes to promptings of the heart:

> Inspirations are the promptings or susceptibilities of the human heart. The promptings of the heart are sometimes satanic. How are we to differentiate them? How are we to tell whether a given statement is an inspiration and prompting of the heart through the merciful assistance or through the satanic agency?[31]

He then suggested that, at the very least, our subjective impressions must be validated against reason, and cannot contravene revealed truth. Furthermore, while personal inspirations and interpretations can provide valuable insights into one's own life and enrich our appreciation of the scriptures, the Bahá'í Writings make it clear that they must never be imposed on others:

> The existence of authoritative interpretations does not preclude the individual from engaging in the study of the Teachings and thereby arriving at a personal interpretation or understanding. A clear distinction is, however, drawn in the Bahá'í Writings between authoritative interpretation and the understanding that each individual arrives at from a study of its Teachings. Individual interpretations based on a person's understanding of the Teachings constitute the fruit of man's rational power and may well contribute to a greater comprehension of the Faith. Such views, nevertheless, lack authority. In presenting their personal ideas, individuals are

cautioned not to discard the authority of the revealed words, not to deny or contend with the authoritative interpretation, and not to engage in controversy; rather they should offer their thoughts as a contribution to knowledge, making it clear that their views are merely their own.[32]

Personal revelation not limited to the priesthood

In the Church of Jesus Christ of Latter-day Saints, only men can hold the priesthood. As previously explained, the priesthood is believed to uniquely enable the man, as patriarch, to spiritually guide his family. Yet Mormon doctrine holds that *all* members of the Church, including women and children, are able to receive personal spiritual guidance:

> The spirit of inspiration, the gift of revelation, does not belong to one man solely; . . . It is not confined to the presiding authorities of the Church, it belongs to every individual member of the Church; and it is the right and privilege of every man, every woman, and every child who has reached the years of accountability, to enjoy the spirit of revelation, and to be possessed of the spirit of inspiration in the discharge of their duties as members of the Church.[33]

In fact, Mormons believe this same definition of 'personal revelation' to apply to all levels of the Church, all the way up to its president. They do not profess a significant difference between the way a church president (who is considered an infallible prophet) receives revelation, and how any other church member experiences it. The primary variation is in the sphere of influence that revelation is assumed to have – the father over his family, the bishop over his ward, and the president over the entire Church.

The infallibility of the head of the faith

In the LDS Church, the writings of its president – who is accepted as the 'living prophet' – can be considered part of the overall body of Mormon scriptures. In a few cases, the canonization of such writings has been done formally, but even without this, the teachings of the presidents of the Church are taken as infallible and scriptural. In the Bahá'í Faith, the same can be said of the writings of Shoghi Effendi and the Universal House of Justice. While these cannot be compared to the Creative Word of the Báb and Bahá'u'lláh, nor to the Writings of 'Abdu'l-Bahá, nonetheless they are seen as divinely inspired and part of the overall body of the Bahá'í Writings.

It is in this light that Mormons see what they refer to as *continuing revelation*: that the head of the faith is continually receiving divine inspiration regarding the direction of the Church. However, as has been noted, this style of revelation is indirect and subjective. Gordon B. Hinckley, president of the LDS Church from 1995 until his death in 2008, described the process as follows:

> Now and again a serious problem arises on which we do need direction and understanding. What do we do? We counsel together as brethren. We pray. We even fast. It's a very sacred thing. An answer comes; I'm satisfied of that. And the results that are achieved from what comes bear out the fact that it was done under inspiration, under revelation. It works. Now, it isn't a constant everyday thing. No. It comes as needed, according to need and opportunity.[34]

If we substitute the word *revelation* in the above statement with *divine guidance*, we find that the process experienced by the Universal House of Justice is remarkably similar. In an address given at the Bahá'í World Centre, Mr Ian Semple – at the time a member of the Universal House of Justice – remarked:

> The authority of the Guardian and the Universal House of Justice go back to the authority of Bahá'u'lláh Himself, so similar principles apply. One should obey them because one knows that they are divinely guided. I can recall more than one occasion on which I found myself either unable to understand or in disagreement with a decision of the Universal House of Justice. You know, the House of Justice doesn't always have unanimous decisions; it has majority decisions sometimes. Such a situation is not surprising of course. The House of Justice is infallible, but individual human beings aren't, so it's only logical that sometimes one should initially disagree with a decision that is reached. In all cases, naturally, I have accepted the decision and after a lapse of time I have always found why the House of Justice was right and I was wrong. The interesting thing is that it isn't only that it was for reasons that I didn't recognize at the time – 'All right, that was what I misunderstood in the consultation, I now know what was right' – but sometimes even because of things that I could not have known at the time the decision was made. The ways of God, again, are mysterious, even when they come through His institutions. One cannot always expect to know everything at the outset.[35]

Notwithstanding the similarities in how the respective heads of these two religions experience inspiration, there are significant differences in how that inspiration is applied. The Universal House of Justice has a clear mandate directly from Bahá'u'lláh, Who outlined its basic role and function in His original Writings. While this mandate gives the Universal House of Justice wide latitude to legislate on matters not specifically mentioned in the Sacred Texts, and the authority to gradually apply the laws of the Kitáb-i-Aqdas, it is clearly limited in that the House can only reverse its own decisions, and can never annul any law or principle enunciated by Bahá'u'lláh. Furthermore, all future decisions must be in accordance with the explicit guidance and authoritative interpretations of 'Abdu'l-Bahá and Shoghi Effendi.

The First Presidency of the LDS Church does not consider itself constrained by any such limitations, and has repeatedly annulled or modified doctrines by prior presidents of the Church, including Joseph Smith himself. Certainly the doctrines on plural marriage and black priesthood fall into this category (see Appendices 1 and 2). On several occasions, the First Presidency has even ordered that actual scriptures be modified or updated, literally altering the written word of their founding prophet.[36]

In a way, these modifications and reversals are not necessarily inconsistent: to Mormons, the current president of the Church is considered every bit as much a prophet as Joseph Smith,[37] so it would be as though Smith himself were to correct or update his own writing. However, the Church is keenly aware of the other side of that argument, namely that any action which is inconsistent with previously established doctrines casts doubt on the infallibility of earlier church presidents. As a result, new doctrines are presented to the faithful as though they were fully in harmony with the utterances of past church leaders, even though they may be diametrically opposed.

Twofold language

Bahá'ís understand that the Holy Scriptures of the world's religions were written in a spiritual language, the meaning of which is gradually unfolded to us as we become more receptive to the truths enshrined in them. Latter-day Saints believe that, for the most part, scripture should be interpreted literally. This belief can be traced back to as early as 1878, when Orson Pratt remarked:

> We do not read the Scriptures as most of the inhabitants of the earth do, thinking that they must be spiritualized. There are scarcely any of the prophecies but what this generation, as well as some of the past generations, interpret as meaning something altogether different from the reading of them . . . The Latter-day Saints . . . learned that the word of God would all be fulfilled, which have not already come to pass, and that

they are to be understood in the same light, and in the same sense as we would understand the writings of uninspired individuals, when plainly and clearly written upon any special subject.[38]

Yet in spite of this focus on the outward meaning of the Word of God, the LDS scriptures also acknowledge that there may be additional, hidden meanings. Concerning a vision in which Joseph Smith and Oliver Cowdery were visited by John the Baptist, Smith wrote:

> Our minds being now enlightened, we began to have the scriptures laid open to our understandings, and the true meaning and intention of their more mysterious passages revealed unto us in a manner which we never could attain to previously, nor ever before had thought of.[39]

The Book of Mormon explains that the writings of those who 'know the mysteries of God' – the prophets – are such that those who harden their hearts will not glean their true significance:

> It is given unto many to know the mysteries of God; nevertheless they are laid under a strict command that they shall not impart only according to the portion of his word which he doth grant unto the children of men, according to the heed and diligence which they give unto him. And therefore, he that will harden his heart, the same receiveth the lesser portion of the word; and he that will not harden his heart, to him is given the greater portion of the word, until it is given unto him to know the mysteries of God until he know them in full. And they that will harden their hearts, to them is given the lesser portion of the word until they know nothing concerning his mysteries; and then they are taken captive by the devil, and led by his will down to destruction. Now this is what is meant by the chains of hell.[40]

Like Bahá'ís, Mormons frequently report that each time they read a certain scripture anew, they glean new truths which they had not noticed before, and which are uniquely applicable to their current situation.

A Bahá'í explanation of twofold language

The Bahá'í Writings point out that all the Messengers of God speak a twofold language. The following passage from the Writings of Bahá'u'lláh explains this concept, and contains a warning very similar to the one previously quoted from the Book of Mormon:

It is evident unto thee that the Birds of Heaven and Doves of Eternity speak a twofold language. One language, the outward language, is devoid of allusions, is unconcealed and unveiled; that it may be a guiding lamp and a beaconing light whereby wayfarers may attain the heights of holiness, and seekers may advance into the realm of eternal reunion . . . The other language is veiled and concealed, so that whatever lieth hidden in the heart of the malevolent may be made manifest and their innermost being be disclosed . . . This is the divine standard, this is the Touchstone of God, wherewith He proveth His servants. None apprehendeth the meaning of these utterances except them whose hearts are assured, whose souls have found favour with God, and whose minds are detached from all else but Him. In such utterances, the literal meaning, as generally understood by the people, is not what hath been intended . . . The people, therefore, must not allow such utterances to deprive them of the divine bounties, but should rather seek enlightenment from them who are the recognized Expounders thereof . . . We perceive none, however, amongst the people of the earth who, sincerely yearning for the Truth, seeketh the guidance of the divine Manifestations concerning the abstruse matters of his Faith. All are dwellers in the land of oblivion, and all are followers of the people of wickedness and rebellion. God will verily do unto them that which they themselves are doing, and will forget them even as they have ignored His Presence in His day. Such is His decree unto those that have denied Him, and such will it be unto them that have rejected His signs. We conclude Our argument with His words – exalted is He – 'And whoso shall withdraw from the remembrance of the Merciful, We will chain a Satan unto him, and he shall be his fast companion.' 'And whoso turneth away from My remembrance, truly his shall be a life of misery.'[41]

Parables

The numerous parables told by Jesus are among the more famous examples of twofold language. Even His Apostles were confounded by at least one of these parables, and so Jesus explained it to them in clear language, along with the qualification that it was due to their special station that He disclosed to them its true meaning. The multitudes, however, would be given only the parable, as a test of their spiritual understanding:

He answered and said unto them, Because it is given unto you to know the mysteries of the kingdom of heaven, but to them it is not given. For whosoever hath, to him shall be given, and he shall have more abundance:

but whosoever hath not, from him shall be taken away even that he hath. Therefore speak I to them in parables: because they seeing see not; and hearing they hear not, neither do they understand. And in them is fulfilled the prophecy of Esaias, which saith, By hearing ye shall hear, and shall not understand; and seeing ye shall see, and shall not perceive:[42] For this people's heart is waxed gross, and their ears are dull of hearing, and their eyes they have closed; lest at any time they should see with their eyes and hear with their ears, and should understand with their heart, and should be converted, and I should heal them. But blessed are your eyes, for they see: and your ears, for they hear.[43]

The LDS *Bible Dictionary* accurately represents the nature and purpose of parables:

Most teachers, especially Oriental teachers, have used some form of parable in their instruction, but none so exclusively as Jesus at one period of his ministry. During part of the Galilean ministry the record states that 'without a parable spake he not unto them' (Mark 4: 34). From our Lord's words (Matt. 13: 13-15; Mark 4: 12; Luke 8: 10) we learn the reason for this method. It was to veil the meaning. The parable conveys to the hearer religious truth exactly in proportion to his faith and intelligence; to the dull and uninspired it is a mere story, 'seeing they see not,' while to the instructed and spiritual it reveals the mysteries or secrets of the kingdom of heaven. Thus it is that the parable exhibits the condition of all true knowledge. Only he who seeks finds.[44]

Bahá'u'lláh confirms that the primary reason for the use of parables is to test the believers' hearts:

Know verily that the purpose underlying all these symbolic terms and abstruse allusions, which emanate from the Revealers of God's holy Cause, hath been to test and prove the peoples of the world; that thereby the earth of the pure and illuminated hearts may be known from the perishable and barren soil. From time immemorial such hath been the way of God amidst His creatures, and to this testify the records of the sacred books.[45]

O Essence of Negligence! Myriads of mystic tongues find utterance in one speech, and myriads of hidden mysteries are revealed in a single melody; yet, alas, there is no ear to hear, nor heart to understand.[46]

Some Mormon commentators have acknowledged that there are underlying spiritual truths to be gleaned from the miracles performed by Jesus Christ, and that these are perhaps even more important than the historical accounts themselves. In the *Questions and Answers* section of a church periodical excerpted below, the author responds to a question about the significance of Jesus and Peter walking on the water. In so doing, he plays down the importance of the literal account in favor of a more meaningful symbolic lesson:

> Jesus spent much of his ministry teaching through parables . . . Perhaps we can learn much by treating the experience of Christ and Peter walking on the water as a kind of dramatized parable. As in Christ's spoken parables, there is more than one level of meaning in this incident. At the surface we have an exciting adventure at sea, where the Lord with supernatural power saves a disciple from drowning and also possibly saves the ship from capsizing.
>
> At another level we contemplate authority, power, and the nature of miracles. We stand in awe of the Son of God as he commands the responsive forces of nature.
>
> At still another level we may see additional significance in what took place that day on the Sea of Galilee, a symbolism that can teach us much about our own experience in life.
>
> Peter and the other disciples embarked upon their journey in response to their master's request. We, too, embarked upon our journey through mortality in willing response to divine will. And, like the disciples on the ship, who were aware of the dangers of traveling on the Sea of Galilee, with its sudden storms, we began our journey with an understanding that there would be perils along the way.
>
> Like Peter, we in this life learn that temporal supports sometimes crumble – or sink – in the face of life's tempests. We find that there are forces capable of upsetting our most carefully improvised plans. But we, like Peter, can discover that our Savior stands nearby, though perhaps dimly seen, ready to help us if we will but reach out to him and accept his divine assistance. We need not struggle alone.
>
> Imagine Peter leaving the boat alone and walking by faith on the water. He is successful in this 'impossible' endeavor because his eyes are fixed steadfastly upon Christ. If we would come to Jesus, we also must forego an inviting reliance on worldly supports. We must determine whether our best opportunity lies in the storm-tossed – though still floating – ship or whether it lies out on the waves with the Savior.[47]

This spiritual explanation of what the commentator calls a 'dramatized parable' can certainly be said to apply to Bahá'ís, as well. Did not Shoghi Effendi remind us that a 'tempest, unprecedented in its violence, unpredictable in its course, catastrophic in its immediate effects, unimaginably glorious in its ultimate consequences, is at present sweeping the face of the earth'[48] and that the 'world, to whichever continent we turn our gaze, to however remote a region our survey may extend, is everywhere assailed by forces it can neither explain nor control'?[49] Are we not assured that our faith will be tested, but that we can attain the seemingly impossible if we detach ourselves from the world and fix our gaze steadfastly on our Beloved?

> O man of two visions! Close one eye and open the other. Close one to the world and all that is therein, and open the other to the hallowed beauty of the Beloved.[50]

> The death of self is needed here, not rhetoric:
> Be nothing, then, and walk upon the waves.[51]

Recent leaders of the LDS Church have suggested that Jesus spoke in parables to make it *easier* for the masses to understand His message. Thomas S. Monson asserted:

> When Jesus walked the dusty pathways of towns and villages that we now reverently call the Holy Land and taught His disciples by beautiful Galilee, He often spoke in parables, in language the people understood best.[52]

If we are to understand the phrase 'in language the people understood best' to refer to Jesus' use of parables (and not to his decision to use Aramaic as opposed to Greek or Hebrew) this statement is somewhat at odds with the *Bible Dictionary* definition previously referred to. While it is true that God's Messengers have always used allegory to bring metaphysical concepts – which the human mind cannot grasp directly – down to the physical plane where mankind can relate to them, the Gospel accounts demonstrate that the true meaning of Jesus' parables was entirely lost on the people of the time. The spoken or written words of a Manifestation of God are seldom directed only at specific individuals; rather, they are for the benefit of all mankind, and valid for all eternity. The parables of Jesus were thus veils for the vast majority of those who heard Him speak, and portals to everlasting life for those detached souls who encountered them long after His ascension.

CHAPTER 5

THE NATURE OF THE SOUL
AND THE AFTERLIFE

In this chapter we examine how Mormons and Bahá'ís understand human nature as it pertains to this earthly existence and beyond. We begin by discussing man's lower nature, and move on from there to explore views on the nature of the eternal soul and the afterlife. It should be noted here that there are significant differences between the two faiths where the afterlife is concerned. These differences are discussed in more detail later in this chapter, but for now we will focus on the similarities.

The lower nature of man

The basic Mormon belief in the nobility of the human spirit has been addressed in the previous discussion about the second Article of Faith (Chapter 3). Here we deal with the other side of that equation, the evil of man's lower nature.

Like the majority of Christians, Mormons believe that Satan is an intelligent being, actively working to lead us astray. However, while they generally see the devil as man's greatest enemy, their scriptures identify an even greater peril:

> For the natural man is an enemy to God, and has been from the fall of Adam, and will be, forever and ever, unless he yields to the enticings of the Holy Spirit, and putteth off the natural man . . . and becometh as a child . . .[1]

> Our first enemy we will find within ourselves. It is a good thing to overcome that enemy first and bring ourselves into subjection to the will of the Father, and into strict obedience to the principles of life and salvation which he has given to the world for the salvation of men.[2]

> A man is his own tormentor and his own condemner. Hence the saying, They shall go into the lake that burns with fire and brimstone. The torment

of disappointment in the mind is as exquisite as a lake burning with fire and brimstone. I say, so is the torment of man.³

The Bahá'í Writings hold the source of all evil to be man's attachments to the world, manifested as selfish desire:

> When a reporter of the New York *Globe* visited 'Abdu'l-Bahá in Haifa, He gave her this message: 'Tell my followers that they have no enemies to fear, no foes to hate. Man's only enemy is himself.'⁴

> 'Abdu'l-Bahá was once asked, 'What is Satan?' He replied in three words: 'The insistent self.'⁵

Conversely, by 'putting off the natural man' and 'becoming like a child,' we allow our spiritual nature to dominate our actions:

> In man there are two natures; his spiritual or higher nature and his material or lower nature. In one he approaches God, in the other he lives for the world alone. Signs of both these natures are to be found in men. In his material aspect he expresses untruth, cruelty and injustice; all these are the outcome of his lower nature. The attributes of his Divine nature are shown forth in love, mercy, kindness, truth and justice, one and all being expressions of his higher nature. Every good habit, every noble quality belongs to man's spiritual nature, whereas all his imperfections and sinful actions are born of his material nature. If a man's Divine nature dominates his human nature, we have a saint.⁶

The preceding quotations demonstrate that while Mormons and Bahá'ís may disagree about the existence of a 'personal Satan,' they can certainly come to agreement on the overriding evil of self and passion. Concerning those who have let their lower nature control their actions, the Book of Mormon and the Bahá'í Writings both promise that their deeds will be exposed in the end. In the words of the Book of Mormon:

> I will bring forth out of darkness unto light all their secret works and their abominations; and except they repent I will destroy them from off the face of the earth; and I will bring to light all their secrets and abominations, unto every nation that shall hereafter possess the land.⁷

While in the Hidden Words we read:

O Children of Fancy! Know, verily, that while the radiant dawn breaketh above the horizon of eternal holiness, the satanic secrets and deeds done in the gloom of night shall be laid bare and manifest before the peoples of the world.[8]

Hell and spiritual death

The Mormon view of hell diverges somewhat from the traditional Christian model. Instead of *hell*, Mormons refer to three separate environments known as *spirit prison*, the *telestial kingdom*, and *outer darkness*. These are thought to be physical places which – while perhaps not geographically or spatially identifiable – are more than simply a state of being. Mormons have a profoundly material view of the afterlife, and interpret the words 'life' and 'death' as found in the Bible in a very literal sense. With this in mind, it is interesting to highlight some LDS scriptures that portray a different notion of hell as a state of spiritual torment resulting from the reflection on our own transgressions, and of life and death as spiritual conditions. The Book of Mormon states:

And if they be evil they are consigned to an awful view of their own guilt and abominations, which doth cause them to shrink from the presence of the Lord into a state of misery and endless torment, from whence they can no more return; therefore they have drunk damnation to their own souls . . . And their torment is as a lake of fire and brimstone, whose flames are unquenchable, and whose smoke ascendeth up forever and ever.[9]

O, my beloved brethren, remember the awfulness in transgressing against that Holy God, and also the awfulness of yielding to the enticings of that cunning one. Remember, to be carnally-minded is death, and to be spiritually-minded is life eternal.[10]

These share a number of similarities with the Bahá'í Writings:

The root cause of wrongdoing is ignorance, and we must therefore hold fast to the tools of perception and knowledge. Good character must be taught. Light must be spread afar, so that, in the school of humanity, all may acquire the heavenly characteristics of the spirit, and see for themselves beyond any doubt that there is no fiercer hell, no more fiery abyss, than to possess a character that is evil and unsound; no more darksome pit nor loathsome torment than to show forth qualities which deserve to be condemned.[11]

They say: 'Where is Paradise, and where is Hell?' Say: 'The one is reunion with Me; the other thine own self, O thou who dost associate a partner with God and doubtest.'[12]

Pre-existence

On the surface, the Bahá'í teachings appear to differ sharply from the Mormon doctrine concerning the pre-existence of souls. When we delve a little deeper, however, we find that there are remarkable undercurrents of similarity. These similarities become more apparent once we distinguish between three forms of pre-existence: of the *individual soul*, of the *Prophets*, and of *mankind*.

Mormon doctrine holds that each human soul is pre-existent, i.e. that it was created in a *pre-mortal spirit world*, but that as part of each soul's natural progression it must obtain a physical body. This physical body is required not only for a soul's earthly experience, but also later on in the Resurrection in order to obtain an *immortal body*:

> Our heavenly parents provided us with a celestial home more glorious and beautiful than any place on earth. We were happy there. Yet they knew we could not progress beyond a certain point unless we left them for a time. They wanted us to develop the godlike qualities that they have. To do this, we needed to leave our celestial home to be tested and to gain experience. We needed to choose good over evil. Our spirits needed to be clothed with physical bodies. We would need to leave our physical bodies at death and reunite with them in the Resurrection. Then we would receive immortal bodies like those of our heavenly parents. If we passed our tests, we would receive the fulness of joy that our heavenly parents have received.[13]

The Bahá'í Writings rule out the pre-existence of the individual human soul. Shoghi Effendi states unequivocally that the 'soul or spirit of the individual comes into being with the conception of his physical body.'[14] However, while ordinary humans may not have a pre-existence, the Bahá'í Writings do confirm the pre-existence of the Manifestations of God:

> The Prophets, unlike us, are pre-existent. The soul of Christ existed in the spiritual world before His birth in this world. We cannot imagine what that world is like, so words are inadequate to picture His state of being.[15]

In addition, the Bahá'í Writings tell us that while each individual soul comes into being at conception, mankind as a whole has always existed, long before it assumed a physical form on this planet:

> . . . it cannot be said there was a time when man was not. All that we can say is that this terrestrial globe at one time did not exist, and at its beginning man did not appear upon it. But from the beginning which has no beginning, to the end which has no end, a Perfect Manifestation always exists. This Man of Whom we speak is not every man; we mean the Perfect Man. For the noblest part of the tree is the fruit, which is the reason of its existence. If the tree had no fruit, it would have no meaning. Therefore, it cannot be imagined that the worlds of existence, whether the stars or this earth, were once inhabited by the donkey, cow, mouse and cat, and that they were without man![16]

In other words, the pre-existence of *mankind* is synonymous with the pre-existence of the *Manifestation*, who is the Perfect Man. Since the Perfect Man has always existed, the same is true for the spiritual creation of mankind in the invisible realm. This could very well be the true meaning of these words by Joseph Smith:

> Man was also in the beginning with God. Intelligence, or the light of truth, was not created or made, neither indeed can be.[17]

To illustrate the difference between the pre-existence of mankind and the coming into existence of the individual soul, consider the example of a car. The author's aged but trusty Geo Prizm did not come into existence until it rolled off the factory floor in 1994, much like the author himself did not come into existence until some time during the 1960s. However, the invention of the automobile has been around for over a century – predating even the earliest prototype – and can be thought of as pre-existent when compared to any specific vehicle. The creation of man has been around from the beginning that has no beginning, while the first appearance of individual human beings on our planet is a relatively recent phenomenon.

The Fall of Adam

Mormon doctrine, like most other Christian doctrines, claims that Adam and Eve were the first people to live on earth:

God prepared this earth as a home for his children. Adam and Eve were chosen to be the first people to live on the earth. Their part in our Father's plan was to bring mortality into the world. They were to be the first parents.[18]

As explained in the previous section, Bahá'ís do not subscribe to the concept of an individual pre-existence; however, it is believed that *mankind* has existed from the beginning of creation, just not always in a physical form. At some point in time, the spiritual essence of man appeared in the temple of the human body. This, according to 'Abdu'l-Bahá, is one of the meanings of the 'Fall of Adam':

Adam signifies the heavenly spirit of Adam, and Eve His human soul . . . The tree of good and evil signifies the human world; for the spiritual and divine world is purely good and absolutely luminous, but in the human world light and darkness, good and evil, exist as opposite conditions. The meaning of the serpent is attachment to the human world. This attachment of the spirit to the human world led the soul and spirit of Adam from the world of freedom to the world of bondage and caused Him to turn from the Kingdom of Unity to the human world. When the soul and spirit of Adam entered the human world, He came out from the paradise of freedom and fell into the world of bondage. From the height of purity and absolute goodness, He entered into the world of good and evil.[19]

Considering that modern humans have roamed the earth for hundreds of millennia, the name 'Adam' here cannot be taken to refer to any prophet that lived within the past 6,000 years. Rather, it is a reference to the 'first man' spoken of in the Bible, which is the spiritual essence of Man. Since the spirit and soul of Adam fell from pre-existent freedom into worldly bondage, this can be taken to signify humanity moving from the invisible spiritual realm, or paradise, into the material world in the form of the human body. The Mormon statement that Adam brought 'mortality into the world' is therefore quite acceptable. However, Mormons understand this to mean that before Adam's transgression, there was no *physical* mortality on earth, meaning that no life form ever experienced death. This doctrine does not account for the possibility that the mortality spoken of is spiritual in nature (and thus refers simultaneously to spiritual death and physical life), nor that it pertains only to humans. This, of course, makes it very difficult to reconcile with scientific evidence that the last dinosaurs became extinct approximately 64 million years before the first humans appeared on the earth.

A spiritual separation from God

The Mormon and Bahá'í scriptures agree that with the Fall of Adam came a spiritual separation from God. The Mormon view is as follows:

> Because Adam and Eve had eaten the fruit of the tree of knowledge of good and evil, the Lord sent them out of the Garden of Eden into the world as we now know it. Their physical condition changed as a result of their eating the forbidden fruit. As God had promised, they became mortal. They were able to have children. They and their children would experience sickness, pain, and physical death. Because of their transgression, Adam and Eve also suffered spiritual death. This meant they and their children could not walk and talk face to face with God. Because Satan had introduced evil into the world, Adam and Eve and their children were separated from God both physically and spiritually.[20]

While 'Abdu'l-Bahá explains that

> . . . the spirit and the soul of Adam, when they were attached to the human world, passed from the world of freedom into the world of bondage, and His descendants continued in bondage. This attachment of the soul and spirit to the human world, which is sin, was inherited by the descendants of Adam, and is the serpent which is always in the midst of, and at enmity with, the spirits and the descendants of Adam. That enmity continues and endures. For attachment to the world has become the cause of the bondage of spirits, and this bondage is identical with sin, which has been transmitted from Adam to His posterity. It is because of this attachment that men have been deprived of essential spirituality and exalted position.[21]

Since each subsequent generation of human souls has likewise been attached to this material world – which, in comparison to the spiritual world, is sin – it can be said that we have all 'inherited the sin of Adam.'

The Fall of Adam was necessary and brought great blessings

Many Christian churches depict the Fall of Adam – or *Adam's transgression* – as a calamitous event for which all of humanity is still paying the price. In sharp contrast, Mormons consider the entire episode a necessary step in the spiritual evolution of man:

> Some people believe Adam and Eve committed a serious sin when they ate

of the tree of knowledge of good and evil. However, latter-day scriptures help us understand that their fall was a necessary step in the plan of life and a great blessing to all of us. Because of the Fall, we are blessed with physical bodies, the right to choose between good and evil, and the opportunity to gain eternal life. None of these privileges would have been ours had Adam and Eve remained in the garden.[22]

Bahá'ís likewise consider this Fall of Adam – or rather the appearance of the human spirit in the physical body of man – a necessary step in acquiring human perfections, and in causing the enlightenment of the world:

> The wisdom of the appearance of the spirit in the body is this: the human spirit is a Divine Trust, and it must traverse all conditions, for its passage and movement through the conditions of existence will be the means of its acquiring perfections. So when a man travels and passes through different regions and numerous countries with system and method, it is certainly a means of his acquiring perfection, for he will see places, scenes and countries, from which he will discover the conditions and states of other nations . . . It is the same when the human spirit passes through the conditions of existence: it will become the possessor of each degree and station. Even in the condition of the body it will surely acquire perfections.
>
> Besides this, it is necessary that the signs of the perfection of the spirit should be apparent in this world, so that the world of creation may bring forth endless results, and this body may receive life and manifest the divine bounties . . . By the appearance of the spirit in the physical form, this world is enlightened. As the spirit of man is the cause of the life of the body, so the world is in the condition of the body, and man is in the condition of the spirit. If there were no man, the perfections of the spirit would not appear, and the light of the mind would not be resplendent in this world. This world would be like a body without a soul.[23]

Free agency
Of crucial importance to Mormons and Bahá'ís alike is the free agency, or free will, of the human soul in whether to accept God's message.

Free agency in the pre-existence
Mormons are taught that in the pre-existence – the spiritual state souls are in prior to conception – each soul must choose between being born into the

physical world, or remaining in heaven. According to this doctrine, Satan attempts to convince these souls to stay in heaven, citing the futility of spending a trial-filled lifetime on earth, only to return whence they came. However, this is contrary to God's plan, which requires that every soul obtain a mortal body and undergo the experiences and trials of a mortal life. These 'pre-mortal' souls are believed to have the freedom to choose either option, and those who choose to forgo life on earth soon discover they have been ensnared by Satan and, deprived of the means to obtain an 'immortal body,' are unable to receive the 'fulness of joy' that comes with exaltation (a concept that will be described in the following section).

Free agency on earth

Mormon doctrine further teaches that while on earth, each soul has the choice of accepting the restored gospel or rejecting it, and will be judged based upon this choice:

> Wherefore, men are free according to the flesh; and all things are given them which are expedient unto man. And they are free to choose liberty and eternal life, through the great Mediator of all men, or to choose captivity and death, according to the captivity and power of the devil; for he seeketh that all men might be miserable like unto himself.[24]

Taken literally, the above verse from the Book of Mormon is quite compatible with the Bahá'í teachings, since each Manifestation of God is considered 'the great Mediator of all men' for His day. Bahá'ís, like Mormons, consider free will to be the primary means by which mankind is judged:

> Suffer not yourselves to be wrapt in the dense veils of your selfish desires, inasmuch as I have perfected in every one of you My creation, so that the excellence of My handiwork may be fully revealed unto men. It follows, therefore, that every man hath been, and will continue to be, able of himself to appreciate the Beauty of God, the Glorified. Had he not been endowed with such a capacity, how could he be called to account for his failure? If, in the Day when all the peoples of the earth will be gathered together, any man should, whilst standing in the presence of God, be asked: 'Wherefore hast thou disbelieved in My Beauty and turned away from My Self,' and if such a man should reply and say: 'Inasmuch as all men have erred, and none hath been found willing to turn his face to the Truth, I, too, following their example, have grievously failed to recognize

the Beauty of the Eternal,' such a plea will, assuredly, be rejected. For the faith of no man can be conditioned by any one except himself.[25]

Literal expectations of the return of Christ are incompatible with free agency

In every age, there have been those who accepted the new Manifestation, and those who did not. This is what is meant by the 'day of reckoning'; we are judged not on our blind adherence to the outward forms and practices of a bygone dispensation, but based on whether we choose to accept or deny the new Message when it is presented to us. Bahá'u'lláh writes:

> How many an embodiment of heedlessness who came unto Us with purity of heart have We established upon the seat of Our acceptance; and how many an exponent of wisdom have We in all justice consigned to the fire. We are, in truth, the One to judge.[26]

Ironically, those who have denied each new Messenger of God have done so because of expectations which, were they to be fulfilled, would have deprived mankind of its free will. For example, the majority of Christians believe that the Second Coming will be a cataclysmic event, the significance of which no one would be able to deny. However, such outward signs would pre-empt man's opportunity to reject or accept the truth of his own accord, as Bahá'u'lláh explains:

> They have even failed to perceive that were the signs of the Manifestation of God in every age to appear in the visible realm in accordance with the text of established traditions, none could possibly deny or turn away, nor would the blessed be distinguished from the miserable, and the transgressor from the God-fearing. Judge fairly: Were the prophecies recorded in the Gospel to be literally fulfilled; were Jesus, Son of Mary, accompanied by angels, to descend from the visible heaven upon the clouds; who would dare to disbelieve, who would dare to reject the truth, and wax disdainful? Nay, such consternation would immediately seize all the dwellers of the earth that no soul would feel able to utter a word, much less to reject or accept the truth.[27]

Mormons, too, believe that Christ's return will be accompanied by physical phenomena. In fact, this is one of the reasons why the Church stockpiles canned food and other emergency supplies. We will discuss Mormon expectations about the Return of Christ in more detail in a later chapter.

Life after death

Although Mormon doctrine bears certain similarities to the Baháʼí teachings on the subject of life after death – particularly with respect to the progression of the soul – these similarities go hand in hand with significant doctrinal differences as to the very nature of the afterlife. Despite these differences, we will uncover some interesting parallels concerning the life beyond.

Knowledge of the afterlife

Mormons claim to have a fairly clear understanding of what the next world (called the *postmortal spirit world*) looks like. For example, it is believed that our spirit bodies will look just like our current material bodies, only in a 'perfected form,' meaning they will be devoid of disease and in a permanent state of young adulthood. Gender, which is thought to be determined in the preexistence, also perpetuates into the postmortal existence. And while Latter-day Saints acknowledge that what lies beyond the veil is hidden from us for a reason, every Mormon temple contains a *celestial room* which is designed to emulate, or at least offer a glimpse of, that celestial glory that is the promise of every faithful member of the Church.

The Baháʼí Writings, on the other hand, explain that we cannot conceptualize the next world any more than a fetus can imagine what the material world looks like while it is still in the womb:

> The nature of the soul after death can never be described, nor is it meet and permissible to reveal its whole character to the eyes of men . . . The world beyond is as different from this world as this world is different from that of the child while still in the womb of its mother.[28]

However, we are promised that the spiritual worlds are indescribably glorious, and were it not for the veil which the Almighty has placed between this world and the next, we would seek to hasten our death:

> O Son of My Handmaid! Didst thou behold immortal sovereignty, thou wouldst strive to pass from this fleeting world. But to conceal the one from thee and to reveal the other is a mystery which none but the pure in heart can comprehend.[29]

Degrees of glory

Mormons do not subscribe to the traditional Christian paradigm of heaven and hell. Rather, they believe that after the soul separates from the body, it enters a temporary *spirit world*. This spirit world contains a *spirit prison* where the souls of those who have committed grave transgressions are confined until after the Resurrection which is to come about upon Christ's Return. After the Resurrection, a soul may attain to one of three general categories, or degrees, of glory, 'according to the deeds done in the body.' From highest to lowest, these are called the *celestial kingdom*, the *terrestrial kingdom*, and the *telestial kingdom*. The following excerpt from the church curriculum book *Gospel Principles* describes each of these postmortal kingdoms in detail:

> **The celestial kingdom**. 'They are they who received the testimony of Jesus, and believed on his name and were baptized . . . that by keeping the commandments they might be washed and cleansed from all their sins, and receive the Holy Spirit.' These are they who overcome the world by their faith. They are just and true so that the Holy Ghost can seal their blessings upon them. Those who inherit the highest degree of the celestial kingdom, who become gods, must also have been married for eternity in the temple. All who inherit the celestial kingdom will live with Heavenly Father and Jesus Christ forever.
>
> **The terrestrial kingdom**. These are they who rejected the gospel on earth but afterward received it in the spirit world. These are the honorable people on the earth who were blinded to the gospel of Jesus Christ by the craftiness of men. These are also they who received the gospel and a testimony of Jesus but then were not valiant. They will be visited by Jesus Christ but not by our Heavenly Father. They will not be part of eternal families; they will live separately and singly forever.
>
> **The telestial kingdom**. These people did not receive the gospel or the testimony of Jesus either on earth or in the spirit world. They will suffer for their own sins in hell until after the Millennium, when they will be resurrected. 'These are they who are liars, and sorcerers, and adulterers, and whoremongers, and whosoever loves and makes a lie.' These people are as numerous as the stars in heaven and the sand on the seashore. They will be visited by the Holy Ghost but not by the Father or the Son.[30]

The LDS *Bible Dictionary* gives a number of scriptural references in support of the theory of multiple heavens. Notwithstanding serious differences in doctrine and scriptural interpretation, the premise of the first sentence in the following quotation is consistent with Bahá'í principles: if we are rewarded according to our earthly deeds, then there must be varying states of spiritual glory in the next world:

> It is apparent that if God rewards everyone according to the deeds done in the body, the term heaven as intended for man's eternal home must include more kingdoms than one. In speaking of man in his resurrected state, Paul tells of glories like the sun, the moon, and the stars (1 Cor. 15: 39-41). He also speaks of the 'third heaven' (2 Cor. 12: 2). Jesus spoke of 'many mansions' or kingdoms (John 14: 2). Latter-day revelation confirms the teaching of the Bible on these matters and verifies that there are three general categories or glories to which the members of the human family will be assigned in the judgment following their resurrection from the grave. These are known as the celestial, terrestrial, and telestial kingdoms, of which the sun, moon, and stars are spoken of as being typical (D&C 76; D&C 88: 20-32; D&C 131: 1-4). In addition to the degrees of glory, there is a place of no glory, called perdition, reserved for those who commit the unpardonable sin.[31]

According to this definition, Mormons recognize yet another postmortal abode known as *outer darkness* or *perdition*, which refers to a realm outside of the three kingdoms.

Eternal progression

Although Mormon doctrine recognizes only three major degrees of glory, there is reference in the LDS scriptures to countless 'heavens.' For example, the Book of Moses states:

> And the Lord God spake unto Moses, saying: The heavens, they are many, and they cannot be numbered unto man; but they are numbered unto me, for they are mine. And as one earth shall pass away, and the heavens thereof even so shall another come; and there is no end to my works, neither to my words.[32]

In addition, the following Bahá'í and Mormon statements on the initial state of the soul and its subsequent progression compare favorably:

> The spiritual grades have infinite degrees and conditions ever ascending upward. It is possible in one step to leave the lowest condition and to enter

the highest. The Blessed Perfection, Bahá'u'lláh, said that the believers will go directly to God, but that all will not be in the same condition, each one will have his degree in accordance with his spiritual progress. When we die we can see those who are in the same condition as ourselves and we can understand those who are in a lower degree, but we cannot understand those who are in conditions above us.[33]

The spirits are classified according to the purity of their lives and their obedience to the will of the Lord while on earth. The righteous and the wicked are separated, but the spirits may progress from one level to another as they learn gospel principles and live in accordance with them.[34]

However, this last statement of Mormon doctrine refers only to the temporary post-mortal world, before the Resurrection after which all souls will be irreversibly consigned to one of the three kingdoms.

The unpardonable sin

Mormons recognize one exception to the ability of a soul to progress – the 'unpardonable sin,' or the denial of Jesus Christ after having accepted him. In his oft-quoted 'King Follett' sermon, Joseph Smith explained:

All sins, and all blasphemies, and every transgression, except one, that man can be guilty of, may be forgiven; and there is a salvation for all men, either in this world or the world to come, who have not committed the unpardonable sin, there being a provision either in this world or the world of spirits. Hence God hath made a provision that every spirit in the eternal world can be ferreted out and saved unless he has committed that unpardonable sin which cannot be remitted to him either in this world or the world of spirits. God has wrought out a salvation for all men, unless they have committed a certain sin; and every man who has a friend in the eternal world can save him, unless he has committed the unpardonable sin . . .

What must a man do to commit the unpardonable sin? He must receive the Holy Ghost, have the heavens opened unto him, and know God, and then sin against him. After a man has sinned against the Holy Ghost, there is no repentance for him. He has got to say that the sun does not shine while he sees it; he has got to deny Jesus Christ when the heavens have been opened unto him, and to deny the plan of salvation with his eyes open to the truth of it; and from that time he begins to be an enemy. This is the case with many apostates of The Church of Jesus Christ of Latter-day Saints.

When a man begins to be an enemy to this work, he hunts me, he seeks to kill me, and never ceases to thirst for my blood. He gets the spirit of the devil – the same spirit that sins against the Holy Ghost. You cannot save such persons; you cannot bring them to repentance; they make open war, like the devil, and awful is the consequence.[35]

It appears that the 'unpardonable sin' thus entails much more than simply withdrawing from the Church, and is equated with apostasy, or actively working to discredit the church while claiming to be a true member of it.

Excepting this sin, the most wicked souls who are confined to the lowest stratum of the afterlife will still get a second chance after the completion of the millennial reign.[36] Those who commit the unpardonable sin, however, are doomed to spend eternity in 'outer darkness,' a world beyond the three kingdoms from which there is no escape:

These are they who had testimonies of Jesus through the Holy Ghost and knew the power of the Lord but allowed Satan to overcome them. They denied the truth and defied the power of the Lord. There is no forgiveness for them, for they denied the Holy Spirit after having received it. They will not have a kingdom of glory. They will live in eternal darkness, torment, and misery with Satan and his angels forever.[37]

The Bahá'í Faith teaches that *all* souls progress in the afterlife through the infinite worlds of God, although not at the same rate and not from the same starting point:

And now concerning thy question regarding the soul of man and its survival after death. Know thou of a truth that the soul, after its separation from the body, will continue to progress until it attaineth the presence of God, in a state and condition which neither the revolution of ages and centuries, nor the changes and chances of this world, can alter. It will endure as long as the Kingdom of God, His sovereignty, His dominion and power will endure. It will manifest the signs of God and His attributes, and will reveal His loving kindness and bounty.[38]

Mrs. S. . . . wished to know whether one would be re-united with those who had gone before immediately after death.

'Abdu'l-Bahá answered that this would depend upon the respective stations of the two. If both had the same degree of development, they would be re-united immediately after death. The questioner then said, how could this state of development be acquired? 'Abdu'l-Bahá replied, by unceasing effort, striving to do right, and to attain spiritual qualities.

The questioner remarked that many differing opinions were held as to the conditions of the future life. Some thought that all would have exactly the same perfections and virtues; that all would be equal and alike.

'Abdu'l-Bahá said there would be variety, and differing degrees of attainment, as in this world.[39]

This latter statement roughly corresponds to the Mormon doctrine that 'spirits are classified according to the purity of their lives and their obedience to the will of the Lord while on earth.'[40] The Bahá'í Writings further clarify that while souls progress indefinitely, it is impossible for a soul to transcend its own state of existence, i.e. the human soul can never hope to reach the same degree of perfection as a Manifestation of God, much less attain a level comparable to that of the Creator. Mormons, on the other hand, believe that once they are accepted into the celestial kingdom, they will themselves put on the mantle of godhood.

Covenant-breaking and apostasy

We have seen that the 'unpardonable sin' in the Mormon faith refers to apostasy. Because the Covenant is an institution unique to the Bahá'í Faith, it is impossible to make a direct comparison between apostasy and Covenant-breaking; however, some similarities can be identified, both in terms of the spiritual consequences of such an act, and in the way the community is instructed to respond.

It is important to draw a distinction between Covenant-breakers, enemies of the Faith, and those who withdraw from the Faith. Regarding the first two designations, Adib Taherzadeh cautioned:

It is necessary here to distinguish between enemies of the Faith and Covenant-breakers. The former attack the Cause of God mainly through ignorance, and perhaps they will be forgiven by God. The latter, however, know where the Source of Truth is, but are unable to turn to it; instead, for their own selfish reasons, they knowingly rise up against it. To inflict harm upon a human being is reprehensible in the sight of God, and perhaps can be forgiven by Him. But to wilfully oppose the Cause of the Almighty and strike at its roots, as the violators of the Covenant do, are grave transgressions which are unforgivable.[41]

This 'unforgivable' sin of Covenant-breaking therefore can be likened to the 'unpardonable sin' referred to by Joseph Smith, which he described as having 'the heavens opened unto him, and know God, and then sin against him.' However, this should not be misconstrued to imply that Covenant-breakers will never advance in the spiritual worlds of God. Such a sin is unforgivable only in the sense that God's forgiveness is conditioned upon the true repentance of the violator:

> These souls are not lost forever. In the Aqdas, Bahá'u'lláh says that God will forgive Mírzá Yahyá* if he repents. It follows, therefore, that God will forgive any soul *if he repents*. Most of them don't want to repent, unfortunately. If the leaders can be forgiven it goes without saying that their followers can also be forgiven . . .[42]

Finally, there are those individuals who at one time declared their belief in Bahá'u'lláh but later, for personal reasons, decide they no longer wish to be Bahá'ís. These are not considered Covenant-breakers. All Bahá'ís accept the Faith through their own free will, and may through that same free will choose to withdraw from it.

In order to be declared a Covenant-breaker, one must openly challenge the validity of the Bahá'í Administrative Order itself and actively work to create divisions in the Faith. Even then, the decision to expel that person from the Faith is not made lightly. Adib Taherzadeh explained:

> It is important to realize that no one is lightly or hurriedly declared a Covenant-breaker by the Centre of the Cause. Great efforts are made to enlighten the individual and guide him to the path of truth. Only when every possible effort to save him from his spiritual downfall has failed will he be expelled from the community.[43]

The LDS term 'apostate' is not as clearly defined as 'Covenant-breaker' is in the Bahá'í Faith. Mormon apostates have included people who published articles or books reporting embarrassing facts about the Church or its leaders, or exposing dubious practices such as scriptural modification. However, it should be emphasized that the Covenant-breakers have always maliciously sought to destroy the very foundations of the Bahá'í Faith through outrageous lies, misrepresentations and duplicitous acts, all of which could be easily exposed

---

* The half-brother of Bahá'u'lláh, and one of the principal Covenant-breakers of the Bahá'í Faith. He made multiple attempts on the life of Bahá'u'lláh, and his duplicity, slander and deceit were responsible for countless miseries visited upon the Blessed Beauty and His companions.

by an objective look at the facts. For a detailed account of these sordid activities, the reader is referred to *The Covenant of Bahá'u'lláh* by Adib Taherzadeh.

In contrast, many of the statements made by those who were eventually excommunicated from the LDS Church can in fact be validated based on the historical record, and were not always designed to discredit the Church.[44] Yet Bahá'ís and Mormons do agree on the potential danger of what the Universal House of Justice has termed 'intellectual pride.'[45] In a statement on individual rights and freedoms in the Bahá'í Faith, the House of Justice drew the distinction between 'open and constructive criticism' and 'ill-directed criticism' leading to 'such concepts as the "loyal opposition:" '

> Apart from the direct access which one has to an Assembly, local or national, or to a Counsellor or Auxiliary Board member, there are specific occasions for the airing of one's views in the community. The most frequent of these occasions for any Bahá'í is the Nineteen Day Feast which, 'besides its social and spiritual aspects, fulfills various administrative needs and requirements of the community, chief among them being the need for open and constructive criticism and deliberation regarding the state of affairs within the local Baha'i community.' At the same time, Shoghi Effendi's advice, as conveyed by his secretary, goes on to stress the point that 'all criticisms and discussions of a negative character which may result in undermining the authority of the Assembly as a body should be strictly avoided. For otherwise the order of the Cause itself will be endangered, and confusion and discord will reign in the community.'
>
> Clearly, then, there is more to be considered than the critic's right to self-expression; the unifying spirit of the Cause of God must also be preserved, the authority of its laws and ordinances safeguarded, authority being an indispensable aspect of freedom. Motive, manner, mode, become relevant; but there is also the matter of love: love for one's fellows, love for one's community, love for one's institutions.[46]

Similar sentiments can be found in the LDS Church. In *Mormon America*, Ostling and Ostling observe:

> ... Apostle James E. Faust, an attorney, stated that there is no concept of a 'loyal opposition' to be found in the church. Each decision by a presiding quorum is unanimous, following private discussion. Similarly, among the membership at large there will be honest differences of opinion, but any questions are to be raised privately with priesthood overseers. 'Those men and women who persist in publicly challenging basic doctrines, practices,

and establishment of the Church sever themselves from the Spirit of the Lord and forfeit their right to place and influence in the Church . . . There is a certain arrogance in thinking that any of us may be more spiritually intelligent, more learned, or more righteous than the Councils called to preside over us.'

In a 1981 *Ensign* article on the subject of apostasy, a high-ranking church official wrote:

When we read about the anti-Christs of former days, we marvel at how perverted their thinking became and we marvel at how successful they were in deceiving men and women. We also wonder why some of the people were so gullible – so easily misled. And with all this marveling and wondering, we tend to niche the anti-Christs in some corner of ancient history and go about our unguarded ways. This is dangerous. It could result in loss of faith; and, in a spiritual sense, it could put us out of existence.

Since the spring of 1820, Lucifer has led a relentless attack against the Latter-day Saints and their leaders. A parade of anti-Christs, anti-Mormons, and apostate groups have appeared on the scene. Many are still among us and have released new floods of lies and false accusations. These faith-killers and testimony-thieves use personal contacts, the printed word, electronic media, and other means of communication to sow doubts and to disturb the peace of true believers.

Two months ago we received a tender letter from a bishop. He informed us that he had been involved in an excommunication of a recent convert. The new convert had fallen under the influence of a very dedicated apostate who was successful in destroying the convert's testimony. It seems that, to discredit Joseph Smith and subsequent prophets, the apostate cited changes made in Church publications over the years.[47]

The first observation about the above excerpt is that Mormons understand the word 'anti-Christ' in the same way that Bahá'ís do: not as the singular personification of evil who is to appear soon before the promised Millennium (as some other Christian groups maintain), but rather as anyone who works to destroy a religion from within. The same article offers a nine-point list of proper responses to acts of apostasy, which closely resemble the attitude Bahá'ís should assume toward Covenant-breakers:

1. *Avoid those who would tear down your faith.* Faith-killers are to be shunned. The seeds which they plant in the minds and hearts of men grow like cancer and

eat away the Spirit. True messengers of God are builders – not destroyers . . .

2. *Keep the commandments.* President Brigham Young promised, 'All we have to do is to go onward and upward, and keep the commandments of our Father and God; and he will confound our enemies.' . . . Moreover, obedience ensures us of the guidance and protection of the Holy Spirit.

3. Follow the living prophets, as we have just been admonished . . .

4. *Do not contend or debate over points of doctrine.* The Master warned that 'the spirit of contention is not of me, but is of the devil' . . .

5. *Search the scriptures.* Few of us would go astray or lose our way if we regarded the scriptures as our personal guide or compass . . .

6. *Do not be swayed or diverted from the mission of the Church.* There are those who would draw you off course and cause you to waste time and energies . . .

7. *Pray for your enemies.* Christ said to the Nephites, 'Love your enemies, bless them that curse you, do good to them that hate you, and pray for them who despitefully use you and persecute you' . . . While on the cross, the Savior pled, 'Father, forgive them; for they know not what they do' . . .

8. *Practice 'pure religion.'* Involve yourself in Christian service. Succor the needs of the sick and poor; visit the fatherless and widows, and be charitable to all whether in the Church or out of the Church . . .

9. *Remember that there may be many questions for which we have no answers and that some things have to be accepted simply on faith* . . . There may be times when we are called upon to climb Mount Moriahs and to sacrifice our Isaacs without a full and prior explanation. Faith is the first principle of the gospel; it is a principle of progress.[48]

Shoghi Effendi described Covenant-breaking as a spiritual disease, warning that those afflicted with it should be shunned (see no. 1, above), while urging prayers on their behalf (see no. 7):

Bahá'u'lláh and the Master in many places and very emphatically have told us to shun entirely all Covenant breakers as they are afflicted with what we might try and define as a contagious spiritual disease; they have also told us, however, to pray for them . . .

Also, it has nothing to do with unity in the Cause; if a man cuts a cancer out of his body to preserve his health and very life, no one would suggest that for the sake of unity it should be reintroduced into the otherwise healthy organism. On the contrary, what was once a part of him has so radically changed as to have become a poison.[49]

THE NATURE OF THE SOUL AND THE AFTERLIFE

And in *Tablets of the Divine Plan*, we read 'Abdu'l-Bahá's admonition (see no. 4, above):

> The text of the divine Book is this: If two souls quarrel and contend about a question of the divine questions, differing and disputing, both are wrong. The wisdom of this incontrovertible law of God is this: That between two souls from amongst the believers of God, no contention and dispute may arise; that they may speak with each other with infinite amity and love. Should there appear the least trace of controversy, they must remain silent, and both parties must continue their discussions no longer, but ask the reality of the question from the Interpreter. This is the irrefutable command![50]

The spiritual consequences of Covenant-breaking, while perhaps not as final as the 'outer darkness' for which Mormon apostates are thought to be destined, are nonetheless of a severity unlike that of any other sin:

> Divine retributive justice is strikingly demonstrated through a series of sudden, rapid, devastating blows sweeping over leaders and henchmen of breakers of Bahá'u'lláh's Covenant foiling the schemes, levelling the hopes, and well-nigh extinguishing the remnants of the conspiring crew which dared challenge the authority, succeeded in inflicting untold sorrow and assiduously plotted to disrupt the Will and Testament of its appointed Center.[51]

> The Supreme Concourse will pray for the one who is adorned with the garment of faithfulness between heaven and earth; but he who breaks the Covenant is cursed by heaven and earth.[52]

And in a parallel to nos. 6 and 8 above, the Will and Testament of 'Abdu'l-Bahá contains the following directive:

> O ye that stand fast in the Covenant! When the hour cometh that this wronged and broken-winged bird will have taken its flight into the Celestial Concourse, when it will have hastened to the Realm of the Unseen and its mortal frame will have been either lost or hidden neath the dust, it is incumbent upon the Afnán,[53] that are steadfast in the Covenant of God and have branched from the Tree of Holiness; the Hands, (pillars) of the Cause of God (the glory of the Lord rest upon them), and all the friends and loved ones, one and all to bestir themselves and arise with heart and soul and in one accord, to diffuse the sweet savors of God, to teach His Cause

and to promote His Faith. It behooveth them not to rest for a moment, neither to seek repose. They must disperse themselves in every land, pass by every clime, and travel throughout all regions. Bestirred, without rest, and steadfast to the end, they must raise in every land the triumphal cry 'Yá Bahá'u'l-Abhá!' (O Thou the Glory of Glories), must achieve renown in the world wherever they go, must burn brightly even as a candle in every meeting and must kindle the flame of Divine love in every assembly; that the light of truth may rise resplendent in the midmost heart of the world, that throughout the East and throughout the West a vast concourse may gather under the shadow of the Word of God, that the sweet savors of holiness may be diffused, that faces may shine radiantly, hearts be filled with the Divine spirit and souls be made heavenly.[54]

A material view of the afterlife

Even though there are few similarities between the Mormon and Bahá'í characterizations of the spiritual worlds of God, the centrality of this theme to the Mormon faith compels us to explore it in some detail. We must keep in mind that although some of the following concepts may seem rather alien – perhaps even blasphemous – to the Bahá'í reader, they are nevertheless deeply held convictions of our Mormon brethren, and are to be respected as such. It may also be of interest to the reader that some of the most controversial doctrines did not come about until the waning years of Joseph Smith's ministry – the idea of God as an 'exalted man' finds its origin in Joseph Smith's 1844 'King Follett Sermon' – while others were introduced only after his death. This may also account for some of the contradictions between current LDS doctrine and the explicit text of the Book of Mormon.

As we shall see, Mormons have a distinctly material view of both this world and the next. They believe that spirit is a form of matter, and that God exists within time, as opposed to the eternal realm as envisioned by Bahá'ís and many Christians.

Spirit bodies

Latter-day Saints believe that in the next life we will have *spirit bodies*, in a very literal sense:

> Spirit beings have the same bodily form as mortals except that the spirit body is in perfect form. Spirits carry with them from earth their attitudes of devotion or antagonism toward things of righteousness. They have the

same appetites and desires that they had when they lived on earth. All spirits are in adult form. They were adults before their mortal existence, and they are in adult form after death, even if they die as infants or children.[55]

This means, for example, that gender is considered a permanent attribute, and if someone is born with a physical deformity or is injured as a result of an accident, his spirit body will not reflect those imperfections. There is a statement in the Bahá'í Writings which refers to a soul assuming a specific form, even though it carries the warning that there is no way to imagine the next world in any material sense:

> The world beyond is as different from this world as this world is different from that of the child while still in the womb of its mother. When the soul attaineth the Presence of God, it will assume the form that best befitteth its immortality and is worthy of its celestial habitation.[56]

Yet even in the Bahá'í Writings we find, at least in allegorical form, examples of a material representation of spirit and the afterlife. In *Memorials of the Faithful*, 'Abdu'l-Bahá recounts a dream in which He is visited by a dear friend who had passed away:

> I loved him very much, for he was delightful to converse with, and as a companion second to none. One night, not long ago, I saw him in the world of dreams. Although his frame had always been massive, in the dream world he appeared larger and more corpulent than ever. It seemed as if he had returned from a journey. I said to him, 'Jináb, you have grown good and stout.' 'Yes,' he answered, 'praise be to God! I have been in places where the air was fresh and sweet, and the water crystal pure; the landscapes were beautiful to look upon, the foods delectable. It all agreed with me, of course, so I am stronger than ever now, and I have recovered the zest of my early youth. The breaths of the All-Merciful blew over me and all my time was spent in telling of God. I have been setting forth His proofs, and teaching His Faith.' (The meaning of teaching the Faith in the next world is spreading the sweet savors of holiness; that action is the same as teaching.) We spoke together a little more, and then some people arrived and he disappeared.[57]

Reunification with resurrected mortal bodies

Latter-day Saints expect that at the Resurrection – around the time when Christ makes Himself manifest – the mortal bodies of the faithful will be literally raised from their graves and reunited with their spirit bodies to form *immortal bodies*. These souls will then become 'living souls' like Christ:

> O how great the plan of our God! For on the other hand, the paradise of God must deliver up the spirits of the righteous, and the grave deliver up the body of the righteous; and the spirit and the body is restored to itself again, and all men become incorruptible, and immortal, and they are living souls, having a perfect knowledge like unto us in the flesh, save it be that our knowledge shall be perfect.[58]

While this basic belief is shared with a number of other Christian denominations, nowhere is it more important than in the LDS Church: righteous souls who obtain their immortal body in the Resurrection are *exalted*, which means that they attain to godhood, along with all of the spiritual and temporal dominion befitting that station.

The Bahá'í teachings dismiss the notion of a material afterlife, and the physical resurrection of the human body, as literalist fallacies. In his definitive introduction to the Bahá'í Faith, *Bahá'u'lláh and the New Era*, J. E. Esslemont states:

> An important part of the Báb's teaching is His explanation of the terms Resurrection, Day of Judgment, Paradise and Hell. By the Resurrection is meant, He said, the appearance of a new Manifestation of the Sun of Truth. The raising of the dead means the spiritual awakening of those who are asleep in the graves of ignorance, heedlessness and lust. The Day of Judgment is the Day of the new Manifestation, by acceptance or rejection of Whose Revelation the sheep are separated from the goats, for the sheep know the voice of the Good Shepherd and follow Him. Paradise is the joy of knowing and loving God, as revealed through His Manifestation, thereby attaining to the utmost perfection of which one is capable, and, after death, obtaining entrance to the Kingdom of God and the life everlasting. Hell is simply deprivation of that knowledge of God with consequent failure to attain divine perfection, and loss of the Eternal Favor. He definitely declared that these terms have no real meaning apart from this; and that the prevalent ideas regarding the resurrection of the material body, a material heaven and hell, and the like, are mere figments of the imagination. He taught that man has a life after death, and that in the afterlife progress towards perfection is limitless.[59]

It is unclear from the Mormon scriptures exactly how a material body (or what remains of it) is expected to rise up from the grave. 'Abdu'l-Bahá, in an unrelated discussion of reincarnation, made the following observation concerning the composition and decomposition of the human body:

Those elements have been decomposed and dispersed; they are dissipated in this vast space. Afterward, other particles of elements have been combined, and a second body has been formed; it may be that one of the particles of the former individual has entered into the composition of the succeeding individual, but these particles have not been conserved and kept, exactly and completely, without addition or diminution, so that they may be combined again, and from that composition and mingling another individual may come into existence. So it cannot be proved that this body with all its particles has returned; that the former man has become the latter; and that, consequently, there has been repetition; that the spirit also, like the body, has returned; and that after death its essence has come back to this world.[60]

In other words, when the deceased human body begins to decompose, the atoms that once comprised it are assimilated into the environment, and subsequently recombined into other life forms. Presumably, this would rule out the possibility of the original body ever being restored to its former state. The Bahá'í Writings clarify the relationship between body and spirit, and explain that once disassociated from the eternal soul, the body is of no further use:

Some think that the body is the substance and exists by itself, and that the spirit is accidental and depends upon the substance of the body, although, on the contrary, the rational soul is the substance, and the body depends upon it. If the accident – that is to say, the body – be destroyed, the substance, the spirit, remains.

Second, the rational soul, meaning the human spirit, does not descend into the body – that is to say, it does not enter it, for descent and entrance are characteristics of bodies, and the rational soul is exempt from this. The spirit never entered this body, so in quitting it, it will not be in need of an abiding-place: no, the spirit is connected with the body, as this light is with this mirror. When the mirror is clear and perfect, the light of the lamp will be apparent in it, and when the mirror becomes covered with dust or breaks, the light will disappear.

The rational soul – that is to say, the human spirit – has neither entered this body nor existed through it; so after the disintegration of the composition of the body, how should it be in need of a substance through which it may exist? On the contrary, the rational soul is the substance through which the body exists.[61]

A body of flesh and bones

In a 1989 *Ensign* magazine article, Donald Q. Cannon, Larry E. Dahl, and John W. Welch discussed a number of Joseph Smith's later revelations, including the notion of the Trinity as being composed of three separate beings, each having a physical manifestation:

> Though most people who believe the Bible accept the idea of a Godhead composed of the Father, Son, and Holy Ghost, Joseph Smith revealed an understanding of the Godhead that differed from the views found in the creeds of his day. The main Christian sects of the nineteenth century taught of 'one God in Trinity, and Trinity in Unity, neither confounding the persons: nor dividing the Substance' and of 'one only living and true God . . . a most pure spirit, invisible, without body, parts, or passions, immutable, immense, eternal, incomprehensible.' Although other churches and individuals held that the Father and the Son are separate entities, Joseph Smith uniquely taught that the Father, Son, and Holy Ghost are three distinct personages, with the Father and the Son having bodies of 'flesh and bones as tangible as man's,' and with the Holy Ghost being a 'personage of Spirit.' (D&C 130:22.)[62]

Cannon, Dahl and Welch then go on to produce a litany of verses from the Bible and various Mormon scriptures to support their argument with respect to each of the components of the Godhead. As the preceding passage shows, Mormons have a distinctly anthropomorphic view of God, believing that since God created man in His image, therefore God must physically resemble a man:

> Because we are made in his image, we know that God has a body that looks like ours. His eternal spirit is housed in a tangible body of flesh and bones. God's body, however, is perfected and glorified, with a glory beyond all description.[63]

Many theologians agree that such a deduction is problematic from a logical perspective, because not only does it appear to reverse causation, it also jumps to the conclusion that the only way to understand the term 'image' is in the physical, corporeal sense. The above statement is somewhat contradictory, as well: the first two sentences describe God in definite terms, but the last sentence characterizes God's glory as 'beyond all description.'

Bahá'ís interpret the 'image' of God as referring to spiritual qualities and characteristics, not outward appearances:

> O Son of Man! Veiled in My immemorial being and in the ancient eternity of My essence, I knew My love for thee; therefore I created thee, have engraved on thee Mine image and revealed to thee My beauty.[64]

> Let us now discover more specifically how he [man] is the image and likeness of God and what is the standard or criterion by which he can be measured and estimated. This standard can be no other than the divine virtues which are revealed in him. Therefore, every man imbued with divine qualities, who reflects heavenly moralities and perfections, who is the expression of ideal and praiseworthy attributes, is, verily, in the image and likeness of God.[65]

Spirit children and Heavenly Mother

Mormon doctrine holds that in the celestial kingdom, the eternal husband and wife can continue to have marital relations, resulting in *spirit children* who may then later be born into the world and obtain a mortal body. This is hailed as one of the greatest benefits of exaltation. In fact, it is believed that neither a man nor a woman can be exalted in the afterlife unless they are married, and sealed by the proper authority on earth. Continuing along this line of reasoning, it follows that both the man and the woman have the ability to become gods. And if our God, as Joseph Smith suggested, 'was once as we are now, and is an exalted Man,'[66] then our God must also be married.

Mormons do in fact believe that God is married, and that there is a Heavenly Mother as well as a Heavenly Father. There is no mention of the terms *Heavenly Mother* or *Heavenly Parents* anywhere in the writings of Joseph Smith, and this doctrine appears to have been introduced after his death. A footnote to a previously quoted article in *Ensign* magazine attempts to legitimize this notion by claiming that the Mormon scriptures 'suggest' the existence of a Heavenly Mother:

> The concepts of husband and wife becoming gods, sharing in their kingdom, and continuing to bear children are delineated in Doctrine and Covenants 131:1-4; 132:19-20. These things suggest the concept of an exalted Mother. Eliza R. Snow's poem 'O My Father,' written in 1843, establishes that the doctrine was known early in Church history.[67]

The spirit world is not far from us

Even amidst these very different beliefs about the nature of God and the afterlife, we still find a striking parallel concerning the relationship between our earthly existence and the world beyond. In the church curriculum book *Gospel Principles*, we read:

> In a funeral sermon, Joseph Smith declared that the spirits of righteous people who have died 'are not far from us, and know and understand our thoughts, feelings, and motions, and are often pained therewith' (Teachings of the Prophet Joseph Smith, p. 326). Other latter-day prophets have made similar statements. President Ezra Taft Benson said: 'Sometimes the veil between this life and the life beyond becomes very thin. Our loved ones who have passed on are not far from us' (in Conference Report, Apr. 1971, p. 18; or Ensign, June 1971, p. 33). President Brigham Young said: 'Where is the spirit world? It is right here' (Discourses of Brigham Young, p. 376).[68]

These characterizations bear more than a passing resemblance to the following words attributed to 'Abdu'l-Bahá:

> In the next world, man will find himself freed from many of the disabilities under which he now suffers. Those who have passed on through death, have a sphere of their own. It is not removed from ours; their work, the work of the Kingdom, is ours; but it is sanctified from what we call 'time and place.' Time with us is measured by the sun. When there is no more sunrise, and no more sunset, that kind of time does not exist for man. Those who have ascended have different attributes from those who are still on earth, yet there is no real separation.[69]

You can *take it with you*

While everyone knows that our possessions do not pass into the next world, the same is not true for our experiences. According to the LDS curriculum book *Gospel Principles*, spirits 'carry with them from earth their attitudes of devotion or antagonism toward things of righteousness.'[70] And in the Doctrine and Covenants we read:

> Whatever principle of intelligence we attain unto in this life, it will rise

with us in the resurrection. And if a person gains more knowledge and intelligence in this life through his diligence and obedience than another, he will have so much the advantage in the world to come.[71]

Similar statements can be found in the Bahá'í Writings:

And now concerning thy question regarding the soul of man and its survival after death. Know thou of a truth that the soul, after its separation from the body, will continue to progress until it attaineth the presence of God, in a state and condition which neither the revolution of ages and centuries, nor the changes and chances of this world, can alter. It will endure as long as the Kingdom of God, His sovereignty, His dominion and power will endure. It will manifest the signs of God and His attributes, and will reveal His loving kindness and bounty.[72]

The personality of the rational soul is from its beginning; it is not due to the instrumentality of the body, but the state and the personality of the rational soul may be strengthened in this world; it will make progress and will attain to the degrees of perfection, or it will remain in the lowest abyss of ignorance, veiled and deprived from beholding the signs of God.[73]

Exaltation

No Mormon belief has other Christians so dismayed as the doctrine of exaltation. Counter to the very core of many Christians' *raison d'être*, Mormons believe that they can themselves become like God, 'with all power in heaven and earth':

All good things come from God. Everything that he does is to help his children become like him – a god.[74]

This is referred to as exaltation, and is believed to be attainable only by righteous followers of the LDS Church who have been *sealed* in the temple. Sealing is a secret ritual performed on a married couple in a Mormon temple, and requires that the husband has first obtained the priesthood. Children can also be sealed to their parents, but only if the parents are still married and are both members of the Church.

The blessings which exalted souls are believed to enjoy can be summarized as follows:

1. They will live eternally in the presence of Heavenly Father and Jesus Christ;

2. They will become gods;

3. They will have their righteous family members with them and will be able to have spirit children also. These spirit children will have the same relationship to them as we do to our Heavenly Father. They will be an eternal family;

4. They will receive a fulness of joy; and

5. They will have everything that our Heavenly Father and Jesus Christ have – all power, glory, dominion, and knowledge.[75]

Many non-Mormon Christians dismiss this doctrine – which holds God to be no different from any ordinary man except in His level of spiritual development – as either polytheistic or pagan, and nearly all consider it open blasphemy. Furthermore, they point out the inconsistency of Joseph Smith's claim that God 'was once as we are now, and is an exalted Man,'[76] with the Book of Mormon's statement that 'God is the same yesterday, today, and forever, and in him there is no variableness neither shadow of changing.'[77] Mormons on their part maintain that the abstract view of God as a transcendent Being is the result of the polluting influence of Greek philosophy on the true religion of Jesus Christ.

Bahá'í analogies to exaltation

Although the Bahá'í Writings certainly do not support the concept of exaltation as the LDS Church portrays it, they nevertheless contain numerous references to the glorified station of the steadfast soul and its nearness to God. The following excerpts are somewhat reminiscent of the LDS descriptions of exaltation:

> Just as the conception of faith hath existed from the beginning that hath no beginning, and will endure till the end that hath no end, in like manner will the true believer eternally live and endure. His spirit will everlastingly circle round the Will of God. He will last as long as God, Himself, will last . . . It is evident that the loftiest mansions in the Realm of Immortality have been ordained as the habitation of them that have truly believed in God and in His signs. Death can never invade that holy seat.[78]

> Thou hast, moreover, asked Me concerning the state of the soul after its separation from the body. Know thou, of a truth, that if the soul of man

hath walked in the ways of God, it will, assuredly, return and be gathered to the glory of the Beloved. By the righteousness of God! It shall attain a station such as no pen can depict, or tongue describe. The soul that hath remained faithful to the Cause of God, and stood unwaveringly firm in His Path shall, after his ascension, be possessed of such power that all the worlds which the Almighty hath created can benefit through him.[79]

Blessed is the soul which, at the hour of its separation from the body, is sanctified from the vain imaginings of the peoples of the world . . . If any man be told that which hath been ordained for such a soul in the worlds of God, the Lord of the throne on high and of earth below, his whole being will instantly blaze out in his great longing to attain that most exalted, that sanctified and resplendent station.[80]

However, while the human soul will continue to progress, this spiritual evolution will remain confined to the realm of human existence. In other words, we can never hope to become greater than human:

Now, as the spirit continues to exist after death, it necessarily progresses or declines; and in the other world to cease to progress is the same as to decline; but it never leaves its own condition, in which it continues to develop. For example, the reality of the spirit of Peter, however far it may progress, will not reach to the condition of the Reality of Christ; it progresses only in its own environment.[81]

If we cannot ascend to the level of Christ, how much less can we hope to become equal in rank with the Almighty Himself! As to the general nature of the world to come, the Bahá'í Writings make it clear that not only are we unable to visualize that world, there is a wisdom in our being veiled from it:

The nature of the soul after death can never be described, nor is it meet and permissible to reveal its whole character to the eyes of men.[82]

Baptism for the dead

One of the more exotic and poorly understood rituals of the Mormon faith is that of *baptism for the dead*. According to Mormon doctrine, souls who left this world prior to Joseph Smith's restoration of the gospel cannot progress to the highest realms of heaven at the time of the Resurrection, as they did not have an opportunity to be baptized by the proper priesthood authority on earth.

To remedy that situation, it is believed that righteous souls in the postmortal spirit world (who accepted the restored gospel while they lived on earth) are now actively engaged in teaching those who died in unawareness or unbelief. These waiting souls then have the free agency to either accept or reject the gospel, and their choice determines whether they will be worthy to enter the celestial kingdom after the Resurrection. However, those who have accepted it must still be baptized in order to fulfill their ultimate destiny, otherwise they will be restricted to the terrestrial kingdom. Since this baptism can obviously no longer be performed in person, it must be done by proxy. Mormons go to the temple to pray for and – vicariously by immersion – baptize their deceased ancestors, so that these ancestors can join them for eternity in the celestial kingdom. And because it is necessary to know the name of the person being baptized, Mormons have become world leaders in the field of genealogy.

While only ancestors are supposed to be baptized in this way, controversy has arisen at various times over certain high-profile celebrities – Abraham Lincoln, for example – being added to the list of souls baptized posthumously. When Ben Gurion, the founder of the state of Israel, was discovered on the list, it created a furor within the Jewish community. Although sporadic violations are occasionally reported, the LDS Church has adamantly prohibited this dubious practice, and urged its members to limit themselves to their immediate ancestry.

Helping souls progress through our actions on earth

While the outward practice of baptism for the dead may be foreign to Bahá'ís, the concept of helping souls progress in the next world is not. Mormons apply their strong sense of family to the need to help their ancestors achieve a higher degree of glory by performing temple ordinances on their behalf:

> Many of our ancestors are among those who died without hearing about the gospel while on the earth. They now live in the spirit world. There they are taught the gospel of Jesus Christ. Those who have accepted the gospel are waiting for the temple ordinances to be performed for them. As we perform these ordinances in the temple for our ancestors, we can share their joy.[83]

For similar reasons, Bahá'ís often pray for the progress of souls that have left this earthly existence. It is believed that these souls, having been newly 'born' into the next world, will need help to grow and develop in that world, and that this help can be given through supplications by righteous souls both in this world and the next:

The rich in the other world can help the poor, as the rich can help the poor here . . . What is their merchandise, their wealth? In the other world what is help and assistance? It is intercession. Undeveloped souls must gain progress at first through the supplications of the spiritually rich; afterwards they can progress through their own supplications.[84]

Implications of baptism for the dead

The Mormon concept of baptism for the dead, upon sincere reflection, could imply a great unfairness in God's treatment of His servants; for how could the countless souls that have roamed the earth since the appearance of Christ be prevented from reaching the highest planes of spiritual development – based on their failure to accept the restored gospel – if that gospel was withheld from them until the 19th century? The following words of Bahá'u'lláh address a similar question:

> How could God, when once the Day-star of the beauty of Jesus had disap-
> peared from the sight of His people, and ascended unto the fourth heaven,
> cause His holy Book, His most great testimony amongst His creatures, to
> disappear also? What would be left to that people to cling to from the set-
> ting of the day-star of Jesus until the rise of the sun of the Muḥammadan
> Dispensation? What law could be their stay and guide? How could such
> people be made the victims of the avenging wrath of God, the omnipotent
> Avenger? How could they be afflicted with the scourge of chastisement
> by the heavenly King? Above all, how could the flow of the grace of the
> All-Bountiful be stayed? How could the ocean of His tender mercies be
> stilled?[85]

Here Bahá'u'lláh specifically addresses the charge, made by some Muslims who were at a loss to find references to Muhammad in the Bible, that 'the genuine text of the heavenly Gospel doth not exist amongst the Christians, that it hath ascended unto heaven.' While this differs somewhat from the Mormon claim that portions of the Gospel – containing 'many plain and precious things' – were lost, the main argument applies equally well in either case.

Even if we consider this injustice to be corrected by the subsequent restora-
tion of the gospel, why should those departed souls be forced to wait for their salvation? Moreover, Mormon doctrine acknowledges that there was sufficient truth in each dispensation to guide man to its acceptance:

> In each dispensation, from the days of Adam to the days of the Prophet

Joseph Smith, the Lord has revealed anew the principles of the gospel. So that while the records of past dispensations, insofar as they are uncorrupted, testify to the truths of the gospel, still each dispensation has had revealed in its day sufficient truth to guide the people of the new dispensation, independent of the records of the past.[86]

Yet it is important to understand how Latter-day Saints view the restoration in relation to baptisms for the dead. From this perspective, humanity brought the great apostasy upon itself, through its heedlessness and gradual departure from the 'original' doctrine of Christ. The restoration of the gospel, along with the institution of baptism for the dead, is thus seen as an act of mercy from Heavenly Father, a corrective measure whereby every soul, regardless of the past, now has equal opportunity to attain the shores of salvation.

Eternal families

Among the various doctrinal differences with respect to the afterlife, one area where there is greater agreement between the Mormon and Bahá'í teachings is *eternal marriage* and the *eternal family*. In the broadest sense, eternal marriage means that the union between two spouses continues for eternity in the afterlife. The phrase 'until death do us part' does not appear as part of any marriage ceremony in either faith. However, Mormons and Bahá'ís differ sharply on the prerequisites for such an eternal bond and the precise nature of the relationship in the afterlife. It is important to remember here that the presence of theological differences should neither be surprising nor disheartening. Rather, the mere fact that these commonalities exist, however superficially, is something to be appreciated and celebrated.

What constitutes eternal marriage?

The adherents of most religions – and certainly the majority of Christians – believe that souls who have loved each other in this life (such as spouses, siblings, parents and children) will, after a brief separation due to the timing of their deaths, be reunited in the afterlife. The LDS Church, however, teaches that such a reunion is possible only if the marriage is *sealed* in a Mormon temple following a very specific set of rituals. This in turn requires that both parties be baptized members of the church:

> Families can be together forever. To enjoy this blessing we must be married in the temple. When people are married outside the temple, the marriage

146

ends when one of the partners dies . . . When we are married in the temple
. . . we are married for time and eternity. Death cannot separate us. If we
obey the commandments of the Lord, our families will be together forever
as husband, wife, and children.[87]

The Bahá'í Writings state that the only requirement for a marriage to last forever is that it is a 'spiritual union.' This standard is not necessarily more liberal
than that set by the LDS Church; on the contrary, in many ways it appears
to be stricter. After all, a couple may be married and sealed in the temple, yet
not have a spiritual marriage. Only God knows the true nature of a relationship, and is able to judge whether two souls are worthy of spending eternity
together. The Bahá'í Writings define true marriage as follows:

The true marriage of Bahá'ís is this, that husband and wife should be united
both physically and spiritually, that they may ever improve the spiritual life
of each other, and may enjoy everlasting unity throughout all the worlds of
God. This is Bahá'í marriage.[88]

The significance of this unity between husband and wife should not be under-
estimated. 'Abdu'l-Bahá has stated that when two people enter into a spiritual
marriage, they become even as one soul:

As to thy question concerning the husband and wife, the tie between them
and the children given to them by God: Know thou, verily, the husband
is one who hath sincerely turned unto God, is awakened by the call of the
Beauty of El-Baha and chanteth the verses of Oneness in the great assemblies; the wife is a being who wisheth to be overflowing with and seeketh
after the attributes of God and His names; and the tie between them is
none other than the Word of God. Verily, it [the Word of God] causeth
the multitudes to assemble together and the remote ones to be united.
Thus the husband and wife are brought into affinity, are united and har-
monized, even as though they were one person. Through their mutual
union, companionship and love great results are produced in the world,
both material and spiritual. The spiritual result is the appearance of divine
bounties. The material result is the children who are born in the cradle of
the love of God, who are nurtured by the breast of knowledge of God, who
are brought up in the bosom of the gift of God, and who are fostered in the
lap of the training of God. Such children are those of whom it was said by
Christ, 'Verily, they are the children of the Kingdom!'[89]

The Bahá'í Writings also suggest that a married couple can remain united even if one of them is not a Bahá'í. Note the inclusiveness of the following statements:

> . . . when two people, husband and wife for instance, have been completely united in this life their souls being as one soul, then after one of them has passed away, this union of heart and soul would remain unbroken.[90]

> . . . the possibility of securing union with his beloved in the next world is one which the Bahá'í Teachings are quite clear about. According to Bahá'u'lláh the soul retains its individuality and consciousness after death, and is able to commune with other souls. This communion, however, is purely spiritual in character, and is conditioned upon the disinterested and selfless love of the individuals for each other.[91]

The eternal nuclear family

The Mormon view of eternal marriage holds that all aspects of marriage are maintained in the afterlife. A 1995 declaration by the First Presidency titled 'The Family: A Proclamation to the World' makes the following assertions:

> All human beings – male and female – are created in the image of God. Each is a beloved spirit son or daughter of heavenly parents, and, as such, each has a divine nature and destiny. Gender is an essential characteristic of individual premortal, mortal, and eternal identity and purpose.
>
> In the premortal realm, spirit sons and daughters knew and worshiped God as their Eternal Father and accepted His plan by which His children could obtain a physical body and gain earthly experience to progress toward perfection and ultimately realize his or her divine destiny as an heir of eternal life. The divine plan of happiness enables family relationships to be perpetuated beyond the grave. Sacred ordinances and covenants available in holy temples make it possible for individuals to return to the presence of God and for families to be united eternally.[92]

Latter-day Saints believe that the nuclear family, made up of father, mother and children, will be reunited in the afterlife and continue to exist as before. This includes marital relations between the husband and wife, which are believed to result in additional *spirit children*. Mormon doctrine teaches that these spirit children must then wait to be born into a physical world, over which the parents will have full dominion. This is why Mormons say that we are *literally* children of God: every soul born on earth is believed to have started out as a spirit child of our 'Heavenly Parents,' who were themselves exalted from another world.

In contrast to a purely spiritual union, which Mormons consider to be somewhat vague and intangible, the prospect of a marriage that continues to exist in heaven exactly as it does on earth is touted as one of the greatest blessings of the Church.

Absent from the discussion is what happens if one partner dies and the other remarries. For if both marriages are sealed in the temple, this would presumably result in a polygamous situation in heaven. Considering the official Church position on plural marriage until 1890, perhaps Mormons assume that this will be, in the words of Brigham Young, 'the restitution of all things.'[93] (For an explanation of this concept, see Appendix 1.) Ironically, this is the exact problem the Sadducees posed to Jesus, in their attempt to prove the nonexistence of an afterlife:

> Then come unto him the Sadducees, which say there is no resurrection; and they asked him, saying, Master, Moses wrote unto us, If a man's brother die, and leave his wife behind him, and leave no children, that his brother should take his wife, and raise up seed unto his brother. Now there were seven brethren: and the first took a wife, and dying left no seed. And the second took her, and died, neither left he any seed: and the third likewise. And the seven had her, and left no seed: last of all the woman died also. In the resurrection therefore, when they shall rise, whose wife shall she be of them? for the seven had her to wife.[94]

The astute reader of the New Testament may observe that the term 'resurrection' in numerous verses throughout the Bible simply refers to the afterlife, particularly when it is followed by 'of the dead.' One of the major doctrinal differences between the Pharisaic and Sadducean sects in the time of Jesus was that the former believed in life after death, while the latter did not:

> For the Sadducees say that there is no resurrection, neither angel, nor spirit: but the Pharisees confess both.[95]

The Sadducees' rejection of the concept of an eternal soul may have been partially due to the Pharisees' material depiction of the next world, including the belief in a bodily resurrection. The accounts in Mark and Luke show Jesus attempting to explain the spiritual nature of the afterlife to the Sadducees.

According to the Bahá'í teachings, there is no doubt that a husband and wife can remain united throughout all the worlds of God. However, this union is of a spiritual nature, and cannot be placed in the context of this material world. In the next life, we shed all physical limitations, including any characteristics of outward appearance or gender. All that remains is the pure essence of our souls, seasoned with the experiences gained in our earthly existence. With this understanding, conjugal relations in the afterlife – or any other traditional notions of marriage – are unthinkable. In the Gospel of Matthew, Jesus makes it clear that no such thing exists; when the Sadducees concocted a convoluted marriage scenario in an attempt to disprove the concept of life after death, Jesus dismissed them:

> Ye do err, not knowing the scriptures, nor the power of God. For in the resurrection they neither marry, nor are given in marriage, but are as the angels of God in heaven.[96]

Luke's account of the same event is even less ambiguous:

> And Jesus answering said unto them, The children of this world marry, and are given in marriage: But they which shall be accounted worthy to obtain that world, and the resurrection from the dead, neither marry, nor are given in marriage: Neither can they die any more: for they are equal unto the angels; and are the children of God, being the children of the resurrection.[97]

In other words, the concept of marriage as it exists on earth is not found in heaven, because the souls, like the angels, associate with each other on a spiritual level, and not based on earthly relationships. The following excerpt from the writings of Shoghi Effendi appears to epitomize the words addressed by Jesus to the Sadducees:

> There is no teaching in the Bahá'í Faith that 'soul mates' exist. What is meant is that marriage should lead to a profound friendship of spirit, which will endure in the next world, where there is no sex, and no giving and taking in marriage; just the way we should establish with our parents, our children, our brothers and sisters and friends a deep spiritual bond which will be ever-lasting, and not merely physical bonds of human relationship.[98]

In an apparent attempt to reconcile his views on eternal marriage with the Bible, Joseph Smith offered a rather creative interpretation of the above-quoted verse from the Gospel of Matthew:

Therefore, when they are out of the world they neither marry nor are given in marriage; but are appointed angels in heaven, which angels are ministering servants, to minister for those who are worthy of a far more, and an exceeding, and an eternal weight of glory. For these angels did not abide my law; therefore, they cannot be enlarged, but remain separately and singly, without exaltation, in their saved condition, to all eternity; and from henceforth are not gods, but are angels of God forever and ever.[99]

Here, Joseph Smith asserts that the angels referred to by Jesus, who 'neither marry nor are given in marriage,' had broken the law and were therefore consigned to the *terrestrial kingdom*. By contrast, those who had met the requirements for eternal marriage would attain to the *celestial kingdom* and become 'gods,' reigning over those very angels. To some, this may come across as a rather egregious twisting of Christ's words, and fails to explain why Jesus extolled these angels as 'the children of the resurrection' and 'they which shall be accounted worthy to obtain that world.'

The eternal extended family

According to the Bahá'í teachings, an eternal bond is not limited to just husband and wife; any two souls who have been closely united in this life – such as siblings or best friends – will remain so in the next life. That suggestion is confirmed by the following excerpt from a Tablet of 'Abdu'l-Bahá:

And know thou for a certainty that in the divine worlds the spiritual beloved ones will recognize one another, and will seek union with each other, but a spiritual union. Likewise a love that one may have entertained for anyone will not be forgotten in the world of the Kingdom, nor wilt thou forget there the life thou hast in the material world.[100]

The ultimate extended family is of course the entire body of the believers. Bahá'ís are promised that in the next world, they 'shall associate in their lives, their aspirations, their aims and strivings as to be even as one soul.'[101] This eternal union also extends to the relationships between parents and children, as they have a special bond with each other from the start. This may explain why a Bahá'í couple wishing to be married must get permission from all living birth parents, whereas the Bahá'í Writings generally confer a greater importance on spiritual parents, i.e. those who raise and educate us.

Our beloved Guardian made it clear that it was the responsibility of the Bahá'í body performing the marriage ceremony to confirm without question the fact that the living natural parents of the two individuals who are being married have given their consent to the marriage.[102]

The close relationship between parent and child is strongly emphasized in the Bahá'í teachings. In *Stories of Bahá'u'lláh*, Hand of the Cause 'Alí-Akbar Furútan quotes Bahá'u'lláh as saying: 'in the Book of God it is recorded that should a person embrace this Faith, his father and mother shall also receive forgiveness.'[103] A prayer for families revealed by 'Abdu'l-Bahá reads:

O Lord! In this Most Great Dispensation Thou dost accept the intercession of children in behalf of their parents. This is one of the special infinite bestowals of this Dispensation. Therefore, O Thou kind Lord, accept the request of this Thy servant at the threshold of Thy singleness and submerge his father in the ocean of Thy grace, because this son hath arisen to render Thee service and is exerting effort at all times in the pathway of Thy love, Verily, Thou art the Giver, the Forgiver and the Kind![104]

Souls are not idle after death

Most people are familiar with the Christian caricature of angels in heaven donning wings and halos, and playing harps for all eternity – a concept which Mark Twain skewered in his comical yet insightful short story, *Captain Stormfield's Visit to Heaven*. Although the Mormon and Bahá'í ideas of the afterlife differ sharply, they do share a common recognition that this traditional Christian view of a 'permanent vacation' is misguided.

The light and the leaven

According to Mormon doctrine, righteous souls after death 'carry the light of the gospel' to those who passed away in ignorance:

According to the prophet Alma, the righteous spirits rest from earthly care and sorrow. Nevertheless, they are occupied in doing the work of the Lord. President Joseph F. Smith saw in a vision that immediately after Jesus Christ was crucified, he visited the righteous in the spirit world. He appointed messengers, gave them power and authority, and commissioned them to 'carry the light of the gospel to them that were in darkness, even to all the spirits of men.'[105]

'Abdu'l-Bahá explained that undeveloped souls in the next world can progress through the supplications of more advanced souls and the intercession of the Manifestations:

> It is even possible that the condition of those who have died in sin and unbelief may become changed – that is to say, they may become the object of pardon through the bounty of God, not through His justice – for bounty is giving without desert, and justice is giving what is deserved. As we have power to pray for these souls here, so likewise we shall possess the same power in the other world, which is the Kingdom of God. Are not all the people in that world the creatures of God? Therefore, in that world also they can make progress. As here they can receive light by their supplications, there also they can plead for forgiveness and receive light through entreaties and supplications. Thus as souls in this world, through the help of the supplications, the entreaties and the prayers of the holy ones, can acquire development, so is it the same after death. Through their own prayers and supplications they can also progress, more especially when they are the object of the intercession of the Holy Manifestations.[106]

The influence of these righteous souls is by no means limited to the next world. Of those who 'at the hour of death, ascend, in the utmost purity and sanctity and with absolute detachment', the Bahá'í Writings say:

> The light which these souls radiate is responsible for the progress of the world and the advancement of its peoples. They are like unto leaven which leaveneth the world of being, and constitute the animating force through which the arts and wonders of the world are made manifest. Through them the clouds rain their bounty upon men, and the earth bringeth forth its fruits. All things must needs have a cause, a motive power, an animating principle. These souls and symbols of detachment have provided, and will continue to provide, the supreme moving impulse in the world of being.[107]

> Know thou, of a truth, that if the soul of man hath walked in the ways of God, it will, assuredly, return and be gathered to the glory of the Beloved . . . Such a soul provideth, at the bidding of the Ideal King and Divine Educator, the pure leaven that leaveneth the world of being, and furnisheth the power through which the arts and wonders of the world are made manifest. Consider how meal needeth leaven to be leavened with. Those souls that are the symbols of detachment are the leaven of the world.[108]

Also, 'Abdu'l-Bahá has explained that the 'meaning of teaching the Faith in the next world is spreading the sweet savors of holiness; that action is the same as teaching.'[109]

An explanation of prodigy

The above words of Bahá'u'lláh may help us to understand how some people can be extraordinarily gifted at an early age; for instance, Mozart wrote his first symphony at age nine, and Albert Einstein as a small child exhibited an unusual curiosity and understanding of the natural world. To those who would point to reincarnation as the only explanation of such innate gifts, the animating influence from the 'concourse on high' on the world of arts and sciences can be offered as a possible alternative.

Some Mormons advance the phenomenon of prodigy as evidence of a pre-existence, proposing that these unusually gifted young children acquired their skills in the premortal world. While this may seem a logical argument on the surface, it does not explain how those skills would have been perfected through practice, such as by playing an instrument or using tools. It might be more logical to suggest that, in Mormon parlance, these very talents are some of the 'godlike qualities' we can develop only through obtaining a mortal life, and are therefore not available to us in the pre-existence. From this stand-point, the idea that departed souls, having obtained earthly experience and talents, 'constitute the animating force through which the arts and wonders of the world are made manifest,' is an attractive and reasonable supposition.

CHAPTER 6

PHYSICAL AND SPIRITUAL HEALTH

There are many similarities between the Bahá'í and Mormon teachings on the subject of health. Health pertains not just to the body, but also to the mind, the heart, and the spirit. In this chapter we'll examine each of these aspects and how the two faiths address them in their scriptures.

Science has long ago discovered that there is a relationship between our physical and our mental health. In many religions, an additional link is made – that between our physical and our *spiritual* health:

> 'Abdu'l-Bahá refers to the effect of 'purity and holiness, cleanliness and refinement' on the exaltation of 'the human condition' and 'the development of man's inner reality'. He states: 'The fact of having a pure and spotless body exercises an influence upon the spirit of man.'[1]

We will see that when it comes to what is good for our body and spirit and what is not, Mormons and Bahá'ís agree on many fronts.

Alcohol, drugs and tobacco

Like Bahá'ís, Mormons are forbidden to drink alcohol. In one sense, the Mormon code of health appears to be even stricter than that of the Bahá'ís, as neither coffee nor tea are forbidden to the latter, and – while it is strongly discouraged – neither is smoking. On the other hand, the language used in the Bahá'í Writings to condemn the use of alcohol, drugs and tobacco is far stronger than any found in the LDS scriptures. Bahá'í law does allow the medical use of alcohol and some drugs, an explicit provision which is not found in the Mormon faith.

Scriptural origins of the Mormon position on alcohol and smoking

In a section of the Doctrine and Covenants generally referred to as the 'Word of Wisdom,' Joseph Smith counsels[2] against the consumption of wine, strong drink, tobacco and what he termed 'hot drinks.' This is generally understood to mean alcoholic beverages of any kind, smoking and other uses of tobacco, as well as coffee and tea (more on this later). An exception is given for wine at the sacrament, as long as it is made by members of the Church and not bought elsewhere:

> That inasmuch as any man drinketh wine or strong drink among you, behold it is not good, neither meet in the sight of your Father, only in assembling yourselves together to offer up your sacraments before him. And, behold, this should be wine, yea, pure wine of the grape of the vine, of your own make. And, again, strong drinks are not for the belly, but for the washing of your bodies. And again, tobacco is not for the body, neither for the belly, and is not good for man, but is an herb for bruises and all sick cattle, to be used with judgment and skill. And again, hot drinks are not for the body or belly . . .
>
> Nevertheless, wheat for man, and corn for the ox, and oats for the horse, and rye for the fowls and for swine, and for all beasts of the field, and barley for all useful animals, and for mild drinks, as also other grain.[3]

Some time during the leadership of Brigham Young, the sacramental wine was replaced by water. This change was justified by Joseph Smith's original indication that 'it mattereth not what ye shall eat or what ye shall drink when ye partake of the sacrament.'[4] An article in *Ensign* magazine elaborates:

> One of the most significant changes was given by revelation in August 1830. The Lord revealed to Joseph Smith that 'it mattereth not what ye shall eat or what ye shall drink when ye partake of the sacrament, if it so be that ye do it with an eye single to my glory – remembering unto the Father my body which was laid down for you, and my blood which was shed for the remission of your sins.
>
> 'Wherefore, a commandment I give unto you, that you shall not purchase wine neither strong drink of your enemies;
>
> 'Wherefore, you shall partake of none except it is made new among you; yea, in this my Father's kingdom which shall be built up on the earth.' (D&C 27:2–4.)
>
> It took a number of years before the congregations of the Saints totally abolished the use of wine in the sacrament, but by the end of President

Brigham Young's administration, the use of water for the sacrament was generally the practice. The point of the revelation was that the sacrament be partaken with an eye single to the glory of the Lord.[5]

Parenthetically, some Mormons have suggested that by 'pure wine of the grape of the vine, of your own make' Joseph Smith really referred to nonalcoholic wine, and that this was the wine used before water was adopted. This is highly unlikely considering that no process existed for removing alcohol from wine, and pasteurized grape juice had not yet been invented. In fact, nothing in the church's official history or curricula supports this notion, and every mention of the former practice simply refers to wine. Moreover, the switch to water would have made little sense if the wine being used was already alcohol-free.

President John Taylor's own memoirs confirm the use of alcoholic wine, in the sacrament as well as for medicinal purposes. Mere days before the fatal jailhouse attack on Joseph and Hyrum Smith, the entire company of prisoners, in what undoubtedly was a moment of deep despair, shared a bottle of wine:

> Sometime after dinner we sent for some wine. It has been reported by some that this was taken as a sacrament. It was no such thing; our spirits were generally dull and heavy, and it was sent for to revive us . . . I believe we all drank of the wine, and gave some to one or two of the prison guards. We all of us felt unusually dull and languid, with a remarkable depression of spirits.[6]

These historical details notwithstanding, all church presidents after Joseph Smith have enjoined the Word of Wisdom on the faithful, explicitly proscribing both alcohol and tobacco.

The Bahá'í position on alcohol and smoking

While the Bahá'í teachings say nothing about coffee and tea – two treasured fixtures of American and Persian culture, respectively – they are quite explicit on the subject of alcohol:

> The drinking of wine is, according to the text of the Most Holy Book, forbidden; for it is the cause of chronic diseases, weakeneth the nerves, and consumeth the mind.[7]

> Drink ye, O handmaidens of God, the Mystic Wine from the cup of My

words. Cast away, then, from you that which your minds abhor, for it hath been forbidden unto you in His Tablets and His Scriptures. Beware lest ye barter away the River that is life indeed for that which the souls of the pure-hearted detest. Become ye intoxicated with the wine of the love of God, and not with that which deadeneth your minds, O ye that adore Him! Verily, it hath been forbidden unto every believer, whether man or woman. Thus hath the sun of My commandment shone forth above the horizon of My utterance, that the handmaidens who believe in Me may be illumined.[8]

Smoking is not expressly prohibited by Bahá'í law. However, it is condemned in terms that are at least as strong as those found in the LDS scriptures. 'Abdu'l-Bahá stated:

> . . . there are other forbidden things which do not cause immediate harm, and the injurious effects of which are only gradually produced: such acts are also repugnant to the Lord, and blameworthy in His sight, and repellent. The absolute unlawfulness of these, however, hath not been expressly set forth in the Text, but their avoidance is necessary to purity, cleanliness, the preservation of health, and freedom from addiction.
>
> Among these latter is smoking tobacco, which is dirty, smelly, offensive – an evil habit, and one the harmfulness of which gradually becometh apparent to all . . .
>
> My meaning is that in the sight of God, smoking tobacco is deprecated, abhorrent, filthy in the extreme; and, albeit by degrees, highly injurious to health. It is also a waste of money and time, and maketh the user a prey to a noxious addiction. To those who stand firm in the Covenant, this habit is therefore censured both by reason and experience, and renouncing it will bring relief and peace of mind to all men.[9]

Notwithstanding this passionate disapproval of the use of tobacco, the small minority of Bahá'ís who do smoke are not vilified in any way, although certain commonsense restrictions are placed on their smoking in Bahá'í gatherings:

> In the case of Nineteen Day Feasts or meetings of Assemblies or committees, it is not right that friends who find smoking offensive should be made to endure it in Bahá'í meetings that they are required or expected to attend. If certain individuals feel that they must smoke, then arrangements, such as a break in the meeting, could be made for their convenience. It would, of course, be entirely inappropriate to smoke during the devotional part of the Feast, or at any other devotional gathering.[10]

While Brigham Young reportedly showed a similar tolerance of tobacco use – so long as it was outside of church meetings – subsequent presidents of the LDS Church have made it clear that all forms of tobacco are off limits to the believers under any condition.[11]

The serving and selling of alcohol

Mormons and Bahá'ís are both strongly discouraged from serving alcohol in social settings, and from owning businesses which involve the sale of alcoholic beverages. Undoubtedly there are instances of members of either faith who, due to social or economic realities, are forced to take certain actions which run contrary to their beliefs. A prominent example of this is the Marriott hotel chain, which is owned by a Latter-day Saint family and serves alcoholic beverages to its patrons.

In an article about the difficulties in applying spiritual principles to every day life, Apostle Dallin H. Oaks mused:

> The consumption of alcohol is increasing among youth. Targeting young audiences, advertisers portray beer and wine as joyful, socially desirable, and harmless. Producers are promoting new types of alcoholic beverages as competitors in the huge soft-drink market. Grocery and convenience stores and gas stations stock alcoholic beverages side by side with soda pop. Can Christians who are involved in this commerce be indifferent to the physical and moral effects of the alcohol from which they are making their profits? . . .
>
> We should also remember that the principle that the Golden Rule governs our earning activities is difficult to apply in practice. We should not consider employees responsible for policies they regret but cannot control. A decision that is made by the owner of a market should not inflict feelings of guilt on a conscientious but powerless Christian who runs the checkout stand. Similarly, a part-owner does not have freedom to impose his standards on business policies if he has partners who do not share his moral concerns. An incorporated business may be controlled by stockholders who have no concern for the destructive human effects of a profitable product or policy.[12]

It could also be argued that the Marriott family is merely following the example of Joseph Smith. Back in Nauvoo, Illinois, Smith owned the Nauvoo Mansion hotel, which counted among its amenities a well-stocked bar. As councilman, and later, mayor of Nauvoo, Smith also passed a number of ordinances giving himself and others the right to sell and serve alcoholic beverages for the comfort of guests:

> I was in the City Council, and moved that any person in the City of Nauvoo be at liberty to sell vinous liquors in any quantity, subject to the city ordinances.[13]

> *Ordinance on the Personal Sale of Liquors.* Section 1. Be it ordained by the City Council of Nauvoo, that the Mayor of the city be and is hereby authorized to sell or give spirits of any quantity as he in his wisdom shall judge to be for the health and comfort, or convenience of such travelers or other persons as shall visit his house from time to time. Passed December 12, 1843. JOSEPH SMITH, Mayor. WILLARD RICHARDS, Recorder.[14]

These actions by Joseph Smith appear to be quite justified and not at all in conflict with his avowed beliefs. In his writings, he only counseled his followers to refrain from drinking, and never vilified others who drank in moderation. He even acknowledged once partaking of a small glass of home-made wine himself.[15] In his early 19th-century American milieu, it would have been offensive in the extreme to entertain visitors who were not members of his church without offering them a drink.

The Bahá'í guidelines, for their part, allow only limited exceptions in social settings where refusing to serve alcohol would be considered offensive, or in businesses that are partly owned by non-Bahá'ís:

> When a Bahá'í is privately entertaining an individual non-Bahá'í or a small group of guests in his own home, he must himself judge whether or not to serve alcohol. This will depend to a great degree on the customs of the country in which he is living, the individuals concerned, and the host's relationship to his guests. Obviously it is better for the Bahá'í not to serve alcohol if possible, but against this he must weigh the probable reaction of the guest in the circumstances which prevail and in the particular situation. In some countries there would be no problem in failing to provide alcohol to a guest; in others it would be regarded as extremely peculiar and anti-social and would immediately raise a barrier to further contact. It is not desirable to make a major issue of the matter.[16]

We have found no explicit text or instruction of the beloved Guardian on such a situation (the sale of alcoholic beverages by a business in which a Bahá'í is a partner with non-Bahá'ís) and feel that it is one in which no hard and fast rules should be drawn at the present time . . . We feel that this is a matter which needs to be decided in each case in the light of the spirit of the teachings and the circumstances of the case, and unless the situation is one which is endangering the good name of the Faith or is obviously a ruse on the part of the believer to evade the Bahá'í law, it should be left to the conscience of the believer concerned who should, of course, be informed of the Bahá'í teachings concerning alcohol and should make every effort to dissociate himself from such an activity.[17]

However, the Bahá'í Writings are unyielding in all other circumstances:

Institutions that are entirely managed by Bahá'ís are, for reasons that are only too obvious, under the obligation of enforcing all the laws and ordinances of the Faith, especially those whose observance constitutes a matter of conscience. There is no reason, no justification whatsoever, that they should act otherwise . . .[18]

Concerning the third question (sale of alcoholic drinks at Bahá'í-owned premises and restaurants), the beloved Guardian has asked me to point out that this practice is highly improper and reprehensible and would be tantamount to encouraging acts that are forbidden in the Faith. It is indeed the conscientious duty of every true Bahá'í to abandon such practices. However, should a Bahá'í owner rent his property without himself taking any part whatever in the business, or giving aid to the tenant, then he would incur no responsibility. Nevertheless the landlord should resort to every possible means to rid his premises of the defilement of this degrading business; how far more injurious if he himself were engaged in such repugnant affairs.[19]

In situations where a Bahá'í is employed by a non-Bahá'í business, the matter is again left up to the conscience of the individual:

Such employments (Bahá'ís who are in the employment of non-Bahá'ís and whose employment involves the serving or selling of alcoholic beverages) cover every wide range of degree in involvement, therefore it is left to the individual to decide whether or not he feels his employment violates the spirit of the Bahá'í law. In cases of doubt he can, of course, consult his Spiritual Assembly for advice . . .[20]

This 'wide range of degree in involvement' refers to the difference between, for example, a grocery store clerk scanning the occasional bottle of wine or liquor, and a bartender who is directly serving alcohol to patrons.

Addictive or habit-forming drugs

In the Bahá'í Writings, the most severe of all condemnations are reserved for addictive drugs, particularly opium and hashish (of which marijuana is a close relative). The following statements by 'Abdu'l-Bahá leave little doubt as to how their Author felt about these substances, and even suggest that drugs inflict permanent harm on the eternal soul:

> As to opium, it is foul and accursed. God protect us from the punishment He inflicteth on the user. According to the explicit Text of the Most Holy Book, it is forbidden, and its use is utterly condemned. Reason showeth that smoking opium is a kind of insanity, and experience attesteth that the user is completely cut off from the human kingdom. May God protect all against the perpetration of an act so hideous as this, an act which layeth in ruins the very foundation of what it is to be human, and which causeth the user to be dispossessed for ever and ever. For opium fasteneth on the soul, so that the user's conscience dieth, his mind is blotted away, his perceptions are eroded. It turneth the living into the dead. It quencheth the natural heat. No greater harm can be conceived than that which opium inflicteth. Fortunate are they who never even speak the name of it; then think how wretched is the user.[21]

> Regarding hashish . . . Gracious God! This is the worst of all intoxicants, and its prohibition is explicitly revealed. Its use causeth the disintegration of thought and the complete torpor of the soul. How could anyone seek the fruit of the infernal tree, and by partaking of it, be led to exemplify the qualities of a monster? How could one use this forbidden drug, and thus deprive himself of the blessings of the All-Merciful?
>
> Alcohol consumeth the mind and causeth man to commit acts of absurdity, but this opium, this foul fruit of the infernal tree, and this wicked hashish extinguish the mind, freeze the spirit, petrify the soul, waste the body and leave man frustrated and lost.[22]

Joseph Smith did not specifically mention drugs, but this is most likely because they were not commonly used in his immediate environment. If asked, he would certainly have disapproved of their use, and subsequent church presidents have spoken out against drugs in unequivocal terms. The general code of health Mormons follow is simple and straightforward:

> We should avoid anything that we know is harmful to our bodies. We should not use any substance that is habit forming . . . We purify our bodies so the Spirit of the Lord can dwell with us.[23]

The same ideas are found in this supplication by 'Abdu'l-Bahá:

> O Divine Providence! Bestow Thou in all things purity and cleanliness upon the people of Bahá. Grant that they be freed from all defilement, and released from all addictions. Save them from committing any repugnant act, unbind them from the chains of every evil habit, that they may live pure and free, wholesome and cleanly, worthy to serve at Thy Sacred Threshold and fit to be related to their Lord. Deliver them from intoxicating drinks and tobacco, save them, rescue them from this opium that bringeth on madness, suffer them to enjoy the sweet savours of holiness, that they may drink deep of the mystic cup of heavenly love and know the rapture of being drawn ever closer unto the Realm of the All-Glorious.[24]

Medical use of alcohol and drugs

The LDS Church does not specifically allow or forbid the use of alcohol or drugs for medical use, although the use of pharmaceuticals as part of professional medical treatment is accepted as a matter of course. It is interesting to note here that Joseph Smith himself did not put a great deal of stock in the benefits of modern medicine – or what was considered modern medicine in the 1840s. In one of his journals, he noted:

> I preached to a large congregation at the stand, on the science and practice of medicine, desiring to persuade the Saints to trust in God when sick, and not in the arm of flesh, and live by faith and not by medicine, or poison; and when they were sick, and had called for the Elders to pray for them, and they were not healed, to use herbs and mild food.[25]

The Baháʼí Writings explain that we must consult medical doctors when necessary, and not rely strictly on spiritual healing:

> Illnesses which occur by reason of physical causes should be treated by doctors with medical remedies; those which are due to spiritual causes disappear

through spiritual means. Thus an illness caused by affliction, fear, nervous impressions, will be healed more effectively by spiritual rather than by physical treatment. Hence, both kinds of treatment should be followed; they are not contradictory. Therefore thou shouldst also accept physical remedies inasmuch as these too have come from the mercy and favour of God, Who hath revealed and made manifest medical science so that His servants may profit from this kind of treatment also.[26]

Resort ye, in times of sickness, to competent physicians; We have not set aside the use of material means, rather have We confirmed it through this Pen, which God hath made to be the Dawning-place of His shining and glorious Cause.[27]

The medical use of alcohol and drugs is explicitly allowed, provided it is part of a specific treatment:

It should be noted that the above prohibition against taking certain classes of drugs does not forbid their use when prescribed by qualified physicians as part of a medical treatment.[28]

Presumably, an over-the-counter remedy containing alcohol would not be permitted, because a qualified physician did not prescribe it. Also, a physician prescribing alcohol or some other drug may only do so as part of a specific medical treatment designed for a particular patient, and not as a blanket exemption. However, the decision as to whether to use a specific medication is considered a matter between the individual and God, and no issue is made of it.

A healthy diet and lifestyle

In addition to discouraging the use of alcohol and tobacco, Joseph Smith prescribed healthy eating, sleeping and working habits to his followers. In his 'Word of Wisdom' (D&C 89) we find the following counsel:

And again, verily I say unto you, all wholesome herbs God hath ordained for the constitution, nature, and use of man. Every herb in the season thereof, and every fruit in the season thereof; all these to be used with prudence and thanksgiving. Yea, flesh also of beasts and of the fowls of the air, I, the Lord, have ordained for the use of man with thanksgiving; nevertheless they are to be used sparingly; And it is pleasing unto me that they should not be used, only in times of winter, or of cold, or famine. All grain is ordained for the use of man and of beasts, to be the staff of life, not only for man but for the beasts of the field, and the fowls of heaven, and all wild animals that run or creep on the earth; And these hath God made for the use of man only in times of famine and excess of hunger. All grain is good for the food of man; as also the fruit of the vine; that which yieldeth fruit, whether in the ground or above the ground.[29]

Cease to be idle; cease to be unclean . . . cease to sleep longer than is needful; retire to thy bed early, that ye may not be weary; arise early, that your bodies and your minds may be invigorated.[30]

One particular characteristic of this Word of Wisdom – the assurance that man is given all good foods to eat, with a caution that meat is 'to be used sparingly' – is also found in the Bahá'í Writings. In one of His tablets, 'Abdu'l-Bahá counsels us:

Thou hast written regarding the four canine teeth in man, saying that these teeth, two in the upper jaw and two in the lower, are for the purpose of eating meat. Know thou that these four teeth are not created for meat-eating, although one can eat meat with them. All the teeth of man are made for eating fruit, cereals and vegetables. These four teeth, however, are designed for breaking hard shells, such as those of almonds. But eating meat is not forbidden or unlawful, nay, the point is this, that it is possible for man to live without eating meat and still be strong. Meat is nourishing and containeth the elements of herbs, seeds and fruits; therefore sometimes it is essential for the sick and for the rehabilitation of health. There is no objection in the Law of God to the eating of meat if it is required. So if thy constitution is rather weak and thou findest meat useful, thou mayest eat it.[31]

Bahá'u'lláh revealed an important tablet on medicine known as the Lawḥ-i-Ṭibb between 1870 and 1872, in honour of Áqá Mírzá Muḥammad-Riḍáy-i-Ṭabíb-i-Yazdí, a physician of the old school of medicine.[32] While no official English translation of this tablet is yet available, a provisional translation dating back to the early 20th century shows that in addition to advising the doctor, Bahá'u'lláh offered a number of 'words of wisdom' concerning our everyday eating habits as well as our general disposition:

He is God!

O God the supreme Knower! The ancient Tongue Speaks that which
will content the wise in the absence of the Doctors. Say: O people, do
not eat except when you are hungry. Do not drink after you have retired
to sleep. Exercise is good when the stomach is empty; it strengthens the
muscles. When the stomach is full, exercise is very bad. Do not neglect
(medical) treatment when it is necessary but leave it off when the body
is in good condition. Do not take nourishment except when digestion is
completed. Do not swallow until you have thoroughly masticated (your
food).

Treat disease first of all through the diet and refrain from medicines.
If you find what you need (for healing) in a single herb, do not use compound medicines. Leave off medicine when the health is good and use it
in case of necessity. If two opposites are put on the table do not mix them,
be content with one of them. Begin first with liquid food before partaking
of solid food. The taking of food before what you have (already eaten) is
digested, is dangerous – avoid this.

When you begin to eat, begin with My Name El Abhá, and finish with
the Name of God the Possessor of the Throne and the earth. When you
have eaten walk a little that the food may settle. What is difficult to masti-
cate is forbidden by the Wise. – Thus the Supreme Pen Commands you.

A little food in the morning is like a light to the body. Leave all harmful habits, they cause unhappiness in the world. Search for the cause of
disease. This saying is the end of this speech.

Be content in all conditions, by this the person is preserved from a bad
condition and from lassitude. Shun grief and sorrow, they cause the greatest misery. Say: Jealousy eats the body and anger burns the liver. Refrain
from these two as you would avoid a lion . . .[33]

Clearly, there is strong agreement between Joseph Smith's Word of Wisdom
and the Bahá'í teachings concerning health and nutrition.

Hot drinks

Most people know that Mormons do not drink coffee. It is less well known
that most kinds of tea fall under the same prohibition. We will examine the
reasons why the LDS Church forbids coffee and black tea, and why there has
been some confusion within the Mormon community about the consumption of herbal teas and caffeinated soft drinks.

Joseph Smith indicated that 'hot drinks' are not for consumption:

And, again, strong drinks are not for the belly, but for the washing of your bodies . . . And again, hot drinks are not for the body or belly.[34]

The question as to what constitutes a 'hot drink' has been the cause of some debate within the Mormon community. Smith never defined this term, and so this task was left to future presidents of the Church. Eventually, Brigham Young settled the issue as follows:

This Word of Wisdom prohibits the use of hot drinks and tobacco. I have heard it argued that tea and coffee are not mentioned therein; that is very true; but what were the people in the habit of taking as hot drinks when that revelation was given? Tea and coffee. We were not in the habit of drinking water very hot, but tea and coffee – the beverages in common use.[35]

There is an interesting anecdote involving the Báb and the consumption of coffee and tea. In the French Persian-language magazine *Páyam-i-Bahá'í*, 'Abdu'l-Hamid Eshrakhavari explains why 'coffee houses' in Iran do not actually serve any coffee. According to Mr Eshrakhvani, at the time of the Báb most Persians drank Turkish coffee. The Báb counseled His followers to drink tea instead, primarily because He deemed the strong Turkish coffee unhealthy. For years, drinking tea was a hallmark of the Bábís, but this custom gradually spread to the rest of the population. While the original name of the Persian coffee house (*ghahve khune*) has remained unchanged, it now serves exclusively tea.[36]

Cola vs. decaf

Some Latter-day Saints remain unsure as to what exactly is prohibited by the Word of Wisdom. The LDS Church has indicated that it is permissible to drink hot soup, cocoa and herbal tea, but it is forbidden to drink regular iced tea, which is cold. No reason was given for allowing herbal tea over black tea, and speculation ensued that it was the caffeine which was prohibited. However, cocoa contains traces of caffeine as well. Some came to believe that decaffeinated coffee was all right to drink, while others considered caffeinated soft drinks to be off limits. Further solidifying this impression are statements such as these by Bruce R. McConkie, as found in his authoritative *Mormon Doctrine*:

. . . there are many other substances which have a harmful effect on the human body, though such particular things are not specifically prohibited by the Word of Wisdom. Certainly the partaking of cola drinks, though not included within the measuring standard here set out, is in violation of the spirit of the Word of Wisdom.[37]

However, the official Church guidance remains that only coffee and black tea are forbidden, regardless of their temperature or caffeine content. Therefore, colas are allowed but decaffeinated coffee is not. Nevertheless, the consumption of caffeinated drinks is generally discouraged because of their potential habit-forming nature:

> There has been no official interpretation of [the] Word of Wisdom except that which was given by the Brethren in the very early days of the Church when it was declared that 'hot drinks' meant tea and coffee.
>
> With reference to cola drinks, the Church has never officially taken a position on this matter, but the leaders of the Church have advised, and we do now specifically advise, against the use of any drink containing harmful habit-forming drugs under circumstances that would result in acquiring the habit. Any beverage that contains ingredients harmful to the body should be avoided.[38]

Interestingly, the entire debate over the habit-forming nature of cola drinks may have originated with a statement dated April 1922 by church president Heber J. Grant:

> I am not going to give any command, but I will ask it as a personal, individual favor to me, to let coca-cola alone. There are plenty of other things you can get at the soda fountains without drinking that which is injurious. The Lord does not want you to use any drug that creates an appetite for itself.[39]

This stern warning about using 'any drug that creates an appetite for itself' may seem somewhat exaggerated until we consider when this statement was made. Prior to its reformulation in 1927, Coca-Cola actually contained a small amount of cocaine – hence the name – and as such carried a significant risk of addiction. Of course, the caffeine which replaced cocaine as Coke's stimulant, while potentially habit forming in very large doses, does not share any of the truly addictive characteristics of cocaine.

In summary, whether or not to drink caffeinated soft drinks is a choice made by each individual member of the Church of Jesus Christ of Latter-day Saints, and the official Church position on the matter is neither to prohibit nor to encourage their consumption.

A matter of obedience

We have seen that the meaning of Joseph Smith's term 'hot drinks' has been interpreted by the Church as referring to coffee and tea. While this interpretation was based on the kinds of hot drinks that were popular in Smith's day, it is difficult to arrive at a scientific or medical reason why coffee and black tea are singled out in this respect. If it's the caffeine that is harmful, then cocoa and caffeinated soft drinks should also be prohibited. If the temperature is the issue, then hot soup and herbal teas should also be off limits. Of course we can't escape the fact that all drinks become hot once they enter the stomach.

Nevertheless, our interest in discovering the reasoning behind this particular rule is not likely to be shared by Latter-day Saints, who value obedience to the teachings of the Church more highly than a full understanding of their purpose. This should be appreciated by Bahá'ís, who unhesitatingly observe a number of Bahá'í laws that are not as yet fully understood by the generality of believers.

Chastity

An essential aspect of spiritual health, according to the teachings of many religions, is chastity. Mormons consider a high standard of chastity to be one of their distinguishing features. They may be surprised, even impressed, to discover that Bahá'í rules of moral conduct are in some ways stricter than their own. On the other hand, both faiths also share the recognition that the powers of procreation are a natural part of married life, and not something to be ashamed of.

Definitions of chastity

The LDS Church defines chastity as follows:

> The law of chastity requires total abstinence before marriage and full fidelity afterward. It is the same for men and women. It is the cornerstone of trust so necessary to the precious happiness of the marriage relationship and family solidarity.[40]

It also warns of the consequences of breaking the law of chastity:

> The law of chastity is one of the most vital importance, both to children, and to men and to women. It is a vitally important principle to the children of God in all their lives, from the cradle to the grave. God has fixed dreadful penalties against the transgression of his law of chastity, of virtue,

of purity. When the law of God shall be in force among men, they will be cut off who are not absolutely pure and unsoiled and spotless – both men and women.[41]

The Bahá'í Writings give a nearly identical warning, and expand the definition of chastity to all areas of conduct:

> O My Friends! Quench ye the lamp of error, and kindle within your hearts the everlasting torch of divine guidance. For erelong the assayers of mankind shall, in the holy presence of the Adored, accept naught but purest virtue and deeds of stainless holiness.[42]

> A chaste and holy life must be made the controlling principle in the behavior and conduct of all Bahá'ís, both in their social relations with the members of their own community, and in their contact with the world at large . . . It must be upheld, in all its integrity and implications, in every phase of the life of those who fill the ranks of that Faith, whether in their homes, their travels, their clubs, their societies, their entertainments, their schools, and their universities . . . Such a chaste and holy life, with its implications of modesty, purity, temperance, decency, and clean-mindedness, involves no less than the exercise of moderation in all that pertains to dress, language, amusements, and all artistic and literary avocations. It demands daily vigilance in the control of one's carnal desires and corrupt inclinations. It calls for the abandonment of a frivolous conduct, with its excessive attachment to trivial and often misdirected pleasures. It requires total abstinence from all alcoholic drinks, from opium, and from similar habit-forming drugs. It condemns the prostitution of art and of literature, the practices of nudism and of companionate marriage, infidelity in marital relationships, and all manner of promiscuity, of easy familiarity, and of sexual vices. It can tolerate no compromise with the theories, the standards, the habits, and the excesses of a decadent age. Nay rather it seeks to demonstrate, through the dynamic force of its example, the pernicious character of such theories, the falsity of such standards, the hollowness of such claims, the perversity of such habits, and the sacrilegious character of such excesses.[43]

Shoghi Effendi, addressing the American believers, additionally stated that these high ideals of chastity, when manifested by the Bahá'ís, are the 'chief propelling forces' driving the growth and protection of the Faith:

A rectitude of conduct, an abiding sense of undeviating justice, unobscured by the demoralizing influences which a corruption-ridden political life so strikingly manifests; a chaste, pure, and holy life, unsullied and unclouded by the indecencies, the vices, the false standards, which an inherently deficient moral code tolerates, perpetuates, and fosters; a fraternity freed from that cancerous growth of racial prejudice, which is eating into the vitals of an already debilitated society – these are the ideals which the American believers must, from now on, individually and through concerted action, strive to promote, in both their private and public lives, ideals which are the chief propelling forces that can most effectively accelerate the march of their institutions, plans, and enterprises, that can guard the honor and integrity of their Faith, and subdue any obstacles that may confront it in the future.[44]

Chastity of mind and heart

The following scriptures from both faiths emphasize the need to cleanse ourselves from earthly desires, pride and other defilements.

And again, thou shalt not be proud in thy heart; let all thy garments be plain, and their beauty the beauty of the work of thine own hands; And let all things be done in cleanliness before me.[45]

He hath chosen out of the whole world the hearts of His servants, and made them each a seat for the revelation of His glory. Wherefore, sanctify them from every defilement, that the things for which they were created may be engraven upon them.[46]

And I give unto you, who are the first laborers in this last kingdom, a commandment that you assemble yourselves together, and organize yourselves, and prepare yourselves, and sanctify yourselves; yea, purify your hearts, and cleanse your hands and your feet before me, that I may make you clean; That I may testify unto your Father, and your God, and my God, that you are clean from the blood of this wicked generation; that I may fulfil this promise, this great and last promise, which I have made unto you, when I will.[47]

Wash yourselves thoroughly, O people of Bahá, from the defilement of the world, and of all that pertaineth unto it.[48]

Chastity of utterance

Mormons are well known for their steadfast refusal to use foul or irreverent language. Less well known is the fact that they are also prohibited from engaging in gossip or backbiting. This philosophy is backed by sound reasoning:

> We are judged by our words every day. Nothing reveals us so intimately as how we use our divine gift of speech. Are we mean, crude, irreverent, thoughtless, smug, self-righteous, pompous? Our tongues will tell. Our language, too, reveals much about our integrity, honesty, kindness, goodness, humility, and decency. Language reveals character.[49]

> And see that there is no iniquity in the church, neither hardness with each other, neither lying, backbiting, nor evil speaking . . .[50]

Virtually the same theme can be found in the Bahá'í Writings:

> Verily I say, the tongue is for mentioning what is good, defile it not with unseemly talk. God hath forgiven what is past. Henceforward everyone should utter that which is meet and seemly, and should refrain from slander, abuse and whatever causeth sadness in men.[51]

> He must never seek to exalt himself above any one, must wash away from the tablet of his heart every trace of pride and vain-glory, must cling unto patience and resignation, observe silence and refrain from idle talk. For the tongue is a smoldering fire, and excess of speech a deadly poison. Material fire consumeth the body, whereas the fire of the tongue devoureth both heart and soul. The force of the former lasteth but for a time, whilst the effects of the latter endureth a century.
>
> That seeker should also regard backbiting as grievous error, and keep himself aloof from its dominion, inasmuch as backbiting quencheth the light of the heart, and extinguisheth the life of the soul.[52]

Kissing and embracing

Romantic kissing between two unmarried people is clearly forbidden to Bahá'ís as well as Mormons:

> What Bahá'u'lláh means by chastity certainly does not include the kissing that goes on in modern society. It is detrimental to the morals of young people, and often leads them to go too far, or arouses appetites which they

cannot perhaps at the time satisfy legitimately through marriage, and the suppression of which is a strain on them. The Bahá'í standard is very high, more particularly when compared with the thoroughly rotten morals of the present world. But this standard of ours will produce healthier, happier, nobler people, and induce stabler marriages.[53]

Kissing has been prostituted and has been degenerated to develop lust instead of affection, honor, and admiration. To kiss in casual dating is asking for trouble.

What is miscalled the soul kiss is an abomination and stirs passion that results in the eventual loss of virtue. Even if timely courtship justifies a kiss, it should be a clean, decent, sexless one.[54]

According to a little-known pilgrim's note, 'Abdu'l-Bahá has raised the standard of chastity another notch by forbidding unmarried women and men to embrace each other. The following quotation is attributed to Him:

The marriage bond is very important . . . Very, very important. Marriage must be strict and pure. You must all be very careful about this . . . Women and men must not embrace each other when not married, or not about to be married. They must not kiss each other . . . Such conduct is not taught in the Bahá'í Revelation . . . If they wish to greet each other, or comfort each other, they may take each other by the hand.[55]

Common sense tells us that the Master is not referring here to an embrace between family members, or for that matter to that most American of social traditions, the friendly 'hug.' Rather, it appears He is condemning the kind of romantic embracing often seen between young people of the opposite sex.

Sexual relations in a marital setting are natural and good

Refreshingly, Mormon doctrine does not promote sexual repression. Like Bahá'ís, Mormons are taught that sexual relations – so long as they are sanctioned by the institution of marriage and with the consent of both parties – are a blessing to mankind. Mormon parents are also encouraged to educate their children about sex:

By the time children reach maturity, parents should have frankly discussed procreation with them. Children should understand that these powers are good and were given to us by the Lord. He expects us to use them within

173

the bounds he has given us . . . The powers of procreation are sacred. God has commanded us that only in marriage are we to have sexual relations. This commandment is called the law of chastity.[56]

The sexual drives which bind men and women together as one are good and necessary. They make it possible to leave one's parents and cleave unto one another. But here, more than almost any other place, we must exercise self-control. These drives which are the fountainhead of human life are to be allowed expression only in the sanctity of marriage.[57]

The Bahá'í Writings similarly acknowledge the blessings of sexual relations in marriage, but warn that we must not become attached to these worldly pleasures:

The Bahá'í Faith recognizes the value of the sex impulse, but condemns its illegitimate and improper expressions such as free love, companionate marriage and others, all of which it considers positively harmful to man and to the society in which he lives. The proper use of the sex instinct is the natural right of every individual, and it is precisely for this very purpose that the institution of marriage has been established. The Bahá'ís do not believe in the suppression of the sex impulse but in its regulation and control.[58]

We are not ascetics in any sense of the word. On the contrary, Bahá'u'lláh says God has created all the good things in the world for us to enjoy and partake of. But we must not become attached to them and put them before the spiritual things. Chastity in the strict sense means not to have sexual intercourse, or sexual intimacies, before marriage. In the general sense it means not to be licentious. This does not mean we Bahá'ís believe sexual relations to be impure or wrong. On the contrary they are natural and should be considered one of God's many blessings . . . But when the world becomes more spiritual there will not be such an exaggerated emphasis on sex, as there is today, and consequently it will be easier for young people to be chaste and control their passions.[59]

Blessings of the law of chastity and consequences of violating it

Those who observe the law of chastity are promised many blessings. According to the LDS Church:

When we obey the law of chastity, we can live without guilt or shame. Our lives and our children's lives are blessed when we keep ourselves pure and spotless before the Lord. Children can look to our example and follow in our footsteps.[60]

While Bahá'u'lláh writes:

We, verily, have decreed in Our Book a goodly and bountiful reward to whosoever will turn away from wickedness and lead a chaste and godly life. He, in truth, is the Great Giver, the All-Bountiful.[61]

Mormons believe 'unchastity' to be 'next to murder in seriousness':

The prophet Alma grieved because one of his sons had broken the law of chastity. Alma said to his son Corianton, 'Know ye not, my son, that these things are an abomination in the sight of the Lord; yea, most abominable above all sins save it be the shedding of innocent blood or denying the Holy Ghost?'. Unchastity is next to murder in seriousness.[62]

Interestingly, in the Kitáb-i-Aqdas (the 'Most Holy Book' containing the most weighty Bahá'í laws), adultery is *literally* listed next to murder:

Ye have been forbidden to commit murder or adultery . . .[63]

Whereas both faiths confirm the spiritual detriment resulting from immorality, Bahá'í law additionally provides for immediate consequences in this world. Both Bahá'u'lláh and 'Abdu'l-Bahá have suggested a monetary fine for adultery and, in the most severe cases, making the infraction public in order to 'shame' the offenders – although these provisions would only apply in a future Bahá'í society and are not currently enforced. Today, flagrant or repeated acts of immorality can result in a Bahá'í being deprived of his administrative rights, including the right to vote in Bahá'í elections, attend the Nineteen Day Feast and contribute to the Bahá'í funds. Bahá'u'lláh issued the following clear rebuke to those who fail to uphold the Bahá'í standard of chastity:

Say: He is not to be numbered with the people of Bahá who followeth his mundane desires, or fixeth his heart on things of the earth. He is My true follower who, if he come to a valley of pure gold, will pass straight through it aloof as a cloud, and will neither turn back, nor pause. Such a man is, assuredly, of Me. From his garment the Concourse on high can inhale the fragrance of sanctity . . . And if he met the fairest and most comely of women, he would not feel his heart seduced by the least shadow of desire for her beauty. Such an one, indeed, is the creation of spotless chastity.[64]

It behoveth the people of Bahá to die to the world and all that is therein, to be so detached from all earthly things that the inmates of Paradise may inhale from their garment the sweet smelling savor of sanctity . . . They that have tarnished the fair name of the Cause of God, by following the things of the flesh – these are in palpable error![65]

However, if an unchaste act has been committed, both faiths teach that forgiveness is available to those who repent. The LDS teachings state:

Peace can come to those who have broken the law of chastity. The Lord tells us, 'If the wicked will turn from all his sins that he hath committed, and keep all my statutes . . . all his transgressions that he hath committed, they shall not be mentioned unto him'. Peace comes only through forgiveness. But forgiveness has a high price.[66]

While Bahá'u'lláh tells his followers that forgiveness lies in God's hands:

Should anyone be afflicted by a sin, it behoveth him to repent thereof and return unto his Lord. He, verily, granteth forgiveness unto whomsoever He willeth, and none may question that which it pleaseth Him to ordain. He is, in truth, the Ever-Forgiving, the Almighty, the All-Praised.[67]

And although God's forgiveness is infinite, Shoghi Effendi cautioned that we 'must be hopeful of God's mercy but not impose upon it.'[68]

CHAPTER 7
FAMILY RESPONSIBILITIES

Mormons place a very high priority on the family. Part of this emphasis is rooted in the conviction that families are eternal. Mormon culture is also conducive to having many children, which fosters a strong bond among the family members. As in the Bahá'í community, Mormon gatherings – whether at home or at church – are characterized by a warm family atmosphere in which children are expected to behave appropriately without being unduly restricted.

At home, Latter-day Saints and Bahá'ís recognize many of the same responsibilities that husbands, wives and children have toward the family. Our investigation into these responsibilities yields a few differences between the LDS and Bahá'í teachings, as well.

The purpose of marriage

Both faiths agree that a primary purpose of marriage is procreation, and that sexual relations are appropriate only within the confines of sanctioned marriage:

> The first commandment that God gave to Adam and Eve pertained to their potential for parenthood as husband and wife. We declare that God's commandment for His children to multiply and replenish the earth remains in force. We further declare that God has commanded that the sacred powers of procreation are to be employed only between man and woman, lawfully wedded as husband and wife.[1]

> The Bahá'í Teachings do not only encourage marital life, considering it the natural and normal way of existence for every sane, healthy and socially-conscious and responsible person, but raise marriage to the status of a Divine institution, its chief and sacred purpose being the perpetuation of the human race – which is the very flower of the entire creation – and its elevation to the true station destined for it by God.[2]

The relationship between husband and wife

The equality of women and men is a major tenet of the Bahá'í Faith, and so it is logical that the same equality governs the relationship between husband and wife:

> The principle of the equality of men and women is transforming relationships within Bahá'í marriages. Because they are equal partners, a status embodied in their identical wedding vows, neither husband nor wife may dominate. Decision-making is to be shared . . . Recognition of equality and the use of consultation allow a husband and wife flexibility to meet the demands of a rapidly changing world. Although men and women have complementary capacities and functions in certain areas, roles are not rigidly defined and may be adjusted, when necessary, to meet the needs of each family member and the family as a whole. While women are encouraged to pursue their careers, it is in a manner that does not conflict with their role as mothers. And fathers are not exempt from household duties and child-rearing.[3]

The LDS Church similarly teaches that husband and wife are equal partners whose duties may be adapted according to necessity. However, there are some important differences concerning the role of the father as patriarch of the family:

> By divine design, fathers are to preside over their families in love and righteousness and are responsible to provide the necessities of life and protection for their families. Mothers are primarily responsible for the nurture of their children. In these sacred responsibilities, fathers and mothers are obligated to help one another as equal partners. Disability, death, or other circumstances may necessitate individual adaptation.[4]

> In marriage neither the man nor the woman is more important than the other. They are equal partners and should work together to provide for the spiritual, emotional, intellectual, and physical needs of the family. . . The father is the patriarch of the family and has important responsibilities that are his alone. He is the priesthood holder and has the duties of priesthood leadership. He should guide his family with humility and kindness rather than with force or cruelty.[5]

On the surface, this statement shares some features with Bahá'í statements pertaining to the responsibilities of the father:

The House of Justice suggests that all statements in the Holy Writings concerning specific areas of the relationship between men and women should be considered in the light of the general principle of equality between the sexes that has been authoritatively and repeatedly enunciated in the Sacred Texts . . .

. . . The atmosphere within a Bahá'í family as within the community as a whole should express 'the keynote of the Cause of God' which, the beloved Guardian has stated, 'is not dictatorial authority, but humble fellowship, not arbitrary power, but the spirit of frank and loving consultation.'

A family, however, is a very special type of 'community'. The Research Department has not come across any statements which specifically name the father as responsible for the 'security, progress and unity of the family' . . . but it can be inferred from a number of the responsibilities placed on him, that the father can be regarded as the 'head' of the family.[6]

However, when we take a closer look at the LDS statement, we discover that the equality it professes is incomplete. According to Mormon doctrine, the 'priesthood leadership' confers upon the man – and the man alone – the ability to receive personal revelation through the Holy Spirit concerning the proper direction of his family, and although he may (and should) consult his wife, she is ultimately expected to defer to his guidance. Any equality enjoyed by the woman is therefore given to her through the man's desire to be a good husband, and not inherently through her rights as a human being. On the other hand, it could be argued that any husband who makes appropriate use of his priesthood blessings to receive divine inspiration will naturally ensure the equal treatment of his wife.

Spiritual education of children

The teachings of the LDS Church and the Bahá'í Faith are remarkably similar with regard to the spiritual education of children, beginning with the fact that such education is considered a sacred obligation on the part of both parents. According to the Bahá'í Writings,

It is the bounden duty of parents to rear their children to be staunch in faith . . . For every praiseworthy deed is born out of the light of religion, and lacking this supreme bestowal the child will not turn away from any evil, nor will he draw nigh unto any good.[7]

While for the LDS Church,

Parents have a sacred duty to rear their children in love and righteousness, to provide for their physical and spiritual needs, to teach them to love and serve one another, to observe the commandments of God and to be law-abiding citizens wherever they live. Husbands and wives – mothers and fathers – will be held accountable before God for the discharge of these obligations.[8]

The LDS Church stipulates that mothers should teach their children the gospel and allow their discovery through play:

A mother needs to spend time with her children and teach them the gospel. She should play and work with them so they can discover the world around them.[9]

'Abdu'l-Bahá similarly taught that mothers should pay attention to their young children's spiritual and moral education, and allow them to learn through play and experience:

The infant, while yet a suckling, must receive Bahá'í training, and the loving spirit of Christ and Bahá'u'lláh must be breathed into him, that he may be reared in accord with the verities of the Gospel and the Most Holy Book.[10]

Beginning in childhood they must receive instruction. They cannot be taught through books. Many elementary sciences must be made clear to them in the nursery; they must learn them in play, in amusement. Most ideas must be taught them through speech, not by book learning.[11]

Both faiths also agree that the best way for parents to teach their children virtues is by setting the example. The LDS Church teaches:

One of the best ways parents can teach their children is by example. Husbands and wives should show love and respect for each other and for their children by both actions and words . . . Parents can provide an atmosphere of reverence and respect in the home if they teach and guide their children with love. Parents should also provide happy experiences for their children.[12]

While 'Abdu'l-Bahá writes:

In this glorious Cause the life of a married couple should resemble the life of the angels in heaven – a life full of joy and spiritual delight, a life of unity and concord, a friendship both mental and physical. The home should be orderly and well-organized . . . Even as two birds they should warble melodies upon the branches of the tree of fellowship and harmony. They should always be elated with joy and gladness and a source of happiness to the hearts of others. They should set an example to their fellow-men, manifest true and sincere love towards each other and educate their children in such a manner as to blazon the fame and glory of their family.[13]

Parents should lovingly and patiently guide their children through the inevitable mistakes:

Parents should understand that sometimes children will make wrong choices even after they have been taught the truth. When this happens, parents should not give up or become discouraged. They should continue to teach their children, to express love for them, to be good examples to them, and to fast and pray for them.[14]

Ye should consider the question of goodly character as of the first importance. It is incumbent upon every father and mother to counsel their children over a long period, and guide them unto these things which lead to everlasting honour.[15]

. . . The child must not be oppressed or censured because it is undeveloped; it must be patiently trained.[16]

Finally, children should be raised with love, kindness and discipline:

Whensoever a mother seeth that her child hath done well, let her praise and applaud him and cheer his heart; and if the slightest undesirable trait should manifest itself, let her counsel the child and punish him, and use means based on reason, even a slight verbal chastisement should this be necessary. It is not, however, permissible to strike a child, or vilify him, for the child's character will be totally perverted if he be subjected to blows or verbal abuse.[17]

It is important to remember that each member of the family is a child of God. Parents should treat their children with love and respect, being firm but kind to them.[18]

Bahá'í parents cannot simply adopt an attitude of non-resistance towards their children, particularly those who are unruly and violent by nature. It is not even sufficient that they should pray on their behalf. Rather they should endeavour to inculcate, gently and patiently, into their youthful minds such principles of moral conduct and initiate them into the principles and teachings of the Cause with such tactful and loving care as would enable them to become 'true sons of God' and develop into loyal and intelligent citizens of His Kingdom.[19]

The role of the father

Although the Bahá'í Faith teaches that the roles of fathers and mothers 'are not rigidly defined and may be adjusted,' there are nevertheless certain duties specifically enjoined on the father, and his failure to fulfill those duties carries with it dire consequences:

The father must always endeavor to educate his son and to acquaint him with the heavenly teachings. He must give him advice and exhort him at all times, teach him praiseworthy conduct and character and enable him to receive training at school and to be instructed in such arts and sciences as are deemed useful and necessary. In brief, let him instill into his mind the virtues and perfections of the world of humanity. Above all he should continually call to his mind the remembrance of God so that his throbbing veins and arteries may pulsate with the love of God.[20]

. . . the father also has the responsibility of educating his children, and this responsibility is so weighty that Bahá'u'lláh has stated that a father who fails to exercise it forfeits his rights of fatherhood.[21]

The above quotations compare favorably with the following statement from *Gospel Principles*:

The father should spend time with each child individually. He should teach his children correct principles, talk with them about their problems and concerns, and counsel them lovingly.[22]

Furthermore, the teachings of both faiths place the primary responsibility for the material support of the family on the father, while allowing flexibility in the actual division of labor between husband and wife:

. . . although the primary responsibility for supporting the family financially is placed upon the husband, this does not by any means imply that
the place of women is confined to the home.[23]

It is also the father's duty to provide for the physical needs of his family,
making sure they have the necessary food, housing, clothing, and education. Even if he is unable to provide all the support himself, he does not
give up the responsibility of the care of his family.[24]

With regard to your question whether mothers should work outside the
home, it is helpful to consider the matter from the perspective of the concept of a Bahá'í family. This concept is based on the principle that the
man has primary responsibility for the financial support of the family,
and the woman is the chief and primary educator of the children. This
by no means implies that these functions are inflexibly fixed and cannot
be changed and adjusted to suit particular family situations, nor does it
mean that the place of the woman is confined to the home. Rather, while
primary responsibility is assigned, it is anticipated that the fathers would
play a significant role in the education of the children and women could
also be breadwinners.[25]

The role of the mother

The LDS Church promotes the model of a traditional family where the husband is the breadwinner and the wife stays at home with the children. In
the Bahá'í Faith, the principle of gender equality requires that husband and
wife consult together on the best way for the family to earn money and raise
spiritual children, with the result that parental roles are not simply divided
along gender lines. However, there are a number of statements in the Bahá'í
Writings that clearly recognize the special strengths and abilities with which
mothers are inherently endowed.

The noblest calling

Both faiths unhesitatingly declare motherhood to be the noblest calling, car-
rying with it the greatest blessings, as well as the greatest responsibility:

. . . motherhood is woman's noblest calling . . . A mother's most important
responsibility is to bring children into the world and to care for and teach
them. Bearing children is one of the greatest of all blessings.[26]

O ye loving mothers, know ye that in God's sight, the best of all ways to worship Him is to educate the children and train them in all the perfections of humankind; and no nobler deed than this can be imagined.[27]

The task of bringing up a Bahá'í child, as emphasized time and again in Bahá'í writings, is the chief responsibility of the mother, whose unique privilege is indeed to create in her home such conditions as would be most conducive to both his material and spiritual welfare and advancement.[28]

To the mothers must be given the divine Teachings and effective counsel, and they must be encouraged and made eager to train their children, for the mother is the first educator of the child. It is she who must, at the very beginning, suckle the new-born at the breast of God's Faith and God's Law, that divine love may enter him even with his mother's milk, and be with him till his final breath.[29]

The Bahá'í Writings further make clear that homemaking is 'of fundamental importance for mankind,' and just as honorable and potentially fulfilling as any other career:

You ask about the admonition that everyone must work, and want to know if this means that you, a wife and mother, must work for a livelihood as your husband does. . . . You will see that the directive is for the friends to be engaged in an occupation which will be of benefit to mankind. Homemaking is a highly honourable and responsible work of fundamental importance for mankind.[30]

O maidservants of the Merciful! It is incumbent upon you to train the children from their earliest babyhood: It is incumbent upon you to beautify their morals! It is incumbent upon you to attend to them under all aspects and circumstances, inasmuch as God – glorified and exalted is He! – hath ordained mothers to be the primary trainers of children and infants. This is a great and important affair and a high and exalted position, and it is not allowable to slacken therein at all!

If thou walkest in this right path, thou wouldst become a real mother to the children, both spiritually and materially.[31]

Women beyond the home

Although the Bahá'í teachings describe motherhood as 'the best of all ways to worship' God, and homemaking as 'a highly honourable and responsible work of fundamental importance,' this in no way implies that women should be confined to the home or limited in their function to that of wife and mother:

> It is not the Bahá'í view, however, that women are to be considered important only in relationship to the rearing of children and attending to the duties of the household. The importance placed on the education of women in the Bahá'í faith is intended to bring about the equality of men and women.[32]

As this statement suggests, the equality of men and women is advanced through the education of women, and inversely, one of the purposes of universal education is so women can become equal participants in society. In 1913 – as women were beginning to win the right to vote in country after country – 'Abdu'l-Bahá proclaimed the full and equal involvement of women in all areas of life:

> In this Revelation of Bahá'u'lláh, the women go neck and neck with the men. In no movement will they be left behind. Their rights with men are equal in degree. They will enter all the administrative branches of politics. They will attain in all such a degree as will be considered the very highest station of the world of humanity and will take part in all affairs. Rest ye assured. Do ye not look upon the present conditions; in the not far distant future the world of women will become all-refulgent and all-glorious, *For His Holiness Bahá'u'lláh Hath Willed It so!* At the time of elections the right to vote is the inalienable right of women, and the entrance of women into all human departments is an irrefutable and incontrovertible question. No soul can retard or prevent it.[33]

It is noteworthy that the territory of Utah (which the LDS Church largely controlled) gave women the right to vote as early as 1870 – a half century before this right was enshrined in the US Constitution by the 19th Amendment. It was only the second territory to do so (after Wyoming) in a time when no American states permitted women to vote. Sarah Young, the grandniece of Brigham Young, allegedly was the first Utah woman to vote in a municipal election. Ironically, the Edmunds–Tucker Act, passed by the US Congress to end Mormon polygamy, rescinded Utah women's right to vote in 1887. It was not restored until Utah gained statehood in 1895.[34]

Women's suffrage notwithstanding, Mormon doctrine teaches that a woman's ultimate and divinely ordained purpose is to be a mother to her children and a helpmeet to her husband. The official church curriculum guidebook for women, *The Latter-day Saint Woman*, warns that professional involvements outside the home could lead to the disintegration of the family:

> Satan seeks to break apart the home and family. One of his many devices is to challenge the role the Lord has given to women. 'Satan and his cohorts … lure women away from their primary responsibilities as wives, mothers, and homemakers' (N. Eldon Tanner, in Conference Report, Oct. 1973, 124; or *Ensign*, Jan. 1974, 7). [35]

While Bahá'ís agree that women should 'pursue their careers . . . in a manner that does not conflict with their role as mothers,'[36] it is another thing entirely to place a woman's desire to fulfill her God-given potential in the context of Satanic temptation. The above excerpt from *The Latter-day Saint Woman* cites a 1973 conference talk by N. Eldon Tanner, who at that time occupied the second-highest office in the LDS Church. While these remarks were made over thirty years ago, the fact that they are quoted in a recently revised (as of 2000) church manual indicates that they are still considered doctrinally valid. The following is a more complete quotation of President Tanner's remarks:

> What woman could want any greater glory or tribute than that which comes from an appreciative and loving husband? The applause and homage of the world fades into insignificance when compared with the approbation of God and expressions of love and appreciation which come from the hearts and lips of those who are nearest and dearest to her.
>
> From the beginning God has made it clear that woman is very special, and he has also very clearly defined her position, her duties, and her destiny in the divine plan. Paul said that man is the image and glory of God, and that woman is the glory of the man; also that the man is not without the woman, neither the woman without the man in the Lord. (See 1 Cor. 11:7, 11.) You will note that significantly God is mentioned in connection with this great partnership, and we must never forget that one of woman's greatest privileges, blessings, and opportunities is to be a co-partner with God in bringing his spirit children into the world.
>
> It is of great concern to all who understand this glorious concept that Satan and his cohorts are using scientific arguments and nefarious propaganda to lure women away from their primary responsibilities as wives,

mothers, and homemakers. We hear so much about emancipation, independence, sexual liberation, birth control, abortion, and other insidious
propaganda belittling the role of motherhood, all of which is Satan's way of
destroying woman, the home, and the family – the basic unit of society.[37]

President Tanner's suggestion that a woman's identity is defined solely in relation to her husband and children fails to acknowledge her right to pursue her
personal dreams and ambitions as well as her responsibility to contribute to
the wider society. 'Abdu'l-Bahá is unequivocal in this regard:

> So it will come to pass that when women participate fully and equally in
> the affairs of the world, when they enter confidently and capably the great
> arena of laws and politics, war will cease . . .[38]

Secondly, the inference that women, once given independence, will somehow
gravitate toward inappropriate behavior cannot be justified on any moral or
scientific grounds.

Bahá'ís, along with the majority of Western society, would seriously
challenge the notion that the emancipation of women engenders sexual
promiscuity, abortion or other social ills. Quite the opposite can be argued:
women who are educated and actively engaged in society gain self-confidence,
and thus have no need to seek validation through casual sexual encounters.
Scientific studies further show that educated women are much less likely to
engage in the kind of risky behavior that would result in unwanted pregnancy.
Moreover, Bahá'ís do not consider a woman's professional aspirations to be
incompatible with motherhood or a healthy family life. On the contrary, it
stands to reason that a woman who is spiritually and emotionally fulfilled
makes for a better mother and wife. But how can women pursue careers or
other occupations while they are mothers? That question is best answered with
another question: 'How can men pursue careers or other occupations while
they are fathers?' Somehow, women are still expected to perform most of the
childrearing and household duties in addition to their jobs outside the home
– the so-called 'double shift.' The Bahá'í teachings, on the other hand, clarify
that it is the duty of both spouses to support each other in all their endeavors,
be they inside or outside the home.

The role of the children

Family responsibilities are not limited to the parents. Children have a vested
interest in the success of the family, and are therefore expected to share in

responsibilities to preserve family unity, and to help in the general mainte-
nance of the home. By obeying their parents and doing chores around the
house, children learn to obey God and to serve mankind. The church curriculum book *Gospel Principles* states:

> Children share with their parents the responsibilities of building a happy
> home. They should obey the commandments and cooperate with other
> family members . . . The Lord has commanded children to obey their
> parents . . . [C]hildren should learn to work and share responsibilities in
> the home and yard. They should be given assignments to keep the house
> neat and clean . . . A loving and happy family does not happen by accident.
> Each person in the family must do his or her part . . . The scriptures teach
> that we must be thoughtful, cheerful, and considerate of others. When we
> speak, pray, sing, or work together, we can enjoy the blessings of harmony
> in our families.[39]

Along the same lines, 'Abdu'l-Bahá identified some of the duties of children,
and urged parents to 'accustom them to hardship.' By this is not meant that
children should be deprived of food or other necessities; rather, it means that
children should be taught about work, sacrifice, and detachment from the
excesses of a decadent society:

> There are also certain sacred duties of children toward parents, which
> duties are written in the Book of God, as belonging to God. The (chil-
> dren's) prosperity in this world and the Kingdom depends upon the good
> pleasure of parents, and without this they will be in manifest loss.[40]

> The son . . . must show forth the utmost obedience towards his father,
> and should conduct himself as a humble and lowly servant. Day and night
> he should seek diligently to ensure the comfort and welfare of his loving
> father and to secure his good-pleasure. He must forgo his own rest and
> enjoyment, and constantly strive to bring gladness to the hearts of his
> father and mother, that thereby he may attain the good-pleasure of the
> Almighty and be graciously aided by the hosts of the unseen.[41]

> While the children are yet in their infancy feed them from the breast of
> heavenly grace, foster them in the cradle of all excellence, rear them in
> the embrace of bounty. Give them the advantage of every useful kind of
> knowledge. Let them share in every new and rare and wondrous craft and
> art. Bring them up to work and strive, and accustom them to hardship.

Teach them to dedicate their lives to matters of great import, and inspire them to undertake studies that will benefit mankind.[42]

* * *

It is clear that the Mormon and Bahá'í views on the family are similar in many ways. Yet Bahá'ís also believe that Bahá'u'lláh has brought new teachings which do not necessarily lend themselves to a direct comparison with other religions. Bahá'í marriage is described as a 'fortress for well-being and salvation,'[43] and the Bahá'í family is viewed not only in terms of the basic building block of society, but also as a divinely ordained institution of the Faith that constitutes the bedrock of the Bahá'í Administrative Order. This has many implications that are beyond the scope of this book, and even further beyond my ability to adequately convey. For an in-depth discussion of this topic, I refer the interested reader to *Bahá'í Families* by Patricia Wilcox.

CHAPTER 8

ACTS OF WORSHIP

Bahá'ís and Mormons share a dedication to daily worship and complete obedience to God's commandments. As we shall see, the similarities also extend into the outward observances of both faith groups.

Prayer

Like the followers of most other faiths, Bahá'ís and Latter-day Saints are told to pray every day. For Bahá'ís, this daily requirement is set forth explicitly in the Kitáb-i-Aqdas – the book of Bahá'í laws – and Bahá'u'lláh revealed three *obligatory prayers* specifically for this purpose. For Mormons, Joseph Smith revealed a number of commandments to pray regularly, although no specific frequency is enjoined. Most make it a habit to offer their supplications at least once or twice each day.

Mormons who are learning about the Bahá'í Faith may take issue with the fact that Bahá'ís primarily recite prayers from a prayer book. There is a perception on the part of Latter-day Saints that it is better if the prayer comes 'from the heart' instead of out of a book. Mormon children are taught how to pray this way from a very early age, although in practice it often comes across as somewhat formulaic and rushed.

There are at least three possible responses to Mormon criticisms about the Bahá'í prayers:

(a) Bahá'ís are not required to read from a prayer book, and pray in many different ways depending on the circumstances.

(b) However, as the revealed Word of God, these 'book' prayers have a special potency that we ourselves cannot duplicate. Shoghi Effendi has indicated that 'prayer can be purely spontaneous, but many of the sentences and thoughts combined in Bahá'í writings of a devotional nature are easy to grasp, and the revealed Word is endowed with a power of its own.'[1]

(c) Without proper guidance, people don't always know what to pray for. For example, most people only pray on behalf of their loved ones, and rarely for their own spiritual advancement. Many of the Bahá'í prayers were specifically revealed to aid us in our spiritual growth and bring us nearer to God. Furthermore, Mormons recognize at least three revealed prayers of their own: the Lord's Prayer, a short prayer recited during the sacrament,[2] and a long Dedicatory Prayer recited at temple dedications.[3] While the first of these three is common to all Christian churches, the latter two are unique to the Mormon faith and can be likened to the Bahá'í 'occasional prayers.' Once this connection has been made, it can be explained that the Bahá'í revealed prayers simply span a wider range of occasions.

Fasting

Most world religions have enjoined a fast on their adherents. However, while the New Testament mentions fasting, it contains no specific guidance on how this form of worship should be practiced. This has resulted in each Christian denomination making up its own rules about fasting, and has caused most to have no prescribed fast at all. Of course, the Catholic Church observes Lent, a kind of fast during which one abstains from certain kinds of food, and other churches have their own unique variations on that theme. The LDS Church is one of the few Christian churches that specifically command a fast requiring complete abstinence from food and drink for a fixed time. Even so, the details of fasting are not set down in its original scriptures, but have been defined in later years.

While the times of fasting are different between the Mormon and Bahá'í faiths, the reasons for fasting, as well as the rules and exemptions, are quite similar.

The Mormon Fast

The fast observed by Latter-day Saints differs from that prescribed by Islam and the Bahá'í Faith in that it is not observed during a specific time of the year. (The Islamic fast, observed during the month of Ramadan, occurs at different times of the solar calendar year, but its timing is fixed relative to the Muslim lunar calendar.) Instead, Mormons fast one day each month by skipping two meals, usually breakfast and lunch:

One Sunday each month Latter-day Saints observe a fast day. On this day we neither eat nor drink for two consecutive meals, thus making a fast of twenty-four hours. If we were to eat our evening meal on Saturday, then we would not eat or drink until the evening meal on Sunday. Everyone who can do so should fast. However, 'many are subject to weakness, others are delicate in health, and others have nursing babies; of such it should not be required to fast. Neither should parents compel their little children to fast.'[4]

This fast is somewhat akin to the Jewish fast on the Day of Atonement (*Yom Kippur*), although the twenty-four hour period is not nearly as rigorously observed. Since there is no strict requirement to wait until sunset to serve dinner after the two missed meals, the Sunday dinner is usually served in the late afternoon or early evening. All Latter-day Saints observe the fast on the same day, typically the first Sunday of the month. An exception can occur if that day is taken up by 'conference' – when the church leadership holds a televised conference consisting of speeches and a musical program – in which case the fasting day is moved to an adjacent Sunday.

Part and parcel of the LDS fast is the *fast offering*. Each month, Mormons are expected to donate the cost of two skipped meals to their ward's local fund. This is primarily to help LDS families in need, but can be used at the discretion of the ward bishop.

The Bahá'í Fast

In the Bahá'í Fast, nineteen fasting days are observed consecutively – as opposed to twelve days spread throughout the year – during which eating and drinking are forbidden from sunrise until sunset. This fasting month (a Bahá'í month comprising 19 days) is comparable to the Muslim month of Ramadan, although it is shorter and always occurs during the same time of the solar year, leading up to the vernal equinox.

The Bahá'í and Mormon rules of fasting are similar in the kinds of exemptions they allow, such as in the case of illness, pregnancy or nursing mothers. This should not be surprising, since these exemptions are mostly based on common sense. However, the Bahá'í Fast does provide an additional exemption for travelers:

The traveller, the ailing, those who are with child or giving suck, are not bound by the Fast; they have been exempted by God as a token of His grace.[5]

Finally, the Bahá'í Fast is enjoined only upon healthy individuals between the ages of 15 and 70:

We have commanded you to pray and fast from the beginning of maturity; this is ordained by God, your Lord and the Lord of your forefathers. He hath exempted from this those who are weak from illness or age, as a bounty from His Presence, and He is the Forgiving, the Generous.[6]

The blessings and purpose of fasting

The Bahá'í and LDS teachings describe the purpose of fasting in similar terms, and extol its many blessings. The LDS *Gospel Principles* state:

Occasional fasting is good for our bodies and helps our minds become more active . . . Fasting helps us gain strength of character . . . When we fast properly, we will learn to control our appetites, our passions, and our tempers . . . When we fast wisely and prayerfully, we develop our faith. With that faith we will have greater spiritual power.[7]

And 'Abdu'l-Bahá wrote to a Bahá'í community:

Ye had written of the fasting month. Fortunate are ye to have obeyed the commandment of God, and kept this fast during the holy season. For this material fast is an outer token of the spiritual fast; it is a symbol of self-restraint, the withholding of oneself from all appetites of the self, taking on the characteristics of the spirit, being carried away by the breathings of heaven and catching fire from the love of God.[8]

Every Sunday is holy to Mormons (it is commonly referred to as the Sabbath), but Fast Sundays are even more so. It is a day of strengthening one's faith, and it is the only day on which any member of the ward is allowed to come forward in the sacrament meeting to give his or her testimony.

Latter-day Saints are proud of their fasting tradition, and will undoubtedly express a sincere interest in learning about the Bahá'í Fast once they hear of it. It is one of the many subjects that can be used as an effective conversation-starter between a Bahá'í and a Mormon.

Daily reading of scripture

The reading of Holy Scripture plays an important role in the lives of Mormons and Bahá'ís alike. While the two religions differ on what is considered scripture, the practice of daily reading and the reasons for doing so are quite similar.

The Bahá'í scriptures

Bahá'ís are required to recite, or read out loud, the Sacred Writings twice each day: once in the morning, and once in the evening. However, the length of the passage is not important. Even a single sentence will suffice, provided it is read 'with joy and radiance' and duly reflected upon:

> Recite ye the verses of God every morn and eventide. Whoso faileth to recite them hath not been faithful to the Covenant of God and His Testament, and whoso turneth away from these holy verses in this Day is of those who throughout eternity have turned away from God . . . Pride not yourselves on much reading of the verses or on a multitude of pious acts by night and day; for were a man to read a single verse with joy and radiance it would be better for him than to read with lassitude all the Holy Books of God, the Help in Peril, the Self-Subsisting. Read ye the sacred verses in such measure that ye be not overcome by languor and despondency. Lay not upon your souls that which will weary them and weigh them down, but rather what will lighten and uplift them, so that they may soar on the wings of the Divine verses towards the Dawning-place of His manifest signs; this will draw you nearer to God, did ye but comprehend.[9]

In its widest possible interpretation, 'the verses of God' might include the Holy Books of every religion – such as the Bible, the Qur'án, the Bhagavad-Gita, the Dhammapada, the Bayán and the Writings of Bahá'u'lláh – all of which are considered by Bahá'ís to be the 'Word of God.' Unverifiable traditions such as the Islamic *hadith* are generally excluded from this definition; however, the epistles of Paul and the other New Testament authors are not treated differently from the four main Gospels.

While the divine Source of these texts is unequivocally confirmed, and all of them are considered equally valid, a distinction is nevertheless made as to their literal accuracy and the power vested in the words themselves. Addressing a perceived inconsistency between the Bible and the Words of Bahá'u'lláh, Shoghi Effendi indicated:

> As to the question raised . . . in connection with Bahá'u'lláh's statement in the *Gleanings* concerning the sacrifice of Ishmael; although His statement does not agree with that made in the Bible, Genesis 12:9, the friends should unhesitatingly, and for reasons that are only too obvious, give precedence to the sayings of Bahá'u'lláh which, it would be pointed out, is fully corroborated by the Qur'án, which book is more authentic than the Bible, including both the New and Old Testaments. The Bible is not wholly

authentic, and in this respect not to be compared with the Qur'án, and should be wholly subordinated to the authentic Sayings of Bahá'u'lláh.[10]

It should not be surprising that those Books which were not committed to writing until long after their divine Authors had left this world, and which subsequently sustained multiple translations and manual transcriptions, may lack some of the outward qualities of those which were dictated or penned directly by the Manifestation Himself. The Writings of the Báb and Bahá'u'lláh are characterized by historical recency, literal accuracy, relevance to the issues facing the world today, a unique directness among all Holy Scriptures owing to a lack of 'veiled' language, as well as a power and influence inherent in the choice and placement of the words themselves. In fact, Bahá'u'lláh promises that the act of reciting these verses has an invisible influence far beyond the ken of the reader:

> Intone, O My servant, the verses of God that have been received by thee, as intoned by them who have drawn nigh unto Him, that the sweetness of thy melody may kindle thine own soul, and attract the hearts of all men. Whoso reciteth, in the privacy of his chamber, the verses revealed by God, the scattering angels of the Almighty shall scatter abroad the fragrance of the words uttered by his mouth, and shall cause the heart of every righteous man to throb. Though he may, at first, remain unaware of its effect, yet the virtue of the grace vouchsafed unto him must needs sooner or later exercise its influence upon his soul. Thus have the mysteries of the Revelation of God been decreed by virtue of the Will of Him Who is the Source of power and wisdom.[11]

Bahá'u'lláh often uses the term 'verses of God' to refer to His own Writings, and makes a connection between this term and the words that issue directly from the pen of a Manifestation of God. In the Kitáb-i-Aqdas, the same term is equated with 'Divine Utterance':

> With regard to the definition of 'verses of God', Bahá'u'lláh states that it refers to 'all that hath been sent down from the Heaven of Divine Utterance'. Shoghi Effendi, in a letter written to one of the believers in the East, has clarified that the term 'verses of God' does not include the writings of 'Abdu'l-Bahá; he has likewise indicated that this term does not apply to his own writings.[12]

As the above note indicates, the writings of 'Abdu'l-Bahá – while believed to be endued with a special power – do not satisfy the Bahá'í requirement for daily reading of scripture. This sets the bar very high, and it would be difficult for a Bahá'í to maintain that the writings of Paul the Apostle, inspired as they were, should occupy a loftier position than the words of 'Abdu'l-Bahá. The 'verses of God' recited daily by Bahá'ís, therefore, are generally limited to the Writings of the Báb and Bahá'u'lláh, and do not include the Bible or scriptures of other religions.

In contrast, texts that are read during the devotional portion of the Nineteen Day Feast, while chiefly from the Writings of the Báb and Bahá'u'lláh, may be taken from any of the Holy Books, as well as from the writings of 'Abdu'l-Bahá.[13]

The LDS scriptures

From early childhood on, Mormons are taught to read the scriptures every day. One children's course teaches:

> Just as your body needs to be fed every day to keep it strong and healthy, your spirit needs daily nourishment to be strong and to stay close to Heavenly Father. One way to do this is by reading the scriptures.[14]

A church magazine article links this 'daily nourishment' to the 'bread of life' that is the Word of God:

> When the Savior showed his disciples how to pray, he included the plea, 'Give us this day our daily bread' (Matt. 6:11). With this supplication, Jesus Christ reminded us of our daily dependence on our Heavenly Father for all the good things of the earth which were 'made for the benefit and the use of man, both to please the eye and to gladden the heart;
>
> 'Yea, for food and for raiment, for taste and for smell, to strengthen the body and to enliven the soul' (D&C 59:18-19).
>
> Like physical nourishment, spiritual food is a gift that comes from God. The Lord explained:
>
> 'I am the bread of life: he that cometh to me shall never hunger; and he that believeth on me shall never thirst' (John 6:35).
>
> As we follow the Savior, we need to recognize that both our bodies and our spirits are nourished and strengthened by our Heavenly Father's bounty – and that both require daily attention and care.[15]

The idea of bread as a spiritual metaphor representing divine revelation reflects an important theme in the Bahá'í Writings:

That which is preeminent above all other gifts, is incorruptible in nature, and pertaineth to God Himself, is the gift of Divine Revelation. Every bounty conferred by the Creator upon man, be it material or spiritual, is subservient unto this. It is, in its essence, and will ever so remain, the Bread which cometh down from Heaven. It is God's supreme testimony, the clearest evidence of His truth, the sign of His consummate bounty, the token of His all-encompassing mercy, the proof of His most loving providence, the symbol of His most perfect grace. He hath, indeed, partaken of this highest gift of God who hath recognized His Manifestation in this Day.[16]

With respect to daily reading requirements, the LDS definition of 'scriptures' encompasses the Old and New Testaments of the Bible, *The Book of Mormon*, *The Doctrine and Covenants* and *The Pearl of Great Price*. In its broadest definition, this may also include the writings of current and past presidents of the Church, who are considered prophets, and whose writings are believed to have the same authority as the Bible. However, for Mormons the term 'scriptures' generally refers to the aforementioned five books.

Like Bahá'ís, Mormons tend to focus more of their attention on 'latter-day' scriptures than on the Old and New Testaments, and for many of the same reasons. Many verses from these older books were elucidated by Joseph Smith and later presidents of the Church, and the Book of Mormon provides an entirely new perspective on both the historical and the spiritual content of the Bible. Nevertheless, the Christian Bible still remains one of the cornerstones of the Mormon faith and is quoted copiously in books and lessons.

Planting the seed of the Word of God in our hearts

The Mormon and Bahá'í scriptures each describe the Word of God as a seed which is planted in our hearts, and which must be given time and nourishment in order to grow and bear the fruit of faith. Bahá'u'lláh counsels us:

O My Brother! Hearken to the delightsome words of My honeyed tongue, and quaff the stream of mystic holiness from My sugar-shedding lips. Sow the seeds of My divine wisdom in the pure soil of thy heart, and water them with the water of certitude, that the hyacinths of My knowledge and wisdom may spring up fresh and green in the sacred city of thy heart.[17]

Incline your hearts, O people of God, unto the counsels of your true, your incomparable Friend. The Word of God may be likened unto a sapling, whose roots have been implanted in the hearts of men. It is incumbent upon you to foster its growth through the living waters of wisdom, of sanctified and holy words, so that its root may become firmly fixed and its branches may spread out as high as the heavens and beyond.[18]

The following excerpt from the Book of Mormon offers a similar analogy:

Now, we will compare the word unto a seed. Now, if ye give place, that a seed may be planted in your heart, behold, if it be a true seed, or a good seed, if ye do not cast it out by your unbelief, that ye will resist the Spirit of the Lord, behold, it will begin to swell within your breasts; and when you feel these swelling motions, ye will begin to say within yourselves – It must needs be that this is a good seed, or that the word is good, for it beginneth to enlarge my soul; yea, it beginneth to enlighten my understanding, yea, it beginneth to be delicious to me . . . And behold, as the tree beginneth to grow, ye will say: Let us nourish it with great care, that it may get root, that it may grow up, and bring forth fruit unto us. And now behold, if ye nourish it with much care it will get root, and grow up, and bring forth fruit. But if ye neglect the tree, and take no thought for its nourishment, behold it will not get any root; and when the heat of the sun cometh and scorcheth it, because it hath no root it withers away, and ye pluck it up and cast it out. Now, this is not because the seed was not good, neither is it because the fruit thereof would not be desirable; but it is because your ground is barren, and ye will not nourish the tree, therefore ye cannot have the fruit thereof. And thus, if ye will not nourish the word, looking forward with an eye of faith to the fruit thereof, ye can never pluck of the fruit of the tree of life. But if ye will nourish the word, yea, nourish the tree as it beginneth to grow, by your faith with great diligence, and with patience, looking forward to the fruit thereof, it shall take root; and behold it shall be a tree springing up unto everlasting life. And because of your diligence and your faith and your patience with the word in nourishing it, that it may take root in you, behold, by and by ye shall pluck the fruit thereof, which is most precious, which is sweet above all that is sweet, and which is white above all that is white, yea, and pure above all that is pure; and ye shall feast upon this fruit even until ye are filled, that ye hunger not, neither shall ye thirst. Then, my brethren, ye shall reap the rewards of your faith, and your diligence, and patience, and long-suffering, waiting for the tree to bring forth fruit unto you.[19]

Sacrament meetings and the Nineteen Day Feast

Mormons, like most other Christians, hold Sunday worship meetings, of which the *sacrament* is an integral part. In most Christian churches, however, the sacrament – also known as *communion* or *Eucharist* – refers to the spiritual 'consumption' of the body and blood of Christ, usually represented by bread and wine. The Mormon sacrament differs slightly in that it is taken 'in remembrance of' the body and blood of Christ, and uses water instead of wine.

There is nothing in the Bahá'í Faith that outwardly resembles the Christian sacrament, although 'Abdu'l-Bahá has likened the Nineteen Day Feast to the Lord's Supper in the spiritual sense:

> The feast (supper) [every nineteen days] is very acceptable and will finally produce good results. The beloved and the maid-servants of the Merciful must inaugurate the feast in such wise as to resurrect the feast of the ancients – namely, the 'lord's supper'.[20]

As we shall see, the LDS sacrament meeting and the Bahá'í Nineteen Day Feast, although they are quite different in nature and purpose, do share a number of features worth noting.

A typical day in the Mormon church

A Sunday at the Mormon church typically consists of a three-hour 'bloc' of worship and education, segmented as follows:[21]

- *Sacrament meeting – 1 hour 15 minutes.* The entire ward (congregation) gathers to pray, sing hymns and partake of the sacrament. Selected individuals also give talks on specific topics.
- *Sunday school – adults 45 minutes, children 1 hour 45 minutes.* A choice of classes is offered, including 'gospel essentials' (an introductory class for seekers and new members), 'gospel doctrine' (an in-depth bible study class) and children's classes separated by age group. All adult classes are open to both men and women. Children go to their respective classes immediately after the sacrament meeting. Young children attend mixed-gender classes, while the older children and youth are separated into boys and girls.
- *Priesthood and Relief Society meetings – 1 hour.* Adult church members split up according to gender and rank in the Church; women attend 'Relief Society' meetings, while men attend a short joint Priesthood meeting (called 'opening exercises'), after which they further break up into groups such as Elder's Quorum and High Priesthood.

The sacrament meeting

The Mormon sacrament meeting begins with what can be termed a devotional portion. This includes prayers and hymns, as well as the sacrament of bread and water. Sometimes guests, newcomers or seekers are asked to introduce themselves to the ward. On rare occasions, someone with a special musical talent is invited to share that gift with the congregation.

The devotional portion of the sacrament meeting is followed by something resembling a business portion, in which a member of the bishopric announces new *callings*, or service assignments. Each assignment is accepted, or *sustained*, by the entire congregation through a show of hands.[22] There is, however, no opportunity for consultation. After a calling is announced, ward members are asked to sustain it 'by the sign of the uplifted hand.' Next, any opposed are asked to 'manifest by the same sign.' This show of hands is little more than a formality as no one ever publicly challenges a calling or any other decision made by the ward leadership.

The rest of the meeting is taken up by prepared talks by adults, youth and children, as well as occasional choir performances and children's class presentations. (As mentioned earlier, an exception occurs on Fast Sundays, when prepared talks and presentations give way to ad hoc testimonies by the general membership.)

The entire sacrament meeting is open to non-Mormons, as long as they are 'earnest' seekers:

> And again I say unto you, ye shall not cast any out of your sacrament meetings who are earnestly seeking the kingdom – I speak this concerning those who are not of the church. And again I say unto you, concerning your confirmation meetings, that if there be any that are not of the church, that are earnestly seeking after the kingdom, ye shall not cast them out.[23]

The Nineteen Day Feast

Since the Bahá'í Feast is intended only for those who have accepted Bahá'u'lláh and are officially enrolled in the Faith, it is not appropriate to invite non-Bahá'ís to the Feast. The Nineteen Day Feast is a fundamental feature of Bahá'í administration, representing the one opportunity each month for the individual members of a local Bahá'í community to engage in open and frank consultation with each other and their elected Local Spiritual Assembly. During such consultation, involving various issues affecting the Faith and the community, recommendations are made to the Assembly, and the Assembly also delivers a financial report to the community.

With this in mind, the Nineteen Day Feast cannot really be compared to a traditional Christian Sunday worship gathering, and more closely resembles a private family meeting. Many families reserve a special night, usually once a month, in which parents and their children discuss important matters affecting only the nuclear family unit, such as finances, family unity, or the division of labor within the home. No one would consider inviting the neighbors to such a meeting, and even most grandparents would feel uncomfortable being privy to these discussions. By the same token, Bahá'ís are strongly discouraged from inviting non-Bahá'í family or friends to any portion of the Nineteen Day Feast. The Universal House of Justice has counseled:

> Regarding the Nineteen Day Feast, the principle universally applicable is that non-Bahá'ís are not invited to attend, and if you are asked about this you can explain that the nature of the Feast is essentially domestic and administrative. During the period of consultation the Bahá'ís should be able to enjoy perfect freedom to express their views on the work of the Cause, unembarrassed by the feeling that all they are saying is being heard by someone who has not accepted Bahá'u'lláh and who might thereby gain a very distorted picture of the Faith. It would also be very embarrassing for any sensitive non-Bahá'í to find himself plunged into the midst of a discussion of the detailed affairs of a Bahá'í community of which he is not a part. A non-Bahá'í who asks to be invited to a Feast will usually understand if this matter is explained to him.[24]

However, if non-Bahá'ís do show up at the Feast, they are not turned back, and most aspects of the Feast can continue unmodified:

> The sharing of local and national news and information about social events, as well as consultation on topics of general interest, such as expansion and the multiplication of core activities, service projects, the fund, and so on, can continue as usual, while discussion of sensitive or problematic issues can be set aside for another occasion when the friends can express themselves freely without being inhibited by the presence of guests.[25]

The distinction between a traditional church gathering and the Bahá'í Feast is anything but academic. Seekers often ask where and how Bahá'ís worship. If a seeker is led to believe that the Nineteen Day Feast is the Bahá'í equivalent of Sunday worship, problems arise as soon as that seeker expresses a desire to attend a Nineteen Day Feast so he or she can learn about the Faith. This inevitably requires an explanation that the Feast is only for Bahá'ís, which may then lead a person unfamiliar with the Faith to incorrectly conclude that Bahá'ís belong to an exclusive or secretive club.

Might there be a better answer to that question about Bahá'í worship practices? Is the Nineteen Day Feast, with its primary administrative function, really an appropriate Bahá'í analogy to the Christian Sunday worship service? Since the Universal House of Justice has identified devotional meetings as one of four core activities Bahá'ís should be engaged in throughout the world, would it not be more correct to say that Bahá'ís host devotional gatherings in many neighborhoods, in which people of diverse religious, cultural and ethnic backgrounds come together to worship God?

Partaking of the Mormon sacrament by non-members

As there is no consultation of any kind in the Mormon sacrament meeting, the presence of non-members there is not an issue. However, non-Mormons are not officially allowed to partake of the bread and water, although this rule is seldom enforced so as not to offend or alienate visitors. Bahá'ís visiting a Mormon church (and unaware of the rule regarding the sacrament) may feel compelled to partake of the sacrament so as not to offend their hosts. The proper thing to do, however, is simply to pass the tray of bread or water to the next person without taking any. Elder Loren C. Dun, answering a question from a youth in a church periodical, explains the LDS position as follows:

> One of the best opportunities for acquainting nonmembers with the spirit and teachings of the gospel is in our church meetings. As part of the non-member friendshiping responsibility each of us has, we should invite our friends and acquaintances to go with us to Sunday School and sacrament meeting as well as the appropriate auxiliary meetings. However, if the sacrament is to be passed, we should explain to the nonmember in advance that the sacrament is for members to renew the covenant of baptism that they made when they joined the Church. Since the nonmember has not yet been baptized, there is no need for him to take the sacrament. One could explain also that quite often we have nonmembers in our meetings, and of course, they don't take the sacrament either, so it is neither unusual nor embarrassing for someone not to take the sacrament.[26]

Tips for attending the Mormon church

Not just the sacrament meeting but the entire three-hour church session is open to non-Mormons. Visiting a Mormon church is a great way to 'consort with the followers' of another religion and advance the cross-pollination of spiritual thought, and it can be a truly rewarding experience. For those Bahá'ís (or other non-Mormons) planning to attend church, here is some general advice:

- On your first visit, it helps to go with a Mormon friend or neighbor. While this isn't required, everyone (especially you) will feel much more at ease when you're the guest of someone who is familiar with the church schedule and building layout. Keep in mind that in the third hour, the meetings are split up by gender. If your host is of the opposite sex, be sure to have him or her introduce you to a friend who can help you find your meeting room.

- During the administration of the sacrament, non-members may not partake of the sacramental bread and water, and should remain in a state of prayerful silence throughout the entire process.

- All non-members in attendance are assumed to be earnest seekers, or 'investigators,' of the Mormon faith. Questions and comments during the Bible study classes as well as the priesthood and Relief Society meetings will be welcomed, but should be offered in a humble posture of learning.

- In the third hour, women attend Relief Society while men join the priesthood meeting. After brief 'opening exercises' (a congregational hymn followed by announcements) the priesthood separates into two different meetings based on rank. At this point, adult men who are not members of the LDS church should join the Elder's Quorum, not the High Priesthood. To be sure you're going to the right place, introduce yourself to the group during the joint meeting – there is a special opportunity to do that – and request that someone show you the way. You'll have no trouble finding eager souls willing to be of assistance.

- On 'Fast Sundays' (usually the first Sunday of each month) both the Elder's Quorum and the High Priesthood break into committees to discuss the needs of specific individuals and families within the ward. Although you may be told there is no need to leave, it would be prudent for non-Mormons to excuse themselves from discussions of a personal nature.

Tithings and offerings

The word *tithe* literally means 'one-tenth,' as in donating one-tenth of one's income to a religious institution. Tithing was prescribed in the Old Testament, but few Christian denominations follow the rule as strictly as do Mormons.

It is considered a matter of course that all active members of the Church contribute ten per cent of their income, and the act of tithing is believed to bring many blessings.

There are a number of similarities between the Mormon tithe and the Bahá'í *Ḥuqúqu'lláh* (Right of God), including the notion that by obeying this law we will bless our affairs. There are also differences.

The Mormon tithe

The tithe is enjoined on all church members:

> And after that, those who have thus been tithed shall pay one-tenth of all their interest annually; and this shall be a standing law unto them forever, for my holy priesthood, saith the Lord. Verily I say unto you, it shall come to pass that all those who gather unto the land of Zion shall be tithed of their surplus properties, and shall observe this law, or they shall not be found worthy to abide among you.[27]

The term 'one-tenth of all their interest' has been interpreted as follows:

> A tithe is one-tenth of our increase. This means that we give one-tenth of all we earn before we pay for our own needs such as food, clothing, and shelter. If our increase is in the form of flocks, herds, or crops rather than money, we give one-tenth of those things.[28]

In other words, a proper tithe is calculated simply as ten per cent of income, before expenses. It is technically left up to the individual whether to calculate the tithe before or after income taxes, although few Mormons would admit to using the lesser amount.

While individual church members are not generally asked for their tithings, the issue does come up in the bishop's interview whenever someone requests permission to visit the Mormon temple or is about to receive an important calling in the ward. Regular tithing is considered one of the requirements for 'temple worthiness,' although this has not always been the case. The tithing requirement for receiving a 'temple recommend' was added in 1910 as a way to boost member participation in the tithe. Today, the Church of Jesus Christ of Latter-day Saints collects an estimated 4 to 5 billion dollars in annual tithing income.[29]

The Bahá'í Ḥuqúqu'lláh

Bahá'ís do not 'tithe' in the literal sense of the word, since that refers explicitly to a one-tenth fraction. Instead, Bahá'ís must pay *Ḥuqúqu'lláh* ('the Right of God'), which is defined as nineteen per cent of one's net worth *after expenses*. The Universal House of Justice clarified the calculation of Ḥuqúqu'lláh as follows:

> Your letter refers to basing the calculation of Ḥuqúqu'lláh on one's income. As you will realize from a study of the texts, however, the computation is made on the net value of one's possessions after deducting a number of exempt items such as residence and necessary furnishings, and on subsequent annual increases to this net property arising from surplus income after the payment of necessary expenses.[30]

> . . . whenever one's income, after all expenses have been paid, increases the value of one's possessions by the amount of at least nineteen mithqáls* of gold, one is to pay nineteen percent of this increase . . .[31]

In other words, the Ḥuqúqu'lláh is calculated based on the *increase in net worth* (or savings), and not on annual income. If one's net worth decreases or its increase does not meet a set minimum, nothing is owed. This ensures that one does not pay more than once for the same money earned, and that those who fall on financial hardship are not burdened even more. Also, there are specific expenses which, like income tax deductions, may be subtracted before calculating the Ḥuqúq. For example, the primary residence, including furnishings, is explicitly exempted. Some expenses incurred as part of generating income may be deducted, as well. Exactly what is covered by these exemptions is left up to the individual believer:

> There is, in fact, a vast range of expenditures which could, or could not, be included under the heading of normal annual expenses which are to be set against income before arriving at the sum assessable to Ḥuqúqu'lláh.[32]

> The devoted believer who is privileged to pay 'the right of God', far from seeking excuses for evading this spiritual obligation, will do his utmost to meet it. On the other hand, inasmuch as obedience to this Law is a matter

---

* A *mithqál* is a unit of measure common to 19th-century Persia, equaling 32.775g. or 0.1170823 troy oz.

of conscience, and payment of Ḥuqúqu'lláh is a voluntary act, it would not be seemly to go beyond informing the . . . friends of their spiritual obligation, and leaving to them to decide what they wish to do about it.

The same principle applies to those friends who spend lavishly on their families, who purchase or build residences and furnish them far in excess of their needs, and rationalize these expenditures in their desire to avoid payment of Ḥuqúqu'lláh.[33]

Whereas tithing is a requirement for temple worthiness in the LDS Church, Bahá'ís need not vouch for their obedience to the law of Ḥuqúqu'lláh in order to be permitted to go on pilgrimage. However, Bahá'u'lláh has clearly expressed His desire that His followers meet their obligations first:

Say: O people, the first duty is to recognize the one true God – magnified be His glory – the second is to show forth constancy in His Cause and, after these, one's duty is to purify one's riches and earthly possessions according to that which is prescribed by God. Therefore it beseemeth thee to meet thine obligation to the Right of God first, then to direct thy steps toward His blessed House. This hath been brought to thine attention as a sign of favour.[34]

The blessings of contributing a portion of our wealth

The Bahá'í law of Ḥuqúqu'lláh is believed to have far-reaching spiritual consequences well beyond those generally associated with the traditional tithe. However, there are strong similarities between the Mormon and Bahá'í teachings in terms of the blessings associated with income- or asset-based contributions. Bahá'u'lláh writes:

It is clear and evident that the payment of the Right of God is conducive to prosperity, to blessing, and to honour and divine protection.[35]

While in the LDS *Gospel Principles* we read:

The Lord promises to bless us as we faithfully pay our tithes and offerings . . .The blessings we have been promised are both material and spiritual. If we give willingly, Heavenly Father will provide our daily needs for food, clothes, and shelter . . . Those who pay their tithes and offerings are greatly blessed. They have a good feeling that they are helping to build the kingdom of God on earth.[36]

And Bahá'u'lláh again writes:

> Ḥuqúqu'lláh is indeed a great law. It is incumbent upon all to make this offering, because it is the source of grace, abundance, and of all good. It is a bounty which shall remain with every soul in every world of the worlds of God, the All-Possessing, the All-Bountiful.[37]

In order for these blessings to have their full effect, contributions must be offered not just willingly, but joyfully:

> When one pays his tithing without enjoyment he is robbed of a part of the blessing. He must learn to give cheerfully, willingly and joyfully, and his gift will be blessed.[38]

> It is incumbent upon everyone to discharge the obligation of Ḥuqúq. The advantages gained from this deed revert to the persons themselves. However, the acceptance of the offerings dependeth on the spirit of joy, fellowship and contentment that the righteous souls who fulfil this injunction will manifest. If such is the attitude acceptance is permissible, and not otherwise.[39]

The act of contributing a portion of our wealth to our faith is considered an act of faith in itself, and a sign of our love for God:

> When we pay tithing we show our faithfulness to the Lord. We also teach our children the value of this law. They will want to follow our example and pay tithing on any money they earn.[40]

> This weighty ordinance, as testified by the Pen of Glory is invested with incalculable benefit and wisdom. It purifies one's possessions, averts loss and disaster, conduces to prosperity and honour and imparts divine increase and blessing. It is a sacrifice offered for and related to God, and an act of servitude leading to the promotion of His Cause. As affirmed by the Centre of the Covenant, Ḥuqúq offerings constitute a test for the believers and enable the friends to become firm and steadfast in faith and certitude.[41]

I'm compelled at this point to recount a story of a personal nature, because it illustrates the true purpose of the tithe as well as the open-mindedness of some of the Mormon clergy. When my wife expressed her desire to pay a regular tithe so that she might be permitted to visit the temple, we decided to consult the ward bishop. Since Sharla did not receive a paycheck, we sought the bishop's guidance on what constituted a proper tithe when the primary breadwinner of the family was not a member of the Church. I explained that the Bahá'í Faith has an institution comparable to the tithe, and if one of the spouses is not a Bahá'í the payments may be based on half of the family's assets. Was there a similar provision in the LDS Church?

I must admit that I was not quite prepared for the bishop's answer. He replied that the tithe is how we show our obedience to the Lord, and that the act of paying the tithe is more important than where we send it, since it's all essentially going to the same place. Therefore, as long as I paid the full amount of Ḥuqúqu'lláh according to the conditions set by the Bahá'í Faith, he would consider that as satisfying the requirement for my wife's temple worthiness. Needless to say, this show of respect for my Faith left me deeply moved.

CHAPTER 9

TEACHING

Bahá'ís are continually reminded in their Sacred Writings of the overarching importance of teaching their Faith to others. To a Bahá'í, teaching is 'the most meritorious of all deeds,' the practice of which is no less a part of Bahá'í life than fasting and daily prayer. In this chapter, we will uncover various similarities as well as a few differences between Mormons and Bahá'ís on the subject of teaching.

Every believer is a teacher

Nearly everyone knows that Mormons use missionaries, both locally and abroad, to spread their faith. It is a lesser-known fact that this responsibility rests not just on 'official' missionaries, but also on every other member of the Church:

> Behold, I sent you out to testify and warn the people, and it becometh every man who hath been warned to warn his neighbor.[1]

> And again, I say unto you, I give unto you a commandment, that every man, both elder, priest, teacher, and also member, go to with his might, with the labor of his hands, to prepare and accomplish the things which I have commanded.[2]

> Every member of the Church is to be a missionary. We should be missionaries even if we are not formally called and set apart. We are responsible to teach the gospel by word and deed to all of our Heavenly Father's children.[3]

The First Presidency has re-emphasized this individual responsibility by publishing a handbook titled *Preach My Gospel*, and instructing local wards to focus on encouraging their members to reach out to friends, family, neighbors and co-workers.

Likewise, every Bahá'í has the sacred responsibility to teach others about the Bahá'í Faith:

Teach ye the Cause of God, O people of Bahá, for God hath prescribed unto everyone the duty of proclaiming His Message, and regardeth it as the most meritorious of all deeds.[4]

Indeed to bring this message to mankind in its darkest hour of need is the paramount duty of every believer. All the agony, the suffering, privation and spiritual blindness afflicting people today everywhere in the world, to a greater or lesser degree, is because they are unaware of, or indifferent to, the Remedy God has sent them. Only those who are aware of it can carry its healing knowledge to others, so that each Bahá'í has an inescapable and sacred duty to perform.[5]

Those who have attended training institutes will be able to help the other Bahá'ís, new and old, to increase their potential for teaching, and so to greatly increase the human resources of the Cause, in which every believer is a teacher.[6]

Much like Bahá'ís, Mormons reach out to others first by living an exemplary life, and then by engaging receptive individuals in earnest conversations about religion. However, once such an 'investigator' (the LDS term for 'seeker') begins to show a genuine interest in the Church, his Mormon teacher is keen to enlist the services of the full-time missionaries in order to confirm him.

A Bahá'í on the other hand would himself, in keeping with the counsel of Shoghi Effendi, continue to

capture the attention, maintain the interest, and deepen the faith, of those whom he seeks to bring into the fold of his Faith . . . until he has infused into his spiritual child so deep a longing as to impel him to arise inde-pendently, in his turn, and devote his energies to the quickening of other souls, and the upholding of the laws and principles laid down by his newly adopted Faith.[7]

The operative word is thus *accompaniment*, as the Bahá'í and his friend walk a path of service together until the new believer is able to 'arise independently' to teach the Faith to others.

Attitude for teaching

As we have seen, Mormon and Bahá'í ideas about the importance of teaching are quite similar. One of the few differences is merely semantic: whereas a Bahá'í would use the term 'teaching opportunity,' a Mormon would say 'missionary opportunity,' demonstrating that missionary activity in the Church encompasses a wide range of efforts to allow others to learn about Latter-day Saints. We will next explore some more of these parallels.

No time to lose

Mormons and Bahá'ís are driven to teach not only by a desire to share the gems of their faith with others, but also by a sober realization that the disintegration of social order in the world is accelerating day by day, and that humanity is desperately crying out for a remedy.

> What a responsibility we have! The whole fate of the world depends on us, according to the revelations of the Almighty. We cannot waste time. We cannot be unrighteous in our living. We cannot let our thoughts dwell on immoral things. We have to be the very best that we can be, you and I, because the very relationship of God our Eternal Father to His children on the earth depends on their accepting what we have come to teach according to His magnificent word.[8]

> Dear friends: That the forces of disintegration are gaining in range and power cannot be ignored. It is equally clear that the community of the Greatest Name has been guided from strength to strength by the Hand of Providence and must now increase in size and augment its resources. The course set by the Five Year Plan is straightforward. How can those of us aware of the plight of humanity, and conscious of the direction in which history is unfolding, not arise to the fullest of our capacity and dedicate ourselves to its aim?[9]

> There is no time to lose. There is no room left for vacillation. Multitudes hunger for the Bread of Life. The stage is set. The firm and irrevocable Promise is given. God's own Plan has been set in motion. It is gathering momentum with every passing day. The powers of heaven and earth mysteriously assist in its execution. Such an opportunity is irreplaceable. Let the doubter arise and himself verify the truth of such assertions. To try, to persevere, is to insure ultimate and complete victory.[10]

Assistance and guidance is assured

There is a shared understanding that our teaching efforts will not go unaided. However, this divine assistance is conditioned upon the teacher's deeds reflecting his words. The LDS Church teaches:

> If we have the Spirit of the Lord to guide us, we can teach any person, no matter how well educated, anyplace in the world. The Lord knows more than any of us, and if we are His servants, acting under His Spirit, He can deliver His message of salvation to each and every soul . . . Teaching by the Spirit requires first that we keep the commandments and be clean before God so His Spirit can dwell in our personal temples. This principle is taught in many scriptures, and it is taught by all the living prophets.[11]

A similar promise and warning are found in the Writings of 'Abdu'l-Bahá:

> O ye servants of the Sacred Threshold! The triumphant hosts of the Celestial Concourse, arrayed and marshalled in the Realms above, stand ready and expectant to assist and assure victory to that valiant horseman who with confidence spurs on his charger into the arena of service. Well is it with that fearless warrior, who armed with the power of true Knowledge, hastens unto the field, disperses the armies of ignorance, and scatters the hosts of error, who holds aloft the Standard of Divine Guidance, and sounds the Clarion of Victory. By the righteousness of the Lord! He hath achieved a glorious triumph and obtained the true victory.[12]

> As to the fundamentals of teaching the Faith: know thou that delivering the Message can be accomplished only through goodly deeds and spiritual attributes, an utterance that is crystal clear and the happiness reflected from the face of that one who is expounding the Teachings. It is essential that the deeds of the teacher should attest the truth of his words. Such is the state of whoso doth spread abroad the sweet savours of God and the quality of him who is sincere in his faith.
>
> Once the Lord hath enabled thee to attain this condition, be thou assured that He will inspire thee with words of truth, and will cause thee to speak through the breathings of the Holy Spirit.[13]

It is clear that in this day, confirmations from the unseen world are encompassing all those who deliver the divine Message. Should the work of teaching lapse, these confirmations would be entirely cut off, since it is impossible for the loved ones of God to receive assistance unless they teach.[14]

And in the words of President Joseph F. Smith:*

> The individual elder is left largely to the guidance of the spirit of his calling, with which he should be imbued. If he fail to cultivate that spirit, which is the spirit of energy and application, he will soon become torpid, indolent and unhappy . . . His mind should be well stored with thoughts worth uttering, worth hearing, worth remembering; then the spirit of inspiration will bring forth the truths of which his auditors are in need, and give to his words the ring of authority.[15]

Meekness in teaching

The attitude of one teaching his faith should be that of utter humility. At no point should the teacher engage in argument or contention:

> And let your preaching be the warning voice, every man to his neighbor, in mildness and in meekness.[16]

> Let God's beloved, each and every one, be the essence of purity, the very life of holiness, so that in every country they may become famed for their sanctity, independence of spirit, and meekness . . . Act ye in such wise, showing forth pure and goodly deeds, and modesty and humility, that ye will cause others to be awakened.[17]

> It is to be earnestly recommended that elders abroad on missions, as indeed Latter-day Saints in general, avoid contentious argument and debate regarding doctrinal subjects. The truth of the gospel does not depend for its demonstration on heated discussion; the message of truth is most effectively delivered when expressed in words of simplicity and sympathy.
> . . . A testimony of the truth is more than a mere assent of the mind, it is a conviction of the heart, a knowledge that fills the whole soul of its recipient.[18]

---

* Joseph F. Smith presided over the LDS Church from 1901-1918 and is not to be confused with Joseph Smith, Jr., the founder of the Church of Jesus Christ of Latter-day Saints, nor with Joseph Fielding Smith, a more recent president of the Church.

The teacher, when teaching, must be himself fully enkindled, so that his utterance, like unto a flame of fire, may exert influence and consume the veil of self and passion. He must also be utterly humble and lowly so that others may be edified, and be totally self-effaced and evanescent so that he may teach with the melody of the Concourse on high – otherwise his teaching will have no effect.[19]

Set forth that which ye possess. If it be favourably received, your end is attained; if not, to protest is vain. Leave that soul to himself and turn unto the Lord, the Protector, the Self-Subsisting. Be not the cause of grief, much less of discord and strife.[20]

Members of the same faith are likewise forbidden to dispute among themselves:

Brethren, leave these themes of profitless discussion alone; keep closely to the teachings of the revealed word, as made plain in the standard works of the Church and through the utterances of the living prophets; and let not a difference of views on abstruse matters of doctrine absorb your attention, lest thereby you become estranged from one another and separated from the Spirit of the Lord.[21]

In brief, O ye believers of God! The text of the divine Book is this: If two souls quarrel and contend about a question of the divine questions, differing and disputing, both are wrong. The wisdom of this incontrovertible law of God is this: That between two souls from amongst the believers of God, no contention and dispute may arise; that they may speak with each other with infinite amity and love. Should there appear the least trace of controversy, they must remain silent, and both parties must continue their discussions no longer, but ask the reality of the question from the Interpreter. This is the irrefutable command![22]

The importance of free will

Both faiths underscore that a teacher's only responsibility is that of sharing the message with those he comes in contact with. Beyond that, it is up to the individual to accept or reject that message according to his own free will. Bahá'u'lláh advises his followers:

Consort with all men, O people of Bahá, in a spirit of friendliness and fellowship. If ye be aware of a certain truth, if ye possess a jewel, of which others are deprived, share it with them in a language of utmost kindliness and goodwill. If it be accepted, if it fulfill its purpose, your object is attained. If anyone should refuse it, leave him unto himself, and beseech God to guide him. Beware lest ye deal unkindly with him. A kindly tongue is the lodestone of the hearts of men. It is the bread of the spirit, it clotheth the words with meaning, it is the fountain of the light of wisdom and understanding.[23]

While the LDS Church teaches:

Our motivation . . . should be a deep love for our friends and neighbors, indeed for every son and daughter of God. Our acquaintances must know that our friendship is not contingent upon their joining the Church. When they feel that we truly care about them, they will begin to recognize that what we are offering them is based upon our love for them, not just a desire to increase the membership of the Church.

Daily seeking the Spirit to attend us in our activities and in our conversations with others will help us be sincere and motivated by Christlike love. We need to be meek and humble if we expect the Spirit to work through us. It is the Holy Spirit that can change a person's heart, not the member or the missionary.[24]

Missionaries

An immediate difference between the LDS and Bahá'í faiths becomes apparent when the discussion turns to missionaries. Although, as we have seen, it is the duty of every Latter-day Saint to teach his faith, in practice the only significant direct teaching work taking place in the LDS Church is shouldered by the full-time missionaries. This is in sharp contrast to the Bahá'í approach to collective teaching, in which individual believers (including youth and children) arise to form teams and embark on periodic intensive teaching campaigns in areas where there are sufficient human resources to sustain a pattern of steady growth. Thus in one sense, there is no such thing as a missionary in the Bahá'í Faith, and in another, every Bahá'í is a missionary.

There are, of course, Bahá'ís who pioneer to foreign lands in order to spread the Message of Bahá'u'lláh, but once there, they teach the Faith in accordance with the needs and plans – as well as the limitations – of the community to which they pioneer, not according to the methods prevalent in their country of origin. Bahá'ís also 'homefront pioneer' to areas within their own country where additional resources are needed to help create and sustain growth. In each case, however, the Baháʼí pioneer aligns his activities with those planned by the local or national community where he has taken up residence.

While the concept of missionary work is certainly not unique to the LDS Church, Mormon missionaries are today one of the most active groups in the field. We will briefly compare their work, as well as their methodology, to that of Baháʼís engaged in the teaching field.

The purpose of Mormon missionary work

The Mormon missionary's primary purpose is to spread the 'restored gospel' across the globe. At the root of this effort are the following scriptural calls to action:

> Yea, verily I say unto you again, the time has come when the voice of the Lord is unto you: Go ye out of Babylon;[25] gather ye out from among the nations, from the four winds, from one end of heaven to the other. Send forth the elders of my church unto the nations which are afar off; unto the islands of the sea; send forth unto foreign lands; call upon all nations, first upon the Gentiles, and then upon the Jews. Yea, let the cry go forth among all people: Awake and arise and go forth to meet the Bridegroom; behold and lo, the Bridegroom cometh; go ye out to meet him. Prepare yourselves for the great day of the Lord.[26]

> And this gospel of the kingdom shall be preached in all the world for a witness unto all nations; and then shall the end come.[27]

Baháʼís and most Christians understand the phrase 'gospel of the kingdom' in the last quotation to refer to the teachings of Jesus Christ as recorded in the New Testament. In this context, Baháʼís point out, it is an indicator of the 'last days' and the coming of a new Manifestation. In his book *Thief of the Night*, William Sears notes:

> A study of the spread of Christianity made by scholars of the 1840s convinced them that the message of Christ had, by their day, already encircled the globe. The Gospel was being taught in all the continents. By 1844 it was being taught even in the interior of Africa, not by solitary missionaries, but on an organized scale. A commercial history of East Africa states: 'Christian missions began their activities amongst the African people in 1844.'[28]

Thus, Bahá'ís believe that this prophecy had been fulfilled by the time the Báb declared His mission in 1844. Mormons, on the other hand, claim to have a new, restored gospel, consisting not only of the Book of Mormon and other scriptures they believe belong in the canon of the Bible, but also the larger notion that God communicates His will to mankind through the 'living prophet,' the president of the LDS Church. They further believe that it is this restored gospel that must be 'preached in all the world,' and so they work diligently to bring about the fulfillment of that prophecy in preparation of the Return of Christ.

Nevertheless, Bahá'ís share a common purpose with Mormons in spreading God's most recent Revelation throughout the planet. 'Abdu'l-Bahá wrote:

> Teachers must continually travel to all parts of the continent, nay, rather, to all parts of the world, but they must travel like 'Abdu'l-Bahá, who journeyed throughout the cities of America. He was sanctified and free from every attachment and in the utmost severance. Just as His Holiness Christ says: Shake off the very dust from your feet . . .
>
> In short, O ye believers of God! Endeavor ye, so that you may take hold of every means in the promulgation of the religion of God and the diffusion of the fragrances of God.[29]

> . . . know ye of a certainty that whosoever arises in this day to diffuse the divine fragrances, the cohorts of the Kingdom of God shall confirm him and the bestowals and the favors of the Blessed Perfection shall encircle him.
>
> O that I could travel, even though on foot and in the utmost poverty, to these regions, and, raising the call of 'Yá Bahá'u'l-Abhá' in cities, villages, mountains, deserts and oceans, promote the divine teachings! This, alas, I cannot do. How intensely I deplore it! Please God, ye may achieve it.[30]

Requirements for teaching and missionary work

A teacher of faith, whether a Bahá'í teacher or a Mormon missionary, must himself embody purity and detachment if his efforts are to bear fruit:

> The intention of the teacher must be pure, his heart independent, his spirit attracted, his thought at peace, his resolution firm, his magnanimity exalted and in the love of God a shining torch. Should he become as such, his sanctified breath will even affect the rock; otherwise there will be no result whatsoever. As long as a soul is not perfected, how can he efface the

defects of others! Unless he is detached from aught else save God, how can he teach the severance to others?[31]

It is deemed inconsistent to send men out into the world to promise to others through obedience to the gospel that which they have not themselves received. Neither is it considered proper to send men out to reform them. Let them first reform at home if they have not been strictly keeping the commandments of God . . .

We want young men . . . who have kept themselves unspotted from the world, and can go into the nations of the earth and say to men, 'Follow me, as I follow Christ.' . . . We expect them to be honest, virtuous, and faithful unto death to their covenants, to their brethren, to their wives, to their fathers and mothers, to their brothers and sisters, to themselves and to God. Where you get men like this to preach the gospel to the world, whether they know much to begin with or not, the Lord will put his Spirit into their hearts, and he will crown them with intelligence and power to save the souls of men. For the germ of life is in them. It has not been vitiated or corrupted; it has not been driven away from them.[32]

A teacher must proceed in this way: he must first teach himself, and then others. If he himself still walks the path of carnal appetites and lusts, how can he guide another to the 'evident signs' of God?[33]

By means of encouraging such detachment, Mormon missionaries – at least those stationed away from home – are prohibited from watching television, going to movies or otherwise engaging in 'frivolous' activities that may distract them from their ultimate goal. To further promote proper attitude and behavior, Mormon missionaries are invariably paired up as part of a 'buddy system.' The two companions keep tabs on one another and remind each other of their sacred duties.

Methods of teaching and the meaning of 'proselytizing'

In the Bahá'í Faith, the term *proselytizing* has taken on a rather negative connotation. Although a general definition of the term is 'to recruit or convert especially to a new faith, institution, or cause,' another, more specific definition is 'to induce someone to convert to one's faith,'[34] in other words, the use of some form of pressure or enticement in order to effect a conversion. It appears to be this latter meaning which Shoghi Effendi had in mind when he cautioned the Bahá'ís:

Care, however, should, at all times, be exercised, lest in their eagerness to further the international interests of the Faith they frustrate their purpose, and turn away, through any act that might be misconstrued as an attempt to proselytize and bring undue pressure upon them, those whom they wish to win over to their Cause.[35]

The Universal House of Justice elaborated:

When teaching among the masses, the friends should be careful not to emphasize the charitable and humanitarian aspects of the Faith as a means to win recruits. Experience has shown that when facilities such as schools, dispensaries, hospitals or even clothes and food are offered to the people being taught, many complications arise. The prime motive should always be the response of man to God's Message, and the recognition of His Messengers. Those who declare themselves as Bahá'ís should become enchanted with the beauty of the Teachings, and touched by the love of Bahá'u'lláh.[36]

This does not mean that Bahá'í pioneers are discouraged from engaging in social and economic development activities. In fact, in a number of developing nations, Bahá'ís have built schools and hospitals where such services are urgently needed. However, these activities are offered purely as a service to humanity and are not used as a way to promote the Faith.

Along the same lines, one of the ways in which Mormon missionary work differs from that of other Christian churches is that very little if any emphasis is placed on combining missionary activity with social and economic development. The missionaries' primary goal is to win converts to the LDS Church, not to establish hospitals or schools. It is believed that the sooner the world accepts the restored gospel of Jesus Christ, the sooner God's kingdom will be established and the root causes of poverty eradicated.

Proselytizing can take many different forms, but the mental image it evokes is that of people aggressively trying to get others to believe their way. Certainly, Bahá'ís are advised not to employ methods that might be construed as pressuring anyone to learn about the Faith. However, the above statements by the Guardian and the Universal House of Justice seem to warn most strongly against the kind of pressure employed all too often by Christian missionaries in the past: providing education and healthcare primarily as an inducement for conversion or as a vehicle for delivering a religious message. Although door-to-door teaching might be perceived by some as too forceful an approach for Bahá'ís, there is nothing inherently undignified about systematic efforts to publicize neighborhood-based activities and services such as devotional gatherings, study circles, children's classes and youth groups, or even to employ direct teaching methods where the population has proven particularly receptive to the Message of Bahá'u'lláh. In a message dated 18 October 2007 to a Local Spiritual Assembly, the Universal House of Justice clarified:

> The statement written on behalf of the Guardian to which you refer appears in a letter dated 20 October 1956 to a National Spiritual Assembly. The letter states that to distribute Baha'i pamphlets from door to door . . . is undignified and might create a bad impression of the Faith' adding that the Guardian 'does not think the best interests of the Cause are served by such a method.' Of paramount consideration, therefore, is whether a particular method of teaching allows for a dignified presentation of the Faith. Cultures differ, and what may be considered dignified in one locality may not be so in another. It should be noted in this respect that, in the context of the Five Year Plan, the friends carry out a wide variety of activities at the level of the neighborhood and village, such as children's classes and study circles, and in many cases it would be quite appropriate to visit the homes of people to explain the nature of these activities and invite them to take part. In still others, paying a visit to the home of someone to see whether they are interested in learning about the Faith would not be regarded as undignified in the least.[37]

Mormon missionaries of course do go door to door with the specific purpose of acquainting souls with 'the teachings of Jesus Christ as restored through Joseph Smith.' Once a pair of missionaries is invited into one's home, they will strive to deliver the first of six standard *missionary talks* aimed at convincing the potential convert of the truth of the restored gospel. For Mormons, the word 'proselytizing' does not have a negative connotation at all, and going around neighborhoods to find receptive souls with whom to share the gospel is seen as a necessary means of spreading God's message for the good of mankind. To be sure, Mormon missionaries apply a good deal more pressure than Bahá'ís in their teaching efforts, but care is taken that the potential convert not be pushed beyond his level of comfort. When confronted with rejection the missionaries will maintain a courteous distance, and if they sense receptivity they will regularly check up to offer their unconditional assistance.

There are a number of similarities in how each faith brings its message to new potential members. Bahá'í teachers are told to adjust their approach based on the receptivity and current beliefs of the individual they are teaching, being careful not to 'water down' the message of the Faith in the process. This personalized approach was used by 'Abdu'l-Bahá Himself:

> It was He, our beloved 'Abdu'l-Bahá, our true and shining Exemplar, who with infinite tact and patience, whether in His public utterances or in private converse, adapted the presentation of the fundamentals of the Cause to the varying capacities and the spiritual receptiveness of His hearers. He never hesitated, however, to tear the veil asunder and reveal to the spiritually ripened those challenging verities that set forth in its true light the relationship of this Supreme Revelation with the Dispensations of the past.[38]

Mormon missionaries are likewise taught to engage with their investigator on a personal level and learn about his current beliefs and spiritual needs in order to discover the most effective approach in presenting their faith. Beyond that, however, the missionary talks themselves are not subject to much variation; each of the six encounters focuses on a particular aspect of Mormon doctrine, beginning with the story of Joseph Smith's *First Vision*.

Yet Bahá'ís are not strangers to standardized messages. One teaching tool that many Bahá'í teachers use to familiarize seekers with the essential verities of their Faith is called *Anna's Presentation*, named after a fictional character in one of the Ruhi Institute courses which focuses on teaching. One lesson in this course tells the story of Anna, a young woman who visits with her friend Emilia to introduce her to the most important aspects of the Bahá'í Faith. The method she uses is simple, straightforward and systematic, yet remains sensitive to Emilia's cultural and religious background, as well as her personal feelings and beliefs. It makes liberal use of quotations from the Writings of Bahá'u'lláh, which Bahá'ís believe to exert a special power of their own to touch the heart of the seeker. Far from a one-sided lecture, *Anna's Presentation* is a dialogue between two souls attracted to the light of God. While one is nominally the teacher and the other the seeker, both are in fact seekers of truth learning from each other. Depending on the seeker's preference, the entire presentation can be given in about an hour, or it can be broken up into various shorter meetings. If a question warrants a more in-depth discussion, it can either be addressed immediately, or postponed until after the presentation so as not to interrupt the flow of love and learning. Bahá'ís often make this presentation as part of a teaching team comprising two members, one of whom is doing the talking while the other remains in silent prayer.

Mormon missionaries are taught to keep things simple and to stay away from in-depth theological discussions if at all possible. They generally limit themselves to the basic message of the Church, including the restoration of the gospel, the truth of the Book of Mormon, and the nature of the premortal and postmortal worlds. Like Bahá'ís, Mormon missionaries are keen to quote from their scriptures, and usually work in pairs with one doing most of the talking and the other remaining mostly silent. After about the third missionary talk, however, the investigator is urged to pray for confirmation. Deeper questions, arising from an investigator's desire to more fully understand a specific concept, are often answered with a call for more ardent prayers. The following passage from a missionary booklet titled *The Plan of Salvation* shows the importance of prayer, as opposed to reason, as the primary means of deciding the truth of the restored gospel:

> You can know for yourself that these things are true by asking Heavenly Father in prayer. He will answer you through the Holy Ghost. The Holy Ghost is also called the Spirit of God, and one of His roles is to witness, or testify, of the truth. The Holy Ghost reveals and confirms truth through feelings, thoughts, and impressions. The feelings that come from the Holy Ghost are powerful, but they are also usually gentle and quiet. As taught in the Bible, 'The fruit of the Spirit is love, joy, peace, longsuffering, gentleness, goodness, faith, meekness, [and] temperance' (Galatians 5:22-23). These feelings are a confirmation from the Holy Ghost that this message is true. You will then need to choose whether you will live in harmony with the teachings of Jesus Christ as restored through Joseph Smith.[39]

Whether or not the investigator continues to express doubt, he is encouraged to set a date for his baptism, with the hope and expectation that in the intervening weeks his prayers will bear fruit. Thus from an LDS perspective, a spiritual conversion resulting from prayer is much preferred over acceptance on intellectual grounds.

While the Bahá'í Writings stress that religious teachings must be conformable to reason, they also explain that it is the human heart which is the receptacle of the love and remembrance of God.[40] Although the process of becoming a Bahá'í is fundamentally different from that of becoming a Mormon, the assumption that one must know every minute detail of the Bahá'í principles, history and laws before accepting Bahá'u'lláh is misguided. Shoghi Effendi has described the process by which a seeker is confirmed in the Faith as follows:

> Let him remember the example set by 'Abdu'l-Bahá, and His constant admonition to shower such kindness upon the seeker, and exemplify to

such a degree the spirit of the teachings he hopes to instill into him, that the recipient will be spontaneously impelled to identify himself with the Cause embodying such teachings. Let him refrain, at the outset, from insisting on such laws and observances as might impose too severe a strain on the seeker's newly awakened faith, and endeavor to nurse him, patiently, tactfully, and yet determinedly, into full maturity, and aid him to proclaim his unqualified acceptance of whatever has been ordained by Bahá'u'lláh.[41]

Whether a rational acceptance of the principles and laws of the Bahá'í Faith occurs early on or later in the seeker's journey, the initial spark of faith is ignited in the heart through a process as mysterious as it is powerful. To protect and feed this delicate flame is one of the sacred duties of the Bahá'í teacher.

CHAPTER 10
SCIENCE AND RELIGION

When comparing the Bahá'í teachings to those of the LDS Church, the question of science evokes both agreement and strong disagreement. In this chapter, we'll examine how the two faiths address the ongoing debate between religious doctrine and scientific discovery. To put our comparison to the test, we'll address one of the most controversial issues in this debate, creationism vs. evolution.

The Bahá'í view of the Creation

The Bahá'í Writings uphold evolution as God's means of manifesting His Creation in the contingent world, where it gradually attains physical perfections over long periods of time. However, they caution against the blind acceptance of Darwinism and all its conclusions, particularly with respect to the origin of man. On the one hand, 'Abdu'l-Bahá explained that the origin of all matter and life in the universe is one and that man evolved through various stages of physical development:

> It is necessary . . . that we should know what each of the important existences was in the beginning – for there is no doubt that in the beginning the origin was one: the origin of all numbers is one and not two. Then it is evident that in the beginning matter was one, and that one matter appeared in different aspects in each element. Thus various forms were produced, and these various aspects as they were produced became permanent, and each element was specialized. But this permanence was not definite, and did not attain realization and perfect existence until after a very long time. Then these elements became composed, and organized and combined in infinite forms; or rather from the composition and combination of these elements innumerable beings appeared.[1]

Then it is clear that original matter, which is in the embryonic state, and the mingled and composed elements which were its earliest forms, gradually grew and developed during many ages and cycles, passing from one shape and form to another, until they appeared in this perfection, this system, this organization and this establishment, through the supreme wisdom of God.[2]

. . . do thou observe that it is evident man has evolved from the mineral world. As long as he was in the mineral kingdom, he could not imagine the vegetable kingdom. He was transferred to the vegetable kingdom. In the vegetable kingdom he could not imagine the animal kingdom. Before he emerged from the animal kingdom he could not imagine the stage of human reason and intelligence, that is, it was impossible for him, he did not have any knowledge thereof.[3]

On the other hand, He expressed disagreement with the theory of the modification of species, clarifying that man has always been a distinct species and not a glorified animal:

Certain European philosophers agree that the species grows and develops, and that even change and alteration are also possible . . . The principal argument is this: that the existence of traces of members proves that they once existed, and as now they are no longer of service, they have gradually disappeared. Therefore, while the perfect and necessary members have remained, those which are unnecessary have gradually disappeared by the modification of the species, but the traces of them continue . . .

. . . let us suppose that there was a time when some animals, or even man, possessed some members which have now disappeared; this is not a sufficient proof of the change and evolution of the species.[4]

In the same way, the embryo of man in the womb of the mother was at first in a strange form; then this body passes from shape to shape, from state to state, from form to form, until it appears in utmost beauty and perfection. But even when in the womb of the mother and in this strange form, entirely different from his present form and figure, he is the embryo of the superior species, and not of the animal; his species and essence undergo no change. Now, admitting that the traces of organs which have disappeared actually exist, this is not a proof of the impermanence and the nonoriginality of the species. At the most it proves that the form, and fashion, and the organs of man have progressed. Man was always a distinct species, a man, not an animal. So, if the embryo of man in the womb of the mother passes from one form to another so that the second form in no way resembles the first, is this a proof that the species has changed? that it was at first an animal, and that its organs progressed and developed until it became a man? No, indeed! How puerile and unfounded is this idea and this thought! For the proof of the originality of the human species, and of the permanency of the nature of man, is clear and evident.[5]

These various statements on the origin of life may seem paradoxical until we recognize that 'Abdu'l-Bahá makes a distinction between a *spiritual* and a *material* creation. The spiritual creation was perfect from the beginning, and man has always stood apart as a separate being; yet this spiritual perfection took a long time to manifest itself in the material world:

All beings, whether large or small, were created perfect and complete from the first, but their perfections appear in them by degrees. The organization of God is one; the evolution of existence is one; the divine system is one. Whether they be small or great beings, all are subject to one law and system. Each seed has in it from the first all the vegetable perfections. For example, in the seed all the vegetable perfections exist from the beginning, but not visibly; afterward little by little they appear. So it is first the shoot which appears from the seed, then the branches, leaves, blossoms and fruits; but from the beginning of its existence all these things are in the seed, potentially, though not apparently . . .

Similarly, the terrestrial globe from the beginning was created with all its elements, substances, minerals, atoms and organisms; but these only appeared by degrees: first the mineral, then the plant, afterward the animal, and finally man. But from the first these kinds and species existed, but were undeveloped in the terrestrial globe, and then appeared only gradually. For the supreme organization of God, and the universal natural system, surround all beings, and all are subject to this rule. When you consider this universal system, you see that there is not one of the beings which at its coming into existence has reached the limit of perfection. No, they gradually grow and develop, and then attain the degree of perfection.[6]

With respect to the time frame in which all this occurred, 'Abdu'l-Bahá has unequivocally proclaimed:

This divine sovereignty is not to be measured by six thousand years. This interminable, illimitable universe is not the result of that measured period.

This stupendous laboratory and workshop has not been limited in its production to six thousand revolutions of the earth about the sun. With the slightest reflection man can be assured that this calculation and announcement is childish, especially in view of the fact that it is scientifically proved the terrestrial globe has been the habitation of man long prior to such a limited estimate.[7]

A common genetic origin

The Bahá'í Writings are silent on the subject of genetics, but they clearly uphold both the uniqueness of the human species as well as the single origin of all beings. With the recent completion of the mapping of the human genome, the common genetic heritage of all life on earth has now been corroborated by strong scientific evidence. According to Dr Francis Collins of the US National Human Genome Research Institute, the makeup of the human gene is 'astonishingly similar' to that of other organisms.[8] For example, humans and mice have over 99 per cent of the same genes in common, and these genes appear in the same sequence more than 80 per cent of the time. We have roughly two-thirds of our DNA in common with ground worms and fruit flies, and humans even share some genetic traits with plant life.

The fact that different organisms share genetic material does not necessarily mean that one evolved directly from the other. Rather, it suggests that all forms of life have a common set of genetic building blocks, and that some developed along parallel evolutionary tracks. 'Abdu'l-Bahá explained:

> . . . the animal having preceded man is not a proof of the evolution, change and alteration of the species, nor that man was raised from the animal world to the human world. For while the individual appearance of these different beings is certain, it is possible that man came into existence after the animal. So when we examine the vegetable kingdom, we see that the fruits of the different trees do not arrive at maturity at one time; on the contrary, some come first and others afterward. This priority does not prove that the later fruit of one tree was produced from the earlier fruit of another tree.[9]

It is now generally accepted that all life, including human life, did evolve from a common set of primitive organisms over the course of billions of years. However, the Bahá'í Teachings reveal the spiritual impetus behind this chemical process, explaining that each creature, having been created spiritually first, traced its own unique evolutionary path through the physical kingdoms, assuming various forms along the way. Thus the evolution of man was destined from the beginning to result in modern man, not an ape, though the two may share a common ancestor. It is also clear that the human spirit could not have entered a material being until that being was a suitable receptacle for it;[10] for example, man's power of reason could not be properly manifested in the world without a fully developed human brain. The very act of the spirit becoming associated with such a body would have produced a unique and original species, mirroring the essence of man in the spiritual realm.

The LDS view of the Creation

On the surface, the LDS scriptures and official doctrine seem impossible to reconcile with the Bahá'í view of the universe. Specifically, they fix the age of the earth at about 6,000 years, something the Bahá'í Writings categorically reject. This 'biblical' age of the earth is actually not found anywhere in the Bible, but rather originated in the 17th century when an Anglican bishop by the name of James Ussher 'calculated' the first day of creation. His entry in *A Geological Miscellany* by G. Y. Craig and E. J. Jones reads:

> James Ussher (1581–1656), Archbishop of Armagh, Primate of All Ireland, and Vice-Chancellor of Trinity College in Dublin was highly regarded in his day as a churchman and as a scholar. Of his many works, his treatise on chronology has proved the most durable. Based on an intricate correlation of Middle Eastern and Mediterranean histories and Holy writ, it was incorporated into an authorized version of the Bible printed in 1701, and thus came to be regarded with almost as much unquestioning reverence as the Bible itself. Having established the first day of creation as Sunday 23 October 4004 BC . . . Ussher calculated the dates of other biblical events, concluding, for example, that Adam and Eve were driven from Paradise on Monday 10 November 4004 BC, and that the ark touched down on Mt Ararat on 5 May 1491 BC 'on a Wednesday'.[11]

This belief in a young earth is also contained within the Mormon scriptures. As reported in the Doctrine and Covenants, Joseph Smith gave the following answer to a question about the Revelation of St John, chapter 5, verse 1:

> Q. What are we to understand by the book which John saw, which was sealed on the back with seven seals?
> A. We are to understand that it contains the revealed will, mysteries, and the works of God; the hidden things of his economy concerning this

earth during the seven thousand years of its continuance, or its temporal existence.[12]

An article in *Ensign* magazine elaborates:

Some of the great truths we learn from section 77 [of the Doctrine and Covenants] include: . . . this earth will have a temporal existence of 7,000 years; . . . the Second Coming will not occur until after the beginning of the seventh 1,000-year period and the completion of the events in Revelation 9 . . .[13]

In other words, the earth's 'temporal existence' will encompass a total of 7,000 years, with the last millennium to coincide with the Second Coming of Christ. Assuming that Christ's return is close at hand, that would mean that the earth is just shy of 6,000 years old today. With respect to scientific evidence in support of a much older earth, a number of church leaders have adamantly maintained in their authoritative writings that any science that does not support the literal text of the LDS scriptures is necessarily faulty. For example, President Joseph Fielding Smith declared:

I will state frankly and positively that I am opposed to the present biological theories and the doctrine that man has been on the earth for millions of years. I am opposed to the present teachings in relation to the age of the earth which declare that the earth is millions of years old. Some modern scientists even claim that it is a billion years old. Naturally, since I believe in modern revelation, I cannot accept these so-called scientific teachings, for I believe them to be in conflict with the simple and direct word of the Lord that has come to us by divine revelation.[14]

Yet when we investigate further, we discover that there is not exactly a true consensus among Latter-day Saints with respect to the history of creation, and that despite the opinions of certain of its past and present leaders, the Church is surprisingly flexible in the face of scientific evidence.

Two creations

The LDS teachings describe two separate creations. According to this doctrine, the Creation as chronicled in the Book of Genesis occurred spiritually first, and the subsequent 'temporal' creation did not come about until much later:

This earth, as with man and all forms of life, was first created spiritually. Thereafter came the temporal creation – the paradisiacal or Edenic creation, the creation of the earth and man and all forms of life as they were before the fall. In that day there was no mortality and no procreation, not for man nor for any form of life. All things were created in a state of paradisiacal immortality.[15]

Mormons have used this to overcome their confusion about the implausible sequence of events described by a literal reading of Genesis, chapter 1. For example, the creation of plants is depicted before the creation of the sun which is the source of photosynthesis. Notwithstanding LDS insistence on the literal interpretation of scripture, the Bahá'í view that Genesis describes a spiritual process and not a scientific or chronological history of the earth is shared by many Mormons.

As early as 1873, Elder Orson Pratt delivered a discourse on the process of creation in which he acknowledged that it may have taken 'many centuries' to complete:

Now these two states of being in which our earth existed are called first, the evening, and second, the morning – and the evening and the morning were the first day. Whether the day here mentioned was a period such as the one to which we now apply that term, we are not informed in the Bible, but from what has been revealed to the Latter-day Saints we have great reason to believe that it was a very long period of time, and that this darkness existed over the face of the great deep for a long time. It might have been for many centuries, we have no definite information on this point . . .

If we had the process of creation unfolded to us, we should probably find that many of the materials of our globe once existed in a dispersed or scattered form, in a state of chaos, and that the Lord, in collecting them together, brought them from a distance in the solar system, and that in so doing, he took his own time and way, and wrought according to his own laws, for, as far as we are acquainted, the Lord works by law, and why not create by law? . . .

These six days in which the Lord performed this work, I do not believe, were each limited to twenty-four hours, as are the periods which we now call day . . .[16]

This shares a number of features with the Bahá'í concept of a spiritual creation that took a long time to come to fruition in the contingent world, and echoes 'Abdu'l-Bahá's explanation that 'original matter . . . gradually grew and developed during many ages and cycles.'[17] Furthermore, it is consistent with scientific evidence that our earth coalesced from an accretion disk that initially surrounded our young sun, and refutes the traditional Christian doctrine of *creatio ex nihilo*, which claims that God fashioned the entire universe from total nonexistence. Indeed, Mormons stress that all matter has existed from the very beginning, and that the Creation represented only the organization of pre-existent material. Not only does this reflect the scientific principle that matter is neither created nor destroyed, it is also quite compatible with the Bahá'í view of the universe:

> If we could imagine a time when no beings existed, this imagination would be the denial of the Divinity of God. Moreover, absolute nonexistence cannot become existence. If the beings were absolutely nonexistent, existence would not have come into being. Therefore, as the Essence of Unity (that is, the existence of God) is everlasting and eternal – that is to say, it has neither beginning nor end – it is certain that this world of existence, this endless universe, has neither beginning nor end. Yes, it may be that one of the parts of the universe, one of the globes, for example, may come into existence, or may be disintegrated, but the other endless globes are still existing; the universe would not be disordered nor destroyed.[18]

However, Elder Pratt, in the same discourse previously quoted, was at pains to reconcile his scientific views with the literal text of the Bible. In so doing, he made a somewhat forced distinction between the organization of the universe and the creation of the earth itself:

> . . . I will refer you to some discoveries that have been made by philosophers and astronomers of the present day. They have invented telescopes that are of such penetrating power that they have discovered systems of worlds at such immense distance in space, that they calculate their light would take six hundred thousand years to reach our system. Very well then, how long must it have been on the journey when the Lord said – 'Let there be light,' so far as this creation is concerned? I answer, that light was traveling five hundred and ninety-four thousand years before that time; consequently light must have existed, at least, half a million years before the Lord said – 'Let there be light,' so far as this globe was concerned.[19]

Here, Pratt appeared to be alluding to two creations of a different kind: first, the appearance of light itself (and presumably the universe in which it travels) hundreds of thousands of years ago; and second, the creation of the earth approximately 6,000 years ago and the first appearance of light upon it. Of course, if Orson Pratt were alive today, he would have to update his estimate of the age of the universe to nearly 14 billion years.

No mortality in the Garden of Eden

As noted in a previous chapter, Mormons interpret the biblical story of Adam and Eve in the Garden of Eden in a very literal sense. The LDS Church teaches that Eden was a physical place, geographically located in what is now the state of Missouri. The various Mormon beliefs surrounding the conditions of that paradisiacal garden are similarly literal in nature. For example, Latter-day Saints are told that prior to the Fall of Adam, the earth knew no physical mortality of any kind. President Joseph Fielding Smith clarified this doctrine as follows:

> According to this [2 Ne 2:22-25] – and it must have been approved by the Lord or it would not be in the Book of Mormon – there was no death of any living creature before the fall of Adam! Adam's mission was to bring to pass the fall and it came upon the earth and living things throughout all nature. Anything contrary to this doctrine is diametrically opposed to the doctrines revealed to the Church! If there was any creature increasing by propagation before the fall, then throw away the Book of Mormon, deny your faith, the Book of Abraham and the revelations in the Doctrine and Covenants! Our scriptures most emphatically tell us that death came through the fall, and has passed upon all creatures including the earth itself. For this earth of ours was pronounced good when the Lord finished it. It became fallen and subject to death as did all things upon its face, through the transgression of Adam.[20]

This doctrine is clearly incompatible with the notion of a mass extinction of dinosaurs millions of years ago. Apostle Bruce R. McConkie – a foremost expert on Mormon doctrine as well as a general authority of the Church – declared:

> There is, of course, no conflict between revealed religion as it has been restored in our day and those scientific realities which have been established as ultimate truth. The mental quagmires in which many students struggle result from the acceptance of unproven scientific theories as ultimate facts, which brings the student to the necessity of rejecting conflicting truths of

revealed religion. If, for example, a student accepts the untrue theory that death has been present on the earth for scores of thousands or millions of years, he must reject the revealed truth that there was no death either for man or animals or plants or any form of life until some 6000 years ago when Adam fell . . .[21]

McConkie described the condition of Eden before the fall as follows:

In that Edenic day, the earth and all life were pronounced very good by the Creator. There was no disease or evil or death. Life was destined to go on forever. The lion ate straw like the ox, and the wolf and the lamb were friends. Light and life and peace and immortality reigned in every department of creation . . .

Then came the fall. Mortality was born; procreation began; disease and death and sorrow covered the earth. The probationary estate had its beginning. Having sinned, man was no longer innocent; he could now feel joy, for he knew misery, and he could do good, for he knew sin.[22]

The original mention of lions eating straw is found in the Book of Isaiah:

The wolf and the lamb shall feed together, and the lion shall eat straw like the bullock: and dust shall be the serpent's meat. They shall not hurt nor destroy in all my holy mountain, saith the LORD.[23]

However, Isaiah referred to the 'last days' of the millennial reign, not to the 'Edenic' past. What's more, most readers of this verse, including a majority of Christians, do not expect this prophecy to be literally fulfilled, and see it instead as a spiritual promise of abiding peace, a world devoid of conflict or strife. Mormon doctrine, on the other hand, follows a strictly literalist approach, and projects a biblical promise of the future onto ancient history. The assertion that lions used to eat straw also brings up a number of thorny questions, such as why their teeth are made for ripping meat, and how their stomachs were able to digest the straw. It cannot be supposed that the animal adapted to its new environment after the Fall of Adam, because that would be tantamount to endorsing Darwinism. Even the very mention of straw (which is dead grass or grain) appears to contradict the Mormon belief that no form of life, including plant life, ever experienced death in the Garden of Eden.

These narrow views of the Creation illustrate some of the same limitations that have held back other religions from reconciling themselves to science: by interpreting scripture literally, and *only* literally, they have painted themselves into a doctrinal corner from which there is no escape, short of disparaging universally accepted scientific principles, discoveries and methods.

Room for agreement

Notwithstanding that the Creation is depicted in two vastly different contexts between the official teachings of the LDS Church and those of the Bahá'í Faith, there appears to be some room for common ground. Whereas Latter-day Saints rarely question the truth of their scriptures, there is a good deal more independent thought among the faithful where science is concerned, and even among the leadership there does not appear to be a unanimous rejection of organic evolution. Many acknowledge, privately or publicly, that dinosaurs once existed and that they became extinct millions of years before the first humans appeared on earth – in direct opposition to the 'no mortality before the fall' doctrine. In the next section we'll look at how Mormons have been able to reconcile some of their religious views with the various scientific findings that appear to contradict them.

The harmony of science and religion

The Bahá'í Writings uphold the harmony of science and religion without the slightest ambiguity and in the strongest terms. At a talk in Pittsburgh, Pennsylvania on May 7, 1912, 'Abdu'l-Bahá declared:

> Any religious belief which is not conformable with scientific proof and investigation is superstition, for true science is reason and reality, and religion is essentially reality and pure reason; therefore, the two must correspond. Religious teaching which is at variance with science and reason is human invention and imagination unworthy of acceptance, for the antithesis and opposite of knowledge is superstition born of the ignorance of man. If we say religion is opposed to science, we lack knowledge of either true science or true religion, for both are founded upon the premises and conclusions of reason, and both must bear its test.[24]

Mormon attitudes toward science are considerably more complex. Among the LDS membership are a sizeable number of truly bright scientists, representing the full spectrum of disciplines. Most consider their faith to be quite compatible with scientific pursuit, yet when the two conflict, the scriptures must trump scientific findings. If that sounds paradoxical, it is nevertheless precisely how science is perceived in the Mormon community. The following quotation from a speech by Bruce R. McConkie – in which he unwittingly echoes 'Abdul-Bahá's statements on the harmony of science and religion – is representative of this sentiment:

> May I say that all truth is in agreement, that true religion and true science bear the same witness, and that in the true and full sense, true science is part of true religion. But may I also raise some questions of a serious nature. Is there any way to harmonize the false religions of the dark ages with the truths of science as they have now been discovered? Is there any way to harmonize the revealed religion that has come to us with the theoretical postulates of Darwinism and the diverse speculations descending therefrom?[25]

The following statement by a University of Utah professor, given in his introduction to President Joseph Fielding Smith's book, *Man . . . His Origin & Destiny*, is even more contradictory:

> Few fields of science come into such direct conflict with the revealed scriptures as the palaeo-sciences – historical geology, palaeoethnology, palaeontology, and palaeogeography. The factual or experimental components of these sciences have contributed much to our knowledge and culture, and their scientists are indispensable in practical applications dealing with the structural and dynamic features of the earth's crust, the discovery of valuable minerals and the evaluation of natural resources, and description and classification of plants and animals. With the author of this book, I believe that much of the theoretical structure of these sciences is incorrect because it is not only in disagreement with the scriptures but is in direct opposition to them. Moreover, I believe that when these sciences are denuded of their theoretical superstructure, they are not found to conflict with the revealed truths of the scriptures. For those who have the patience to await the great event, when the final chapters of theory in these and other sciences are written, I am confident that they also will square with the pre-eminent science of our Savior. The great challenge thus confronts the scientist with faith in divine revelation to attempt each in his own field to write his theories to include not only the facts of direct experimental observation but also those generally more significant ones revealed by the Omnipotent Scientist, the Creator of the world and Savior of mankind.[26]

It is this tentative embrace of the scientific method that is so intriguing to the outside observer. Latter-day Saints are encouraged to be fully engaged in scientific discovery, so long as their findings do not appear to conflict with Church doctrine:

> We ought to judge everything by gospel standards, not the reverse. Do not take a scientific principle, so-called, and try to make the gospel conform to it. Take the gospel for what it is, and, insofar as you can, make other things conform to it, and if they do not conform to it, forget them. Forget them; do not worry. They will vanish away eventually. In the true sense of the word, the gospel embraces all truth. And everything that is true is going to conform to the principles that God has revealed.[27]

> From the earliest days of the Christian church, spurious gospels have been taught – not really gospels, as Paul pointed out, for there is only one gospel of Christ. Today is not different. We are surrounded by frustrations and advances in thought and learning which raise questions and doubts. These seem to drag men down and destroy faith and morality . . .
>
> I believe we can be modern and enjoy the fruits of a modern world and its high standard of living, and I believe we can have the benefits of modern scholarship and scientific advances without turning to the theories of the modernist. I believe the principles of the gospel announced by the Savior in his personal ministry were true when they were given and are true today. Truth is eternal and never changing, and the gospel of Jesus Christ is ever contemporary in a changing world.[28]

> President Joseph F. Smith said: 'Our young people are diligent students. They reach out for truth and knowledge with commendable zeal, and in so doing they must necessarily adopt for temporary use, the theories of men. As long, however, as they recognize them as scaffolding useful for research purposes, there can be no special harm in them. It is when these theories are settled upon as basic truth that trouble appears, and the searcher then stands in grave danger of being led hopelessly from the right way.'[29]

The Bahá'í Writings dismiss the notion that 'advances in thought and learning' can 'destroy faith and morality,' or that scientific conclusions that contradict religious dogma can lead people 'hopelessly from the right way.' On the contrary, they maintain that religious doctrines which deny or suppress clear scientific observations actually promote irreligion:

> Inasmuch as the blind imitations or dogmatic interpretations current among men do not coincide with the postulates of reason, and the mind

and scientific investigation cannot acquiesce thereto, many souls in the human world today shun and deny religion. That is to say, imitations, when weighed in the scales of reason, will not conform to its standard and requirement. Therefore, these souls deny religion and become irreligious, whereas if the reality of the divine religions becomes manifest to them and the foundation of the heavenly teachings is revealed coinciding with facts and evident truths, reconciling with scientific knowledge and reasonable proof, all may acknowledge them, and irreligion will cease to exist. In this way all mankind may be brought to the foundation of religion, for reality is true reason and science, while all that is not conformable thereto is mere superstition.[30]

Yet Bahá'ís are also cautioned that the validity of scientific evidence does not warrant the blind acceptance of every conclusion the scientific community draws from that evidence:

The House of Justice feels that Bahá'í scholars must beware of the temptations of intellectual pride. 'Abdu'l-Bahá has warned the friends in the West that they would be subjected to intellectual tests, and the Guardian reminded them of this warning. There are many aspects of western thinking which have been exalted to a status of unassailable principle in the general mind, that time may well show to have been erroneous or, at least, only partially true. Any Bahá'í who rises to eminence in academic circles will be exposed to the powerful influence of such thinking. One of the problems of modern times is the degree to which the different disciplines have become specialized and isolated from one another. Thinkers are now faced with a challenge to achieve a synthesis, or at least a coherent correlation, of the vast amount of knowledge that has been acquired during the past century. The Bahá'ís must be aware of this factor and of the moderation and all-embracing nature of this Revelation.[31]

Latter-day Saints generally accept that scientific discovery is necessary for the progress of man, and that many questions about his origin are as yet unanswered. Boyd K. Packer of the Quorum of the Twelve Apostles addressed a 1988 symposium with these words:

. . . let me tell you how I feel about you who study or teach or work in the fields of science. I envy your opportunity to work in fields of scientific discovery: anthropology, paleontology, geology, physics, biology, physiology, chemistry, medicine, engineering and many others. Just think of the opportunity to study the laws of the physical universe and harness the power inherent in obeying them for the good of mankind . . . No Latter-day Saint should be hesitant to pursue any true science as a career, a hobby, an interest, or to accept any truth established through those means of discovery. Nor need one become a scientist at the expense of being a Latter-day Saint of faith and spiritual maturity.

Science is seeking; science is discovery. Man finds joy in discovery. If all things were known, man's creativity would be stifled. There could be no further discovery, no growth, nothing to decide – no agency.

All things not only are not known but must not be so convincingly clear as to eliminate the need for faith. That would nullify agency and defeat the purpose of the plan of salvation. Tests of faith are growing experiences. We all have unanswered questions. Seeking and questioning, periods of doubt, in an effort to find answers, are part of the process of discovery. The kind of doubt which is spiritually dangerous does not relate to questions so much as to answers. For that and other reasons, it is my conviction that a full knowledge of the origin of man must await further discovery, further revelation . . .[32]

In a 1912 talk, 'Abdu'l-Bahá extolled scientific discovery as 'the greatest virtue' of man's 'faculty of intellectual investigation':

God has conferred upon and added to man a distinctive power – the faculty of intellectual investigation into the secrets of creation, the acquisition of higher knowledge – the greatest virtue of which is scientific enlightenment.

This endowment is the most praiseworthy power of man, for through its employment and exercise the betterment of the human race is accomplished, the development of the virtues of mankind is made possible and the spirit and mysteries of God become manifest.[33]

The Lord shall reveal all things

The following excerpt from a 1972 First Presidency message by Harold B. Lee is noteworthy for several reasons. First, it indicates that Mormons have been looking to harmonize their beliefs with scientific findings for a number of years; secondly, it highlights some of their leaders' disdain for those same findings if they are not in complete accord with the official doctrine; and lastly, it explains the Church's own approach in attempting to reconcile its doctrinal views with scientific evidence:

238

I was somewhat sorrowed recently to hear someone, a sister who comes from a church family, ask, 'What about the pre-Adamic people?' Here was someone who I thought was fully grounded in the faith.

I asked, 'What about the pre-Adamic people?'

She replied, 'Well, aren't there evidences that people preceded the Adamic period of the earth?'

I said, 'Have you forgotten the scriptures that says, "And I, the Lord God, formed man from the dust of the ground, and breathed into his nostrils the breath of life; and man became a living soul, the first flesh upon the earth, the first man also . . ." ' (Moses 3:7.) I asked, 'Do you believe that?'

She wondered about the creation because she had read the theories of the scientists, and the question that she was really asking was: How do you reconcile science with religion? The answer must be, If science is not true, you cannot reconcile truth with error.

Missionaries going out into the field often ask how we reconcile the teachings of the scriptures with the teachings of the scientists in accordance with the temple ordinances. In reply I occasionally refer to the revelation given to the Prophet Joseph Smith in Kirtland in 1833, concerning the great event that is to take place at the commencement of the millennial reign when the Lord shall come; the Lord said:

'Yea, verily I say unto you, in that day when the Lord shall come, he shall reveal all things –

'Things which have passed, and hidden things which no man knew, things of the earth, by which it was made, and the purpose and the end thereof –

'Things most precious, things that are above, and things that are beneath, things that are in the earth, and upon the earth, and in heaven.' (D&C 101:32-34)

Then I say, 'If you and I are there when the Lord reveals all this, then I'll answer your questions – how the earth was made, how man came to be placed upon the earth. Until that time till we have is the support and security that we have in the scriptures, and we must accept the rest by faith.'[34]

In other words, the LDS Church has adopted a 'wait and see' approach wherever science and religion appear to clash, confident that Christ will explain everything when He returns. Ironically, this may have resulted in a fairly relaxed attitude about such sensitive topics as geology and paleontology. In 1987, an *Ensign* magazine feature titled 'I Have a Question' asked, 'Do we know how the earth's history as indicated from fossils fits with the earth's history as the scriptures present it?' In answer to this question, Morris S. Petersen, professor of geology at Brigham Young University, suggested that religion and science address two different questions concerning the Creation, and that neither provides a clear enough picture to contradict the other:

> Foremost, the scriptures testify of Jesus Christ and how we may receive the blessings of salvation and exaltation through his atonement. They reveal why (not necessarily how) the earth was created, and what laws and principles a person must follow to obtain eternal life. The goal of science, on the other hand, is to learn how (not why) the world was made and to understand the laws and principles governing the physical world.
>
> The different roles science and religion play is illustrated in a study of the dinosaurs. From the fossil record we learn that the dinosaurs were the dominant animals on earth between 225 and 67 million years ago. ...
>
> The existence of these animals is indisputable, for their remains have been found in rocks all over the earth. What eternal purpose they played in the creation and early history of the earth is unknown. The scriptures do not address the question, and it is not the realm of science to explore the issue of why they were here. We can only conclude, as Elder Talmage did, that 'the whole series of chalk deposits and many of our deep-sea limestones contain the skeletal remains of animals. These lived and died, age after age, while the earth was yet unfit for human habitation.' ...
>
> The relationship between scripture and what is currently understood in science is ever changing. Science continually learns more about the history of life on earth, and we have every reason to believe that much more will be learned as research continues.
>
> The struggle to correlate a passage in scripture with a specific portion of scientific research has been a challenge for centuries. But experience has shown that what a person understands today will be modified by tomorrow's discoveries. Patience and humility will eventually resolve all questions – if not in this life, then in the next.
>
> Fortunately, we need not know all the details of the Creation to take advantage of the essential saving ordinances of the gospel and conform to divine standards of progression. The scriptures and the inspired counsel of the prophets are sufficient to lead us back to God.
>
> But this does not mean that science has no place in our eternal pursuit of truth. The more we learn of God's handiwork, the more we come to know him and love his works. As a Latter-day Saint geologist, I consider myself fortunate indeed to have the opportunity to study rocks and fossils as evidences of God's creation of our earth. Everything I have learned of

the grandeur of the Creation has strengthened my resolve to learn more of our Heavenly Father and live as He would have me live.[35]

Although the article in which this answer appeared was prefaced by a disclaimer that these were questions 'of general gospel interest answered for guidance, not as official statements of Church policy,' the fact that it was printed in an official church magazine twenty years ago hints at a possible, if subtle shift in position on the part of the Church of Jesus Christ of Latter-day Saints.

Regarding the ultimate harmonization of science and religion, Apostle Bruce R. McConkie predicted:

As a matter of fact, from the eternal perspective, true science is part of the gospel itself; in its broadest signification the gospel embraces all truth. When the full blessings of the millennium are poured out upon the earth and its inhabitants, pseudo-science and pseudo-religion will be swept aside, and all supposed conflicts between science and religion will vanish away.[36]

Has this not occurred with the appearance of Bahá'u'lláh? Has He not revealed things 'which have passed, and hidden things which no man knew, things of the earth, by which it was made, and the purpose and the end thereof'?[37] Has He not spoken in plain language concerning these things?

Technological advances

Bahá'ís believe that there is a definite causal relationship between the birth of their Faith (marked by the Declaration of the Báb on the eve of May 23, 1844) and the explosion of scientific and technological advances that humanity has witnessed ever since. On the very next day, half a world away, Samuel Morse sent his famous telegraph message from Washington to Baltimore. The content of the message: a verse from the Book of Numbers – 'What hath God wrought!'[38]

Joseph Smith mentioned the telegraph in his writings as early as August 1840:

The electric telegraph is beginning to be used on the Great Western Railroad in England, between Drayton and Paddington, by which intelligence is communicated at the rate of two hundred thousand miles per second.[39]

It is clear from this and other historical information that the invention of the telegraph was an evolutionary process involving many bright minds and numerous patents, each improving on the previous design. The culmination of this process was the aforementioned transmission over a considerable distance by Samuel Morse on May 24, 1844. The appearance of this note in Joseph Smith's daily journal of the Church also suggests he recognized the significance of that invention.

It is a generally accepted notion among Bahá'ís that with the coming of this new Revelation from God, a shockwave was sent throughout the world in fulfillment of a prophecy from the Book of Daniel:

> But thou, O Daniel, shut up the words, and seal the book, even to the time of the end: many shall run to and fro, and knowledge shall be increased.[40]

But Bahá'ís are not the only ones to make such a claim. The Mormon faith was founded two decades earlier, in the 1820s, and Joseph Smith was martyred on June 27, 1844, just over a month after the Declaration of the Báb. The indisputable technological advances that have taken place since are considered by Mormons to be a sign of 'the Fullness of Times,' and a direct result of the 'restoration of the gospel.' During a 1926 speech, Joseph Fielding Smith declared:

> . . . I maintain that had there been no restoration of the gospel, and no organization of the Church of Jesus Christ of Latter-day Saints, there would have been no radio; there would have been no airplane, and there would not have been the wonderful discoveries in medicine, chemistry, electricity, and the many other things wherein the world has been benefited by such discoveries. Under such conditions these blessings would have been withheld, for they belong to the Dispensation of the Fulness of Times of which the restoration of the gospel and the organization of the Church constitute the central point, from which radiates the Spirit of the Lord throughout the world. The inspiration of the Lord has gone out and takes hold of the minds of men, though they know it not, and they are directed by the Lord. In this manner he brings them into his service that his purposes and his righteousness, in due time, may be supreme on the earth . . . I do not believe for one moment that these discoveries have come by chance, or that they have come because of superior intelligence possessed by men today over those who lived in ages that are past. They have come and are coming because the time is ripe, because the Lord has willed it, and because he has poured out his Spirit on all flesh.[41]

An age of renewal

Bahá'ís consider it a matter of course that the enormous acceleration of discovery, invention and social and spiritual awakening that occurred in the mid-19th century was a direct result of the stupendous energy released into the world by the Bahá'í Revelation. Although there was a gradual buildup in the first few decades of that century, this energy was released in full force in 1844, the year in which the Báb declared His mission. Of this year, Hand of the Cause William Sears wrote:

> I was intrigued to discover that certainly some creative power had 'brought to light' the 'hidden things' during that epoch of 1844. My search through secular history revealed the astonishing fact that beginning in that decade an entirely new spirit of invention and discovery had made itself apparent
> . . .
>
> I also read the report given by an official of the United States Patent Office who, in 1844, stated that in his opinion everything worthwhile had already been invented, and the Patent Office might as well close its doors. From that time on the Patent Office was overwhelmed with new inventions and discoveries . . .
>
> The endless stream of wonders still continues. The whole concept of life has altered. Newspapers, magazines, books, radio, television, telephone, telegraph, schools, education, travel – have all vastly increased man's knowledge and information.[42]

Many Bahá'ís see the advent of the Internet as yet another product of God's plan for the unification of the planet, as Shoghi Effendi envisaged on March 11, 1936:

> A mechanism of world inter-communication will be devised, embracing the whole planet, freed from national hindrances and restrictions, and functioning with marvellous swiftness and perfect regularity.[43]

These momentous advances in every area of human interaction – social, artistic, scientific – are thus considered part of the new creation that is the Bahá'í Revelation:

> Should the Will of God assist Us, there would flow out from the Pen of the Divine Expounder a lengthy exposition of that which hath been mentioned, and there would be revealed, in the field of arts and sciences, what would renew the world and the nations.[44]

In the estimation of historians this radiant [20th] century is equivalent to one hundred centuries of the past. If comparison be made with the sum total of all former human achievements, it will be found that the discoveries, scientific advancement and material civilization of this present century have equaled, yea far exceeded the progress and outcome of one hundred former centuries . . . Reflect upon the miracles of accomplishment which have already characterized it: the discoveries in every realm of human research. Inventions, scientific knowledge, ethical reforms and regulations established for the welfare of humanity, mysteries of nature explored, invisible forces brought into visibility and subjection – a veritable wonder-world of new phenomena and conditions heretofore unknown to man now open to his uses and further investigation. The East and West can communicate instantly. A human being can soar in the skies or speed in submarine depths. The power of steam has linked the continents. Trains cross the deserts and pierce the barriers of mountains; ships find unerring pathways upon the trackless oceans. Day by day discoveries are increasing. What a wonderful century this is! It is an age of universal reformation.[45]

'Abdu'l-Bahá made this last statement nearly 100 years ago. What marvelous new inventions the world has witnessed since!

It is clear that both religious communities share a deep conviction that the changes this world has undergone in the past century and a half are by no means accidental. Mormons and Bahá'ís not only recognize the hand of God in these various developments, but also associate them with the 'last days' as prophesied by the prophet Daniel. The only difference lies in the two groups' understanding of the specific events on earth which ushered in these changes.

The existence of other worlds

Mormons and Bahá'ís share another belief not generally held by other organized religions: that God has created worlds beside ours, each with its own creatures. While the two faiths differ in their reasons for acknowledging the existence of extraterrestrial life, the following quotations – the first from *The Pearl of Great Price* (which Mormons claim contains additional revelations from Moses) and the next two from the Writings of Bahá'u'lláh – show more than a superficial resemblance:

And behold, the glory of the Lord was upon Moses, so that Moses stood in the presence of God, and talked with him face to face. And the Lord

244

God said unto Moses: For mine own purpose have I made these things. Here is wisdom and it remaineth in me. And by the word of my power, have I created them . . . And worlds without number have I created; and I also created them for mine own purpose; . . . But only an account of this earth, and the inhabitants thereof, give I unto you. For behold, there are many worlds that have passed away by the word of my power. And there are many that now stand, and innumerable are they unto man; but all things are numbered unto me, for they are mine and I know them . . . And the Lord God spake unto Moses, saying: The heavens, they are many, and they cannot be numbered unto man; but they are numbered unto me, for they are mine. And as one earth shall pass away, and the heavens thereof even so shall another come; and there is no end to my works, neither to my words.[46]

Verily I say, the creation of God embraceth worlds besides this world, and creatures apart from these creatures. In each of these worlds He hath ordained things which none can search except Himself, the All-Searching, the All-Wise.[47]

Through His potency the Trees of Divine Revelation have yielded their fruits, every one of which hath been sent down in the form of a Prophet, bearing a Message to God's creatures in each of the worlds whose number God, alone, in His all-encompassing Knowledge, can reckon.[48]

Although these last two utterances of Bahá'u'lláh can certainly be understood to refer to the infinite *spiritual* worlds through which we are told we will progress, the following statement is a clear reference to *physical* worlds:

The learned men, that have fixed at several thousand years the life of this earth, have failed, throughout the long period of their observation, to consider either the number or the age of the other planets. Consider, moreover, the manifold divergencies that have resulted from the theories propounded by these men. Know thou that every fixed star hath its own planets, and every planet its own creatures, whose number no man can compute.[49]

Every planet its own creatures?

Notwithstanding the high statistical probability that this immense universe harbors other manifestations of life, the above-quoted verse by Bahá'u'lláh sometimes evokes strong reactions on the part of non-Bahá'ís, who correctly point out that of the planets we have thus far surveyed, the vast majority appear to be incapable of supporting life as we imagine it. This becomes even more challenging in light of 'Abdu'l-Bahá's declaration that if 'statements and teachings of religion are found to be unreasonable and contrary to science, they are outcomes of superstition and imagination.'[50]

However, there are several possible explanations for this apparent contradiction. The first concerns what might be termed *scriptural hyperbole*: a form of poetic license employed by the Divine Authors to contrast two opposing ideas. For example, Jesus told His disciples: 'And again I say unto you, It is easier for a camel to go through the eye of a needle, than for a rich man to enter into the kingdom of God.'[51] Taken out of context, this suggests that one has to become destitute in order to be accepted into the Kingdom, as a camel obviously could never pass through the eye of a needle. Yet Jesus' subsequent assurance that 'with God all things are possible' makes it clear that He was using a form of stylistic exaggeration to get a point across, namely that it is a man's attachment to his riches, not necessarily his net worth, that prevents his entry. Shoghi Effendi described as 'exaggerated emphasis' a similar dichotomy presented by 'Abdu'l-Bahá Who, in answer to a question about pantheism, stated that the 'Divine Reality is sanctified from singleness, then how much more from plurality.'[52] The Guardian clarified that, far from denying the singleness of God,

> The Master uses this term . . . in order to forcibly impress us with the fact that the Godhead is unknowable, and that to define it is impossible . . . He uses the method of exaggerated emphasis in order to drive home His thought that we know the sun indirectly through its rays, the Godhead indirectly through the Manifestation of God.[53]

In like manner, it would not be unreasonable to suggest that in the aforementioned verse about life on other planets, Bahá'u'lláh was using a similar device to contrast the 'theories' of 'learned men, that have fixed at several thousand years the life of this earth' to the scientific reality that over the course of billions of years innumerable stars and planets have formed, some of which are undoubtedly capable of sustaining life.

Secondly, the Bahá'í Writings clearly differentiate between the spiritual foundation of man that has 'existed from all eternity,' and his eventual appearance in the world of matter perhaps a million years ago. Likewise, all of creation is considered perfect in its original design, but at various stages of development in its physical perfections:

... it is clear that this terrestrial globe in its present form did not come into existence all at once, but that this universal existence gradually passed through different phases until it became adorned with its present perfection.[54]

The searing mass of molten rock and metal that was our Earth four and a half billion years ago would have seemed, to an outside observer, to be at best an implausible host of living organisms. By the same token, we cannot say with certainty that millions or billions of years from now, other planets will not develop their own creatures, however elemental. In a letter to an individual believer, the Universal House of Justice explained:[55]

> As you rightly state, Bahá'u'lláh affirms that every fixed star has its planets, and every planet its own creatures. The House of Justice states however, that it has not discovered anything in the Bahá'í Writings which would indicate the degree of progress such creatures may have attained. Obviously, as creatures of earth have managed to construct space probes and send them into outer space, it can be believed that creatures on other planets may have succeeded in doing likewise . . .[56]

Lastly, we cannot tell what creatures, if any, exist in a higher state of existence beyond our own limited three-dimensional window on the universe, and are thus undetectable through ordinary means.

LDS belief in other worlds based on doctrine of exaltation

The Mormon belief in the existence of other worlds is not based on scientific principle; rather, at its origin is the theological doctrine that God was once a man on another planet who became 'exalted' to the level of godhood, and thus inherited our world as His dominion. An article in *New Era* magazine states:

> Long before our God began his creations, he dwelt on a mortal world like ours, one of the creations that his Father had created for him and his brethren. He, with many of his brethren, was obedient to the principles of the eternal gospel. One among these, it is presumed, was a savior for them, and through him they obtained a resurrection and an exaltation on an eternal, celestial world. Then they gained the power and godhood of their Father and were made heirs of all that he had, continuing his works and creating worlds of their own for their own posterity – the same as their Father had done before, and his Father, and his Father, and on and on.[57]

Mormon doctrine thus holds that our God had a father of His own, suggesting a hierarchy of divine beings not unlike that postulated by some metaphysical theories. However, the use of the word *God* in the preceding quotation seems difficult to relate to the Being who said, 'And worlds without number have I created; and I also created them for mine own purpose . . .'[58] For if it is God the exalted man who has created innumerable worlds, where are the worlds created by his father? Is there a parallel universe, or did these worlds pass away before the creation of our world? Who created the first such world, and the first being to dwell upon it?

These questions lead to the logical conclusion that there must exist a higher Being, an Unknowable Essence Who is the Source and Creator of *all* the worlds and *all* creatures that roam them, Who is without origin, and without any direct relationship to His creation. It is this all-highest Essence, the Supreme Creator, Whom Bahá'ís call God.

CHAPTER 11

SOME ADDITIONAL BAHÁ'Í THEMES

Up to this point we have primarily focused on established Mormon principles, and attempted to build a framework of comparison to the Bahá'í Faith
using the scriptures of both religions as a guide. In this last chapter on doctrinal and behavioral similarities we will turn things around a bit by discussing
some distinctively Bahá'í principles, and examining how they are reflected in
the Mormon teachings.

The oneness of religion

One of the most significant principles of the Bahá'í Faith is the oneness of
religion. According to this principle, all the world's great religions have issued
from the same divine Source. These religions were sent down by God at different times in history through chosen Messengers or *Manifestations*. Each of
these Manifestations, like a polished mirror reflecting the sun, was a perfect
image of God's spiritual qualities, and His words were synonymous with the
Word of God. The differences between the various religions are due to the age
in which they appeared and the needs of the people to whom they were given,
in accordance with their understanding and spiritual receptivity. All religions
are thus seen as progressive stages in the gradual unfolding of *the same religion*:
the religion of God. Abraham, Krishna, Moses, Zoroaster, the Buddha, Jesus,
Muhammad, the Báb, Bahá'u'lláh[1] – all are considered exponents of that same
religion, and each was entrusted with a particular mission to help humanity
progress to the next stage of its collective spiritual development. On one level,
the Manifestations of God were unique individuals with different names and
distinct messages. On another level, all of them were as one soul representing
that same eternal Spirit Christians know as 'the Word' that 'was in the beginning with God.'[2]

By way of analogy, the earth can be likened to an elementary school, in
which humanity must learn lessons and pass tests in order to progress from
one grade to the next. In one respect, every teacher (Divine Educator) is con-

sidered an individual, with specific course materials (scriptures) suited to the grade he is teaching. In another sense, all teachers work from the same overall school curriculum whose ultimate purpose it is to prepare students for graduation. Once we start to view the various religions as grade levels of the same school, we come to see the folly of religious prejudice. Can a second grader honestly say he has no need of the third grade, while rejecting fractions and long division as nonsense because he does not understand these concepts? Should a sixth grader have contempt for the fifth grade teacher because his lesson plan doesn't include algebra? What if a student refused to advance to the next grade because he wanted to keep his old teacher?

The following excerpts from the Bahá'í Writings explain the oneness of all religions:

> The holy Manifestations Who have been the Sources or Founders of the various religious systems were united and agreed in purpose and teaching . . . there is no differentiation possible in Their mission and teachings; all are reflectors of reality, and all are promulgators of the religion of God. The divine religion is reality, and reality is not multiple; it is one. Therefore, the foundations of the religious systems are one because all proceed from the indivisible reality . . .[3]

> Contemplate with thine inward eye the chain of successive Revelations that hath linked the Manifestation of Adam with that of the Báb. I testify before God that each one of these Manifestations hath been sent down through the operation of the Divine Will and Purpose, that each hath been the bearer of a specific Message, that each hath been entrusted with a divinely-revealed Book and been commissioned to unravel the mysteries of a mighty Tablet. The measure of the Revelation with which every one of them hath been identified had been definitely fore-ordained.[4]

> There can be no doubt whatever that the peoples of the world, of whatever race or religion, derive their inspiration from one heavenly Source, and are the subjects of one God. The difference between the ordinances under which they abide should be attributed to the varying requirements and exigencies of the age in which they were revealed. All of them . . . were ordained of God, and are a reflection of His Will and Purpose. Arise and, armed with the power of faith, shatter to pieces the gods of your vain imaginings, the sowers of dissension amongst you.[5]

The Mormon scriptures on the oneness of religion

We have already observed that the Church of Jesus Christ of Latter-day Saints considers itself to be the only true religion of God, and 'every system of religion in the world today' to be 'born of religious syncretism.'[6] Yet in the Book of Mormon there are strong acknowledgments of the divine origin of all the world's religions:

> All things which are good cometh from God. Everything which inviteth and enticeth to do good, and to serve him, is inspired of God.[7]

> Thou fool, that shall say: A Bible, we have got a Bible, and we need no more Bible. Have ye obtained a Bible save it were by the Jews? Know ye not that there are more nations than one? Know ye not that I, the Lord your God, have created all men, and that I remember those who are upon the isles of the sea; and that I rule in the heavens above and in the earth beneath; and I bring forth my word unto the children of men, yea, even upon all the nations of the earth? Wherefore murmur ye, because that ye shall receive more of my word? Know ye not that the testimony of two nations is a witness unto you that I am God, that I remember one nation like unto another? Wherefore, I speak the same words unto one nation like unto another. And when the two nations shall run together the testimony of the two nations shall run together also. And I do this that I may prove unto many that I am the same yesterday, today, and forever; and that I speak forth my words according to my own pleasure.[8]

> For behold, the Lord doth grant unto all nations, of their own nation and tongue, to teach his word, yea, in wisdom, all that he seeth fit that they should have; therefore we see that the Lord doth counsel in wisdom, according to that which is just and true.[9]

Compare the above verse from the Book of Mormon to these Words of Bahá'u'lláh:

> Unto the cities of all nations He hath sent His Messengers, Whom He hath commissioned to announce unto men tidings of the Paradise of His good pleasure, and to draw them nigh unto the Haven of abiding security, the Seat of eternal holiness and transcendent glory.[10]

The oneness of mankind

Notwithstanding the Church's controversial history and scriptures with respect to race (see Appendix 2), elsewhere in the Mormon scriptures the oneness of mankind is firmly upheld. The following two verses – the first from the Book of Mormon and the second from the Hidden Words of Bahá'u'lláh – use identical metaphors to make their point:

> And now, my brethren, I have spoken unto you concerning pride; and those of you which have afflicted your neighbor, and persecuted him because ye were proud in your hearts, of the things which God hath given you, what say ye of it? Do ye not suppose that such things are abominable unto him who created all flesh? And the one being is as precious in his sight as the other. And all flesh is of the dust; and for the selfsame end hath he created them, that they should keep his commandments and glorify him forever.[11]

> O Children of Men! Know ye not why We created you all from the same dust? That no one should exalt himself over the other. Ponder at all times in your hearts how ye were created. Since We have created you all from one same substance it is incumbent on you to be even as one soul, to walk with the same feet, eat with the same mouth and dwell in the same land, that from your inmost being, by your deeds and actions, the signs of oneness and the essence of detachment may be made manifest. Such is My counsel to you, O concourse of light! Heed ye this counsel that ye may obtain the fruit of holiness from the tree of wondrous glory.[12]

Having observed that all men were created from the same dust, the sacred writings of both faiths conclude that all of mankind is equal in the sight of God:

> Now my brethren, we see that God is mindful of every people, whatsoever land they may be in; yea, he numbereth his people, and his bowels of mercy are over all the earth. Now this is my joy, and my great thanksgiving; yea, and I will give thanks unto my God forever.[13]

> O Thou kind Lord! Thou hast created all humanity from the same stock. Thou hast decreed that all shall belong to the same household. In Thy Holy Presence they are all Thy servants, and all mankind are sheltered beneath Thy Tabernacle; all have gathered together at Thy Table of Bounty; all are illumined through the light of Thy Providence.[14]

For none of these iniquities come of the Lord; for he doeth that which is good among the children of men; and he doeth nothing save it be plain unto the children of men; and he inviteth them all to come unto him and partake of his goodness; and he denieth none that come unto him, black and white, bond and free, male and female; and he remembereth the heathen; and all are alike unto God, both Jew and Gentile.[15]

There are no whites and blacks before God. All colors are one, and that is the color of servitude to God. Scent and color are not important. The heart is important. If the heart is pure, white or black or any color makes no difference. God does not look at colors; He looks at the hearts. He whose heart is pure is better. He whose character is better is more pleasing. He who turns more to the Abhá Kingdom is more advanced.[16]

Unity

Unity is unquestionably *the* central theme of the Bahá'í Faith. The oneness of God, of religion and of humanity are foremost among its tenets; world peace is its ultimate goal; and the unity of the Bahá'í world community itself is safeguarded by that most unique of institutions, the Covenant of Bahá'u'lláh. This Covenant has its origin in Bahá'u'lláh's Will and Testament, and marks the first time in recorded history that the founder of a religion has named his successor as head of the faith *in writing*. The result is an unbroken chain of authority in the Bahá'í Faith which prevents it from splintering into countless sects or factions.

Although there is nothing remotely akin to the Covenant in the LDS Church, its scriptures contain clear statements about unity:

And he commanded that there should be no contention one with another, but that they should look forward with one eye, having one faith and one baptism, having their hearts knit together in unity and in love one towards another.[17]

And there shall be no disputations among you, as there have hitherto been; neither shall there be disputations among you concerning the points of my doctrine, as there have hitherto been. For verily, verily I say unto you, he that hath the spirit of contention is not of me, but is of the devil, who is the father of contention, and he stirreth up the hearts of men to contend with anger, one with another.[18]

The same sentiments are expressed in Bahá'u'lláh's unequivocal verdict:

> Every eye, in this Day, should seek what will best promote the Cause of God. He, Who is the Eternal Truth, beareth Me witness! Nothing whatever can, in this Day, inflict a greater harm upon this Cause than dissension and strife, contention, estrangement and apathy, among the loved ones of God. Flee them, through the power of God and His sovereign aid, and strive ye to knit together the hearts of men, in His Name, the Unifier, the All-Knowing, the All-Wise.[19]

> Beware lest ye prefer yourselves above your neighbors. Fix your gaze upon Him Who is the Temple of God amongst men. He, in truth, hath offered up His life as a ransom for the redemption of the world. He, verily, is the All-Bountiful, the Gracious, the Most High. If any differences arise amongst you, behold Me standing before your face, and overlook the faults of one another for My name's sake and as a token of your love for My manifest and resplendent Cause. We love to see you at all times consorting in amity and concord within the paradise of My good-pleasure, and to inhale from your acts the fragrance of friendliness and unity, of loving-kindness and fellowship.[20]

However, the Bahá'í teachings carry the concept of unity a step further. Unity is not simply limited to the body of believers; it is considered the ultimate goal and destiny of all mankind. 'Abdu'l-Bahá implored:

> The aim of the appearance of the Blessed Perfection – may my life be a sacrifice for His beloved ones! – was the unity and agreement of all the people of the world. Therefore, my utmost desire, firstly, is the accord and union and love of the believers and after that of all the people of the world. Now, if unity and agreement is not established among the believers, I will become heartbroken and the afflictions will leave a greater imprint upon me. But if the fragrance of love and unity among the believers is wafted to my nostrils, every trial will become a mercy, every unhappiness a joy, every difficulty an expansion, every misery a treasure and every hardship a felicity.[21]

> Wherefore, O ye beloved of the Lord, bestir yourselves, do all in your power to be as one, to live in peace, each with the others: for ye are all the drops from but one ocean, the foliage of one tree, the pearls from a single shell, the flowers and sweet herbs from the same one garden. And achieving that, strive ye to unite the hearts of those who follow other faiths.[22]

Diversity

'Unity in Diversity' is not just another catchphrase. This deceptively simple concept has far-reaching implications for how we view those who are different from us. With deep roots in the Bahá'í Writings, unity in diversity represents a radical departure from what has traditionally been considered an 'appropriate' attitude toward different races and cultures.

More and more people are beginning to realize that the familiar metaphor of America as a cultural 'melting pot' is slightly off the mark. When gold jewelry is melted down, it loses its original beauty and individuality, and is reduced to a form of currency; candles of differing sizes, shapes and colors turn into a homogeneous mass of brownish wax. With the possible exception of cheese fondue, few things are made better by melting them together. Rather, a salad bowl might be a better way to symbolize America's diverse population: while all the vegetables and fruits retain their individual flavor, color and shape, they blend together to make a delicious and visually pleasing dish.

It has also been said that people should become 'color blind' with respect to other races, as a way to end race-based discrimination. However, this opinion acknowledges only the historically negative consequences of racial distinctions, and entirely ignores their positive potential. After all, if God had desired for man to be color blind, why would He have caused humanity to abound in color? Could it be that the true purpose of our diversity is to make the world a more beautiful place?

The Bahá'í Writings show that there is another way to eliminate discrimination while still embracing the things that make us different. Although our society has only recently come to appreciate diversity, 'Abdu'l-Bahá introduced these principles to the American continent nearly a century ago. At a 1912 talk in Chicago, He stated:

Bahá'u'lláh has proclaimed the oneness of the world of humanity. He has caused various nations and divergent creeds to unite. He has declared that difference of race and color is like the variegated beauty of flowers in a garden. If you enter a garden, you will see yellow, white, blue, red flowers in profusion and beauty – each radiant within itself and although different from the others, lending its own charm to them. Racial difference in the human kingdom is similar. If all the flowers in a garden were of the same color, the effect would be monotonous and wearying to the eye.

Therefore, Bahá'u'lláh hath said that the various races of humankind lend a composite harmony and beauty of color to the whole. Let all associate, therefore, in this great human garden even as flowers grow and blend together side by side without discord or disagreement between them.[23]

Interracial marriage is of course the ultimate expression of unity in diversity. 'Abdu'l-Bahá wholeheartedly encouraged such marriages as a way to accelerate the unification of the races:

> If it be possible, gather together these two races, black and white, into one Assembly, and put such love into their hearts that they shall not only unite but even intermarry. Be sure that the result of this will abolish differences and disputes between black and white.[24]

Diversity in the LDS Church

Over the past decades, the LDS Church leadership has come to see racial diversity as a positive influence, and has issued a number of statements affirming the oneness of humanity and extending a warm welcome to people of all races, nationalities, and cultural backgrounds. It has also recognized that the appreciation of the diversity of the human race is a key ingredient in fostering universal brotherhood. In 1973, President Marion G. Romney, speaking to a culturally diverse group of college students at the Hawaii campus of Brigham Young University, remarked:

> This college is a living laboratory in which individuals who share the teachings of the Master Teacher have an opportunity for developing an appreciation, tolerance, and esteem for one another. For what can be done here interculturally in a small way is what mankind must do on a large scale if we are ever to have real brotherhood on this earth.[25]

Fueled by the Church's rapid expansion to all corners of the world, the issue of diversity has forced itself into the collective consciousness of the American LDS community, as well. Among individual Saints, diversity is generally seen as having a positive effect on their religion, although attitudes differ on the merits of diversity as a goal in itself. This is evidenced by the varied opinions given in church magazines, some of which are very much in line with Bahá'í principles:

> Whether we recognize it or not, diversity is now a part of the Church, and it is increasing daily. If our experience in linking and unifying diverse members is . . . successful, . . . an institution of color, beauty, and deep spiritual unity can develop. To succeed, we will need unifying ideas taught by thoughtful leaders. Stakes and wards whose members can eagerly greet

and make welcome diverse membership – putting brothers and sisters to work in meaningful service – will hasten the unification process . . . Experience teaches me that we must work hard at creating unity in diversity. We must do it with active and strong leadership. Unity in diversity will not happen if we let nature take its course. Isolation and discrimination are still capable of surfacing in every location of the Church. We each need to assign ourselves as a 'committee of one' to create the attitudes of inclusion, acceptance, and unity wherever we find ourselves. It needs to be a high priority with us. We especially need leaders to show the way by precept and example. Each of us should be fair to everyone, especially the victims of discrimination, isolation, and exclusion. Let us be careful not to consider as funny any joke that demeans or belittles others because of religious, cultural, racial, national, or gender differences. All are alike unto God. We should walk away or face up to the problem when confronted with these common and unworthy practices. Each should do his or her part . . . May we look for every opportunity, therefore, to decrease isolation, increase inclusion of all, and enrich our lives with this human diversity within the bonds of unifying doctrinal beliefs . . . let us find the common bond that links us through love and through Christ and His gospel. May the happy result be the emergence of unity in diversity.[26]

In contrast, the following excerpt from a more recent talk by Elder Dallin Oaks reflects old tendencies to see unity and diversity as mutually exclusive principles:

Our Church has an approach to the obvious cultural and ethnic diversities among our members. We teach that what unites us is far more important than what differentiates us. Consequently, our members are asked to concentrate their efforts to strengthen our unity – not to glorify our diversity. For example, our objective is not to organize local wards and branches according to differences in culture or in ethnic or national origins, although that effect is sometimes produced on a temporary basis when required because of language barriers. Instead, we teach that members of majority groupings (whatever their nature) are responsible to accept church members of other groupings, providing full fellowship and full opportunities in Church participation. We seek to establish a community of Saints – 'one body,' the Apostle Paul called it (1 Cor. 12:13) – where everyone feels needed and wanted and where all can pursue the eternal goals we share. Consistent with the Savior's command to 'be one,' we seek unity.[27]

Although Elder Oaks appears to have mistakenly equated diversity to the ethnic segregation of the community, his greater point is valid: members of 'majority groupings' in the Church should accept minorities in their midst, and treat them as their equals. However, this does not mean that these minorities should have to sacrifice their cultural identity in order to be fully assimilated into the Church.

In the United States, the Church's ideal of diversity has proved rather elusive. While there are a large number of Latino Mormons, these usually attend special 'Spanish wards' that are separated from the rest of the community by cultural and language barriers. And while the number of Asian believers appears to be on the rise, the number of African American and Native American believers remains statistically insignificant.[28]

Cultural identity

In the Bahá'í Faith, the encroachment of religious rituals is assiduously avoided. Each individual believer is free to worship God in his own way, but may never attempt to influence another's expression of devotion. Even the administration of the Nineteen Day Feast – the Bahá'í equivalent of the sacrament – is not cast in stone:

> Even though the observance of the Feast requires strict adherence to the threefold aspects in the sequence in which they have been defined, there is much room for variety in the total experience. For example, music may be introduced at various stages, including the devotional portion; 'Abdu'l-Bahá recommends that eloquent, uplifting talks be given; originality and variety in expressions of hospitality are possible; the quality and range of the consultation are critical to the spirit of the occasion. The effects of different cultures in all these respects are welcome factors which can lend the Feast a salutary diversity, representative of the unique characteristics of the various societies in which it is held, and therefore conducive to the upliftment and enjoyment of its participants.[29]

This lack of conformity to a specific worship formula leaves room for a good deal of cultural expression. The slogan 'unity in diversity' not only suggests that members of different races can live in harmony with each other, but also that people from vastly different cultures can come together in one Faith while retaining their unique cultural identity. Rather than abandon the riches of their ethnic and cultural heritage, they instead bring them to the table for everyone to enjoy. A statement submitted by the Bahá'í International

Community to the United Nations reads:

> Such a definition envisages a unified world – but not a uniform world.
> The diversity of the human family is both its glory and its strength, for
> the diversity of humanity (both physical and cultural) is proof of the suc-
> cess with which man has adapted to the diverse conditions existing on
> his planet. Modes of life, of dress, of construction, of diet, of husbandry
> – all have their roots in the natural environment of a particular nation or
> people. A development plan which recognizes this fact will draw upon
> traditional local knowledge, and will seek to improve existing methods and
> to increase local resources by means which are compatible with the existing
> culture and environment.[30]

The Bahá'í Feast and other devotional gatherings may include various forms
of music from virtually all cultural backgrounds and genres – even popular
music styles such hip hop, so long as the message is in accordance with Bahá'í
principles. (An exception to this are the Bahá'í Houses of Worship, where
music is restricted to *a cappella* music.) As to proper attire at worship services,
a Bahá'í's clothing must be modest and clean, but otherwise can be of any
style. At some special celebrations, Bahá'ís are in fact encouraged to dress in
the traditional style of their native country in order to promote an atmosphere
of diversity.

By contrast, Mormon worship services throughout the world allow only
classical instruments, and the music must be 'reverent' in nature. Although
a local ward may sometimes accommodate special performances to promote
cultural diversity, musical selections are usually limited to a standard canon of
solemn 19th-century hymns accompanied by a pipe organ, and there are no
drums or dancing of any kind. Gospel-style music is not found in Mormon
churches. Regardless of the local customs, women are required to wear dresses
or skirts that fall below the knee, and men are expected to wear slacks, a (pref-
erably white) dress shirt and a tie.

Notwithstanding the apparent homogeneity of the Mormon community
and its worship practices, LDS wards periodically sponsor events or parties to
highlight a particular culture, for example by hosting a Hawaiian luau featuring traditional hula dancing. As the following excerpt from a church magazine
article shows, Latter-day Saints recognize that being Mormon does not mean
necessarily having to submit to 'the life-style and psychological references' of
19th-century Utah and that eventually, some of our old attachments – including those of cultural and national identity – must yield to a greater religious
identity:

Of course, the gospel does not eliminate the preferential differences in dress, music, and the arts. In fact, it even seeks to preserve and promote the vast stores of cultural wisdom and beauty which reinforce gospel ideals and give infinite variety and flavor to a people. But gone are the days when we saw the gospel as a culture itself, usually characterized by the life-style and psychological references of the Wasatch front. We really do believe now that the gospel embraces a set of spiritual values that transcends the mere emotional allegiances to the ways things are said and done in a particular environment. This means that deep change is both desirable and inevitable in the wake of full conversion and that some cultural elements will be and ought to be superseded and lost. We stress that we are followers of Christ first and foremost, Latter-day Saints, a fraternity of priesthood which is more infinitely precious and meaningful than any cultural institution or national identity.[31]

The Kingdom of God on earth

Bahá'ís and Mormons share a similar vision of a world that will eventually become united, and subject to the universal law of God. In 1844, Joseph Smith declared that the 'government of God' must eventually replace all the governments of the world. An *Ensign* magazine article elaborates:

> This restored kingdom of Jesus Christ was revealed in a day when other kingdoms on the earth were rapidly being eliminated. There are only a few kingdoms left, and these are principally constitutional monarchies. The day will soon come when the only kingdom to survive will be that ecclesiastical kingdom of Jesus Christ which is to replace all other kingdoms on the face of the earth.[32]

Excepting the specific reference to Jesus Christ, this statement can be favorably compared to the following utterance of 'Abdu'l-Bahá:

> Bahá'u'lláh through the power of heaven has brought the East and the West together. Erelong we shall know that they have been cemented by the power of God. The oneness of the kingdom of humanity will supplant the banner of conquest, and all communities of the earth will gather under its protection. No nation with separate and restricted boundaries – such as Persia, for instance – will exist. The United States of America will be known only as a name. Germany, France, England, Turkey, Arabia – all these various nations will be welded together in unity. When the people

of the future are asked, 'To which nationality do you belong?' the answer will be, 'To the nationality of humanity. I am living under the shadow of Bahá'u'lláh. I am the servant of Bahá'u'lláh. I belong to the army of the Most Great Peace.' The people of the future will not say, 'I belong to the nation of England, France or Persia'; for all of them will be citizens of a universal nationality – the one family, the one country, the one world of humanity – and then these wars, hatreds and strifes will pass away.[33]

Man is powerless to effect the regeneration of the world

In a stunning evaluation of man's failure to the present day – and his inevitable helplessness in the future – to establish peace in the world without divine assistance, LDS President John Taylor in his book *The Government of God* (1852) made the following astute observations:

I purpose in this Chapter to shew the incompetency of the means made use of by man for the accomplishment of the purposes of God – the establishment of His Kingdom, or Millennial reign.

Now, if it is the kingdom of God that is to be established, it must be introduced by God. He must not only be the originator of it, but the controller also; and any means short of these must fail of the object designed.

The great evils that now exist in the world are the consequences of man's departure from God. This has introduced this degeneracy and imbecility, and nothing but a retracing of his steps, and a return to God can bring about a restitution.

God gave to man a moral agency, as head of the world, under himself. Man has usurped the sole authority, and taken upon himself to reign and rule without God. The natural consequence is, that we have inherited all the evils of which I have spoken, and nothing but the wisdom, goodness, power, and compassion of God, can deliver us therefrom, restore the earth to its pristine excellence, and put man again in possession of those blessings which he has forfeited by his transgression. Emperors, kings, princes, potentates, statesmen, philosophers, and churches, have tried for ages to bring this state of things about; but they have all signally failed, not having derived their wisdom from the proper source. And all human means made use of at the present time to ameliorate the condition of the world must fail, as all human means have always done.[34]

Note how the above argument parallels these words of Bahá'u'lláh:

That which God hath ordained as the sovereign remedy and mightiest instrument for the healing of the world is the union of all its peoples in one universal Cause, one common Faith. This can in no wise be achieved except through the power of a skilled, an all-powerful, and inspired Physician. By My life! This is the truth, and all else naught but error. Each time that Most Mighty Instrument hath come, and that Light shone forth from the Ancient Dayspring, He was withheld by ignorant physicians who, even as clouds, interposed themselves between Him and the world. It failed therefore, to recover, and its sickness hath persisted until this day. They indeed were powerless to protect it, or to effect a cure, whilst He Who hath been the Manifestation of Power amongst men was withheld from achieving His purpose, by reason of what the hands of the ignorant physicians have wrought.[35]

John Taylor, an Englishman, roundly dismissed claims that Christianity as we know it can ever hope to bring about universal peace. In support of his argument, he highlighted the utter failures of various churches – notwithstanding their considerable influence and autonomy – to maintain peace within their respective dominions and amongst each other:

There are some who suppose that the influence of Christianity, as it is now preached and administered, will bring about a Millennial reign of peace. We will briefly examine the subject.

First, we will take the Greek and Catholic Churches as they have existed for ages – without an examination of their doctrines, whether right or wrong – for they form two of the largest branches of the Christian Church. They have, more or less, governed a great portion of Europe at different times; and what is the situation of the people and nations where they have held sway?

We have noticed the effects, and already briefly touched upon the evils that prevail in those countries; and if Greece and Russia, or any other country where the Greek Church has held sway, be a fair specimen of the influence of that church, we have very little prospect, if that religion were more widely diffused or extended, that the results would be more beneficial, for if it has failed in a few nations to ameliorate their condition, it would necessarily fail to benefit the earth if extended over it.

Nor do we turn with any better prospect to the Catholic religion. Of what benefit has it been to nations where it has prevailed the most? Has there been less war, less animosity, less butchery, less evil of any kind under its empire? It cannot be said that it has been crippled in its progress or its operations. It has held full sway in Spain, Rome, and a great portion of Italy, in France and Mexico for generations, not to mention many smaller states. Has it augmented the happiness of those nations of the world? I need not here refer to the history of the Waldenses, and Albigenses, and Huguenots, to that of the Crusades, wherein so many Christian kings engaged; nor to the unhappy differences, the wars and commotions, the bloodshed and carnage, that have existed among these people, for their history is well known. And the present position of both the Greek and Roman churches, presents a spectacle that is anything but encouraging to lead us to hope, that if the world were under their influence, a Millennial reign of peace and righteousness would ensue . . .

But, methinks I hear the Protestants say, we fully accord with you thus far, but we have placed Christianity on another footing. Let us examine this subject for a moment.

The question would naturally follow, What have the reformations of Calvin, Luther, and other reformers, done for the world? We may notice that Denmark, Sweden, Prussia, with a great part of Germany, Holland, and Switzerland, as also England and the United States, are Protestant. What can we say of them? That they are a part of the disorganized world, and have manifested the same unhappy dispositions as other portions. Reform has not altered their dispositions or circumstances. We see among them the same ambitious, grasping, reckless disposition manifested, and consequently the same wars, bloodshed, poverty, misery, and distress; and millions of human beings have been sacrificed to their pride, ambition, avarice, and thirst for national fame and glory.

The Reformation of the Church of England is anything but creditable to that church. I refer to Henry VIII, and the vacillating course taken by some of its early reformers; and its persecution of those who were opposed to it in religious faith.

. . . If we look at Christian nations as a whole, we see a picture that is truly lamentable; a miserable portrait of poor, degenerated, fallen humanity. We see Christian nations arrayed against Christian nations in battle, with the Christian ministers of each Christian nation calling upon the Christian's God to give them each the victory over their enemies! Christians! and worshippers of the same God!!

Hence, Christian England has been arrayed against Christian France; Christian Russia against Christian Prussia; Christian Spain against Christian Holland; Christian Austria against Christian Hungary; Christian England against Christian United States; and Christian United States against Christian Mexico. Not to mention the innumerable aggressions and conquests of some of the larger nations, not only upon their Christian brethren, but against other nations of the earth.

Before those several nations have engaged in their wars, their ministers have presented their several prayers before the same God; and if He had been as infatuated as they, and listened to their prayers, they would long ago have been destroyed, and the Christian world depopulated. After their prayers they have met in deadly strife; foe has rushed against foe with mortal energy, and the clarion of war, the clang of arms, and the cannon's roar have been followed by dying groans, shattered limbs, carnage, blood, and death; and unutterable misery and distress, desolate hearths, lonely widows, and fatherless children.

And yet these are all Christian nations, Christian brethren, worshippers of the same God. Christianity has prevailed more or less for eighteen hundred years. If it should still continue and overspread the world in its present form, what would it accomplish? The world's redemption and regeneration? No, verily. Its most staunch supporters, and most strenuous advocates would say, No. For like causes always produce like effects: and if it has failed to regenerate the nations where it has had full sway for generations, it must necessarily fail to regenerate the world. If it has failed in a small thing, how can it accomplish a large one?[36]

John Taylor's palpable disdain for the ecclesiastical wars which have pitted Christian against Christian is shared by 'Abdu'l-Bahá and Shoghi Effendi:

There are five hundred million people who call themselves Christians. If you compare their deeds with the text of the Gospels, you will find no likeness thereto. The real Christians are rare. The Christ exhorted men to be kind. The Christians are fighting and killing one another, leading their young men into war, shedding blood, destroying dwellings, causing mothers to lose their sons and children their fathers. What has all this to do with the teachings of Christ? Is a man whose highest aim is bloodshed a Christian? Christ suffered in order to teach kindness. 'O Father, forgive them, for they know not what they do.' Thus he pardoned his murderers. How merciful he was![37]

What a sorry spectacle of impotence and disruption does this fratricidal war, which Christian nations are waging against Christian nations – Anglicans pitted against Lutherans, Catholics against Greek Orthodox, Catholics against Catholics, and Protestants against Protestants – in support of a so-called Christian civilization, offer to the eyes of those who are already perceiving the bankruptcy of the institutions that claim to speak in the name, and to be the custodians, of the Faith of Jesus Christ! The powerlessness and despair of the Holy See to halt this internecine strife, in which the children of the Prince of Peace – blessed and supported by the benedictions and harangues of the prelates of a hopelessly divided church – are engaged, proclaim the degree of subservience into which the once all-powerful institutions of the Christian Faith have sunk, and are a striking reminder of the parallel state of decadence into which the hierarchies of its sister religion have fallen . . .

Such is the pass to which the Christian clergy have come – a clergy that have interposed themselves between their flock and the Christ returned in the glory of the Father. As the Faith of this Promised One penetrates farther and farther into the heart of Christendom, as its recruits from the garrisons which its spirit is assailing multiply, and provoke a concerted and determined action in defense of the strongholds of Christian orthodoxy, and as the forces of nationalism, paganism, secularism and racialism move jointly towards a climax, might we not expect that the decline in the power, the authority, and the prestige of these ecclesiastics will be accentuated, and further demonstrate the truth, and more fully unfold the implications, of Bahá'u'lláh's pronouncement predicting the eclipse of the luminaries of the Church of Jesus Christ.[38]

Order amid chaos

Bahá'ís believe that God has established His kingdom on earth 'as it is in heaven' not instantaneously by force, but rather as a perfect blueprint to be carried out by all humanity – Bahá'ís consciously so, and the rest of the world without direct knowledge of its Source. This blueprint comprises the Bahá'í Administrative Order and the Covenant of Bahá'u'lláh, and its inevitable realization is impeded only by the free will of those in charge of implementing it. Bahá'ís therefore remain aloof from politics and concern themselves primarily with raising this all-important edifice, in the hope that after the promised world upheavals, its institutions will have developed to the point of delineating a clear path to lasting world peace and providing spiritual shelter for a distraught populace. Like a phoenix rising from the ashes of chaos and destruction, the World Order of Bahá'u'lláh will stand ready to lead the world to its destined glory. Shoghi Effendi offered these sobering words:

The prophetic voice of Bahá'u'lláh warning, in the concluding passages of the Hidden Words, 'the peoples of the world' that 'an unforeseen calamity is following them and that grievous retribution awaiteth them' throws indeed a lurid light upon the immediate fortunes of sorrowing humanity. Nothing but a fiery ordeal, out of which humanity will emerge, chastened and prepared, can succeed in implanting that sense of responsibility which the leaders of a new-born age must arise to shoulder.[39]

A similar scenario is envisioned by the LDS Church. In *Mormon America*, we find the following characterization of future LDS expectations:

> The kingdom of God is the church, and before the Lord does return there will be chaos on earth and all earthly kingdoms will disintegrate. Then the church will be there, ready to provide order amid chaos.[40]

Indeed, when a Mormon is asked, 'When will the kingdom of God be established?' he will answer, 'It is already here. It is the Church of Jesus Christ of Latter-day Saints.'

An LDS vision of lasting peace

Whether or not it is reflected in the original scriptures of the LDS Church or in the explicit words of its presidents, there are souls within that organization who recognize the true destiny of our planet and express a sincere wish to help bring it about. In 2002, Russell M. Nelson, a member of the Quorum of the Twelve Apostles – a body second in rank only to the First Presidency – expressed these heartfelt sentiments:

> Because of the long history of hostility upon the earth, many feel that peace is beyond hope. I disagree. Peace is possible. We can learn to love our fellow human beings throughout the world. Whether they be Jewish, Islamic, or fellow Christians, whether Hindu, Buddhist, or other, we can live together with mutual admiration and respect, without forsaking our religious convictions. Things we have in common are greater than are our differences. Peace is a prime priority that pleads for our pursuit. Old Testament prophets held out hope and so should we. The Psalmist said, 'God is our refuge and strength, a very present help in trouble.' 'He maketh wars to cease unto the end of the earth.' . . .
>
> Isaiah prophesied of hope for our day. Speaking of the gathering of Israel and the Restoration of the Church through the Prophet Joseph Smith, Isaiah wrote:
>
> 'It shall come to pass in that day, that the Lord shall set his hand again the second time to recover the remnant of his people . . .

'And he shall set up an ensign for the nations, and shall assemble the outcasts of Israel, and gather together the dispersed of Judah from the four corners of the earth.'

These prophecies of hope could materialize if leaders and citizens of nations would apply the teachings of Jesus Christ. Ours could then be an age of unparalleled peace and progress. Barbarism of the past would be buried. War with its horrors would be relegated to the realm of maudlin memory. Aims of nations would be mutually supportive. Peacemakers could lead in the art of arbitration, give relief to the needy, and bring hope to those who fear. Of such patriots, future generations would shout praises, and our Eternal God would pass judgments of glory.[41]

And the venerable Brigham Young himself remarked:

Whoever lives to see the Kingdom of God fully established upon the earth will see a government that will protect every person in his rights. If that government was now reigning . . . you would see the Roman Catholic, the Greek Catholic, the Episcopalian, the Presbyterian, the Methodist, the Baptist, the Quaker, the Shaker, the [Hindu], the [Muslim], and every class of worshipers most strictly protected in all their municipal rights and in the privileges of worshiping who, what, and when they pleased, not infringing upon the rights of others. Does any candid person in his sound judgment desire any greater liberty?[42]

Indeed, do not these sentiments evoke the vision of a future Bahá'í State, of which it is promised that 'the rights of non-Bahá'í religious minorities would be rigorously protected by the Bahá'ís'?[43]

CHAPTER 12

FULFILLMENT OF PROPHECY

Now that we have explored a great many similarities between the LDS Church and the Bahá'í Faith, it is time to consider another, perhaps the most intriguing, connection between these two faiths: *prophecy*.

In examining the various prophecies contained within the Mormon scriptures, we should remind ourselves that the Church of Jesus Christ of Latter-day Saints is at its root a Christian church, one which not only considers the Bible an integral part of its canon, but whose own unique scriptures have liberally borrowed from that Holy Book – major portions of the Book of Mormon are direct quotations from the King James Bible. As most Bahá'ís are already familiar with the many Bible prophecies concerning the current dispensation, we should distinguish between prophecies unique to Mormonism and those that find their origin in the Old and New Testaments. In the following pages we look first at some Mormon predictions about the Coming of the Son of Man, and then at various Bible prophecies that have either been emphasized or recast in the LDS scriptures.

It is evident that Joseph Smith – though a fallible human being with all of the weaknesses that ordinary humans possess – exhibited extraordinary sensitivity to 'the spiritual currents flowing . . . directly from the appearance of the Báb and Bahá'u'lláh.'[1] While it may be true that, especially toward the close of his ministry, many of Smith's writings and utterances seem to get lost in a never-ending cycle of reinterpretations and rationalizations, the overall spirit of his words evinces a deep love of Christ and a conviction that His Return was near. Furthermore, sprinkled throughout Smith's writings are indications of a very real clairvoyance, prophecies which, unbeknownst to his millions of current followers, appear to point directly to the Báb and Bahá'u'lláh.[2] And although we should take care not to make too much of these prophecies or assume any definite link to the Bahá'í Faith – after all, it is clear from Joseph Smith's writings that he did not expect anything but the physical return of Jesus Christ – it is nevertheless striking how closely they correlate to significant events in the inauguration of the Bahá'í Dispensation.

The coming of the Son of Man

Joseph Smith was acutely aware that the Second Coming of Christ was close at hand. Yet when he was approached by a group of young Millerites (followers of William Miller, founder of what is now the Seventh-day Adventist Church), Smith made it clear that he did not agree with Miller's prediction – based on a numerical analysis of biblical events and prophecies – that Christ would return between the years 1843 and 1845:

> Seven or eight young men came to see me, part of them from the city of New York. They treated me with the greatest respect. I showed them the fallacy of Mr. Miller's *data* concerning the coming of Christ and the end of the world, or as it is commonly called, Millerism, and preached them quite a sermon; that error was in the Bible, or the translation of the Bible; that Miller was in want of correct information upon the subject, and that he was not so much to blame as the translators. I told them the prophecies must all be fulfilled; the sun must be darkened and the moon turned into blood, and many more things take place before Christ would come.[3]

Dismissive as he was of William Miller's claims, Joseph Smith frequently inquired of the Lord about this very subject. As his writings indicate, he received not one, but several answers through prayer. Though some non-Mormon Christians, unaware of the events that took place in 19th-century Persia, scoff at these predictions and hold them up as proof that Joseph Smith was a 'false prophet,' to the Bahá'í reader they present compelling evidence of Smith's spiritual powers of perception.

American Civil War to usher in the coming of the Son of Man

In *The Doctrine and Covenants* we find the following startling prophecy by Joseph Smith:

> I prophesy, in the name of the Lord God, that the commencement of the difficulties which will cause much bloodshed previous to the coming of the Son of Man will be in South Carolina. It may probably arise through the slave question. This a voice declared to me, while I was praying earnestly on the subject, December 25th, 1832.[4]

From a Bahá'í viewpoint, Smith could not have been more correct. In January 1861 – more than twenty-eight years from the time of this revelation and nearly seventeen years after Smith's death – South Carolina became the first state to secede from the Union over the issue of slavery. In all, seven states seceded, forming the Confederacy and sparking the American Civil War. On January 1, 1863, US President Abraham Lincoln issued the Emancipation Proclamation, officially abolishing human slavery and declaring the basic equality of all men before God without regard to race, nationality or previous condition of servitude.

Less than four months later, on April 21, 1863, Bahá'u'lláh declared His mission in Baghdad, an act which Bahá'ís consider to be one of the most significant events in the history of the Faith. It was this moment when Bahá'u'lláh, hitherto known only as a preeminent leader of the Bábí community, revealed His true station as the Promised One of all religions, and the One hailed by the Báb as 'Him Whom God will make manifest.' Of that day Bahá'u'lláh wrote:

> Rejoice with exceeding gladness, O people of Bahá, as ye call to remembrance the Day of supreme felicity, the Day whereon the Tongue of the Ancient of Days hath spoken, as He departed from His House, proceeding to the Spot from which He shed upon the whole of creation the splendors of His name, the All-Merciful. God is Our witness. Were We to reveal the hidden secrets of that Day, all they that dwell on earth and in the heavens would swoon away and die, except such as will be preserved by God, the Almighty, the All-Knowing, the All-Wise.[5]

Back in America, from May until July of that same year, the Union army scored key victories at Vicksburg and Gettysburg, turning the tide against the Confederacy and eventually sealing the Union's triumph.[6]

Joseph Smith would 'see the face of the Son of Man' in 1890

Joseph Smith made another prediction concerning the time of the Return:

> I was once praying very earnestly to know the time of the coming of the Son of Man, when I heard a voice repeat the following: Joseph, my son, if thou livest until thou art eighty-five years old, thou shalt see the face of the Son of Man; therefore let this suffice, and trouble me no more on this matter. I was left thus, without being able to decide whether this coming referred to the beginning of the millennium or to some previous appearing, or whether I should die and thus see his face.[7]

Since Smith was born in 1805, the 'time of the coming of the Son of Man' would have coincided with the year 1890 – the first year any Westerner was able to attain the presence of Bahá'u'lláh. By his own admission, Smith was unsure about the exact meaning of this revelation and suggested three possible explanations. Let's examine them in reverse order:

- '*I should die and thus see his face.*' Since Joseph Smith died in 1844, it is obvious that he did not 'die and thus see' the face of the Son of Man in 1890, and so this explanation can be eliminated.
- '*this coming referred . . . to some previous appearing.*' Smith clearly inquired of the Lord about a future event, and the revelation he received mentioned the age of eighty-five. Since Smith did not believe in reincarnation, it is extremely unlikely that this could have referred to 'some previous appearing.' Therefore, the only plausible explanation is that
- '*this coming referred to the beginning of the millennium,*' the ushering in of the thousand-year reign of Christ during which Satan will be bound.

Incidentally, Bahá'u'lláh has fixed the minimum duration of His Dispensation at 1,000 years, and promised that this day 'shall not be followed by night,' meaning that the Bahá'í Faith will not suffer the same corruption and degradation that has befallen previous religions.

Fifty-six years should wind up the scene

A rather obscure entry in the compilation *History of the Church* notes that on February 14, 1835, referring to the Return of Christ, Joseph Smith declared that 'fifty-six years should wind up the scene.'[8] Adding 56 to 1835 yields 1891, by which year Smith boldly predicted the entire Second Coming would be a *fait accompli*!

This time frame correlates closely to the completion of Bahá'u'lláh's forty-year Mission and the first signs of the spread of His Cause to the West. In 1889, Bahá'u'lláh marked the conclusion of His mighty work with the following words:

> Praise be to God that whatever is essential for the believers in this Revelation to be told has been revealed. Their duties have been clearly defined, and the deeds they are expected to perform have been plainly set forth in Our Book. Now is the time to arise and fulfill their duty. Let them translate into deeds the exhortations We have given them.[9]

On February 15, 1891 (fifty-six years and a day after Joseph Smith's prediction), Professor Edward Granville Browne, a British orientalist who was granted four historic interviews with Bahá'u'lláh only the previous year, gave a talk to the South Place Ethical Society in Finsbury, London – constituting one of the first public mentions of the Bahá'í Faith in the West.[10] That same year Bahá'u'lláh made His last visit to Mt Carmel and marked the spot where the sacred remains of the Báb should be interred and a Shrine erected in His honor. In a tablet addressed to that holy mountain, Bahá'u'lláh revealed:

> Call out to Zion, O Carmel, and announce the joyful tidings: He that was hidden from mortal eyes is come! His all-conquering sovereignty is manifest; His all-encompassing splendour is revealed. Beware lest thou hesitate or halt. Hasten forth and circumambulate the City of God that hath descended from heaven, the celestial Kaaba round which have circled in adoration the favoured of God, the pure in heart, and the company of the most exalted angels. Oh, how I long to announce unto every spot on the surface of the earth, and to carry to each one of its cities, the glad-tidings of this Revelation – a Revelation to which the heart of Sinai hath been attracted, and in whose name the Burning Bush is calling: 'Unto God, the Lord of Lords, belong the kingdoms of earth and heaven.' Verily this is the Day in which both land and sea rejoice at this announcement, the Day for which have been laid up those things which God, through a bounty beyond the ken of mortal mind or heart, hath destined for revelation. Ere long will God sail His Ark upon thee, and will manifest the people of Bahá who have been mentioned in the Book of Names.[11]

Bahá'u'lláh left this earthly existence in the early morning hours of May 29, 1892.

'One mighty and strong' to appear at Joseph Smith's death

Another entry in the *History of the Church* suggests that Joseph Smith would live until the time of Christ's Second Coming. On January 23, 1833, Smith's father, Joseph Sr, gave his son a patriarchal blessing in which he declared that Joseph Jr 'should continue in the Priest's office until Christ comes.'[12] Two months earlier, on November 27, 1832, Joseph Smith prophesied the appearance of 'one mighty and strong' at the same time as a man called of God would 'fall by the shaft of death':

> And it shall come to pass that I, the Lord God, will send one mighty and

strong, holding the scepter of power in his hand, clothed with light for a covering, whose mouth shall utter words, eternal words; while his bowels shall be a fountain of truth, to set in order the house of God, and to arrange by lot the inheritances of the saints whose names are found, and the names of their fathers, and of their children, enrolled in the book of the law of God; While that man, who was called of God and appointed, that putteth forth his hand to steady the ark of God, shall fall by the shaft of death, like as a tree that is smitten by the vivid shaft of lightning.[13]

Joseph Smith continued 'in the Priest's office' until he fell 'by the shaft of death' on June 27, 1844, a mere 35 days after the Báb ushered in the Bahá'í Era, uttering 'eternal words . . . to set in order the house of God'.

Joseph Smith to prepare the way for two Manifestations

Joseph Smith clearly indicated that the Return of Christ was to be preceded by another Return, namely that of Elijah. According to the Mormon scriptures, the angel Moroni told Joseph Smith:

Behold, I will reveal unto you the Priesthood, by the hand of Elijah the prophet, before the coming of the great and dreadful day of the Lord. And he shall plant in the hearts of the children the promises made to the fathers, and the hearts of the children shall turn to their fathers. If it were not so, the whole earth would be utterly wasted at his coming.[14]

And in another verse from the Doctrine and Covenants, Jesus tells Joseph:

Thou art blessed, for thou shalt do great things. Behold thou wast sent forth, even as John, to prepare the way before me, and before Elijah which should come, and thou knewest it not.[15]

As the preceding two quotations indicate, first Joseph Smith is to prepare the way before Elijah, and only *after* Elijah will come 'the great and dreadful day of the Lord.' While the Mormon mention of a 'dual return' in the last days is not unique, its clear and unambiguous language is distinctive among Christian prophecies.

The Bahá'í Faith claims to have not one founding Prophet, but two. While the Báb's mission in certain respects was very similar to that of John the Baptist, the Bible does not attribute any statements to John that identify his mission with that of Christ – although the four evangelists certainly sought to establish that connection (in Mark 1:1-14 the ministry of John is portrayed as 'the beginning of the gospel'). The Báb indicated that His Cause and that of 'Him Whom God shall make manifest' were one and the same:

> At the time of the appearance of Him Whom God shall make manifest, wert thou to perform thy deeds for the sake of the Point of the Bayán, they would be regarded as performed for one other than God, inasmuch as on that Day the Point of the Bayán is none other than Him Whom God shall make manifest . . .[16]

This essential unity between the Bábí and Bahá'í Dispensations is further elucidated in a letter written on behalf of Shoghi Effendi:

> Shoghi Effendi feels that the unity of the Bahá'í Revelation as one complete whole embracing the Faith of the Báb should be emphasized . . . The Faith of the Báb should not be divorced from that of Bahá'u'lláh. Though the teachings of the Bayán have been abrogated and superseded by the laws of the Aqdas, yet due to the fact that the Báb considered Himself as the Forerunner of Bahá'u'lláh, we would regard His Dispensation together with that of Bahá'u'lláh as forming one entity, the former being introductory to the advent of the latter.[17]

However, Mormons are told that the prophet Elijah came to Joseph Smith and Oliver Cowdery in a vision in 1836, along with Jesus, Moses, and another prophet named Elias,[18] thus fulfilling Mormon prophecies about him. No explanation is given as to why Elijah's promised return was satisfied by a mere appearance in a vision, while the return of Jesus – Who appeared in that same vision – is still pending.

The end of a cycle

One remarkable observation made by Joseph Smith, and supported by the Bahá'í Writings, is that a new dispensation, which 'is now beginning to usher in,' will encompass every previous dispensation from Adam through today. On September 6, 1842, Joseph Smith wrote:

> . . . for it is necessary in the ushering in of the dispensation of the fulness of times, which dispensation is now beginning to usher in, that a whole and complete and perfect union, and welding together of dispensations, and keys, and powers, and glories should take place, and be revealed from

the days of Adam even to the present time. And not only this, but those things which never have been revealed from the foundation of the world, but have been kept hid from the wise and prudent, shall be revealed unto babes and sucklings in this, the dispensation of the fulness of times.[19]

Bahá'ís believe Bahá'u'lláh to be a Universal Manifestation in the sense that His Dispensation closes out the 'prophetic cycle' which began with the Adam mentioned in Genesis, and simultaneously opens up a new 'cycle of fulfillment' that will last for at least half a million years. Shoghi Effendi described the Revelation of Bahá'u'lláh as a 'Revelation, hailed as the promise and crowning glory of past ages and centuries, as the consummation of all the Dispensations within the Adamic Cycle, inaugurating an era of at least a thousand years' duration, and a cycle destined to last no less than five thousand centuries, signalizing the end of the Prophetic Era and the beginning of the Era of Fulfillment . . .'[20] Concerning the 'babes and sucklings' mentioned by Joseph Smith, the Báb promised:

The newly born babe of that Day excels the wisest and most venerable men of this time, and the lowliest and most unlearned of that period shall surpass in understanding the most erudite and accomplished divines of this age . . .[21]

Furthermore, 'those things which . . . have been kept hid from the wise and prudent' are reminiscent of the epilogue to the Hidden Words, which are now being memorized by young children the world over:

The mystic and wondrous Bride, hidden ere this beneath the veiling of utterance, hath now, by the grace of God and His divine favor, been made manifest even as the resplendent light shed by the beauty of the Beloved. I bear witness, O friends! that the favor is complete, the argument fulfilled, the proof manifest and the evidence established. Let it now be seen what your endeavors in the path of detachment will reveal. In this wise hath the divine favor been fully vouchsafed unto you and unto them that are in heaven and on earth. All praise to God, the Lord of all Worlds.

The light will come from the East and shine on the West

According to the LDS scriptures – and the Bible as well – the Lord will come from the East and spread His influence throughout the West. Even the trumpet-blowing angel statues adorning Mormon temples are positioned facing east, ready to announce His Coming:

Behold, I have told you before; wherefore, if they say unto you: Behold, he is in the desert; go not forth; Behold, he is in the secret chambers; believe it not; for as the light of the morning cometh out of the east, and shineth even unto the west, and covereth the whole earth, so shall the coming of the Son of Man be.[22]

John Whitmer's *History of the Church* mentions a vision experienced by Elder Lyman Wight as he was being ordained to the High Priesthood in 1831:

And the Spirit fell upon Lyman, and he prophesied concerning the coming of Christ. He said that there were some in the congregation that should live until the Savior should descend from heaven with a shout, with all the holy angels with Him. He said the coming of the Savior should be like the sun rising in the east, and will cover the whole earth . . . He said that God would work a work in these last days that tongue cannot express and the mind is not capable to conceive. The glory of the Lord shone around.[23]

During a talk in New York in 1912, 'Abdu'l-Bahá referred to this Bible prophecy, and alluded to its fulfillment by the Faith spreading to America and Europe:

In the Holy Books it is recorded that when the Sun of Truth dawns, it will appear in the East, and its light will be reflected in the West. Already its dawning has taken place in the East, and its signs are appearing in the West. Its illumination shall spread rapidly and widely in the Occident. The Sun of Truth has risen in Persia, and its effulgence is now manifest here in America. This is the greatest proof of its appearance in the horizon of the world, as recorded in the heavenly Books. Praise be to God! That which is prophesied in the Holy Books has been fulfilled.[24]

According to the LDS Doctrine and Covenants, the Lord gave a commandment to gather from the east and establish His faith in the west:

Wherefore I, the Lord, have said, gather ye out from the eastern lands, assemble ye yourselves together ye elders of my church; go ye forth into the western countries, call upon the inhabitants to repent, and inasmuch as they do repent, build up churches unto me.[25]

From a Bahá'í perspective, such a call could be seen as having been literally answered by the thousands of believers who scattered from their native Persia to spread the Faith westward. However, Mormons deem 'eastern lands' and 'western countries' to refer to places within the continental United States. Since the Church of Jesus Christ of Latter-day Saints was founded in upstate New York, expanded westward through Ohio, Missouri, Illinois, and finally settled in Utah, Mormons claim that this migration fulfilled that commandment.

The Greatest Name

In April 1843, Joseph Smith referred to the following verse from the Revelation of St John:

> He that hath an ear, let him hear what the Spirit saith unto the churches; To him that overcometh will I give to eat of the hidden manna, and will give him a white stone, and in the stone a new name written, which no man knoweth saving he that receiveth it.[26]

Smith wrote:

> Then the white stone mentioned in Revelation 2:17, will become a Urim and Thummim[27] to each individual who receives one, whereby things pertaining to a higher order of kingdoms will be made known; And a white stone is given to each of those who come into the celestial kingdom, whereon is a new name written, which no man knoweth save he that receiveth it. The new name is the key word.[28]

This reference to a new name has often been interpreted to mean that *each new believer* will receive a new name. The LDS Church reads the above verse literally, so a worthy Mormon as part of his temple 'endowment', or initiation, receives a *temple name* (often after a figure in the Bible or the Book of Mormon), which is not to be revealed to anyone. Joseph Smith emphasizes that this new name is 'the key word.' Mormons believe that on Resurrection Day, the husband must call his wife from the grave by using her temple name. This is one reason why women cannot attain 'exaltation' without being married, as there would be no one to call her up to the celestial kingdom. And while a husband is required to know his wife's temple name, a wife may not know her husband's.

Although no such practice is found in the Bahá'í Faith, the history of the Faith offers numerous examples of prominent believers receiving a new name in honor of their spiritual distinction. The Báb gave special names or titles to some of His most notable followers: to His first believer, Mullá Ḥusayn, He gave the title of Bábu'l-Báb ('Gate of the Gate'), and upon Zarrín-Táj

– later named Ṭáhirih, 'the pure,' by Bahá'u'lláh – He conferred the name Qurratu'l-'Ayn ('solace of the eyes'). Among the other well-known believers who were similarly honored by Bahá'u'lláh were Quddús ('most holy') and Badí' ('wondrous'). 'Abdu'l-Bahá extended the practice to Western believers, including Thornton Chase (Thábit, 'the firm'), Lady Blomfield (Sitarih, or star), and Mrs Thornburgh-Cropper (Maryam, the Persian name for Mary). And when Shoghi Effendi married Mary Sutherland Maxwell, he gave her the name Rúḥíyyih Khánum (Rúḥíyyih meaning 'spirit,' and Khánum being a term of respect, i.e. 'Lady').

An entirely different interpretation of the above verse from Revelation is that this 'new name' is *a single name* revealed to *all* believers; a name engraved on a stone, which is not understood except by those who have accepted its source. The collection *'Abdu'l-Bahá in London* gives the following account:

> Someone wished to know if it were a good custom to wear a symbol, as, for instance, a cross. He ['Abdu'l-Bahá] said: 'You wear the cross for remembrance, it concentrates your thoughts; it has no magical power. Bahá'ís often wear a stone with the greatest name engraved on it: there is no magical influence in the stone; it is a reminder, and companion. If you are about to do some selfish or hasty action, and your glance falls on the ring on your hand, you will remember and change your intention.'[29]

Could it be that this new name mentioned in the New Testament, and underscored by Joseph Smith, is none other than the Greatest Name, *Yá Bahá'u'l-Abhá*? This phrase translates to 'O Glory of the Most Glorious,' and is also another name for *Bahá'u'lláh* ('the Glory of God'). One of the calligraphical representations of this name is known as the *ringstone symbol*. 'Abdu'l-Bahá further suggests that only through meditating upon the divine verses of Bahá'u'lláh can we hope to unravel the 'concealed mystery' of the Most Great Name:

> I hope that thou shalt discover the hidden significances of divine verses, and through the bounty of the Almighty, thou mayest become informed of the concealed mystery and recondite symbol of the stone of the Most Great Name. These mysteries can neither be written nor uttered. Whenever the eye of insight is opened, the reality of meanings is understood.[30]

Bahá'ís do know at least one of the outward meanings of this ringstone symbol, which can roughly be described as three parallel horizontal lines intersected by a single perpendicular line, flanked on either side by a five-pointed star.

The uppermost horizontal line symbolizes the realm of God, the Unknowable Essence; the bottom line signifies the world of man; and the line in the middle represents the Manifestation of God, that essential Mediator between the Creator and His Creation. The vertical line intersecting the three horizontal lines can be said to represent the Holy Spirit, God's grace flowing through the Manifestation to the world of humanity in the form of Revelation; it is the lifeline connecting mankind to its Creator. The two five-pointed stars on either side of the central symbol represent the Twin Manifestations, the Báb and Bahá'u'lláh.

There is another, albeit more tenuous allusion to the Greatest Name in the Mormon scriptures. In the Doctrine and Covenants Joseph Smith prays:

> That your incomings may be in the name of the Lord, that your outgoings may be in the name of the Lord, that all your salutations may be in the name of the Lord, with uplifted hands unto the Most High . . .[31]

One variant of the Most Great Name of the Lord, *Alláh'u'Abhá*, is not only used as a Bahá'í salutation – for 'incomings' as well as 'outgoings' – it is also said as part of the long obligatory prayer, with uplifted hands.

Other Mormon prophecies fulfilled by Bahá'u'lláh

Consider the following selections from the Mormon scriptures, and how they have been fulfilled by Bahá'u'lláh. Many of these prophecies are also found in the Bible, and some appear to be direct quotations from the King James Version. Wherever possible, both the Mormon scriptural reference and the biblical source are provided in the endnote.

The work of the Father

The Book of Mormon indicates that in the last days, 'the work of the Father' will begin, implying that the establishment of the Kingdom is not an instantaneous event. Mormons believe that they are currently engaged in this work in preparation of Christ's Second Coming. In 3 Nephi, chapters 20 and 21, the following words are attributed to Jesus Christ:

> Behold, my servant shall deal prudently; he shall be exalted and extolled and be very high. As many were astonished at thee – his visage was so marred, more than any man, and his form more than the sons of men – So shall he sprinkle many nations; the kings shall shut their mouths at him, for that which had not been told them shall they see; and that which they had not heard shall they consider. Verily, verily, I say unto you, all these things shall surely come, even as the Father hath commanded me. Then shall this covenant which the Father hath covenanted with his people be fulfilled; and then shall Jerusalem be inhabited again with my people, and it shall be the land of their inheritance.[32]

> For in that day, for my sake shall the Father work a work, which shall be a great and a marvelous work among them; and there shall be among them those who will not believe it, although a man shall declare it unto them. But behold, the life of my servant shall be in my hand; therefore they shall not hurt him, although he shall be marred because of them. Yet I will heal him, for I will show unto them that my wisdom is greater than the cunning of the devil.[33]

> And then shall the work of the Father commence at that day, even when this gospel shall be preached among the remnant of this people. Verily I say unto you, at that day shall the work of the Father commence among all the dispersed of my people, yea, even the tribes which have been lost, which the Father hath led away out of Jerusalem . . . Yea, and then shall the work commence, with the Father among all nations in preparing the way whereby his people may be gathered home to the land of their inheritance. And they shall go out from all nations; and they shall not go out in haste, nor go by flight, for I will go before them, saith the Father, and I will be their rearward.[34]

Note the many allusions to Bahá'u'lláh and the dawning of the Bahá'í Era:

- *His visage was marred.* This is not a uniquely Mormon prophecy, but a Judeo-Christian one.[35] Bahá'u'lláh carried the scars from the heavy chains of the Síyáh-Chál[36] with him for the rest of His life.

- *They shall not hurt him.* Bahá'u'lláh endured countless cruelties and hardships, including forty years of imprisonment and banishment, as well as several attempts on His life, chief among them being poisoned by His own half-brother, Mírzá Yaḥyá. While this poisoning had lasting effects on His health, Bahá'u'lláh died of natural causes at the age of 74.

- *The kings shall shut their mouths at him.* Bahá'u'lláh wrote numerous epistles to the kings and rulers of the earth, calling on them to recognize His station, to reconcile their differences, and to rid themselves of all armaments 'except what the protection of your cities and territories demandeth.' He further warned them: 'If ye pay no heed unto the counsels which, in peerless and unequivocal language, We have revealed in this Tablet, Divine chastisement shall assail you from every direction, and the sentence of His justice shall be pronounced against you. On that day ye shall have no power to resist Him, and shall recognize your own impotence.'[37]

- *The Father among all nations will gather his people.* Bahá'u'lláh referred to His station as that of the Father, and declared His Cause to be the one destined to bring together all nations in peace: 'Blessed be the Lord Who is the Father! He, verily, is come unto the nations in His most great majesty.'[38]

- *Jerusalem shall be inhabited again with my people.* Jerusalem, the 'land of inheritance' spoken of by Isaiah, was virtually inaccessible to Jews until the opening of the Bahá'í Era. This 'gathering of Israel' has continued ever since, culminating in the establishment of the State of Israel in 1948.

The lawgiver

Bahá'u'lláh laid out the body of laws applicable to Bahá'ís in the *Kitáb-i-Aqdas*, or *Most Holy Book*. These new laws, according to their Author, supersede all other religious laws that were given to humanity in the past, such as in the Qur'án, the Gospel, or the Torah. Furthermore, the World Order of Bahá'u'lláh envisions a future where the affairs of the world are administered by a world federation of nations guided by the principles of the Bahá'í Faith. In this light, the following passage from the Doctrine and Covenants could certainly refer to Bahá'u'lláh:

But, verily I say unto you that in time ye shall have no king nor ruler, for I will be your king and watch over you. Wherefore, hear my voice and follow me, and you shall be a free people, and ye shall have no laws but my laws when I come, for I am your lawgiver, and what can stay my hand?[39]

God himself to come down in the form of a man

In the Book of Mormon, Abinadi asks the following questions concerning the latter days:

> Have they [all the prophets] not said that God himself should come down among the children of men, and take upon him the form of a man, and go forth in mighty power upon the face of the earth?[40]

This was never fulfilled by the First Coming of Jesus Christ, Who always referred to Himself as the Son in relation to the Father. Latter-day Saints might suggest that this was fulfilled by Joseph Smith's 'First Vision,' in which he describes being visited by two personages, one of whom was God the Father. Yet if God's appearance in a vision were the extent of 'going forth in mighty power upon the face of the earth,' then one must hold Jesus Christ – the other personage from that vision – to the same standard, and consider the Second Coming complete.

Mormons believe that the Father, the Son and the Holy Ghost are three separate beings, or 'gods,' making up the 'Godhead' of the Trinity, and therefore see Jesus as neither equal to God, nor the incarnation of His essence. However, that prophecy was spiritually fulfilled by Bahá'u'lláh, Who in His epistle to the Czar of Russia proclaimed:

> He, verily, is come with His Kingdom, and all the atoms cry aloud: 'Lo! The Lord is come in His great majesty!' He Who is the Father is come, and the Son (Jesus), in the holy vale, crieth out: 'Here am I, here am I, O Lord, My God!' whilst Sinai circleth round the House, and the Burning Bush calleth aloud: 'The All-Bounteous is come mounted upon the clouds! Blessed is he that draweth nigh unto Him, and woe betide them that are far away.'[41]

However, this should not be misconstrued as a claim that God incarnated Himself in the body of Bahá'u'lláh:

> To every discerning and illuminated heart it is evident that God, the unknowable Essence, the Divine Being, is immensely exalted beyond every human attribute, such as corporeal existence, ascent and descent, egress and regress . . . He is, and hath ever been, veiled in the ancient eternity of

His Essence, and will remain in His Reality everlastingly hidden from the sight of men.[42]

Joseph Smith expected the imminent Return of Christ

As noted earlier, the Return of Christ is a predominant theme throughout Joseph Smith's writings, and this Return was expected to occur at any moment. The Book of Mormon is replete with direct quotations from the Book of Isaiah concerning the 'latter days' – far outnumbering other quotations from the Bible – suggesting that the Second Coming is a central theme of that book. Here are but a few of the countless references to the imminent Return of Christ that occur throughout the LDS scriptures:

... and ye need not say that the Lord delays his coming unto the children of Israel.[43]

Wherefore the voice of the Lord is unto the ends of the earth, that all that will hear may hear: Prepare ye, prepare ye for that which is to come, for the Lord is nigh; And the anger of the Lord is kindled, and his sword is bathed in heaven, and it shall fall upon the inhabitants of the earth.[44]

A great and marvelous work is about to come forth unto the children of men. Behold, I am God; give heed unto my word, which is quick and powerful, sharper than a two-edged sword, to the dividing asunder of both joints and marrow; therefore give heed unto my words. Behold, the field is white already to harvest; therefore, whoso desireth to reap, let him thrust in his sickle with his might, and reap while the day lasts, that he may treasure up for his soul everlasting salvation in the kingdom of God. Yea, whosoever will thrust in his sickle and reap, the same is called of God.[45]

For behold, the field is white already to harvest; and it is the eleventh hour, and the last time that I shall call laborers into my vineyard.[46]

Wherefore, be faithful, praying always, having your lamps trimmed and burning, and oil with you, that you may be ready at the coming of the Bridegroom. For behold, verily, verily, I say unto you, that I come quickly.[47]

For behold, verily, verily, I say unto you, the time is soon at hand that I shall come in a cloud with power and great glory.[48]

And verily, verily, I say unto you, I come quickly.[49]

Lift up your hearts and be glad, your redemption draweth nigh. Fear not, little flock, the kingdom is yours until I come. Behold, I come quickly.[50]

For the time is at hand; the day or the hour no man knoweth; but it surely shall come.[51]

Verily, I say unto you, I am Jesus Christ, who cometh quickly, in an hour you think not.[52]

And again, be patient in tribulation until I come; and, behold, I come quickly, and my reward is with me, and they who have sought me early shall find rest to their souls.[53]

Ye cannot behold with your natural eyes, for the present time, the design of your God concerning those things which shall come hereafter, and the glory which shall follow after much tribulation. For after much tribulation come the blessings. Wherefore the day cometh that ye shall be crowned with much glory; the hour is not yet, but is nigh at hand. Remember this, which I tell you before, that you may lay it to heart, and receive that which is to follow. Behold, verily I say unto you, for this cause I have sent you that you might be obedient, and that your hearts might be prepared to bear testimony of the things which are to come; And also that you might be honored in laying the foundation, and in bearing record of the land upon which the Zion of God shall stand . . .[54]

Pray always, that ye may not faint, until I come. Behold, and lo, I will come quickly, and receive you unto myself.[55]

Behold, the great day of the Lord is at hand; and who can abide the day of his coming, and who can stand when he appeareth?[56]

Yea, I would that ye would come forth and harden not your hearts any longer; for behold, now is the time and the day of your salvation; and therefore, if ye will repent and harden not your hearts, immediately shall the great plan of redemption be brought about unto you. For behold, this life is the time for men to prepare to meet God; yea, behold the day of this life is the day for men to perform their labors.[57]

Considering the sheer preponderance of these warnings, not to mention their severity, it is difficult to fathom how they could have been ignored. In the prospectus of the first foreign publication of the LDS Church, the British periodical *The Millennial Star*, we catch a glimpse of the immense hope pinned upon the imminent arrival of the promised Millennium:

> The *Millennial Star* will stand aloof from the common political and commercial news of the day. Its columns will be devoted to the spread of the fulness of the Gospel – the restoration of the ancient principles of Christianity – the gathering of Israel – the rolling forth of the kingdom of God among the nations – the signs of the times – the fulfillment of prophecy – recording the judgments of God as they befall the nations whether signs in the heavens or in the earth, blood fire or vapor of smoke – in short, whatever is shown forth indicative of the coming of the 'Son of Man' and ushering in of his universal reign upon the earth.[58]

Joseph Smith limited the time frame of the Second Coming

As if the many references to Christ's imminent return were not enough, Joseph Smith limited the time frame within which this momentous event was to occur. As we have already seen, Smith estimated that 'fifty-six years should wind up the scene,' referring to the completion of the Lord's work by the year 1891. Likewise, he predicted that Christ would return during the Civil War (1861–1865), and that he himself would 'see the face of the Son of Man' if he lived to see the year 1890. By Joseph Smith's own account, the Second Coming should have been completed over a hundred years ago, and yet people are still waiting.

In an interesting parallel, the Báb limited the time of His own Dispensation, and prophesied the immediate arrival of another Manifestation. Addressing 'Him Whom God will make manifest,' the Báb wrote:

> . . . do Thou grant a respite of nineteen years as a token of Thy favour so that those who have embraced this Cause may be graciously rewarded by Thee . . .[59]

Bahá'u'lláh declared His mission in 1863, exactly nineteen years after the start of the Báb's ministry, thereby fulfilling the latter's prophecy. However, whereas the majority of Bábís eventually became Bahá'ís, Mormons – like the Millerites and a number of other Christian sects in 1844 when Christ did not appear as expected – have found ways to explain away these clear indications concerning the time of the Second Coming.

Christ in our midst

On January 2, 1831, Joseph Smith attributed the following words to Christ:

> But behold, verily, verily, I say unto you that mine eyes are upon you. I am in your midst and ye cannot see me; But the day soon cometh that ye shall see me, and know that I am; for the veil of darkness shall soon be rent, and he that is not purified shall not abide the day. Wherefore, gird up your loins and be prepared.[60]

On that very day, the Báb was 11 years old, and Bahá'u'lláh was 13. They were walking in our midst – in the streets of Shiraz and Tehran, respectively – but we could not 'see' them, as They had not yet made Their purpose known to mankind. However, that would soon change, and although Joseph Smith had no direct knowledge of the exact time, place or manner of the Lord's appearance, he clearly considered it his duty to prepare his followers lest 'he that is not purified shall not abide the day.' In fact, the entire purpose of Joseph Smith's calling could be summarized in the following verse from the Book of Mormon, in which the younger Alma addresses his son Corianton:

> And now, my son, this was the ministry unto which ye were called, to declare these glad tidings unto this people, to prepare their minds; or rather that salvation might come unto them, that they may prepare the minds of their children to hear the word at the time of his coming.[61]

There is of course nothing to suggest that Mormons were somehow destined to be America's first Bahá'ís; yet would it not seem possible that a determined seeker, after reading Smith's prophecies, might have 'connected the dots' and started looking for a person of eastern origin claiming to be the Promised One between 1844 and 1891?

Repeated warnings from Joseph Smith to his followers

Joseph Smith warned his own followers in clear and unequivocal language about their potential failure to recognize Christ. The following counsel, given in the voice of Christ, is directed specifically at the members of his Church, including its leaders:

> And I give unto you, who are the first laborers in this last kingdom, a commandment that you assemble yourselves together, and organize yourselves,

and prepare yourselves, and sanctify yourselves; yea, purify your hearts, and cleanse your hands and your feet before me, that I may make you clean; That I may testify unto your Father, and your God, and my God, that you are clean from the blood of this wicked generation; that I may fulfil this promise, this great and last promise, which I have made unto you, when I will.[62]

Hearken, O ye people of my church, to whom the kingdom has been given; hearken ye and give ear to him who laid the foundation of the earth, who made the heavens and all the hosts thereof, and by whom all things were made which live, and move, and have a being. And again I say, hearken unto my voice, lest death shall overtake you; in an hour when ye think not the summer shall be past, and the harvest ended, and your souls not saved . . . Hearken, O ye people of my church, and ye elders listen together, and hear my voice while it is called today, and harden not your hearts . . .[63]

Would he have issued this grave a warning if Christ's return was going to be as obvious – accompanied by all manner of physical phenomena – as many Mormons think? One could imagine Bahá'u'lláh addressing these people in the following words:

Retrace your steps, O My servants, and incline your hearts to Him Who is the Source of your creation . . . With ears that are sanctified from vain-glory and worldly desires hearken unto the counsels which I, in My merciful kindness, have revealed unto you, and with your inner and outer eyes contemplate the evidences of My marvelous Revelation . . .[64]

Judge ye fairly the Cause of God, your Creator, and behold that which hath been sent down from the Throne on high, and meditate thereon with innocent and sanctified hearts. Then will the truth of this Cause appear unto you as manifest as the sun in its noon-tide glory. Then will ye be of them that have believed in Him.[65]

O the pity! that man should deprive himself of this goodly gift, this imperishable bounty, this everlasting life. It behooveth him to prize this food that cometh from heaven, that perchance, through the wondrous favours of the Sun of Truth, the dead may be brought to life, and withered souls be quickened by the infinite Spirit. Make haste, O my brother, that while there is yet time our lips may taste of the immortal draught, for the breeze of life, now blowing from the city of the Well-Beloved, cannot last, and the streaming river of holy utterance must needs be stilled, and the portals of the Riḍván cannot for ever remain open.[66]

The Book of Mormon warns against complacency and denial among the believers:

> Wo unto them that turn aside the just for a thing of naught and revile against that which is good, and say that it is of no worth! For the day shall come that the Lord God will speedily visit the inhabitants of the earth; and in that day that they are fully ripe in iniquity they shall perish . . . For behold, at that day shall he [Satan] rage in the hearts of the children of men, and stir them up to anger against that which is good . . . And others will he pacify and lull them away into carnal security, that they will say: All is well in Zion; yea, Zion prospereth, all is well – and thus the devil cheateth their souls, and leadeth them away carefully down to hell . . . Therefore, wo be unto him that is at ease in Zion! Wo be unto him that crieth: All is well! Yea, wo be unto him, that hearkeneth unto the precepts of men, and denieth the power of God, and the gift of the Holy Ghost! Yea, wo be unto him that saith: We have received, and we need no more![67]

Mormons often use the name 'Zion' to refer to the body of believers, or the LDS Church as a whole. Although it may appear that this verse – purportedly written around 550 BC – has been taken out of context, it is part of a series of prophecies concerning the 'last days,' and was clearly written for the benefit of the Latter-day Saints.

Barriers to Mormons' acceptance of Bahá'u'lláh

In light of all these warnings and admonitions by Joseph Smith, why do Mormons not actively seek the return of their Lord? Why are they resigned to waiting patiently for Christ to seek them out instead? Let's look at some of the barriers that stand in the way of the recognition of the One Whose advent they are still awaiting.

Scriptures not to be spiritualized

For many people, the first step in the recognition of the station of Bahá'u'lláh is to gain an understanding of the spiritual nature of the Sacred Word. Christians, including Mormons, understand that Jesus spoke in parables, a form of spiritual language that cannot and should not be taken literally. For example, most Christians are familiar with the following story about Jesus:

> Then answered the Jews and said unto him, What sign shewest thou unto us, seeing that thou doest these things? Jesus answered and said unto them, Destroy this temple, and in three days I will raise it up. Then said the Jews, Forty and six years was this temple in building, and wilt thou rear it up in three days? But he spake of the temple of his body.[68]

According to this story, the Jewish divines asked Jesus to show them a physical miracle, and He promised them a spiritual one, namely His resurrection after three days. But because they interpreted Jesus' words literally, they failed to understand that He was referring to His human temple, not a building of stone. Christians also recognize that the authors of the New Testament pointed to specific prophecies in the Old Testament – the book of Isaiah in particular – to prove Jesus' station as the promised Messiah. Yet there is almost no literal correlation between those prophecies and the way in which Jesus appeared – even His own name is different from the promised *Immanuel*.[69] For example, few Christians would interpret the following verse to mean that the entire coastal region of Capernaum was engulfed in physical darkness, and that the sun only began to shine when Jesus came there to preach:

> And leaving Nazareth, he came and dwelt in Capernaum, which is upon the sea coast, in the borders of Zabulon and Nephthalim: That it might be fulfilled which was spoken by Esaias the prophet, saying, The land of Zabulon, and the land of Nephthalim, by the way of the sea, beyond Jordan, Galilee of the Gentiles; The people which sat in darkness saw great light; and to them which sat in the region and shadow of death light is sprung up.[70]

According to Mormon doctrine, the Bible is to be understood only in its outward meaning, and if an event described in it has not literally come to pass, it has yet to occur:

> We do not read the Scriptures as most of the inhabitants of the earth do, thinking that they must be spiritualized. There are scarcely any of the prophecies but what this generation, as well as some of the past generations, interpret as meaning something altogether different from the reading of them . . . The Latter-day Saints . . . learned that the word of God would all be fulfilled, which have not already come to pass, and that

they are to be understood in the same light, and in the same sense as we would understand the writings of uninspired individuals, when plainly and clearly written upon any special subject.[71]

This doctrine, developed in the mid-19th century, appears to have been a reaction to the many conflicting 'spiritualized' interpretations offered by various sects of the time. While the problem was obvious, the solution – simply declaring that all spiritual interpretations are false – did not take into account these words of Isaiah:

And the vision of all is become unto you as the words of a book that is sealed, which men deliver to one that is learned, saying, Read this, I pray thee: and he saith, I cannot; for it is sealed: And the book is delivered to him that is not learned, saying, Read this, I pray thee: and he saith, I am not learned.[72]

Those who deny all spiritual interpretations perhaps fail to recognize that the true meaning of these verses can only be unsealed by a Manifestation of God:

I beheld till the thrones were cast down, and the Ancient of days did sit, whose garment was white as snow, and the hair of his head like the pure wool: his throne was like the fiery flame, and his wheels as burning fire. A fiery stream issued and came forth from before him: thousand thousands ministered unto him, and ten thousand times ten thousand stood before him: the judgment was set, and the books were opened.[73]

A belief in the literal fulfillment of prophecy – no matter its scientific improbability or spiritual irrelevance – largely persists today among Latter-day Saints. The degree to which such beliefs are held may pose a barrier to a deeper appreciation of the spiritual nature of the Word of God, and its consequences for accepting a new Messenger. Another potential obstacle to Mormons' acceptance of the spiritual meaning of certain Bible verses is the fact that they consider many of these same verses to be inaccurate. Some of the 'corrected' versions provided by the Joseph Smith Translation, in an attempt to clarify the literal meaning of the original text, have effectively rendered their intended spiritual meaning null and void.

Mormons expect a supernatural Second Coming

Because of their belief in the literal interpretation of scripture, Mormons are expecting Christ's Second Coming to be very much like His appearance as described in the Book of Mormon, that is to say, a distinctly supernatural event:

> And it came to pass, as they understood they cast their eyes up again towards heaven; and behold, they saw a Man descending out of heaven; and he was clothed in a white robe; and he came down and stood in the midst of them; and the eyes of the whole multitude were turned upon him, and they durst not open their mouths, even one to another, and wist not what it meant, for they thought it was an angel that had appeared unto them . . . And it came to pass that the multitude went forth, and thrust their hands into his side,[74] and did feel the prints of the nails in his hands and in his feet; and this they did do, going forth one by one until they had all gone forth, and did see with their eyes and did feel with their hands, and did know of a surety and did bear record, that it was he, of whom it was written by the prophets, that should come. And when they had all gone forth and had witnessed for themselves, they did cry out with one accord, saying: Hosanna! Blessed be the name of the Most High God! And they did fall down at the feet of Jesus, and did worship him.[75]

Interestingly, the Bible prophecy that 'he shall come even to thee from Assyria [Iraq], and from the fortified cities, and from the fortress even to the river, and from sea to sea, and from mountain to mountain'[76] is never considered. That prophecy was literally fulfilled by Bahá'u'lláh.

Mormon artwork depicting the scene described above shows Jesus descending from the sky standing atop a cloud. This image can be traced back to several prophecies from the Old and New Testaments:

> I saw in the night visions, and, behold, one like the Son of man came with the clouds of heaven, and came to the Ancient of days, and they brought him near before him.[77]

> And then shall appear the sign of the Son of man in heaven: and then shall all the tribes of the earth mourn, and they shall see the Son of man coming in the clouds of heaven with power and great glory.[78]

> Jesus saith unto him, Thou hast said: nevertheless I say unto you, Hereafter

shall ye see the Son of man sitting on the right hand of power, and coming in the clouds of heaven.[79]

And Jesus said, I am: and ye shall see the Son of man sitting on the right hand of power, and coming in the clouds of heaven.[80]

While 'the Son of man,' 'clouds' and 'heaven' appear in each of these verses, nothing in them suggests that Jesus would literally descend from the sky and touch down upon earth. In fact, the Book of Daniel mentions the Son of Man being brought near before the Ancient of days, not down toward earth. Besides, there are enough textual differences among these verses that no single literal meaning can be said to apply to all of them. In light of this, could these verses be understood in a spiritual sense? Bahá'u'lláh explained:

And now regarding His words, that the Son of man shall 'come in the clouds of heaven.' By the term 'clouds' is meant those things that are contrary to the ways and desires of men. Even as He hath revealed in the verse already quoted: 'As oft as an Apostle cometh unto you with that which your souls desire not, ye swell with pride, accusing some of being impostors and slaying others.' These 'clouds' signify, in one sense, the annulment of laws, the abrogation of former Dispensations, the repeal of rituals and customs current amongst men, the exalting of the illiterate faithful above the learned opposers of the Faith. In another sense, they mean the appearance of that immortal Beauty in the image of mortal man, with such human limitations as eating and drinking, poverty and riches, glory and abasement, sleeping and waking, and such other things as cast doubt in the minds of men, and cause them to turn away. All such veils are symbolically referred to as 'clouds.'

. . . Even as the clouds prevent the eyes of men from beholding the sun, so do these things hinder the souls of men from recognizing the light of the divine Luminary. To this beareth witness that which hath proceeded out of the mouth of the unbelievers as revealed in the sacred Book: 'And they have said: "What manner of apostle is this? He eateth food, and walketh the streets. Unless an angel be sent down and take part in His warnings, we will not believe. " ' . . .

It is evident that the changes brought about in every Dispensation constitute the dark clouds that intervene between the eye of man's understanding and the divine Luminary which shineth forth from the dayspring of the divine Essence. Consider how men for generations have been blindly imitating their fathers, and have been trained according to such ways and manners as have been laid down by the dictates of their Faith. Were these men, therefore, to discover suddenly that a Man, Who hath been living in their midst, Who, with respect to every human limitation, hath been their equal, had risen to abolish every established principle imposed by their Faith – principles by which for centuries they have been disciplined, and every opposer and denier of which they have come to regard as infidel, profligate and wicked, – they would of a certainty be veiled and hindered from acknowledging His truth. Such things are as 'clouds' that veil the eyes of those whose inner being hath not tasted the Salsabíl of detachment, nor drunk from the Kawthar of the knowledge of God. Such men, when acquainted with these circumstances, become so veiled that without the least question, they pronounce the Manifestation of God an infidel, and sentence Him to death. You must have heard of such things taking place all down the ages, and are now observing them in these days.[81]

Furthermore, even if these signs of the Second Coming were to be literally fulfilled, there is no guarantee that this would result in a lasting transformation of mankind. The Book of Mormon recounts that shortly after Christ's appearance on the American continent – during which he descended upon a cloud and performed many miracles – both the Nephite and Lamanite peoples became converted to the Church of Christ. Yet it also states that barely three centuries later, both of these groups had become 'exceedingly wicked one like unto another.'[82] In the end, the Nephites were completely wiped off the face of the earth, and only the Lamanites remained in a state of degeneracy. If the Nephites – who had for six hundred years been promised that Jesus Christ would appear in their midst, and who had witnessed that appearance exactly according to their expectations – could not remain faithful for another three hundred years, what hope would humanity have to maintain peace upon this earth for an entire millennium? It is clear that an enduring transformation of humanity must come from within each individual based on the rational acceptance of divinely revealed truths, and cannot simply be brought about by a spectacular display of supernatural power.

No need to seek diligently

The belief in the literal fulfillment of prophecy also carries with it the danger of complacency. After all, if one believes that one knows precisely how Christ will make Himself manifest, it is easy to forget Joseph Smith's admonitions about being taken unawares and to 'seek me diligently.'[83] In the same book containing these warnings, Mormons have also been promised that as long as they are members of the Church, they need not worry:

Therefore, whosoever belongeth to my church need not fear, for such shall inherit the kingdom of heaven.[84]

As mentioned earlier, shortly after Joseph Smith's death the priorities of the Church shifted from the preparation for Christ's return to the survival and organization of the Church itself. The urgency of Smith's warnings has waned through the years, and Mormons now seem more concerned with the consolidation and expansion of their organization, in the relative comfort and confidence that either they or their leaders will recognize Christ when the time comes.

Mormon expectations of the Return

In our dialogue with Mormon friends, it is important to be familiar with Mormon expectations about the Return of Christ, so that we are neither taken aback by the level of detail to which these expectations have been defined, nor by their apparent improbability. We must at all times remember that these are strongly held beliefs, and to challenge them directly would cause offense. Rather, it may be best – as always – to invite a sincerely interested friend to study Christ's First Coming, and how it failed to literally fulfill the expectations of the people of His day.

The gospel preached in all the world

The Gospel of Matthew contains the following prophecy by Jesus:

> And this gospel of the kingdom shall be preached in all the world for a witness unto all nations; and then shall the end come.[85]

As a matter of record, this actually came to pass around the year 1844, when it was determined that the message of Christ had been spread by Christian missionaries to every country on the globe, including some that had until recently been 'off limits' for geopolitical reasons. Mormons, however, do not consider this prophecy as necessarily having been fulfilled; since they believe the Book of Mormon to be an integral part of the 'restored' gospel of Jesus Christ, they are working diligently to spread it throughout the world in order to hasten Christ's return.

He comes in great glory

According to Mormon doctrine, when Jesus was born in Bethlehem He 'did not come in glory,' because he was obviously devoid of earthly riches and power. The Sunday school curriculum book *Gospel Principles* states:

> When Jesus Christ first came to the earth, he did not come in glory. He was born in a lowly stable and laid in a manger of hay. He did not come with great armies as the Jews had expected of their Savior.[86]

While this is true in a literal sense, this rationale, rather than pointing out the spiritual blindness of the people of the time, seems to be apologizing for it. Furthermore, the New Testament affirms that Jesus *did* in fact come in glory:

> For we have not followed cunningly devised fables, when we made known unto you the power and coming of our Lord Jesus Christ, but were eye-witnesses of his majesty. For he received from God the Father honour and glory, when there came such a voice to him from the excellent glory, This is my beloved Son, in whom I am well pleased.[87]

Even the Mormon scriptures state unequivocally that Jesus came 'in power and great glory.' In the Book of Mormon, Nephi relates a vision he had of Jesus' appearance in the Holy Land:

> And I beheld that he went forth ministering unto the people, in power and great glory; and the multitudes were gathered together to hear him; and I beheld that they cast him out from among them.[88]

And in the Doctrine and Covenants, Joseph Smith attributes the following words to John the Baptist:

> And I, John, bear record that I beheld his glory, as the glory of the Only Begotten of the Father, full of grace and truth, even the Spirit of truth, which came and dwelt in the flesh, and dwelt among us . . . And I, John, bear record, and lo, the heavens were opened, and the Holy Ghost descended upon him in the form of a dove, and sat upon him, and there came a voice out of heaven saying: This is my beloved Son. And I, John, bear record that he received a fulness of the glory of the Father; And he received all power, both in heaven and on earth, and the glory of the Father was with him, for he dwelt in him.[89]

Consider the words spoken to the Virgin Mary by the angel Gabriel prior to the birth of Jesus:

> He shall be great, and shall be called the Son of the Highest: and the Lord God shall give unto him the throne of his father David: And he shall reign over the house of Jacob for ever; and of his kingdom there shall be no end.[90]

How could Mary, or any of her contemporaries, correlate this with the temporal life of Jesus? Would they not have been bitterly disappointed by His brief and seemingly inconsequential ministry, which left but a handful of disciples to carry on the work? In fact, His true sovereignty did not become apparent in this world until centuries after His death. Yet from the above verse it would have been easy to assume that these things should come to pass all at once. Bahá'u'lláh explained:

> It hath, therefore, become manifest and evident that within the tabernacles of these Prophets and chosen Ones of God the light of His infinite names and exalted attributes hath been reflected, even though the light of some of these attributes may or may not be outwardly revealed from these luminous Temples to the eyes of men. That a certain attribute of God hath not been outwardly manifested by these Essences of Detachment doth in no wise imply that they who are the Day Springs of God's attributes and the Treasuries of His holy names did not actually possess it. Therefore, these illuminated Souls, these beauteous Countenances have, each and every one of them, been endowed with all the attributes of God, such as sovereignty, dominion, and the like, even though to outward seeming they be shorn of all earthly majesty . . .[91]

Mormons believe that the Second Coming of Christ will cause devastation to the world and will be patently obvious to all. Joseph Smith in his journal noted various news items about earthquakes, meteor showers, violent storms, and even a 'shower of flesh and blood,' a mysterious blood-colored rain that reportedly fell over Tennessee in 1841.[92] All these are indications that Smith was actively looking for outward signs of the Return.

Curiously, Christ's promise that the Day of the Lord would come 'as a thief in the night'[93] is altogether missing from Mormon conjectures about the nature of this event. Bahá'ís consider this prophecy to be one of the most telling, for several reasons: (1) when a thief has been in our home, we usually do not find out about it until after he has left; (2) when we discover the unlawful entry, we feel upset and violated; and (3) we don't know who the thief is until we thoroughly investigate the evidence left behind. These observations apply to many people today: only a few Bahá'ís were privileged to know about the new Revelation from God during Bahá'u'lláh's lifetime, and the vast majority did not discover it until after He had left this earthly existence; some who are confronted with the Bahá'í Faith discover that their most cherished traditions and outward observances have been annulled, causing great consternation in their hearts; and it is only through the evidence of Sacred Writings and transformed lives that we can grasp the true significance of the Bahá'í Dispensation.

Mormons expect that Christ's second appearance will be very different from the first:

> When Jesus comes again, he will come in power and great glory . . . All things that are corrupt will be burned, and the earth will be cleansed by fire . . . When Jesus was born, very few people knew that the Savior of the world had come. When he comes again, there will be no doubt who he is.[94]

The New Testament recounts that Jesus rebuked James and John for drawing similar conclusions about His First Coming:

> And when his disciples James and John saw this, they said, Lord, wilt thou that we command fire to come down from heaven, and consume them, even as Elias did? But he turned, and rebuked them, and said, Ye know not what manner of spirit ye are of. For the Son of man is not come to destroy men's lives, but to save them.[95]

He likewise explained that the coming of the Kingdom is not outwardly visible:

> And when he was demanded of the Pharisees, when the kingdom of God should come, he answered them and said, The kingdom of God cometh not with observation: Neither shall they say, Lo here! or, lo there! for, behold, the kingdom of God is within you.[96]

Yet are we not in the midst of a world conflagration, the purpose of which we currently do not understand, but which will surely result in a cleansing? Are not the wars and rumors of wars that have persisted ever since the mid-19th century a clear sign that we are living in the 'last days,' the Day of Resurrection, at this very moment? Indeed, Bahá'u'lláh's clear warnings, quoted by Shoghi

Effendi in *The Promised Day is Come*, bear witness to the great convulsions that the world must endure before the establishment of that promised Bahá'í World Order:

'The time for the destruction of the world and its people,' Bahá'u'lláh's prophetic pen has proclaimed, 'hath arrived.' 'The hour is approaching,' He specifically affirms, 'when the most great convulsion will have appeared.' 'The promised day is come, the day when tormenting trials will have surged above your heads, and beneath your feet, saying: "Taste ye what your hands have wrought!"' 'Soon shall the blasts of His chastisement beat upon you, and the dust of hell enshroud you.' And again: 'And when the appointed hour is come, there shall suddenly appear that which shall cause the limbs of mankind to quake.' 'The day is approaching when its [civilization's] flame will devour the cities, when the Tongue of Grandeur will proclaim: "The Kingdom is God's, the Almighty, the All-Praised!"' 'The day will soon come,' He, referring to the foolish ones of the earth, has written, 'whereon they will cry out for help and receive no answer.' 'The day is approaching,' He moreover has prophesied, 'when the wrathful anger of the Almighty will have taken hold of them. He, verily, is the Omnipotent, the All-Subduing, the Most Powerful. He shall cleanse the earth from the defilement of their corruption, and shall give it for an heritage unto such of His servants as are nigh unto Him.'[97]

Resurrection of the dead

If we distance ourselves for a moment from well-known Christian preconceptions of the Resurrection of Jesus Christ, we might notice that the word *resurrection* as it appears in the Bible can be taken to refer to one of two concepts, neither of which describes the physical reanimation of the body of Jesus. This is a startling claim that will certainly be rejected by many Christians, but the skeptical reader is encouraged to verify it, armed with a searchable electronic Bible or an old-fashioned concordance.[98]

In one sense, the New Testament uses the phrase 'resurrection of the dead,' or simply 'resurrection,' to refer to the passing of the soul from the physical into the spiritual world at the time of death; in other words, it refers to the afterlife:

There is one glory of the sun, and another glory of the moon, and another glory of the stars: for one star differeth from another star in glory. So also is the resurrection of the dead. It is sown in corruption; it is raised in incorruption: It is sown in dishonour; it is raised in glory: it is sown in weakness; it is raised in power: It is sown a natural body; it is raised a spiritual body. There is a natural body, and there is a spiritual body.[99]

The other use of the word *resurrection* is in the context of the Return of a Manifestation of God. For example, in the Gospel of John, Jesus proclaims Himself to be the promised Return:

Martha saith unto him, I know that he shall rise again *in the resurrection at the last day.* Jesus said unto her, *I am the resurrection,* and the life: he that believeth in me, though he were dead, yet shall he live: And whosoever liveth and believeth in me shall never die.[100]

The Book of Mormon, however, seems to confuse these two meanings, claiming that at or around the time of the Resurrection (Return) of Jesus, the souls of the dead will be reunited with their bodies, which are to physically come forth (resurrect) from their graves:

And behold, again it hath been spoken, that there is a first resurrection, a resurrection of all those who have been, or who are, or who shall be, down to the resurrection of Christ from the dead. Now, we do not suppose that this first resurrection, which is spoken of in this manner, can be the resurrection of the souls and their consignation to happiness or misery. Ye cannot suppose that this is what it meaneth. Behold, I say unto you, Nay; but it meaneth the reuniting of the soul with the body, of those from the days of Adam down to the resurrection of Christ.[101]

This belief is not strictly a Mormon phenomenon, but one that is shared by many Christian denominations. It can be traced back to a literal interpretation of the following verse from the Bible:

And the graves were opened; and many bodies of the saints which slept arose, And came out of the graves after his resurrection, and went into the holy city, and appeared unto many.[102]

Bahá'u'lláh has explained that the opening of the graves and the arising of the saints symbolize the quickening and spiritual rejuvenation of mankind; the *resurrection* denotes the Return of the Manifestation; and the *holy city* is the city of the nearness of God. Furthermore, this verse from the Gospel of Matthew, written in the past tense, appears at a point in the narrative when

Christ is still on the cross, making it unlikely that the word 'resurrection' refers to the reanimation of His body on the third day.

The idea that Christ's Return will somehow precipitate a bodily resurrection of the faithful poses a logistical dilemma as well, beyond the obvious one relating to the reanimation of decomposed human remains: what about people who are still alive at the time of the Resurrection? Do they have to die first so they can be resurrected? The Book of Mormon offers a creative if rather inelegant solution, namely a *delayed resurrection*:

> Now there must be a space betwixt the time of death and the time of resurrection . . . Now, whether the souls and the bodies of those of whom has been spoken shall all be reunited at once, the wicked as well as the righteous, I do not say; let it suffice, that I say that they all come forth; or in other words, their resurrection cometh to pass before the resurrection of those who die after the resurrection of Christ. Now, my son, I do not say that their resurrection cometh at the resurrection of Christ; but behold, I give it as my opinion, that the souls and the bodies are reunited, of the righteous, at the resurrection of Christ, and his ascension into heaven. But whether it be at his resurrection or after, I do not say; but this much I say, that there is a space between death and the resurrection of the body, and a state of the soul in happiness or in misery until the time which is appointed of God that the dead shall come forth, and be reunited, both soul and body, and be brought to stand before God, and be judged according to their works.[103]

It then offers an elaborate description of what happens to these souls between the time of death and their eventual resurrection. In the most simplified terms, Mormons believe that at physical death, there is a separation of the mortal body from the spiritual body, and that at the Resurrection, the two are reunited, producing an *immortal body*. Furthermore, Jesus is believed to have been the first to do this. *Gospel Principles* states in this regard:

> He [Jesus] will complete the Resurrection. Those who have obtained the privilege of coming forth in the Resurrection of the Just will rise from their graves. They will be caught up to meet the Savior as he comes down from heaven. After Jesus Christ rose from the dead, other righteous people who had died were also resurrected. They appeared in Jerusalem and also on the American continent. This was the beginning of the First Resurrection. Some people have been resurrected since then. Those who already have been resurrected and those who will be resurrected at the time of his

coming will all inherit the glory of the celestial kingdom . . . When all these people have been resurrected, the First Resurrection will be completed. The wicked who are living at the time of the second coming of the Lord will be destroyed in the flesh. They, along with the wicked who are already dead, will have to wait until the end of the Millennium before they can come forth from their graves. At the end of the Millennium, the Second Resurrection will take place. All of the remaining dead will rise to meet God. They will either inherit the telestial kingdom or be cast into outer darkness with Satan.[104]

This refers to both a first and a second resurrection, describing the former as an ongoing process that began when Christ rose from the dead nearly two thousand years ago, and which will culminate in His Second Coming.

Conclusion

From the foregoing descriptions it becomes clear that there are significant differences in understanding between Mormons and Bahá'ís concerning the nature of the Second Coming of Christ. Bahá'ís would do well to make a concerted effort to further acquaint themselves with Mormon doctrine so that they are able to engage, where appropriate, in constructive dialogue with their LDS friends regarding the spiritual character of the Word of God.

CHAPTER 13

LEARNING FROM MORMONS

Without doubt, Latter-day Saints have been spectacularly successful in the expansion and consolidation of their organization, especially in the United States. Regardless of any theological or philosophical differences, Bahá'ís would be remiss not to study the extraordinary ways in which the Church of Jesus Christ of Latter-day Saints has fostered a spirit of obedience, consecration and sacrifice at every level of its hierarchy, the undaunted application of religious convictions – no matter how contrary to the norms of society – to every aspect of life, strong family and community bonds, and a structured curriculum for the spiritual education of children and adults alike. As our own Bahá'í communities grow in size and complexity, we can gain inspiration from these successes, while remaining true to the teachings and principles of our own Faith.

Spiritual education

'Abdu'l-Bahá has stressed the importance of the spiritual education of children starting at a very early age:

> There are certain pillars which have been established as the unshakeable supports of the Faith of God. The mightiest of these is learning and the use of the mind, the expansion of consciousness, and insight into the realities of the universe and the hidden mysteries of Almighty God.
>
> To promote knowledge is thus an inescapable duty imposed on every one of the friends of God. It is incumbent upon that Spiritual Assembly, that assemblage of God, to exert every effort to educate the children, so that from infancy they will be trained in Bahá'í conduct and the ways of God, and will, even as young plants, thrive and flourish in the soft-flowing waters that are the counsels and admonitions of the Blessed Beauty.[1]

This call is answered in countless Bahá'í communities through neighborhood-based children's classes, and is being applied ever more systematically across the globe. A distinguishing feature of these classes is that they are offered to the general public – in fact, a number of such classes are established with only non-Bahá'í children attending – yet they all use a distinctly Bahá'í curriculum that encourages the memorization of Bahá'í prayers and Writings, teaches virtues through stories about the Central Figures of the Faith, and demonstrates those virtues through games and other activities.

Older children can join Bahá'í junior youth groups, where the curriculum focuses on the life skills they so urgently need to maintain their individual identity and withstand the onslaught of materialism and peer pressure. While these groups have a written curriculum, a significant portion of the time is spent engaged in group activities involving the arts, sports and recreation, service projects, and the exploration of different cultures through crafts, history, music and cuisine. Junior youth groups are guided by trained 'animators,' usually older youth or young adults who mentor the group, facilitate consultation among its members, and organize its various activities. The term 'animator' attests to that individual's multifaceted role, which is to foster the spiritual identity of the members in the group, empower them to serve humanity, develop their powers of expression, enhance their spiritual and intellectual capacities, help create a moral structure in their lives, and prepare them to participate effectively in the affairs of their community.

Starting at the age of 15 – the age of spiritual maturity in the Bahá'í Faith – youth are challenged to become full participants in the Divine Plan. Like their adult coreligionists, the youth are encouraged to acquire specific skills through completing a sequence of training courses, and to hone those skills by applying them in real-life situations that involve teaching the Faith. For example, one training course focuses on the life of the spirit, and develops the skill of holding devotional gatherings in the neighborhood. Other skills developed through these courses include conducting home visits (to establish social and spiritual bonds among neighbors), teaching neighborhood children's classes (to instill virtues and an understanding of spiritual concepts), telling stories about the history and Central Figures of the Bahá'í Faith (useful in teaching the Faith to others), and participating in collective teaching efforts. Although all Bahá'ís are encouraged to participate in these courses, the youth are uniquely positioned, owing to their relative lack of worldly commitments, to be at the forefront of these activities.

From the very beginning, children and youth are empowered to become active servants of their community. This means, for example, that a seven-year-old boy could teach the Faith to his friends and invite them to join his children's class; a twelve-year-old girl could be a teacher's assistant in her younger brother's children's class; or a group of high school friends could form a teaching team to establish junior youth groups in their neighborhood.

Church-based education

Latter-day Saints share the Bahá'ís' commitment to the spiritual education of children and youth, although this education is not actively promoted to the general public. The structured religious instruction of Mormon children begins at eighteen months and continues through college, gradually intensifying as the student grows in mental and spiritual capacity, and tailored to the specific needs of each age group. Mormon churches, where most of the early education takes place, also foster a family-oriented environment. Before a child has reached the minimum age for the nursery class, mother and father usually alternate watching the infant during their own Sunday-school classes. And although the Church encourages traditional gender roles, taking care of the children is clearly identified as a shared responsibility between the two parents. It is quite refreshing to see a proud father quietly entertaining or rocking a baby to sleep during a priesthood meeting.

Beginning at eighteen months, toddlers attend a *nursery* class where they play with toys, sing songs, and hear stories about the Bible or the Book of Mormon. This is a fertile age for learning; by the time my daughter was two years old, she had memorized several complete Mormon songs and hymns. Virtues such as kindness, reverence and obedience are taught using stories and activities. Starting at age three, children attend *primary*, where they receive more direct instruction on church doctrine.

Virtues make up an important part of the lesson plan regardless of age group. The LDS Church has coined (and trademarked) the motto *Choose The Right*, or *CTR* – a reference to choosing the right path of Christ – and markets CTR signet rings, T-shirts, posters, wrist bands, and a host of related paraphernalia.

From age 12 through 18, boys and girls receive separate instruction as part of the *Young Men's* and *Young Women's* programs. Here, strong emphasis is placed on chastity, modesty of dress, and a rejection of the various excesses and promiscuities of society in general, such as drinking, smoking, drugs, and inappropriate sexual contact. Pre-teens and teens attend regular firesides,[2] go on camping trips and other outings – separated by gender – and take part in service projects designed specifically for youth. All activities are organized and supervised by the adults who make up the Young Men's and Young Women's presidencies, and whose relationship to their charges is characterized by a careful mix of camaraderie and mentorship.

Seminaries and institutes

LDS parents of high-school-aged teens are strongly encouraged to enroll their sons and daughters in *seminary*. As with many other Mormon terms, this does not describe anything like a traditional Christian theological institute of higher learning. Rather, the LDS seminary is an institution for the continued spiritual education of youth, and acts as both supplement and counterbalance to secular high school education. In most parts of the world, a single seminary building serves a wide area, requiring students to rise well before dawn in order to attend their seminary class and still get to school on time. However, in places with large Mormon populations (such as Utah, Idaho and Arizona), some major public high schools have a seminary or church building located within walking distance of campus, allowing Mormon students not only to attend their seminary classes as part of their regular school day, but also to meet for lunch and after-school activities. This fosters a spirit of fellowship with other LDS students, provides a safe haven from the usual campus intrigues, and keeps youth firmly rooted in the doctrines of the Church during the most vulnerable and tumultuous time of their lives.

The seminary experience does not end with high school. Located near major universities and community colleges, LDS *institutes of religion* provide a form of higher education in the principles of the restored gospel to college students and other adults. Learning takes place in a traditional classroom environment, and the instructors are usually among the more learned Mormons in the community.

Family Home Evening

Every LDS husband/father/priest has a sacred duty to provide for the spiritual and moral education of his children, and to work together with his wife to foster a spirit of unity within the family. In 1964, the LDS Church created a vehicle for this kind of education and family bonding, called *Family Home Evening*. Each year the Church publishes manuals, videos and other resources that help parents teach their children about Mormon principles, doctrine and history, geared to various age groups. In addition, it has designated Monday night as official Family Home Evening night, and decreed that no church meetings should be planned during that time.

Family Home Evening, aside from providing spiritual and moral education for all family members and reinforcing church doctrine, also includes a strong service component and promotes consultation among family members. It is an especially effective tool for keeping lines of communication open between parents and their teenage children, and for the resolution of conflicts between siblings.

This concept is, in my view, worthy of emulation. Several years ago, my wife and I decided to offer our children an experience similar to Family Home Evening we call 'Family Fun Night.' Rather than use the LDS materials, our family has traditionally allowed the children to choose a virtue from the *Family Virtues Guide* by Linda Kavelin Popov which, although written by a Bahá'í, celebrates the divine origin of all virtues without promoting a specific religious agenda. One evening each week, we would gather to discuss a new virtue, and afterwards enjoy some family games and a special treat. Over time, use of the *Family Virtues Guide* has gradually diminished in favor of having the kids come up with their own topic for discussion. Our children have always looked forward to this tradition, and have seemed to enjoy the discussion of the virtue as much as the games that follow.

Latter-day Saints have devised a successful system of spiritual education incorporating children and youth of all ages and genders, and extending from the church into the home. While this system may not be suitable as a direct model for Bahá'í education, it is nevertheless worthy of admiration, and deserves close examination as we prepare ourselves for entry by troops.

Strong social bonds in the community

Latter-day Saints have developed a system of communal ties, and a sense of kinship, the likes of which are found in few other religious communities. Mormon families visit each other regularly just to socialize, and often baby-sit each other's children. In other words, they are part of a neighborhood-based support system. Of course, such a support system comes naturally in cities with a large Mormon presence. In places such as Mesa, Arizona – where in some neighborhoods three out of five homes are LDS – most members of a ward live within walking distance from each other, and such close proximity encourages social interaction. In areas where the membership is more spread out, Mormons do whatever they can to maintain their social bonds, such as organize picnics, parties, and other social gatherings.

While Latter-day Saints are quite serious about their faith, their piety in no way translates into asceticism. Mormons know how to have fun – good, wholesome, clean fun. Church buildings are suitable for having parties, parking lot barbecues, dances, and even indoor basketball games. A spirit of fellowship and Mormon identity is fostered among children and youth by including them in all activities.

Unlike the Bahá'í Faith, the LDS Church urges its members to marry within the faith. To this end, it creates regular opportunities for single people of all ages to meet in both social and worship settings. One of these is the weekly church-sponsored (and chaperoned) dance night for youth. The Church also sponsors special 'fireside' gatherings for young single adults, and each stake has a separate 'singles ward' where everyone attending the sacrament and Sunday school is unattached.

Lest we unfairly judge our own Bahá'í communities for any perceived lack of social interaction, it should be noted that in places where there are large concentrations of Bahá'ís (such as in Iran, India, and a number of Asian, African and South American countries), similar support systems have thrived from the very beginning. Even in the United States, one need only look at larger Bahá'í communities to see examples of a vibrant social network. Yet to see how Mormons take care of each other is inspiring, and Bahá'ís should not hesitate to bridge physical and emotional distances to strengthen the social fabric of their own communities.

As Bahá'ís strive to turn their communities into nurturing families in which everyone feels welcome, the need for more interaction on a social as well as spiritual level, and the resulting feeling of belonging and identity, are abundantly clear.

Home teaching and visiting teaching

A very effective tool the LDS Church uses in reinforcing social and spiritual bonds in the community is that of *home teaching* and *visiting teaching*. These terms refer to a similar function for different genders – men are home teachers, women are visiting teachers. However, whereas home teachers can share a short lesson with the entire family, visiting teachers generally meet only with the women in the household. Each month, active men and women in the Church are assigned a list of families to visit. The purpose of these thirty-minute visits is threefold:

(1) *To share a lesson.* Each month, the church periodical *Ensign* contains a short lesson for home and visiting teachers to share with their assigned families. This is a way for the Church to ensure that every member of the community receives some doctrinal education on a regular basis.

(2) *To provide social interaction.* Home and visiting teachers usually spend a little time socializing with their families, if appropriate. To this end, they sometimes bring a plate of cookies or other snacks.

(3) *To offer assistance.* Home and visiting teachers take a sincere interest in their families' well-being, and offer their assistance if needed. For

example, if a family is moving, the home or visiting teacher will organize a group of volunteers to help with the move. If a person is ill, he or she will volunteer to help out with shopping and transportation.

Home teaching visits are not geared specifically to active or inactive members of the ward; all members are contacted about these visits, although priority is sometimes given to families who do not attend regularly or may have fallen away from the Church.

On the administrative level, two main features of home and visiting teaching stand out. Firstly, each member of the Priesthood or Relief Society is randomly assigned one or more families or individuals whom they are required to visit at least once per month. The second distinguishing feature is diligent follow-up. Home and visiting teachers receive frequent reminders about meeting their assigned goals, and a monthly accounting is done of the actual families visited.

Home visits in the Baháʼí community

Are there any principles of LDS home teaching that apply to the Baháʼí community? Indeed, the Universal House of Justice has identified 'home visits' among Baháʼís and receptive seekers as being an essential component of community development and systematic growth. In a letter outlining the Second Five Year Plan, it wrote:

> Even an act of service as simple as visiting the home of a new believer, whether in a village in the Pacific Islands or in a vast metropolitan area like London, reinforces ties of fellowship that bind the members of the community together. Conceived as a means for exposing believers to the fundamentals of the Faith, 'home visits' are giving rise to an array of deepening efforts, both individual and collective, in which the friends are delving into the Writings and exploring their implications for their lives.[3]

The International Teaching Centre elaborated:

> The importance of home visits in the current framework for growth reaches to the heart of what it means to build a Baháʼí community and a new civilization. Although raising up a new world order is concerned with governance and other social principles, it is fundamentally about building a global society based on justice and love. Is it sufficient to call people to a center for meetings and expect them to come, or do we need to visit

one another and talk about spiritual matters and aspirations? Home visits have proven effective because they lend themselves to promoting a Baháʼí conversation – discussions on spiritual concerns that strengthen bonds of fellowship, love and unity.[4]

Clearly, the motivating principles underpinning LDS 'home teaching' and the Baháʼí 'home visits' are the same – to expose believers 'to the fundamentals of the Faith' and to 'strengthen bonds of fellowship, love and unity' in the community. The beauty of the Baháʼí home visit lies in its ability to fulfill a wide range of needs according to the stage of development of each local Baháʼí community.

In communities where there is not yet a large influx of new believers, home visits are an important means for building unity and growing the 'active core' among the existing membership. The simple act of contacting one or more families or individuals on a regular basis, even if only for a brief visit, certainly helps the entire community feel more like a family unit. Baháʼís who are not often seen at the Nineteen Day Feast might appreciate having someone visit with them and check on their health. The visitor might discover that the extended absence is due to a lack of transportation, which could lead to arranging for a ride to the Feast; or the individual might have become somewhat isolated and disaffected from the Baháʼí community, in which case regular social interaction can serve as a process for their gradual reintegration.

As the Baháʼís in a community become more effective teachers of the Cause, they will attract new souls to the Faith and their ranks will increase. The newly declared believers will need to be welcomed into the community and given an opportunity to become more familiar with essential Baháʼí concepts such as the Covenant of Baháʼuʼlláh, the distinguishing features of the life of Baháʼuʼlláh, the importance of unity in the Baháʼí community, the Nineteen Day Feast, the Baháʼí fund, and the role of teaching in the life of the individual and the community. Regular home visits to these new believers can serve to deepen them in these topics, as well as make them feel part of a loving family in which they can thrive spiritually through collective worship, deepening, and service, and in which their children can receive a spiritual education. Through loving interaction and spiritual conversations in the comfort of their own home, new Baháʼís will come to understand how these needs are addressed by Feasts, Holy Day celebrations, and the four core activities identified by the Universal House of Justice – neighborhood-based devotional gatherings, study circles, children's classes and junior youth groups.

Developing an outward-looking orientation

One of the stated purposes of Bahá'í home visits is to reinforce 'ties of fel-lowship that bind the members of the community together.' Does the word 'community' here refer just to the Bahá'í community, or are we called upon to build fellowship in the community at large? What if a Bahá'í were to actively seek out new friendships among his neighbors, or strengthen ties with his existing friends and relatives and elevating those friendships to a more spiritual level? Could home visits be a means to engage people in spiritual conversa-tions that lead to a discussion of the Faith and the solutions it offers to the world's problems? Can they be an effective tool for preparing these friends and neighbors to participate in (and even host) devotional meetings, study circles and children's classes? When we consider that Bahá'u'lláh has brought His Revelation as a healing medicine to all of mankind, the answer to these questions becomes abundantly clear. Through developing an 'outward-look-ing orientation'[5] and actively inviting non-Bahá'ís to join us in our activities, we come to realize that these 'core activities, which at the outset were devised principally to benefit the believers themselves, are naturally becoming portals for entry by troops.'[6]

Community support

The LDS Church provides a robust economic support system for its mem-bers, and also reaches out to others in need regardless of their religion. We'll take a look at how this support system operates, and how it benefits both individual members and the Church as a whole.

Emergency preparedness

Because Mormons expect the Return of Christ to be accompanied by cataclys-mic phenomena – possibly involving earthquakes and other natural disasters – the Church of Jesus Christ of Latter-day Saints advises its members to pre-pare for the worst. The general recommendation is for each family to have one or two years' worth of food and heating supplies in storage. Illustrative of the importance of emergency preparedness is former church president Ezra Taft Benson's statement that the 'revelation to produce and store food may be as essential to our temporal welfare today as boarding the ark was to the people in the days of Noah.'[7]

Since no one knows exactly when disaster will strike, individual Mormons are encouraged to maintain the freshness of their supply by rotating out the oldest food – including flour and powdered milk – and using it in every-day cooking. Furthermore, church leadership has moved away from a purely apocalyptic rationale, and embraced a more pragmatic message of economic preparedness: if a family suffers a loss of income, it can subsist for months on its own store of food before it needs to draw on outside assistance.

Self-sufficiency and welfare

This emphasis on self-sufficiency, both of individual families and of the Church as a whole, is a recurring theme throughout the history of the LDS Church. Early Mormons were frequent targets of persecution, and it became increasingly important to build a self-sustaining economy within the Church so they would not become dependent on their enemies. The theocratic gov-ernment of Nauvoo, Illinois, with its own political and economic systems – not to mention a full-blown army – was a prime example of self-sufficiency in action. This continued in Salt Lake City, Utah, where Mormons avoided business dealings with the 'Babylon' of the outside world for many years. However, in the late 19th century the Church found itself on life support when all of its properties were placed in government receivership over the issue of polygamy. The trauma of that time seems to have steeled the Church's resolve to never again have to rely on any outside entity for its survival or that of its members.

Today, the LDS Church runs an impressive network of food produc-tion, processing, storage and distribution facilities under its Welfare Services umbrella. On the production side, food staples such as corn and wheat are grown on thousands of acres of farm land. Fruits and vegetables are likewise grown, harvested and canned. All of it is stored in capacious grain elevators and warehouses. On the distribution side, the Church operates a chain of thrift stores under the name *Deseret Industries*. Deseret's stated purpose is to foster the self-sufficiency of the Latter-day Saints, to which end it provides both employment opportunities and food assistance to those in need. Used clothing and household articles, regardless of condition, can be dropped off at special donation centers. Saleable items are sold in the adjacent thrift store, and the remainder is donated or recycled. In addition to used clothing, furni-ture and appliances, Deseret Industries sells canned food and other items the Church seeks to rotate out of its vast storehouses.

Staffing the various canneries, warehouses and thrift stores is a steady stream of volunteers. Ward members regularly gather for communal canning projects, where they not only help the Church maintain inventory levels, but also learn how to do their own canning. Simple mechanical canning machines are easily set up in a garage, and can provide a low-cost solution to building an emergency food supply.

Self-sufficiency is the primary motivation for Mormon families to maintain their own year's supply of food. In hard economic times, those same families are expected to get by on what they've saved, and failing that, get assistance through the Church's Welfare Services and Deseret Industries. However, that assistance is not free. Being 'on the dole' is considered demeaning, and those in need are required to perform some kind of labor to safeguard their own sense of self-worth as well as minimize the Church's reliance on salaried employees. Through its production–distribution department, LDS Welfare Services has a job for just about anyone, ranging from picking corn or canning fruits and vegetables, to sorting donated items at Deseret Industries. Even if a person is disabled, local Church leaders are encouraged to engage him in whatever meaningful activity he is able to perform. Reliance on government assistance is looked upon with disdain, and acceded to only as a last resort. An *Ensign* magazine article explains:

> Production projects are nonprofit activities that are operated by wards, stakes, or regions for the purpose of providing food and nonfood commodities to care for the poor and the needy of the kingdom. Food projects such as farms, orchards, dairies, ranches, feed-lot operations, canneries, and bakeries, and nonfood projects such as rug-making, handicrafts, furniture making, and sewing projects also provide a few of many opportunities where those receiving assistance may work as best they can, thereby maintaining their integrity in an age when there is more and more reliance upon so-called 'free' government assistance. The projects also provide opportunities for families to learn to work together and to learn to sacrifice and to consecrate their energies to provide for those who are less fortunate.[8]

The Bahá'í reader may have noticed that the LDS emphasis on self-sufficiency and universal productivity closely resembles the Bahá'í principle requiring all believers to occupy themselves with 'what will profit you and others.'[9] In fact, the Bahá'í Writings both extol the benefits of work, and condemn the bane of idleness and sloth:

> O people of Bahá! It is incumbent upon each one of you to engage in some occupation – such as a craft, a trade or the like. We have exalted your engagement in such work to the rank of worship of the one true God. Reflect, O people, on the grace and blessings of your Lord, and yield Him thanks at eventide and dawn. Waste not your hours in idleness and sloth,

but occupy yourselves with what will profit you and others. Thus hath it been decreed in this Tablet from whose horizon hath shone the day-star of wisdom and utterance.[10]

The Guardian expounded:

> With reference to Bahá'u'lláh's command concerning the engagement of the believers in some sort of profession; the teachings are most emphatic on this matter, particularly the statement in the *Aqdas* to this effect which makes it quite clear that idle people who lack the desire to work can have no place in the new World Order. As a corollary of this principle, Bahá'u'lláh further states that mendicity should not only be discouraged but entirely wiped out from the face of society. It is the duty of those who are in charge of the organization of society to give every individual the opportunity of acquiring the necessary talent in some kind of profession, and also the means of utilizing such a talent, both for its own sake and for the sake of earning the means of his livelihood. Every individual, no matter how handicapped and limited he may be, is under the obligation of engaging in some work or profession, for work, especially when performed in the spirit of service, is according to Bahá'u'lláh, a form of worship. It has not only a utilitarian purpose, but has a value in itself, because it draws us nearer to God, and enables us to better grasp His purpose for us in this world.[11]

In the future, Bahá'í Houses of Worship, eventually to be erected in every town and village, will form the administrative as well as the physical hubs of an intricate support structure, involved not only in medical and welfare services for all of humanity, but also in education and scientific research. In their current state of maturity, however, most of the Bahá'í institutions in the world are as yet unable to provide material welfare on any significant scale. Where social and economic development projects do exist, they are mostly aimed at the general population, and do not specifically target Bahá'ís in need.

Even prior to the advent of the promised Golden Age of the Faith – in which a global economic system based on spiritual principles will make poverty and hunger obsolete – the Bahá'í Writings promise that the day will come when Bahá'í communities have sufficient financial resources at their disposal to ensure that every one of its members has food, clothing, shelter and education, and is given an opportunity to serve the Faith in whatever capacity they can. The Bahá'í funds, and particularly the institution of Ḥuqúqu'lláh, will be central to this future capacity:

As to the specific concern that prompted your inquiry, the use of funds from Ḥuqúqu'lláh, the disbursement of which is entirely at the discretion of the Head of the Faith, entails a wide range of applications that will eventually address various needs of society in ways that will also contribute to the solution of economic problems. However, it is much too early in the worldwide observance of the Law, and is not possible in the current state of the Bahá'í community or of society, for the House of Justice to elaborate on these details. For the time being, the Ḥuqúqu'lláh is used principally for the work of the Bahá'í community, which, of course, includes its initial efforts at social and economic development.[12]

This should not prevent individuals with the necessary means from establishing small-scale social and economic development projects that would benefit those in need, including Bahá'ís. In this context, the LDS Welfare Services department serves as a praiseworthy model, particularly in that it promotes a strong work ethic and is financially self-sustaining.

Everyone has a calling

Mormons do not accept idleness in their communities; nearly everyone, whether young or old, man or woman, able-bodied or handicapped, is put to work in some capacity at least some of the time. Activities in service of the Church are referred to as 'callings,' and are assigned by the ward bishopric.

Callings can range from the trivial (handing out sacrament programs at the door) to the intensely challenging (managing the Boy Scouts or Young Women's programs). When the bishop 'calls' a youth or adult to service, it is considered a divine bestowal and a great bounty which must not be turned down. Even if the task seems overwhelming, there is a sense of trust that God will not burden a soul beyond its capacity, and the way will be opened. Most Mormons therefore accept their callings with a spirit of gratitude and obedience.

The Universal House of Justice has repeatedly urged local institutions to involve all members of their communities, including children and youth, in some service to the Faith. In its message at Riḍván 2000, the House stressed the need to integrate young people, and particularly 'junior youth' between the ages of 12 and 14, into the life and activities of the community:

They represent a special group with special needs as they are somewhat in between childhood and youth when many changes are occurring within them. Creative attention must be devoted to involving them in programmes of activity that will engage their interests, mold their capacities for teaching and service, and involve them in social interaction with older youth. The employment of the arts in various forms can be of great value in such activity.[13]

Since then, this guidance has given rise to special junior youth groups, led by dedicated 'animators,' which focus on preparing adolescents to become servants of humanity.

Depending on the size of the Bahá'í community and its level of maturity, there are a number of steps local Assemblies can take to encourage more active involvement on the part of individual believers of all ages. Assuming that the community is considerably larger than the minimum of nine – in which all adult members already serve on the Assembly – there are likely significant human resources that remain untapped. While much of the involvement in Bahá'í activities on every level is dependent on individual initiative, Assemblies play a crucial role in encouraging the members of their communities to arise and serve. In an August 2007 letter to Local Spiritual Assemblies, the National Spiritual Assembly of the Bahá'ís of the United States wrote:

> The chief duty of Local Spiritual Assemblies is to promote the teaching work. We therefore call upon you to rise to the challenge of the hour by making support of the Plan your top priority. Prominent features of your leadership of the community in this arena should include . . . constant encouragement of the believers to enter this field of action . . . You can also help the community to avoid unnecessary distractions, allocating its precious resources, both human and financial, 'according to priorities wisely set.'[14]

The Local Spiritual Assembly, as the spiritual parent of the community, is uniquely empowered to inspire the believers to arise and serve. Certainly the most effective form of encouragement is to lead by example. Many current Assembly members have either completed or are in the process of completing the Ruhi sequence of training courses, and are applying the skills they have thus learned to actively take part in teaching projects or tutor study circles. This in turn has inspired other believers to overcome any obstacles or feelings of inadequacy and to engage more fully in the promotion of the Divine Plan.

'A peculiar people'

One of the greatest challenges facing Bahá'ís is maintaining a life in harmony with Bahá'í principles on one hand, while being actively engaged in a thoroughly material world on the other. As it is our sacred duty to spread the teachings of Bahá'u'lláh over the entire planet, we cannot simply seclude ourselves in enclaves, safely protected from corrupting outside influences. In order to build His Kingdom, we must roll up our sleeves and join the world without becoming attached to it. 'Abdu'l-Bahá described this condition as being 'in the world but . . . not of it':

> Saints are men who have freed themselves from the world of matter and who have overcome sin. They live in the world but are not of it, their thoughts being continually in the world of the spirit. Their lives are spent in holiness, and their deeds show forth love, justice and godliness. They are illumined from on high; they are as bright and shining lamps in the dark places of the earth. These are the saints of God.[15]

Of course, this is a formidable task, fraught with challenges and obstacles. In the closing year of his earthly life, Shoghi Effendi issued this dire warning:

> The Bahá'ís should realize that today's intensely materialistic civilization, alas, most perfectly exemplified by the United States, has far exceeded the bounds of moderation, and, as Bahá'u'lláh has pointed out in His Writings, civilization itself, when carried to extremes, leads to destruction. The Canadian friends should be on their guard against this deadly influence to which they are so constantly exposed, and which we can see is undermining the moral strength of not only America, but indeed of Europe and other parts of the world to which it is rapidly spreading.[16]

Considering that, in the Guardian's estimation, the world had already 'far exceeded the bounds of moderation' by 1957, one can only wonder what he might have said about today's state of affairs, assuming he could find the words to describe it. While seclusion is not an acceptable defense against this 'deadly influence,' we must strive to provide a safe and healthy environment in which to raise our children. A strong Bahá'í identity, fostered by warm and loving Bahá'í communities, and demonstrated by steadfastness of faith and the tenacious observance of Bahá'í law, is the compass that allows us to navigate these treacherous waters and set an example for the rest of mankind:

> By the sublimity and serenity of their faith, by the steadiness and clarity of their vision, the incorruptibility of their character, the rigor of their discipline, the sanctity of their morals, and the unique example of their community life, they can and indeed must in a world polluted with its incurable corruptions, paralyzed by its haunting fears, torn by its devas-

tating hatreds, and languishing under the weight of its appalling miseries demonstrate the validity of their claim to be regarded as the sole repository of that grace upon whose operation must depend the complete deliverance, the fundamental reorganization and the supreme felicity of all mankind.[17]

Indeed, we should constantly strive to manifest these words quoted by Bahá'u'lláh: 'A lover feareth nothing and no harm can come nigh him: Thou seest him chill in the fire and dry in the sea.'[18]

Proud to be different

Like Bahá'ís, Latter-day Saints are keenly aware of the corrupting influences of a culture that appears to promote greed, sex, violence and a plethora of addictive behaviors. They endeavor to live up to the standards of the Gospel, and try to provide a safe social environment for their members without isolating themselves from the rest of society. The practice by some Mormon families of shunning 'non-member' neighbors – even to the point of forbidding their children to associate with children of other faiths – is condemned by the current LDS leadership as narrow-minded and irrational.

Whenever possible, Mormons avoid working on Sundays, instead choosing to devote their Sabbath Day to worship and family activities. They refuse to use swear words or take the Lord's name in vain, and are not embarrassed to ask for a soft drink at a mostly alcoholic cocktail party. Latter-day Saints feel happy, even proud, to be different from the world around them, so much so that they have adopted for themselves the biblical designation of 'a peculiar people,' a term which occurs in both the Old and New Testaments, and appears to be synonymous with 'chosen people.'[19] Although Mormons sometimes half jokingly observe that a lot of people indeed find them peculiar, what they really mean is that they see themselves as 'distinctive in nature or character from others,'[20] in other words, a people set apart. This positive sense of peculiarity is inculcated in LDS children from a very early age. Along these same lines, 'Abdu'l-Bahá exhorted the friends to follow His example, to live a Bahá'í life, and thus become distinguished and recognizable among all the peoples of the world:

O army of God! Through the protection and help vouchsafed by the Blessed Beauty – may my life be a sacrifice to His loved ones – ye must conduct yourselves in such a manner that ye may stand out distinguished and brilliant as the sun among other souls. Should any one of you enter a city, he should become a centre of attraction by reason of his sincerity, his faithfulness and love, his honesty and fidelity, his truthfulness and loving-kindness towards all the peoples of the world, so that the people of that city may cry out and say: 'This man is unquestionably a Bahá'í, for his manners, his behaviour, his conduct, his morals, his nature, and disposition reflect the attributes of the Bahá'ís.' Not until ye attain this station can ye be said to have been faithful to the Covenant and Testament of God. For He hath, through irrefutable Texts, entered into a binding Covenant with us all, requiring us to act in accordance with His sacred instructions and counsels.[21]

In a society where peer pressure is not merely confined to the world of adolescence, Bahá'ís can foster within themselves – and their children in particular – a strong sense of identity not only with Bahá'í principles, but also with the Cause of Bahá'u'lláh itself. Such an identity entails an unabashed love of our religion, its principles, and its Founders. It also gives rise to a special virtue mentioned by the Universal House of Justice on numerous occasions – *audacity*, or the courage to speak up when an opportunity presents itself.

As Bahá'í communities grow and mature, their members will solidify social and spiritual bonds with each other, thus providing a safe environment for children and creating that all-important sense of Bahá'í identity. And while we must be careful not to hide out from the world, we can strive to distinguish ourselves through our words and deeds. Knowing that Mormons have come to terms with being different from the rest of society can be a comfort and an inspiration to Bahá'ís who experience a lack of acceptance among their non-Bahá'í families and peers.

A personal testimony

The term *personal testimony*, as understood by most Mormons, refers simultaneously to an individual's personal conviction in his avowed beliefs, and his willingness and ability to share that conviction with others. Accordingly, there are two aspects to every personal testimony: an internal striving for certitude, and an external product of that certitude, manifested in words and deeds.

The personal testimony plays a supreme role, both individually and collectively, in the lives of Latter-day Saints. Its importance is established in the Book of Mormon, wherein countless prophets testify to the future appearance of Jesus Christ on the American continent. But the clearest directive to build a testimony is attributed to Jesus Christ himself, later in that same book, when upon his promised arrival in America he exhorts the people to testify of his appearance:

And again, more blessed are they who shall believe in your words because that ye shall testify that ye have seen me, and that ye know that I am. Yea, blessed are they who shall believe in your words, and come down into the depths of humility and be baptized, for they shall be visited with fire and with the Holy Ghost, and shall receive a remission of their sins.[22]

Devout Mormons continually strive to strengthen their testimony, letting their faith take root in their hearts, while honing their skills in announcing the restored gospel to those around them – the deeper the conviction, the stronger the testimony, and the greater the effect on the hearer. An essential part of this growth process is living a holy life and remaining obedient to God's commandments. Most importantly, a true testimony is unique to each individual, gained not through blind imitation, but rather through individual prayer, study, and experience. In a recent *Ensign* magazine article titled 'The Power of a Strong Testimony,' a member of the Quorum of the Twelve Apostles offered the following insights into the nature and significance of the Mormon testimony:

> In this uncertain world, there are some things that never change: the perfect love of our Heavenly Father for each of us; the assurance that He is there and will always hear us; the existence of absolute, unchanging truths; the fact that there is a plan of happiness; the assurance that success in life is attained through faith in Jesus Christ and obedience to His teachings because of the redemptive power of His Atonement; the certainty of life after death; the reality that our condition there is set by how we live here. Whether one does or does not accept these truths does not alter their reality. They are the fundamental building blocks of a living testimony . . .
>
> These and the other truths are certainties. However, your conviction of their reality must come from your own understanding of truth, from your own application of divine law and your willingness to seek the confirming witness of the Spirit. Your testimony may begin from acknowledgment that the teachings of the Lord seem reasonable. But it must grow from practicing those laws. Then your own experience will attest to their validity and yield the results promised. That confirmation will not all come at once. A strong testimony comes line upon line, precept upon precept. It requires faith, time, consistent obedience, and a willingness to sacrifice.
>
> A strong testimony cannot be built upon a weak foundation. Therefore, don't pretend you believe something when you are not sure of it. Seek to receive a ratifying witness. Wrestle in mighty prayer, living righteously, and ask for a spiritual confirmation. The beauty of the teachings of the Lord is

that they are true and that you can confirm them for yourself. Hone your spiritual susceptibility by being constantly alert to the guidance that will come through the still, small voice of the Spirit. Let your Father in Heaven know of your feelings, your needs, your concerns, your hopes and aspirations. Speak to Him with total confidence, knowing that He will hear and respond. Then patiently go forth in your life doing those things you know are correct, walking with confidence born of faith and righteousness, patiently waiting for the response that will come in the manner and at the time the Lord considers most appropriate . . .

For enduring peace and security, at some time in life, in quiet moments of reflection, you must come to know with a surety that there is a God in heaven who loves you, that He is in control and will help you. That conviction is the core of strong testimony.[23]

Mormon children, almost as soon as they are able to speak, are taught to 'gain a testimony of the Church,' and occasionally to give this testimony during a sacrament meeting. It usually starts out as a simple memorization, such as: '*I'd like to bear my testimony. I know this Church is true. I love my parents, and I love my brothers and sisters . . . In the name of Jesus Christ, Amen.*'

Over time, children are given additional suggestions to include in their testimony, such as an affirmation that the current president of the Church is a prophet. The seeds of personal testimony are thus sown in early childhood, nourished through the study of the scriptures and doctrine of the LDS Church, and watered with a deep sense of love and gratitude for the person of Jesus Christ. By early adulthood, the outward expression of this testimony will, in most cases, have flowered into an eloquent, heartfelt, and often emotional declaration of faith. Many LDS women – as well as some men – break into tears or weep openly while giving their testimony during the sacrament meeting. For this reason, the lectern at the front of the chapel is invariably outfitted with a box of tissues.

Several of the distinguishing features of the Mormon testimony – faith, study, prayer, purity of heart, and the independent search for confirmation – are also to be found in the Bahá'í Writings:

O My Brother! Hearken to the delightsome words of My honeyed tongue, and quaff the stream of mystic holiness from My sugar-shedding lips. Sow the seeds of My divine wisdom in the pure soil of thy heart, and water them with the water of certitude, that the hyacinths of My knowledge and wisdom may spring up fresh and green in the sacred city of thy heart.[24]

Only when the lamp of search, of earnest striving, of longing desire, of passionate devotion, of fervid love, of rapture, and ecstasy, is kindled within the seeker's heart, and the breeze of His loving-kindness is wafted upon his soul, will the darkness of error be dispelled, the mists of doubts and misgivings be dissipated, and the lights of knowledge and certitude envelop his being. At that hour will the mystic Herald, bearing the joyful tidings of the Spirit, shine forth from the City of God resplendent as the morn, and, through the trumpet-blast of knowledge, will awaken the heart, the soul, and the spirit from the slumber of negligence. Then will the manifold favours and outpouring grace of the holy and everlasting Spirit confer such new life upon the seeker that he will find himself endowed with a new eye, a new ear, a new heart, and a new mind. He will contemplate the manifest signs of the universe, and will penetrate the hidden mysteries of the soul. Gazing with the eye of God, he will perceive within every atom a door that leadeth him to the stations of absolute certitude. He will discover in all things the mysteries of divine Revelation and the evidences of an everlasting manifestation.[25]

I now assure thee, O servant of God, that, if thy mind become empty and pure from every mention and thought and thy heart attracted wholly to the Kingdom of God, forget all else besides God and come in communion with the Spirit of God, then the Holy Spirit will assist thee with a power which will enable thee to penetrate all things, and a Dazzling Spark which enlightens all sides, a Brilliant Flame in the zenith of the heavens, will teach thee that which thou dost not know of the facts of the universe and of the divine doctrine. Verily, I say unto thee, every soul which ariseth today to guide others to the path of safety and infuse in them the Spirit of Life, the Holy Spirit will inspire that soul with evidences, proofs and facts and the lights will shine upon it from the Kingdom of God . . .[26]

Perhaps the purest example of the importance of testimony in the Bahá'í Faith is given in the Short Obligatory Prayer, to be recited once each day:

I bear witness, O my God, that Thou hast created me to know Thee and to worship Thee. I testify, at this moment, to my powerlessness and to Thy might, to my poverty and to Thy wealth.

There is none other God but Thee, the Help in Peril, the Self-Subsisting.[27]

We are promised that through earnest search, study of the Writings and daily prayer, we can attain to certitude and steadfastness in our Faith, and receive proofs and testimonies through the confirmation of the Holy Spirit. Do we not receive these things that we may acquaint others with the wondrous signs of this age?

> It is incumbent upon thee, by the permission of God, to cleanse the eye of thine heart from the things of the world, that thou mayest realize the infinitude of divine knowledge, and mayest behold Truth so clearly that thou wilt need no proof to demonstrate His reality, nor any evidence to bear witness unto His testimony.[28]

> O thou seeker of the kingdom of God! If thou wishest thy speech and utterance to take effect in the hardened hearts, be thou severed from all attachment to this world and turn unto the Kingdom of God. Enkindle the fire of the love of God in the heart with such intensity that thou mayest become a flame of fire and a luminous lamp of guidance. At that time thy speech will take effect within the hearts, through the confirmation of the Holy Spirit.[29]

Bahá'í teaching should not be limited to explaining the essential verities of our Faith. A number of people, while sympathetic to its unifying message, may not fully appreciate the significance of this momentous Revelation based solely on its basic principles, as these have, over the years, become nearly universally accepted. That these principles were nothing short of revolutionary in the time and place in which they were first proclaimed, or that their acceptance by the generality of mankind is a quite recent phenomenon, may be of little consequence to them. What may resonate more with these souls, apart from being exposed to the Creative Word itself, is an eloquent testimony of how the Bahá'í Faith has affected us personally. 'Abdu'l-Bahá explained that the transformation of the individual believer is the ultimate proof of the truth of Bahá'u'lláh's mission:

> Verily, ye are the proofs of Bahá'u'lláh. Verily, Bahá'u'lláh is the True One, for He has trained such souls as these, each one of which is a proof in himself.[30]

If we were not born into a Bahá'í family, what was our spiritual condition prior to discovering the Faith? How did it initially capture our attention, and later inspire us to investigate it? What was it that finally led us to accept the station of Bahá'u'lláh? Was there a defining moment of truth, or a gradual process toward recognition? Regardless of our religious background, what effect has the Faith had on our lives, and how has it transformed our inner being? In what ways has it answered our questions, allayed our fears or dispelled our doubts? How has it influenced our outlook on the world? As we meditate on these and other questions, the answers we receive can form the basis for a strong testimony of faith.

We should not underestimate the power of testimony in our teaching efforts; perhaps some small detail about what attracts us to the Faith will stir similar sentiments in our audience. Likewise, should we not encourage our children to consider what the Faith means to them, and instill in them the ability to articulate those thoughts?

> Strain every nerve to acquire both inner and outer perfections, for the fruit of the human tree hath ever been and will ever be perfections both within and without. It is not desirable that a man be left without knowledge or skills, for he is then but a barren tree. Then, so much as capacity and capability allow, ye needs must deck the tree of being with fruits such as knowledge, wisdom, spiritual perception and eloquent speech.[31]

In our efforts to gain a greater appreciation and understanding of our Faith and to translate our inner testimony into words and actions, we may well take some cues from our Mormon friends.

A framework for action

So far we have identified a number of successful achievements by the Church of Jesus Christ of Latter-day Saints, and perhaps discovered among them even some concepts worthy of emulation. However, the Bahá'í Revelation brings unique instructions for mankind which are not found in any other religion, and which have only been manifested through the Persons of the Báb and Bahá'u'lláh. Mere emulation, therefore, is insufficient to bring about a true transformation of the Bahá'í community, much less the world at large. For this, we must turn to Bahá'u'lláh Himself, as well as His representatives on earth, the Universal House of Justice. As they apply the 'framework for action' set forth by their Supreme Institution, Bahá'ís may well draw inspiration from the successes our Mormon friends have attained through their own systematic programs, aided by a strong sense of community and a love for their Creator.

323

CHAPTER 14

THE NEXT STEP

We have now reached the end of this book, but the journey is only beginning. Having explored the countless commonalities between Mormons and Bahá'ís, we have no more excuses to remain aloof from our Mormon brothers and sisters. To be sure, many of these shared beliefs are not so much a blessed convergence between two specific religions as they are a natural outcome of the oneness of all religions. But which is more important: that a point of agreement between two faiths is due to their uniqueness, or to their common origin?

We've also seen that these similarities go hand in hand with a number of dissimilarities. Notwithstanding the many things we have in common, to discount the differences that exist between Mormon doctrine and the Bahá'í teachings would be disingenuous. The LDS Church's literal and sometimes perplexing interpretations of the Bible pose a considerable obstacle to a productive dialogue about prophecy, and there are obvious disagreements with respect to the concepts of pre-existence, the nature of God, spirit children and exaltation, to name a few.

Is there any way to resolve these differences? If not, what is the best way for Mormons and Bahá'ís to come to a better appreciation of each other's faith?

The Mormon scriptures

One way that Bahá'ís can start to build a bridge of understanding is to familiarize themselves with the Mormon scriptures. Of course, while Joseph Smith was clearly 'sensitive to the spiritual currents flowing . . . from the appearance of the Báb and Bahá'u'lláh,'[1] it is impossible for Bahá'ís to accept the Book of Mormon as the direct Word of God, not least because parts of it are in outward conflict with the Bahá'í teachings. Likewise, we cannot accept the divine origin of the Doctrine and Covenants or of any other distinctly Mormon scriptural work, as this would necessitate a belief in the prophethood of Joseph Smith – a position which runs counter to explicit statements made by Shoghi Effendi. However, as mentioned before, we need not accept the LDS scriptures as being divinely inspired in order to appreciate the many truths enshrined in them. The Book of Mormon is a spiritual book with a noble message, carried by an intriguing narrative. The spiritual principles it conveys, such as honesty and detachment from worldly desires, are essentially those contained within the Bible, a book which Bahá'ís do accept as the Word of God. In addition, the Book of Mormon and the other LDS scriptures advance many new ideas which Bahá'ís share. William Collins perhaps expressed it best when he stated:

> The Bahá'í, it seems safe to say, may posit that Joseph Smith, along with William Miller and many other religious prodigies, enunciated a number of ideas that had formed in the collective unconscious of mankind over a long period of incubation, finally to emerge in the early nineteenth century. That the expression of these ideas should occur at the appearance of the Báb and Bahá'u'lláh is a monumental coincidence. Joseph Smith, in founding a highly successful missionary movement and in tapping and channeling the spiritual current of a new age, showed himself to be a religious genius of a most profound kind. Bahá'ís may regard Joseph Smith not as a prophet, but as a seer – one endowed with extraordinary powers of insight. This understanding is a result of viewing Joseph Smith's 'revelatory' experience as being different in kind from that of messengers of God. The Book of Mormon, the Doctrine and Covenants, and *Pearl of Great Price* can be seen by Bahá'ís as repositories of a certain amount of relevant truth, though not necessarily as documents recording historical fact or produced by supernatural means.[2]

Mormons and Bahá'ís also find common ground in Paul's admonition to 'despise not prophesyings' and to 'hold fast that which is good.' The thirteenth Article of Faith states that 'If there is anything virtuous, lovely or of good report or praiseworthy, we seek after these things.'

The futility of theological debate

'Abdu'l-Bahá called on the believers to 'speak out, expound the proofs, set forth clear arguments, draw irrefutable conclusions establishing the truth of the manifestation of the Sun of Reality.'[3] Does this mean that we should engage our Mormon friends in theological discussions in order to show them the clear proofs concerning the Bahá'í Faith?

This is a thorny question whose answer depends on individual circumstances. For example, many Bahá'ís feel that when Mormon missionaries come to visit them, they would be remiss not to acquaint them with the Faith, as long as it is done with humility. Some missionaries may be truly interested in learning about our Faith, while others may politely listen and wait for the right teaching moment of their own. Either way, there can be little harm in seizing the opportunity to blazon the name of Bahá'u'lláh and bring out the essential verities of the Faith. However, some well-intentioned Bahá'ís may be tempted to confront Mormon missionaries with perceived inconsistencies in their church's doctrine, or take them to task for its history on race or polygamy. While most missionaries will take such disputations in stride – they are trained to be impervious to criticism and rejection – this approach obviously does not cultivate an attitude of mutual respect. The sincere Bahá'í has no need, nor should he have the desire, to undermine another's faith by pointing out flaws in that person's religion or its leaders, current or past. Rather, we are promised much greater success by extolling the greatness of the day in which we live:

> It ill beseemeth thee to turn thy gaze unto former or more recent times. Make thou mention of this Day and magnify that which hath appeared therein. It will in truth suffice all mankind. Indeed expositions and discourses in explanation of such things cause the spirits to be chilled. It behoveth thee to speak forth in such wise as to set the hearts of the true believers ablaze and cause their bodies to soar.[4]

> This is the Day in which God's most excellent favors have been poured out upon men, the Day in which His most mighty grace hath been infused into all created things. It is incumbent upon all the peoples of the world to reconcile their differences, and, with perfect unity and peace, abide beneath the shadow of the Tree of His care and loving-kindness.[5]

The observance of tact and wisdom is even more important when dealing with Mormon friends and neighbors, including those we meet in church. Unlike the full-time missionaries, our friends do not deliberately set out to convert us, and may be taken aback by an overly forward approach on our part. Certainly, each individual will respond differently to the Bahá'í Faith; however, attempts to convince Mormons of the truth of the Cause by overwhelming them with theological facts and figures will likely have an adverse effect. Latter-day Saints generally place more stock in spiritual experiences than in philosophical arguments, and are told to eschew 'inappropriate intellectualism':

> One activity which often leads a member to be critical is engaging in inappropriate intellectualism. While it would seem the search for and discovery

of truth should be the goal of all Latter-day Saints, it appears some get more satisfaction from trying to discover new uncertainties. I have friends who have literally spent their lives, thus far, trying to nail down every single intellectual loose end rather than accepting the witness of the Spirit and getting on with it. In so doing, they are depriving themselves of a gold mine of beautiful truths which cannot be tapped by the mind alone.[6]

Furthermore, Mormons expect Satan to try and destroy their testimony through persuasive arguments:

How does Satan operate? What are his tactics? Using his superior knowledge, his unique powers of persuasion, half-truths, and complete lies, the evil one uses the spirit children who followed him (which were many), plus mortal beings who have yielded to his evil ways, to wage war against Jehovah and his followers; and they will, if they can, influence us to become critical and to rebel against God and his work. Thus he destroys the souls of men.[7]

. . . if force will not achieve his ends, Satan is quick to use more subtle and enticing means. He presents his principles and arguments in the most approved style, with great charm and grace. He is very careful to integrate himself into the favor of the powerful and influential among mankind. He unites with popular movements and programs, only to use them as a means of doing that which ultimately oppresses and takes away God-given freedoms . . .

Satan will not ordinarily appear himself to do his dirty work. Rather, he will most often act through friends or acquaintances in whom we have confidence. Being disobedient themselves, they will attempt to persuade us to violate the standards of the Church and the commandments of God.[8]

Of course, Bahá'ís do not consider Satan to be a real person, but rather, as 'Abdu'l-Bahá put it, a manifestation of 'the Insistent Self.'[9] This does not mean that they play down the threat that 'Satan' poses. On the contrary, Bahá'ís believe that to have the enemy wrapt up within our own selves is infinitely more pernicious than if the evil came from outside. Like the Trojan horse, it is precisely the belief that Satan is external to ourselves that makes us forget to look inside for danger. This also means that we cannot abdicate our responsibility by claiming that 'Satan made me do it.' Ours is a continuing struggle between the innate nobility of the soul and the evil promptings of the human heart.

Unfortunately, Bahá'í attempts to convince their Mormon friends that

Satan is not an intelligent being, and therefore is not acting 'through friends and acquaintances' to lead them astray, will likely fail. The previously quoted magazine article continues:

> Satan lives. We must realize that he lives just as certainly as God lives and as we live. Those who teach that there is no devil are either ignorant of the facts or are deceivers.[10]

A discussion of Old and New Testament prophecies concerning the Báb and Bahá'u'lláh may not have much effect either, as Mormons are aware of many of these prophecies and believe them to be fulfilled by Joseph Smith. All of this suggests that even the most logical and skillfully presented arguments and proofs may well be rejected.

Tact and wisdom

The Bahá'í Writings prescribe tact and wisdom in all human interactions, and especially when expounding the verities of the Faith. We are told that our words will have a profound effect on the listener, but that this effect can be either positive or negative. The utmost care must be taken never to offend anyone, nor to overwhelm a person with information he is not able to fully digest:

> Every word is endowed with a spirit, therefore the speaker or expounder should carefully deliver his words at the appropriate time and place, for the impression which each word maketh is clearly evident and perceptible. The Great Being saith: One word may be likened unto fire, another unto light, and the influence which both exert is manifest in the world. Therefore an enlightened man of wisdom should primarily speak with words as mild as milk, that the children of men may be nurtured and edified thereby and may attain the ultimate goal of human existence which is the station of true understanding and nobility. And likewise He saith: One word is like unto springtime causing the tender saplings of the rose-garden of knowledge to become verdant and flourishing, while another word is even as a deadly poison. It behoveth a prudent man of wisdom to speak with utmost leniency and forbearance so that the sweetness of his words may induce everyone to attain that which befitteth man's station.[11]

> You should exercise your judgement and tact in delivering the message. You should make an effort to understand the character and mind of the seeker before you speak to him on the Cause.[12]

Set forth that which ye possess. If it be favourably received, your end is attained; if not, to protest is vain. Leave that soul to himself and turn unto the Lord, the Protector, the Self-Subsisting.[13]

In accordance with the divine teachings in this glorious dispensation we should not belittle anyone and call him ignorant, saying: 'You know not, but I know'. Rather, we should look upon others with respect, and when attempting to explain and demonstrate, we should speak as if we are investigating the truth, saying: 'Here these things are before us. Let us investigate to determine where and in what form the truth can be found.' The teacher should not consider himself as learned and others ignorant. Such a thought breedeth pride, and pride is not conducive to influence. The teacher should not see in himself any superiority; he should speak with the utmost kindliness, lowliness and humility, for such speech exerteth influence and educateth the souls.[14]

'Not everything that a man knoweth can be disclosed, nor can everything that he can disclose be regarded as timely, nor can every timely utterance be considered as suited to the capacity of those who hear it.'[15]

Love is the secret

If we are to turn any heart to Bahá'u'lláh, we must humbly show forth the highest respect for other faiths, and not be too concerned with theological minutiae. Our greatest teaching tool is the love we have for all mankind, since it not only prompts us to reach out to our fellowman, but also enables our friends and acquaintances to feel that love and to open their hearts and minds as a result. 'Abdu'l-Bahá taught:

Love ye all religions and all races with a love that is true and sincere and show that love through deeds and not through the tongue; for the latter hath no importance, as the majority of men are, in speech, well-wishers, while action is the best.[16]

Know thou of a certainty that Love is the secret of God's holy Dispensation, the manifestation of the All-Merciful, the fountain of spiritual outpourings. Love is heaven's kindly light, the Holy Spirit's eternal breath that vivifieth the human soul. Love is the cause of God's revelation unto man, the vital bond inherent, in accordance with the divine creation, in the realities of things. Love is the one means that ensureth true felicity both in this world and the next. Love is the light that guideth in darkness, the living link that uniteth God with man, that assureth the progress of every illumined soul. Love is the most great law that ruleth this mighty and heavenly cycle, the unique power that bindeth together the divers elements of this material world, the supreme magnetic force that directeth the movements of the spheres in the celestial realms. Love revealeth with unfailing and limitless power the mysteries latent in the universe. Love is the spirit of life unto the adorned body of mankind, the establisher of true civilization in this mortal world, and the shedder of imperishable glory upon every high-aiming race and nation.[17]

If a soul is touched by this love and is thereby attracted to the Message of Bahá'u'lláh, even the gravest theological differences will fade against the light of truth:

Shoghi Effendi . . . fully agrees . . . that different people must be approached in different ways and that valuable work for the Bahá'í Cause can be done within the Christian Churches by promoting the 'Christianity of Christ'. 'Abdu'l-Bahá said that when people become true Christians, they will find themselves Bahá'ís. One or two of the best Bahá'ís I know were very earnest, sincere, devoted Christians and accepted the Bahá'í teachings with very little difficulty and without any intervening period of religious scepticism, as an amplification and fulfilment of the teachings and prophesyings of Christ and the prophets.[18]

There are no accidents in God's plan; everything happens for a reason. Could it not be that the LDS Church, like other Christian churches that sprang up during that remarkable spiritual revival of the early 1800s, may yet prove to be a necessary stepping stone for some who would eventually accept the Bahá'í Revelation?

What I have attempted to convey throughout this book is that as Bahá'ís, we can look beyond outward differences and probe deeper to discover the many hidden gems of shared conviction. In one place we may happen upon a small nugget, in another we may strike the mother lode. Our awareness of these common themes allows us not only to feel closer in spirit to our Mormon brethren, but also to engage in more meaningful dialogue with them. Whether this results in any Mormons accepting the Bahá'í Faith is immaterial; that is a matter between each individual and God. The true purpose in this is that the cause of religious tolerance and unity is advanced by our very association with people of other faiths, in a spirit of true brotherly love and fellowship.

I leave you with these exalted Words of Bahá'u'lláh:

> The second Ṭaráz [Ornament] is to consort with the followers of all religions in a spirit of friendliness and fellowship, to proclaim that which the Speaker on Sinai hath set forth and to observe fairness in all matters.
>
> They that are endued with sincerity and faithfulness should associate with all the peoples and kindreds of the earth with joy and radiance, inasmuch as consorting with people hath promoted and will continue to promote unity and concord, which in turn are conducive to the maintenance of order in the world and to the regeneration of nations. Blessed are such as hold fast to the cord of kindliness and tender mercy and are free from animosity and hatred.
>
> This Wronged One exhorteth the peoples of the world to observe tolerance and righteousness, which are two lights amidst the darkness of the world and two educators for the edification of mankind. Happy are they who have attained thereto and woe betide the heedless.[19]

APPENDIX 1

THE HISTORY OF POLYGAMY IN THE LDS CHURCH

By now, most people realize that Mormons no longer practice polygamy, or *plural marriage*, as the Church prefers to call it. However, this fact is somewhat obscured by a number of 'orthodox' splinter groups which persist in this practice, against the law and against the official teachings of the Church. It should be noted that these groups are not recognized by the Church of Jesus Christ of Latter-day Saints, which resents even a passing association with those who practice polygamy, and is loath to describe them as Mormon fundamentalists lest doing so would acknowledge them as Mormons.

The Church's current policies notwithstanding, almost every Mormon family tree going back to the 19th century includes a polygamous marriage, and many people still involuntarily link the practice to Mormonism. Let us briefly examine its origins, as well as the events surrounding its eventual discontinuance (it was never officially abolished by the LDS Church, although it is unlikely to be revived in the future).

Current practices of plural marriage

A little over a century ago, the Church of Jesus Christ of Latter-day Saints not only tolerated plural marriage, it specifically enjoined the practice as an integral part of *celestial marriage*, and thus a requirement for attaining the highest stratum of heaven, the *celestial kingdom*. Today, anyone who engages in the practice is summarily excommunicated. The thousands of Mormon fundamentalist families in Utah that continue to contract plural marriages – much to the chagrin of the LDS Church – help to perpetuate the association between Mormonism and polygamy. Church leaders respond by washing their hands of the entire affair:

> I wish to state categorically that this Church has nothing whatever to do with those practicing polygamy. They are not members of this Church.

Most of them have never been members. They are in violation of the civil law. They know they are in violation of the law. They are subject to its penalties. The Church, of course, has no jurisdiction whatever in this matter.[1]

One polygamist sect, the Fundamentalist Church of Jesus Christ of Latter-day Saints (FLDS), has gained notoriety over its alleged practice of forcing teenaged girls to marry older men who already had other wives, under the auspices of the group's former leader and self-proclaimed prophet, Warren Jeffs. Already under scrutiny from Utah and Arizona law enforcement authorities, the FLDS church in 2005 moved some of its members into the Yearning for Zion (YFZ) Ranch, a large compound it constructed near Eldorado, Texas. There, polygamous families could remain out of the public eye, although the ranch's very presence created some uneasiness in the surrounding community. In 2007, Jeffs was arrested and convicted of rape as an accomplice for his role in arranging the marriage of a 14-year-old girl to her older cousin. The following year, responding to a report of child sexual abuse inside the YFZ Ranch, Texas state authorities raided the compound and forcibly removed 416 children accompanied by about 100 women, including several pregnant teenagers. However, the raid was criticized – even by some unsympathetic to the FLDS church – as an exaggerated response. It also created a logistical dilemma; the church's inconsistent record-keeping made it difficult to establish which children belonged to which mothers, or whether any of the young mothers were of legal age. In addition, since children had been separated from their mothers and few of the women were willing to cooperate with the investigation, questions arose whether the state had violated the civil rights of the families. Despite previous reports of sexual abuse in the FLDS community, the state's actions were seen by some as religiously motivated, and it did not help that the emergency call that triggered the raid on the YFZ Ranch turned out to have probably been a hoax. In the end, the Texas Supreme Court ordered the families' return to the ranch, citing insufficient evidence of immediate danger to the children. The FLDS church, for its part, agreed to officially renounce underage marriage.

This episode echoes a similar incident that occurred more than a half century before. In 1953, Arizona law enforcement officials descended on the Mormon fundamentalist enclave of Short Creek and took nearly the entire town into custody – around 400 people including 236 children. The raid backfired spectacularly. Because the only people who avoided arrest were those who denied being Mormon fundamentalists, the state was accused of religious persecution. Pictures of children being taken from their mothers aroused public sympathy for the families, and generated negative media attention for the state of Arizona – including its governor, who was voted out of office the following year. Even the Church of Jesus Christ of Latter-day Saints, which had supported the raid, came under widespread criticism for condoning the heavy-handed treatment of religious dissidents. Eventually most of the Short Creek residents were able to return home, although it took some parents as much as two years to regain custody of their children.

In light of events such as these, it is sometimes easy to forget that the majority of polygamous Mormon families do not live in compounds or isolated towns far removed from civilization. Most reside in Utah's Salt Lake Valley, lead surprisingly mundane lives, and send their children to public schools. Many of these families, which see themselves as upholding God's commandment as it was originally given to Joseph Smith, have specific rules designed to maintain family unity and protect individual rights, even to the point of establishing a protocol for the courtship of a potential new wife. The American television series 'Big Love' (produced by Home Box Office) portrays just such a family, and was deemed by Mormon polygamist reviewers to offer 'a more realistic view of a polygamous family than most people have known.'[2]

Scriptural justification

In earlier times, both the validity and necessity of plural marriage were basic tenets of the Church of Jesus Christ of Latter-day Saints, and the practice was widely adopted by its members, especially in the higher ranks of the Church. The primary scriptural justification for this practice is found in the original revealed writings of Joseph Smith as canonized in Section 132 of *The Doctrine and Covenants*:

> And again, as pertaining to the law of the priesthood – if any man espouse a virgin, and desire to espouse another, and the first give her consent, and if he espouse the second, and they are virgins, and have vowed to no other man, then is he justified; he cannot commit adultery for they are given unto him; for he cannot commit adultery with that that belongeth unto him and to no one else. And if he have ten virgins given unto him by this law, he cannot commit adultery, for they belong to him, and they are given unto him; therefore is he justified. But if one or either of the ten virgins, after she is espoused, shall be with another man, she has committed adultery, and shall be destroyed; for they are given unto him to multiply and replenish the earth, according to my commandment, and to fulfil the promise which was given by my Father before the foundation

of the world, and for their exaltation in the eternal worlds, that they may bear the souls of men; for herein is the work of my Father continued, that he may be glorified.[3]

According to Smith, then, plural marriage was commanded to 'multiply and replenish the earth,' and was a requirement for 'exaltation in the eternal worlds,' namely the attainment of the celestial kingdom, or highest realm in heaven. What's more, it was considered an eternal law of God, sent 'to fulfil the promise which was given . . . before the foundation of the world.' In *Our Heritage: A Brief History of the Church of Jesus Christ of Latter-day Saints* this point is further clarified:

> While working on the translation of the Bible in the early 1830s, the Prophet Joseph Smith became troubled by the fact that Abraham, Jacob, David, and other Old Testament leaders had more than one wife. The Prophet prayed for understanding and learned that at certain times, for specific purposes, following divinely given laws, plural marriage was approved and directed by God. Joseph Smith also learned that with divine approval, some Latter-day Saints would soon be chosen by priesthood authority to marry more than one wife. A number of Latter-day Saints practiced plural marriage in Nauvoo, but a public announcement of this doctrine and practice was not made until the August 1852 general conference in Salt Lake City. At that conference, Elder Orson Pratt, as directed by President Brigham Young, announced that the practice of a man having more than one wife was part of the Lord's restitution of all things.[4]

Thus 'the Lord's restitution of all things' included the revelation of the law of plural marriage, which had existed from the beginning, and which was to endure to the end. As Heber C. Kimball expressed it in a January 28, 1866 letter to his sons in England:

> Plurality is a law which God established for his elect before the world was formed, for a continuation of seeds forever. It would be as easy for the United States to build a tower to remove the sun, as to remove polygamy, or the Church and kingdom of God.[5]

Practical justification

Within today's LDS community – especially in response to questions from children and youth – the explanation is sometimes given that plural marriage was practiced for a time because many men had perished during the Illinois and Missouri persecutions and the subsequent migration westward, or as part of the 'Mormon Battalion March' to Mexico in 1846 to assist in the war effort. Plural marriage during this period is thus portrayed as a necessary evil, instituted so that the remaining men could take care of the widows and their children. In reality, there is no evidence whatsoever to support that claim. While the long and perilous trek to the west certainly left casualties in its wake, there is no mention in Mormon history of a disproportionate number of men dying. And while several of the 500 men in the Mormon Battalion took to illness, none perished. A church magazine notes:

> On December 11 the battalion fought its only engagement of the Mexican War – one with wild bulls. One man was gored in the leg and sixty to eighty bulls were killed.[6]

Furthermore, the Church's own historical records boldly assert that plural marriage was ordained by God as a requirement for attaining to the highest degrees of glory. In 1878, Joseph F. Smith, a later church president, dispelled any doubts as to the significance of plural marriage to God's plan of salvation:

> Some people have supposed that the doctrine of plural marriage was a sort of superfluity, or non-essential to the salvation or exaltation of mankind. In other words, some of the Saints have said, and believe, that a man with one wife, sealed to him by the authority of the Priesthood for time and eternity, will receive an exaltation as great and glorious, if he is faithful, as he possibly could with more than one. I want here to enter my solemn protest against this idea, for I know it is false. There is no blessing promised except upon conditions, and no blessing can be obtained by mankind except by faithful compliance with the conditions, or law, upon which the same is promised. The marriage of one woman to a man for time and eternity by the sealing power, according to the law of God, is a fulfillment of the celestial law of marriage in part – and is good so far as it goes – and so far as a man abides these conditions of the law, he will receive his reward therefor, and this reward, or blessing, he could not obtain on any other grounds or conditions. But this is only the beginning of the law, not the whole of it. Therefore, whoever has imagined that he could obtain the fullness of blessings pertaining to this celestial law, by complying with only a portion of its conditions, has deceived himself. He cannot do it.[7]

Earlier still in 1873, then-president Brigham Young related the law of plural marriage to Jesus' parable of the talents:

> Now, where a man in this Church says, 'I don't want but one wife, I will live my religion with one,' he will perhaps be saved in the celestial kingdom; but when he gets there he will not find himself in possession of any wife at all. He has had a talent that he has hid up. He will come forward and say, 'Here is that which thou gavest me, I have not wasted it, and here is the one talent,' and he will not enjoy it, but it will be taken and given to those who have improved the talents they received, and he will find himself without any wife, and he will remain single for ever and ever.[8]

Joseph Smith's practice of plural marriage

As previously noted, Section 132 of the Doctrine and Covenants appears to be Joseph Smith's official enjoinder of plural marriage, and while evidence suggests he himself had engaged in the practice for some time, it was neither well known nor widespread during his ministry. The preface to this section reads:

> Although the revelation was recorded in 1843, it is evident from the historical records that the doctrines and principles involved in this revelation had been known by the Prophet since 1831.

It appears that Smith kept his ideas concerning plural marriage a secret for many years, even to the point of denying its existence.[9] In an introduction to the official compilation *History of the Church*, B. H. Roberts explains:

> The date in the heading of the Revelation on the Eternity of the Marriage Covenant, including the Plurality of Wives, notes the time at which the revelation was committed to writing, not the time at which the principles set forth in the revelation were first made known to the Prophet. This is evident from the written revelation itself which discloses the fact that Joseph Smith was already in the relationship of plural marriage, as the following passage witnesses:
>   'And let mine handmaid, Emma Smith, receive all those that have been given unto my servant Joseph, and who are virtuous and pure before me.'[10]

There are clear indications that Emma Hale Smith did not readily accede to her husband's unconventional ideas about marriage. The first such evidence is

D&C 132 itself, in which Joseph, speaking in the voice of Christ, appears to rebuke Emma for resisting his revelation concerning the plurality of wives:

> And I command mine handmaid, Emma Smith, to abide and cleave unto my servant Joseph, and to none else. But if she will not abide this commandment she shall be destroyed, saith the Lord; for I am the Lord thy God, and will destroy her if she abide not in my law.[11]

B. H. Roberts additionally quotes an 1874 account by William Clayton – to whom Joseph Smith originally dictated the above revelation – describing Emma's reaction:

> On the morning of the 12th of July, 1843; Joseph and Hyrum Smith came into the office in the upper story of the brick store, on the bank of the Mississippi river. They were talking on the subject of plural marriage. Hyrum said to Joseph, 'If you will write the revelation on celestial marriage, I will take it and read it to Emma, and I believe I can convince her of its truth, and you will hereafter have peace.' Joseph smiled and remarked, 'You do not know Emma as well as I do.' Hyrum repeated his opinion, and further remarked, 'The doctrine is so plain, I can convince any reasonable man or woman of its truth, purity and heavenly origin,' or words to that effect. Joseph then said, 'Well, I will write the revelation and we will see'
> . . .
> Hyrum then took the revelation to read to Emma. Joseph remained with me in the office until Hyrum returned. When he came back, Joseph asked him how he had succeeded. Hyrum replied that he had never received a more severe talking to in his life, that Emma was very bitter and full of resentment and anger.
> Joseph quietly remarked, 'I told you you did not know Emma as well as I did.' Joseph then put the revelation in his pocket, and they both left the office.
> The revelation was . . . carefully copied the following day by Joseph C. Kingsbury. Two or three days after the revelation was written Joseph related to me and several others that Emma had so teased, and urgently entreated him for the privilege of destroying it, that he became so weary of her teasing, and to get rid of her annoyance, he told her she might destroy it and she had done so, but he had consented to her wish in this matter to pacify her, realizing that he knew the revelation perfectly, and could rewrite it at any time if necessary.[12]

An obscure note in *History of the Church* may even point to the possibility that at least initially, Joseph Smith considered himself to be the only one authorized by God to have multiple wives:

> Evening, at home, and walked up and down the streets with my scribe. Gave instructions to try those persons who were preaching, teaching, or practicing the doctrine of plurality of wives; for, according to the law, I hold the keys of this power in the last days; for there is never but one on earth at a time on whom the power and its keys are conferred; *and I have constantly said no man shall have but one wife at a time, unless the Lord directs otherwise.*[13]

Some church leaders have later suggested that the revelation contained within D&C 132 was of a personal nature and that its canonization into the official scriptures was both premature and unwise.

The Reorganized view

The LDS Church contends that Joseph Smith's commandment to engage in plural marriage at first met with some resistance from his own followers, including Brigham Young, but that Smith eventually succeeded in winning them over. However, the Reorganized Church of Jesus Christ of Latter Day Saints – a Missouri sect which has Joseph Smith as its prophet but is not associated with the so-called 'Utah Mormons,' and which has recently renamed itself *Community of Christ* – originally denied that Smith himself ever engaged in or condoned plural marriage, and accused Brigham Young of introducing it as church doctrine. The Reorganized Church, as an organization, has never embraced plural marriage, and claims it broke away from the mainstream church over this issue, among others. However, it has since recognized, in the face of strong evidence, that Joseph Smith did in fact practice polygamy:

> The issues of polygamy and whether Joseph Smith Jr. was connected with its inception at Nauvoo, Illinois, in the 1840s have been of considerable interest to Community of Christ members and others through the years. The early RLDS Church (1860–1960) consistently opposed the doctrine and fought against the assertion by the Church of Jesus Christ of Latter-day Saints that Joseph Smith Jr. advocated this practice as part of a divine plan. Joseph Smith III, son of the founding prophet and first prophet-president of the RLDS Church (1860–1914), spent much of his life trying to clear his father's name from the stigma of polygamy and polygamous doctrine,

even though there were leaders in the early RLDS Church who believed otherwise. While it is clear that Joseph Smith III sincerely believed that his father was innocent, he was heard to affirm on more than one occasion that even if his father was guilty, he was wrong.

Today the Community of Christ takes into account the growing body of scholarly research and publications depicting the polygamous teachings and practices of the Nauvoo period of church history (1840–1846). The context of these developments included a time of religious and cultural experimentation in the United States and the emergence of a system of secret temple ordinances in Nauvoo that accented the primacy of family connections, both in this life and the next. The practice of plural marriage emerged from that context and involved a select cadre of key leaders entering into polygamous marriage rituals and covenants. The research findings seem to increasingly point to Joseph Smith Jr. as a significant source for plural marriage teaching and practice at Nauvoo. However, several of Joseph Smith's associates later wrote that he repudiated the plural marriage system and began to try to stop its practice shortly before his death in June 1844.[14]

The Book of Mormon condemns plural marriage

Paradoxically, the Book of Mormon, which was published before Joseph Smith first 'became aware' of the law of plural marriage, unequivocally condemns the idea:

> Behold, David and Solomon truly had many wives and concubines, which thing was abominable before me, saith the Lord . . . Wherefore, my brethren, hear me, and hearken to the word of the Lord: For there shall not any man among you have save it be one wife; and concubines he shall have none . . .[15]

Of course this begs the question: how did Joseph Smith reconcile these conflicting teachings, both of which he claimed were divinely revealed? To this end, it seems he employed a rather creative interpretation of scripture. He began by explaining that Abraham and David were commanded by God to have multiple wives and were therefore justified in doing so:

> Verily, thus saith the Lord unto you my servant Joseph, that inasmuch as you have inquired of my hand to know and understand wherein I, the Lord, justified my servants Abraham, Isaac, and Jacob, as also Moses,

David and Solomon, my servants, as touching the principle and doctrine of their having many wives and concubines –

... God commanded Abraham, and Sarah gave Hagar to Abraham to wife. And why did she do it? Because this was the law; and from Hagar sprang many people. This, therefore, was fulfilling, among other things, the promises. Was Abraham, therefore, under condemnation? Verily I say unto you, Nay; for I, the Lord, commanded it.[16]

Incidentally, one of the people who 'sprang' from Hagar was Ishmael, of whom the Prophet Muhammad was a descendant. Some Mormons have unofficially claimed – in an apparent effort to discredit Muhammad – that Ishmael was the product of an illegitimate union between Abraham and Hagar. This is clearly contradicted by the above verses from the Doctrine and Covenants.

Next, Joseph Smith suggested that at least some of the actions of David and Solomon were 'abominable' because in addition to the wives and concubines *given to them*, they sinned with *other men's wives*:

David also received many wives and concubines, and also Solomon and Moses my servants, as also many others of my servants, from the beginning of creation until this time; and in nothing did they sin save in those things which they received not of me. David's wives and concubines were given unto him of me, by the hand of Nathan, my servant, and others of the prophets who had the keys of this power; and in none of these things did he sin against me save in the case of Uriah and his wife; and, therefore he hath fallen from his exaltation, and received his portion; and he shall not inherit them out of the world, for I gave them unto another, saith the Lord.[17]

In an interesting twist to the legitimacy of Ishmael, this statement condemning the union between David and the wife of Uriah as sinful might be used to discredit Jesus, since His genealogy includes Solomon, the product of that union:

And Jesse begat David the king; and David the king begat Solomon of *her that had been the wife of Urias* . . .[18]

Of course, we should remember that this genealogy ends with Joseph who, Mormons and Bahá'ís agree, was not the biological father of Jesus.

Plural marriage discontinued in 1890

An official LDS statement about the Church's former practice of plural marriage reads:

> Some early leaders and members of the Church entered into plural marriages during the latter half of the nineteenth century. After receiving a revelation, Church President Wilford Woodruff declared the practice should be discontinued in 1890 . . . Members of the Church who enter into plural marriage today face Church disciplinary action, including excommunication.[19]

This suggests that God somehow intervened to discontinue a misguided or obsolete practice within the Church, contrary to the expressed declarations of earlier church leaders that plural marriage was God's eternal plan for the 'restitution of all things.' Also, whereas recent church president Gordon B. Hinckley (quoted at the beginning of this appendix) denounced polygamy as a 'violation of civil law,' the Church has never shied away from defiantly vindicating any doctrine that ran afoul of the law. Referring to federal laws instituted against plural marriage during the 1870s and 80s – and their rather enthusiastic enforcement by government officials – a 1978 church magazine article charges:

> These laws were designed to discriminate solely against Latter-day Saints. Federal officials sent into Utah, along with anti-Mormons already living in the state, vigorously worked to identify and prosecute Church members who were living the law of plural marriage. Wives and children were forced to testify in court against their own husbands and fathers. As a result, men who were law abiding were forced to go into hiding. Among these were many Church leaders, including President Taylor, and his first counselor, President George Q. Cannon.[20]

The above statement does not impart the slightest notion that plural marriage was morally wrong – it refers to its practitioners as 'law abiding' – and gives little if any deference to civil law. Indeed, this same attitude is evident from the following 1879 discourse by Orson Pratt:

> Now in regard to plurality of wives, why is that a crime? Only because Congress passed a law making it criminal. Does the Bible make it criminal? No. Does the Book of Mormon make it criminal? No. Does the Doctrine

THE HISTORY OF POLYGAMY IN THE LDS CHURCH

and Covenants make it criminal? No. Why is it criminal? Is there a law of our nature that makes it criminal? No.[21]

In the same year, the aforementioned George Q. Cannon proclaimed:

I do not believe in being defiant. Men that marry more wives than one should be able to bear the penalty of it if there be any attached thereto, or they should not take them. A man that enters this Church ought to be able to die for its principles if necessary, and certainly should be able to go to prison for them without crying about the matter. If you are sentenced to prison for marrying more wives than one, round up your shoulders and bear it like men and no murmuring about it; prepare yourselves to take the consequences.[22]

Seven years later George Q. Cannon was arrested on polygamy charges. After posting bail, he went into hiding until finally giving himself up in 1888. He eventually served a 175-day jail sentence and paid a $450 fine.[23]

Reasons for discontinuing plural marriage

We are told that plural marriage was discontinued in 1890 as a result of direct revelation received by church president Wilford Woodruff, at the time a recent successor to John Taylor. However, in *Our Heritage: A Brief History of the Church of Jesus Christ of Latter-day Saints* we discover an additional motivation for this change in doctrine:

As the 1880s drew to a close, the United States government passed additional laws that deprived those who practiced plural marriage of the right to vote and serve on juries and severely restricted the amount of property the Church could own. Latter-day Saint families suffered as even more fathers went into hiding. President Woodruff pleaded with the Lord for guidance. On the evening of 23 September 1890, the prophet, acting under inspiration, wrote the Manifesto, a document that ended plural marriage for Church members. The Lord showed President Woodruff in vision that unless the practice of plural marriage was ended, the United States government would take over the temples, thus ending work for the living and the dead . . . Following the Church's action, federal officials issued pardons to Latter-day Saint men convicted of violating the antipolygamy laws and much of the persecution stopped.[24]

Anticipating the argument that the Church changed its policy under government pressure and not by divine revelation, *Our Heritage* continues:

> President Woodruff explained: 'I should have let all the temples go out of
> our hands; I should have gone to prison myself, and let every other man
> go there, had not the God of heaven commanded me to do what I did
> do; and when the hour came that I was commanded to do that, it was all
> clear to me. I went before the Lord, and I wrote what the Lord told me
> to write.' God, not the United States Congress, brought about the official
> discontinuance of plural marriage.[25]

Nonetheless, in an emotional address by Wilford Woodruff shortly after this
revelation, there are clear references to a decision made under threat:

> The question is this: Which is the wisest course for the Latter-day Saints to
> pursue – to continue to attempt to practice plural marriage, with the laws
> of the nation against it and the opposition of sixty millions of people, and
> at the cost of the confiscation and loss of all the Temples, and the stopping
> of all the ordinances therein, both for the living and the dead, and the
> imprisonment of the First Presidency and Twelve and the heads of families
> in the Church, and the confiscation of personal property of the people (all
> of which of themselves would stop the practice); or, after doing and suf-
> fering what we have through our adherence to this principle to cease the
> practice and submit to the law, and through doing so leave the Prophets,
> Apostles and fathers at home, so that they can instruct the people and
> attend to the duties of the Church, and also leave the Temples in the hands
> of the Saints, so that they can attend to the ordinances of the Gospel, both
> for the living and the dead?[26]

On the day that his *Manifesto* discontinuing plural marriage was issued,
President Woodruff wrote in his private journal:

> I have arrived at a point in the history of my life as the President of the
> Church of Jesus Christ of Latter-day Saints, where I am under the neces-
> sity of acting for the temporal salvation of the church.[27]

Exactly what kind of threat was the Church facing? Three years earlier, in
1887, the U.S. Congress passed the *Edmunds–Tucker Act*, providing for the
dissolution of the corporation of the Church of Jesus Christ of Latter-day
Saints, with all assets to be disposed of by the Department of the Interior. The

Church went into receivership while it fought a bitter legal battle all the way up to the Supreme Court, which in 1890 handed down a devastating ruling supporting the government's position and effectively sealing the Church's fate.[28] By issuing his 1890 manifesto, Wilford Woodruff narrowly averted total ruin for the Church. Official historical sources additionally suggest that this action may have been a condition for Utah gaining statehood:

> The polygamy prosecutions of the 1880s caused immense disruptions in Utah society and greatly exacerbated the already raw feelings between Utah Mormons and the nation at large. Now, during the turbulent nineties, Utah had begun a wholesale reversal of its cross-grained traditions in order to gain statehood.[29]

In spite of the 1890 decision, however, it took a number of years for the practice of plural marriage to be abandoned, and the Church did not begin to aggressively excommunicate polygamists until around 1930.

Today's Mormons are monogamous

While all of this background may be of keen interest to the student of Mormon history, we should bear in mind that these details are of little use in our everyday conversations with Mormon friends and acquaintances. In most cases, decisions by a president of the LDS Church are taken at face value without any further discussion. And because he is considered the mouthpiece of God, changes in doctrine are not questioned; rather, it is assumed that such changes must be part of some greater plan, the details of which are as yet unknown.

Today, all members of the Church of Jesus Christ of Latter-day Saints are staunchly monogamous, although this has apparently not lessened their desire to 'replenish the earth': it is not uncommon for a Mormon family to include six or more children. Nevertheless, recent changes in the Church's position on birth control now leave it up to a couple to decide how many children to have and when, very much in line with the Bahá'í position on procreation. In a 1983 speech, church president Gordon B. Hinckley stated:

> Much has been said . . . about birth control. I like to think of the positive side of the equation, of the meaning and sanctity of life, of the purpose of this estate in our eternal journey, of the need for the experiences of mortal life under the great plan of God our Father, of the joy that is to be found only where there are children in the home, of the blessings that come of good posterity. When I think of these values and see them taught and

345

observed, then I am willing to leave the question of numbers to the man and the woman and the Lord.[30]

The Bahá'í Faith and plural marriage

Those who have read the Kitáb-i-Aqdas, the book containing the most weighty Bahá'í laws and principles, may remember stumbling upon the following verse:

> God hath prescribed matrimony unto you. Beware that ye take not unto yourselves more wives than two. Whoso contenteth himself with a single partner from among the maidservants of God, both he and she shall live in tranquillity.[31]

While this ordinance may seem on the surface to allow a man to have more than one wife, upon closer inspection we discover that it does not. The note referenced by that paragraph perhaps provides the best explanation:

> While the text of the Kitáb-i-Aqdas appears to permit bigamy, Bahá'u'lláh counsels that tranquillity and contentment derive from monogamy. In another Tablet, He underlines the importance of the individual's acting in such a way as to 'bring comfort to himself and to his partner'. 'Abdu'l-Bahá, the authorized Interpreter of the Bahá'í Writings, states that in the text of the Aqdas monogamy is in effect enjoined. He elaborates this theme in a number of Tablets, including the following:
>
> 'Know thou that polygamy is not permitted under the law of God, for contentment with one wife hath been clearly stipulated. Taking a second wife is made dependent upon equity and justice being upheld between the two wives, under all conditions. However, observance of justice and equity towards two wives is utterly impossible. The fact that bigamy has been made dependent upon an impossible condition is clear proof of its absolute prohibition. Therefore it is not permissible for a man to have more than one wife.'
>
> Polygamy is a very ancient practice among the majority of humanity. The introduction of monogamy has been only gradually accomplished by the Manifestations of God. Jesus, for example, did not prohibit polygamy, but abolished divorce except in the case of fornication; Muhammad limited the number of wives to four, but making plurality of wives contingent on justice, and reintroducing permission for divorce; Bahá'u'lláh, Who was revealing His Teachings in the milieu of a Muslim society, introduced

the question of monogamy gradually in accordance with the principles of wisdom and the progressive unfoldment of His purpose. The fact that He left His followers with an infallible Interpreter of His Writings enabled Him to outwardly permit two wives in the Kitáb-i-Aqdas but uphold a condition that enabled 'Abdu'l-Bahá to elucidate later that the intention of the law was to enforce monogamy.[32]

The Covenant of Bahá'u'lláh is unique in organized religion in that it prevents the breakup of the Bahá'í Faith into divergent sects, something that would nullify the very purpose of a Cause that seeks to unite the entire planet. One consequence of this Covenant is that no law laid down by Bahá'u'lláh can be viewed in isolation from the interpretation of 'Abdu'l-Bahá, the further explication by Shoghi Effendi, and the prerogative of the Universal House of Justice to graduate its implementation. In this particular case, 'Abdu'l-Bahá's emphatic statement concerning the illegality of bigamy has rendered any further explanations or actions moot.

When we closely examine the statement, quoted above, that 'Muhammad limited the number of wives to four ... contingent on justice' we find that this seemingly paradoxical juxtaposition – allowing for polygamy only under impossible conditions – did not originate in the Bahá'í Faith. In the Qur'án, Muhammad provided for plural marriage under specific circumstances, permitting men to 'marry of the women, who seem good to you, two or three or four' but warned that in a monogamous marriage 'it is more likely that ye will not do injustice.'[33] Later on in the same chapter, Muhammad clarified that the conditions of justice required for a polygamous marriage are actually impossible to attain: 'Ye will not be able to deal equally between (your) wives, however much ye wish (to do so).'[34] Thus it was Muhammad who was the first to prescribe monogamy, in the same indirect manner as Bahá'u'lláh. In both religions, the reason for this indirectness has been to gradually introduce monogamy to the part of the world in which they appeared.

APPENDIX 2

RACISM IN THE LDS CHURCH

The Church of Jesus Christ of Latter-day Saints has been much maligned for its policies and attitudes concerning race, and its history is indeed problematic in this respect. Yet as we shall see, this is also the aspect of traditional Mormon 'culture' which the Church is working hardest to reverse. Before engaging our Mormon friends and neighbors, we should come to terms with this issue by first investigating the origins of the LDS Church's unique racial doctrine, and then comparing historical Mormon attitudes to those prevalent among Latter-day Saints today.

Blacks and the priesthood

Although membership in the Church of Jesus Christ of Latter-day Saints has never been closed to blacks, prior to 1978 members of African descent could not be ordained to the priesthood that is believed to be the calling of every male member of the Church. Mormon doctrine did provide for blacks eventually gaining the priesthood, but not until after every non-black person on earth had done so. Interestingly, a small number of African Americans did join the Church prior to 1978, being so attracted to the message of the restored gospel that they were willing to accept the restrictions placed upon them.

To a Mormon, being deprived of the blessings of the priesthood is a serious matter. Without the priesthood, a Mormon family would be considered lacking in spiritual guidance, like a ship without a rudder. A church member would not be able to perform temple ordinances such as baptisms for the dead, or hold leadership positions within the church. But most importantly, there are eternal ramifications. Without the priesthood being conferred on the father and husband, a family cannot be 'sealed' in the temple in order to obtain 'exaltation' to a state of godhood in the highest realms of heaven – the *celestial kingdom* – after the Resurrection. Consequently, keeping the priesthood closed to blacks would, following Mormon doctrine to its own conclusions, amount to establishing a kind of race-based class hierarchy in the afterlife, with 'black' souls confined to the lower *terrestrial kingdom* – the postmortal abode of goodhearted souls who nevertheless failed to recognize the truth of the restored gospel – and in a subservient position to those in the celestial kingdom who will have attained to godhood. The church curriculum book *Gospel Principles* describes the denizens of this terrestrial kingdom as follows:

> These are they who rejected the gospel on earth but afterward received it in the spirit world. These are the honorable people on the earth who were blinded to the gospel of Jesus Christ by the craftiness of men. These are also they who received the gospel and a testimony of Jesus but then were not valiant. They will be visited by Jesus Christ but not by our Heavenly Father. They will not be part of eternal families; they will live separately and singly forever. [1]

Not only would such souls, after passing from this earthly existence, be prevented from consorting with their Heavenly Father and the inhabitants of the celestial kingdom, but spouses and other family members would be separated from each other for eternity.

Early black members of the priesthood

It appears that Joseph Smith himself had no qualms about ordaining black men to the priesthood: at least two African American men – Elijah Abel and Walker Lewis – were ordained during his lifetime.[2] In J. Christopher Conkling's *A Joseph Smith Chronology* we find the following entry:

> Mar. 3, 1836. Elijah Abel, a Negro, is ordained an elder and receives his patriarchal blessing from Joseph Smith, Sr.[3]

It is unlikely that Joseph Smith, Jr was unaware of the ordination of a black man performed by his own father, who was also the patriarch of the Church.

Abel was not only an elder in the Melchizedek priesthood, he had been elevated to the high rank of Seventy, a position he held until his death in 1884. Abel was greatly respected by Joseph Smith, and was sustained as a member of the Third Quorum of Seventies by both Brigham Young and Joseph F. Smith (a later Church president), despite occasional challenges from other church leaders. However, by 1908 the Church's 'Negro policy' of denying blacks the priesthood had taken firm root, and Elijah Abel's priesthood ordination was posthumously declared 'null and void,' ironically by the same Joseph F. Smith who had come to his defense thirty years before.[4] It was not until recently that Elijah Abel was once again publicly acknowledged by the Church. In the January 2003 issue of *Ensign* magazine, the following news item was published under the headline 'Monument Honors African–American Pioneer':

> Baptized in 1832, Elijah Abel was one of the earliest members of the Church. He was also a former slave and one of the few African–Americans to join the Church in his day. Brother Abel and his family traveled west with the Saints, and he lived in Salt Lake City until his death in 1884. He was characterized as a true, pure, and spiritual man, and his memory was recently honored with the dedication of a monument at his grave site in a Salt Lake City cemetery.[5]

Curiously, this statement makes no mention of Abel's 1836 ordination to the Melchizedek priesthood, let alone his high position in the Church.

Scriptural justification for denying the priesthood to blacks

While many Christian churches have at various times discriminated against people of color, the LDS Church is unique in that its reasons for doing so are fixed in its scriptures, which hold that the seed of Cain was cursed with a black skin and a state of servitude:

> For behold, the Lord shall curse the land with much heat, and the barrenness thereof shall go forth forever; and there was a blackness came upon all the children of Canaan, that they were despised among all people.[6]

> And Enoch also beheld the residue of the people which were the sons of Adam; and they were a mixture of all the seed of Adam save it was the seed of Cain, for the seed of Cain were black, and had not place among them.[7]

These verses, purported to have been translated from writings of Moses not recorded in the Pentateuch, were used by Joseph Smith's successors to justify the denial of the priesthood to blacks, and even to criticize the abolitionist movement. Whereas Joseph Smith had been a strong proponent of buying slaves their freedom, Brigham Young was at the very least ambivalent about abolition, and in many of his writings appeared to openly support slavery. In an 1844 article, Smith wrote:

Petition, also, ye goodly inhabitants of the slave states, your legislators to abolish slavery by the year 1850, or now, and save the abolitionist from reproach and ruin, and infamy and shame. Pray Congress to pay every man a reasonable price for his slaves out of the surplus revenue arising from the sale of the public lands, and from the deduction of pay from the members of Congress. Break off the shackles from the poor black man, and hire him to labor like other human beings; for an hour of virtuous liberty is worth a whole eternity of bondage.[8]

This is contrasted by the following remark, made in 1863 by Brigham Young, concerning the American Civil War:

What is the cause of all this waste of life and treasure? To tell it in a plain, truthful way, one portion of the country wish to raise their negroes or black slaves, and the other portion wish to free them, and, apparently, to almost worship them. Well, raise and worship them, who cares? I should never fight one moment about it, for the cause of human improvement is not in the least advanced by the dreadful war which now convulses our unhappy country.[9]

The curse of the Lamanites

The LDS canon contains additional scriptural references to a darkening of the skin as a curse upon a people. According to the Book of Mormon, shortly after a tribe of Israelites under the leadership of a man named Lehi arrived on the American continent, a rift occurred between two of Lehi's sons, Nephi and Laman. In a parallel to the story of Cain and Abel, Laman and his followers, refusing to submit to the will of the righteous Nephi, founded a new people known as the Lamanites, after which endless wars ensued between the generally God-fearing Nephites and the habitually heedless Lamanites. These same Lamanites are considered by Mormons to be the forefathers of today's Native American cultures, and some Mormons boldly refer to American Indians as 'Lamanites.' Native peoples, the Book of Mormon explains, owe their red skin to the transgression of their forefathers:

And the skins of the Lamanites were dark, according to the mark which was set upon their fathers, which was a curse upon them because of their transgression and their rebellion against their brethren . . .[10]

Later in the same book it is written:

And it came to pass that those Lamanites who had united with the Nephites were numbered among the Nephites; And their curse was taken from them, and their skin became white like unto the Nephites; And their young men and their daughters became exceedingly fair, and they were numbered among the Nephites, and were called Nephites.[11]

And then shall they rejoice; for they shall know that it is a blessing unto them from the hand of God; and their scales of darkness shall begin to fall from their eyes; and many generations shall not pass away among them, save they shall be a pure and a delightsome people.[12]

That the LDS Church has become more sensitive to the racial implications of the Book of Mormon is evidenced by the fact that the original text of the above verse was altered in 1981 at the behest of the First Presidency under Spencer W. Kimball. It used to end with ' . . . they shall be a *white* and a delightsome people.'[13]

In any case, it would appear that a curse on an entire branch of humanity runs afoul of the Church's Second Article of Faith, which proclaims that 'men will be punished for their own sins, and not for Adam's transgression.' By corollary, one could argue, men will not be punished for Cain's or Laman's transgression, either. Besides, the Book of Mormon appears to forbid discrimination based on skin color, even if it was the result of a curse:

Wherefore, a commandment I give unto you, which is the word of God, that ye revile no more against them because of the darkness of their skins; neither shall ye revile against them because of their filthiness; but ye shall remember your own filthiness, and remember that their filthiness came because of their fathers.[14]

And the following verse proclaims all the races equal before God:

For none of these iniquities come of the Lord; for he doeth that which is good among the children of men; and he doeth nothing save it be plain unto the children of men; and he inviteth them all to come unto him and partake of his goodness; and he denieth none that come unto him, black and white, bond and free, male and female; and he remembereth the heathen; and all are alike unto God, both Jew and Gentile.[15]

Little explanation is given as to why African Americans and Native Americans were treated differently in this respect. The Mormon scriptures describe both races as having been cursed with a dark skin, yet only blacks were, until some thirty years ago, denied the priesthood. In contrast, American Indians have never been subject to this exclusion, and have in fact been enthusiastically targeted by missionaries, albeit with disappointing results. One possible reason for the unique treatment of American Indians is that they are considered long-lost descendants of the Israelites:

> The interest of the Saints in American Indians grows out of the knowledge that they have of their forefathers, revealed through the Book of Mormon. From the historical parts of that book they learned the origin of these Indians; that they are of the house of Israel: from the prophetic parts of the book they learn of their future, that it is to be glorious; that fallen as their fortunes now are, they will not always remain so; extinction is not their fate, but before many generations shall pass away they will become a white and delightsome people, favored of God, and prominent in bringing to pass His purposes in the land of Zion – the two Americas.[16]

The above passage's promise of a glorious future for Native Americans bears a resemblance to these words of 'Abdu'l-Bahá:

> Attach great importance to the indigenous population of America. For these souls may be likened unto the ancient inhabitants of the Arabian Peninsula, who, prior to the Mission of Muhammad, were like unto savages. When the light of Muhammad shone forth in their midst, however, they became so radiant as to illumine the world. Likewise, these Indians, should they be educated and guided, there can be no doubt that they will become so illumined as to enlighten the whole world.[17]

In fact, the LDS Church went to unprecedented lengths to bring about the fulfillment of the Book of Mormon prophecies concerning the 'Lamanite' people. From 1954 until 1996, it sponsored the *Indian Student Placement Program*. Native children, mostly Navajos from Arizona, spent nine months out of each year away from home to live with white Mormon foster families in Utah, where they not only attended public school, but were also exposed to traditional Mormon religious and cultural values. These children were taught that they were ancient descendants of the Israelites, that a curse of dark skin had been placed upon their forefathers, but that their race had a glorious future through the restoration of the Gospel. A 1971 church magazine article described the purpose of this program as follows:

It has already been noted that more than five thousand youngsters from reservations throughout the United States and Canada spent the last school year with non-Lamanite Latter-day Saint families. Even though there are some problems and frustrations, this great program widens the vision of the Indian youngster and helps to narrow the opportunity gap that exists between the Anglo society and the Indian society.

Placement program administrators feel that one of the major results of the program is to give the Indian student a better concept of himself, not to make him into a white man, as is sometimes charged. Further, these young people scattered throughout the Church cannot help but break down the barriers of prejudice that may exist among the whites.[18]

Over 20,000 American Indian children were baptized into the Church as a result of the Indian Student Placement Program. For the foster families, taking in a child was an act of charity and faith. To the Native parents, it presented a rare opportunity for their children to receive a quality education and learn the skills of the dominant society. Yet in a number of interviews conducted for a radio documentary about this controversial program,[19] some former foster children expressed bitterness for having been taken away from their families and for having lost an important part of their Native heritage. A few, upon returning home, discovered that they did not fit well into either culture. This serves as an important reminder that religious education should be respectful of cultural diversity. One of the great tragedies of human history has been the repeated institutional attempts by religion and government to bring about unity through uniformity.

Bahá'í references to 'white' and 'black' faces

Interestingly, the Bahá'í Writings also refer to faces turning white or black, although this is clearly not to be taken literally. In the following prayers, references to 'white' and 'black' faces are spiritually discerned:

> ... I beseech Thee by Thy Name, through which the faces of them that are nigh unto Thee have turned white, and the hearts of such as are devoted to Thee have winged their flight towards Thee, to grant that I may, at all times and under all conditions, lay hold on Thy cord, and be rid of all attachment to anyone except Thee ...[20]

Blessed is the man that turneth towards Thee, and woe betide him who standeth aloof from Thee, who denieth Thee and repudiateth Thy signs in this

Revelation wherein the faces of the exponents of denial have turned black and the faces of the exponents of truthfulness have turned white . . .'[21]

These are understood to describe one's inner state of being as opposed to outward appearance, not least because a literal interpretation would be contrary to every Bahá'í principle from the oneness of mankind to the harmony of science and religion. One thing to keep in mind is that Bahá'u'lláh, in many of His Writings, addressed a predominantly Muslim audience, and He appears to be referring here to a verse from the Qur'án regarding 'Clear Signs':

Let there arise out of you a band of people inviting to all that is good, enjoining what is right, and forbidding what is wrong: They are the ones to attain felicity. Be not like those who are divided amongst themselves and fall into disputations after receiving Clear Signs: For them is a dreadful penalty, – On the Day when some faces will be (lit up with) white, and some faces will be (in the gloom of) black: To those whose faces will be black, (will be said): 'Did ye reject Faith after accepting it? Taste then the penalty for rejecting Faith.' But those whose faces will be (lit with) white, – they will be in (the light of) God's mercy: therein to dwell (for ever).[22]

Thus, 'white' and 'black' faces are a metaphor for the acceptance or denial of certain clear signs concerning the new revelation from God. Those whose faces have turned white are 'people inviting to all that is good, enjoining what is right, and forbidding what is wrong,' or in the Words of Bahá'u'lláh, 'the exponents of truthfulness.' Conversely, those whose faces have turned black are equated with 'those who are divided amongst themselves and fall into disputations after receiving Clear Signs,' or 'the exponents of denial.'

It is tempting to suggest that a spiritual interpretation could likewise be applied to some of the LDS scriptures quoted previously. However, the specific mention of skin changing color appears to rule out this possibility, and in any case, church leaders have from the outset upheld only the literal interpretation.

Historical attitudes of the Church

The Church of Jesus Christ of Latter-day Saints did not develop in a religious or cultural vacuum. When discussing historical attitudes about race, we should keep in mind that the LDS Church's record is not notably worse than that of other Christian churches during the same time period. Virtually all mainstream American churches – though initially eager to convert former

355

slaves to Christianity – persistently denied black Christians the right to associate with their white brethren, limited the influence of black church leaders,
and either openly or tacitly promoted segregation until well into the 1960s.
Jessie L. Embry, professor of history at Brigham Young University, describes
widespread racial discrimination among different churches throughout the
first century of emancipation:

> Some blacks have always belonged to traditionally white churches.
> Following the Civil War the Northern Methodist Episcopal church sent
> missionaries to the South, and by 1896 nearly 250,000 blacks had joined.
> In 1900 they appealed to the national convention for black bishops, but
> the general conference did not respond. According to [*Modern American
> Religion* author Martin E.] Marty, those who remained in the Methodist
> Episcopal church were essentially assigned to a 'world-within-a-world,' and
> were never fully accepted . . . This separate unit remained until 1966 . . .
>
> Other churches also accepted black members only with strict limits.
> When northern Presbyterians and Cumberland Presbyterians of the mid-
> South discussed a merger in 1900, race was an issue. According to Marty,
> 'Cumberlanders said that the northerners recognized the absolute necessity
> of a separation of the races in the South.' Although a church publication,
> the *Afro-American Presbyterian*, denounced segregation as having no 'just
> ground . . . in law, morals or Christianity,' the Special Committee on the
> Territorial Limits of Presbyteries adopted a policy that blacks were 'inferior
> to the whites in culture, mental and moral development' and needed 'the
> stronger race for help and guidance' . . .
>
> Catholics were also segregated or limited from full participation. The
> church ordained few blacks to the priesthood until the 1920s, and those
> who were installed encountered prejudice and misunderstanding. Some
> dioceses voted against 'colored' priests. Others, according to Dorothy
> Liptak's history of Catholic immigrants, simply had 'an unwritten policy
> concerning the preparation of black men for the priesthood.'[23]

From this evidence we must conclude that at least until the mid-1960s, it
would have been quite unfair to single out the Church of Jesus Christ of
Latter-day Saints as somehow being more racist than other churches.

While historically, Mormons' secular attitudes towards African Americans
have been similar to those of the nation as a whole, two things set the Church
of Jesus Christ of Latter-day Saints apart from other Christian churches in
America. The first and most obvious is that racial bias is embedded within the
canon of Mormon scriptures. These scriptures have tragically served as justifi-

cation to early church leaders for making racist remarks in public speeches, not just concerning the role of African Americans in the Church but also in government and society in general. Particularly the words of Brigham Young – who in addition to being president of the LDS Church also held the governorship of the territory of Utah – had influence well beyond the walls of church buildings. It is this well-documented history that is proving difficult for Latter-day Saints to escape, notwithstanding unprecedented efforts on the part of the Church to redefine itself as an organization supporting racial diversity.

The second difference – and arguably the most damaging to the Church's image today – is that while other predominantly white Christian churches officially removed racial barriers in the 1950s and 1960s, the LDS Church continued to resist full integration of blacks into its ranks until 1978. By way of contrast, the Reorganized Church of Jesus Christ of Latter Day Saints, which had Joseph Smith's son, Joseph III, as its President starting in 1860, officially allowed all races into the priesthood as early as 1865, although this did not prevent the racial segregation characteristic of the time.[24] In *Mormon America*, Ostling and Ostling write:

> On May 4, 1865, just after the Civil War ended, Joseph Smith III gave his young church the third of his fifteen revelations, declaring in God's voice that 'it is expedient in me that you ordain priests unto me, of every race who receive the teachings of my law, and become heirs according to the promise.' Reflecting the caution of the day, the revelation added, 'Be not hasty in ordaining men of the Negro race,' and stated that they were to be 'ministers of their own race,' although RLDS segregation has long since disappeared.[25]

In *Black Saints*, Embry elaborates:

> In 1866 the RLDS Quorum of the Twelve Apostles decided blacks should worship with whites, declaring, 'As the Author of Life and Salvation does not discriminate among His rational creatures on account of Color neither does the [Reorganized] Church of Jesus Christ of Latter Day Saints.' This idealistic policy, however, ran into practical difficulties in a world divided by segregation. In the South RLDS blacks had separate congregations. Joseph Smith III conceded in 1893: 'Custom and the natural barriers in the way must have their weight . . . Any attempt to urge the unrestrained intercourse of all classes, races, and conditions will stir up strife and contention far more dangerous to the welfare and unity of the church, than the principle contended for will justify.'[26]

This *de facto* segregation in the Reorganized Church of Jesus Christ of Latter Day Saints remained in effect until at least 1956.

Mormon attitudes toward slavery and segregation

The precise historical attitude of the LDS Church toward slavery and segregation is difficult to ascertain, as various church leaders have issued conflicting opinions over time. As previously noted, Joseph Smith appeared to have been an abolitionist at heart. From a remark he made in 1843, we can surmise that he subscribed to the 'separate but equal' philosophy concerning blacks:

> Elder Hyde inquired the situation of the negro. I replied, they came into the world slaves, mentally and physically. Change their situation with the whites, and they would be like them. They have souls, and are subjects of salvation. Go into Cincinnati[27] or any city, and find an educated negro, who rides in his carriage, and you will see a man who has risen by the powers of his own mind to his exalted state of respectability. The slaves in Washington are more refined than many in high places, and the black boys will take the shine off many of those they brush and wait on . . . Had I anything to do with the negro, I would confine them by strict law to their own species, and put them on a national equalization.[28]

However, Smith's attitude toward slavery may have evolved somewhat over time. Five years earlier in 1838, he published a list of questions and answers about Mormon beliefs. Among these was the question, 'Are the Mormons abolitionists?' Smith answered: 'No, unless delivering the people from priest-craft, and the priests from the power of Satan, should be considered abolition. But we do not believe in setting the negroes free.'[29] Furthermore, the minutes of an 1835 general assembly of the church, incorporated into the Doctrine and Covenants, reflect the following declaration:[30]

> We believe it just to preach the gospel to the nations of the earth, and warn the righteous to save themselves from the corruption of the world; but we do not believe it right to interfere with bond-servants, neither preach the gospel to, nor baptize them contrary to the will and wish of their masters, nor to meddle with or influence them in the least to cause them to be dissatisfied with their situations in this life, thereby jeopardizing the lives of men; such interference we believe to be unlawful and unjust, and dangerous to the peace of every government allowing human beings to be held in servitude.[31]

This public declaration may have been partly aimed at easing tensions between the Mormon community and the population at large, especially in the South. An identical declaration was made at a public meeting held on July 1, 1836 in Clay County, Missouri in response to a citizens' proposal that the Latter-day Saints 'move into another part of the state.'[32] Indeed, Mormons were looked upon with deep suspicion by Missourians, concerned that this group of New England immigrants might harbor abolitionist sentiments. In his introduction to the official *History of the Church*, originally published in 1930, B. H. Roberts explains:

> In 1831 the sentiment for the positive abolition of slavery had made such progress in Massachusetts, that William Lloyd Garrison established in Boston 'The Liberator', a paper which advocated 'the immediate and unconditional emancipation of every slave in the United States.' As a result of this agitation anti-slavery societies were formed and active measures taken to advocate these opinions by means of lectures and pamphlets. These extreme measures against slavery did not meet with the approval of all or even a majority of the people of New England, much less with the approval of the people of other northern states. Still this agitation arose and was chiefly supported in New England. It will not be difficult to understand, therefore, that any considerable number of people from that section of the Union immigrating into a slave state would arouse suspicion; especially when that immigration was into a slave state upon which, when as a territory she had made application for admission into the Union, prohibition of slavery was sought to be enforced by the northern members of the National Congress. Nor will it be sufficient to dispel this suspicion to aver that these particular immigrants from New England, and other northern states are not abolitionists; that they take no part with, and do not share the fanatical sentiments of, the abolitionists; that their objects and purposes are of an entirely different and larger character. [33]

Dispelling the popular notion, circulated by a number of Mormons today, that the persecutions of Latter-day Saints were the result of their opposition to slavery, Roberts continues:

> I do not refer to this question of slavery in connection with the persecution of the Saints in Missouri in order to set it down as one of the causes of that persecution; because, as a matter of fact, the views of the Saints, and especially of the leading Elders of the Church on that question were such that they could never be truthfully charged with being a menace to that institution.[34]

Joseph Smith's personal sensibilities aside, the above excerpts make it clear that the majority of Mormons of the day were not particularly interested in promoting abolition, and that the suspicions of the Missouri populace were unwarranted. Among those who were opposed to the freeing of slaves was Brigham Young:

> In the providences of God their ability is such that they cannot rise above the position of a servant, and they are willing to serve me and have me dictate their labor. Then let them do service to me, and it is my duty to treat them kindly and reward them accordingly.[35]

Yet in the writings of John Taylor – Brigham Young's successor and one of only two survivors of the jailhouse attack on Joseph and Hyrum Smith – we find a number of clear references to the oneness of mankind, of which the following is representative:

> How does God feel towards the human family? He feels that they are his children. What, all? Yes, the white, the black, the red, the Jew, the gentile, the heathen, the Christian, and all classes and grades of men. He feels interested in all. He has done so from the beginning and will continue to do so to the end. He will do all that lies in his power for the benefit, blessing, and exaltation of the human family, both in time and eternity . . .[36]

The Negro doctrine

The first half of the 20th century saw the 'Negro doctrine' take hold in earnest, as church leaders began to portray the separation of the races not just as a temporal issue, but as a much deeper, spiritual one. According to LDS doctrine, all souls were created in a pre-mortal spirit world long before being born into this world. Rather than question the unequal treatment of African Americans on moral grounds, church leaders of the time supposed that a soul born into a black family must have done something wrong in the pre-existence to deserve his unfortunate placement. In a 1915 conference speech, Elder Melvin J. Ballard maintained:

> My brethren and sisters, we are here reaping the reward of our former labors, and we are going hereafter to reap the consequences of our lives and works here. We know, from the doctrines that we have received, that men and women have existed before coming into this life, for countless ages, and that we have been developing certain qualities, and the reason we are

separated into great classes, as the Negro race and the other races on the earth, is not a matter of caprice. God did not take three beautiful children yesterday morning, and say to one, You go to the Negro woman, and to another one, You go to that Chinese mother, and to another, You go down to that beautiful Christian home. In my opinion, there were classes and races, and separation into different groups and conditions before we came to this world, and all are getting what they are entitled to receive here.[37]

Specifically, a great war between good and evil is thought to have occurred in the pre-existence, and the presumption was made that these 'black' souls must not have been sufficiently 'valiant in the fight.' In 1939, Elder George F. Richards remarked:

The negro is an unfortunate man. He has been given a black skin. But that is as nothing compared with that greater handicap that he is not permitted to receive the Priesthood and the ordinances of the temple, necessary to prepare men and women to enter into and enjoy a fulness of glory in the celestial kingdom. What is the reason for this condition, we ask, and I find it to my satisfaction to think that as spirit children of our Eternal Father they were not valiant in the fight . . . I cannot conceive our Father consigning his children to a condition such as that of the negro race, if they had been valiant in the spirit world in that war in heaven.[38]

This principle – that any injustices heaped upon black people were a sort of karmic retribution for transgressions in a previous existence – was given doctrinal weight on August 17, 1949, when the First Presidency issued the following official declaration:

The attitude of the Church with reference to negroes remains as it has always stood. It is not a matter of the declaration of policy but of direct commandment from the Lord, on which is founded the doctrine of the Church from the days of its organization, to the effect that negroes may become members of the church but that they are not entitled to the priesthood at the present time . . .

The position of the Church regarding the Negro may be understood when another doctrine of the Church is kept in mind; namely, that the conduct of spirits in the pre-mortal existence has some determining effect upon the conditions and circumstances under which these spirits take on mortality, and that while the details of the principle have not been made known, the principle itself indicates that the coming to this earth and taking on mortality is a privilege that is given to those who maintain their first estate; and that the worth of the principle is so great that spirits are willing to come to earth and take on bodies no matter what the handicap may be as to the kind of bodies they are to secure; and that among the handicaps, failure of the right to enjoy in mortality the blessings of the priesthood, is a handicap which spirits are willing to assume in order that they might come to earth. Under this principle there is no injustice whatsoever involved in this deprivation as to the holding of the Priesthood by Negroes.[39]

Putting it into perspective

It is undeniable that all of these opinions constitute a form of racism. Yet in my view we should not attempt to hold these statements to the standard of the Bahá'í Faith, which has stood alone in its historical rejection of racial discrimination, but rather examine them against the backdrop of American society during the first half of the 20th century. In this light, the Church of Jesus Christ of Latter-day Saints expressed no more racism than most other 'white' churches of the time, and was well ahead of its contemporaries in accepting other non-European people such as Pacific Islanders and Native Americans into its ranks. Also, the official church position on blacks and the priesthood was not necessarily shared by all Latter-day Saints. In the 1950s, Stewart Udall – at the time the US Secretary of the Interior as well as a church member – published a letter in the independent Mormon journal *Dialogue* which included this rather prophetic statement: 'My fear is that the very character of Mormonism is being distorted and crippled by adherence to a belief that denies the oneness of mankind. We violate the rights and dignity of our Negro brothers, and for this we bear a measure of guilt; but surely we harm ourselves even more.'[40]

The Church today

In June 1978, the LDS Church at long last abandoned its 'Negro doctrine,' making it possible not only for African Americans, but for all people of African descent, to obtain the Mormon priesthood. The basic belief that God cursed certain peoples with dark skin is not openly rejected by today's Latter-day Saints, as it is enshrined in their scriptures and thus beyond question. However, it may be supposed that some Mormons have either rejected that doctrine in their hearts, or simply compartmentalized their thoughts on the matter. In any case, those scriptural references are no longer used to justify racial prejudice in the Church. The official LDS web site simply states:

Until 1978, black male members of the Church were not ordained to the lay priesthood. That position was changed by revelation on 8 June 1978, when Spencer W. Kimball, the 12th president of the Church, announced that the 'long-promised day has come when every faithful, worthy man in the Church may receive the holy priesthood.'[41]

This suggests that it had always been the Church's intention to allow blacks into the priesthood, but that there was a certain wisdom in delaying this privilege. Although this is at odds with earlier church teachings that blacks would never be allowed into the priesthood – at least not in their lifetimes – it is important to understand how Mormons view such changes in policy by their leadership. Because the president of the LDS Church is at once its 'prophet, seer and revelator,' every decision he makes is believed to be divinely inspired, and every word the unquestioned truth. When the Church finally decided to allow blacks into the priesthood, the underlying assumption was that God had a greater plan that was not yet fully understood, and that even such a clear reversal of doctrine was part of that plan. This line of reasoning was enunciated at a recent LDS fireside[*] featuring one of the more famous African American converts to the Mormon faith, R&B recording artist Gladys Knight. At the conclusion of the fireside, a high-ranking church member compared the 1978 revelation allowing blacks into the priesthood to a well-known revelation described in the New Testament:

'Why does the Lord work in stages in taking the gospel across the earth? Why did He initially send the Twelve only to the house of Israel and not to others during His ministry? Why did it take a special revelation to Peter following the Lord's Ascension to expand the work to the Gentiles? Why has the Lord phased His work in this dispensation? It is clear that the Lord has a divine timetable,' Elder Bateman concluded. 'We are all God's children, and the great plan of redemption is organized so that every person who has lived, now lives, or will live on this planet will have an opportunity to accept it.'[42]

This of course implies that prior presidents of the Church – each of whom was considered infallible – were unaware of the Lord's 'divine timetable,' in light of their emphatic declarations that the doctrine on blacks was eternal and unchangeable. This seeming paradox is illustrated by Apostle Bruce R.

---

[*] An LDS fireside, unlike its Bahá'í namesake, is a large event geared toward youth including various speakers and often some form of entertainment.

McConkie, who in earlier editions of his *Mormon Doctrine* had maintained that 'Negroes in this life are denied the priesthood' and that 'under no circumstances can they hold this delegation of authority from the Almighty.'[43] Two months after the 1978 revelation, McConkie made this remarkable admission:

> There are statements in our literature by the early brethren which we have interpreted to mean that the Negroes would not receive the priesthood in mortality. I have said the same things . . . All I can say to that is that it is time disbelieving people repented and got in line and believed in a living, modern, prophet. Forget everything that I have said, or what President Brigham Young or President George Q. Cannon or whomsoever has said in days past that is contrary to the present revelation. We spoke with a limited understanding and without the light and knowledge that now has come into the world. We get our truth and our light line upon line and precept upon precept. We have now had added a new flood of intelligence and light on this particular subject, and it erases all the darkness, and all the views and all the thoughts of the past. They don't matter any more. It doesn't make a particle of difference what anybody ever said about the Negro matter before the first day of June of this year [1978]. It is a new day and a new arrangement, and the Lord has now given the revelation that sheds light out into the world on this subject. As to any slivers of light or particles of darkness of the past, we forget about them. We now do what meridian Israel did when the Lord said the gospel should go to the gentiles. We forget all the statements that limited the gospel to the house of Israel, and we start going to the gentiles.[44]

No less significant than McConkie's reference to the 'limited understanding' of prior prophets of the Church is his suggestion that the 'light and knowledge' of racial equality only came into the world in 1978. Has this light not always been in the world, notwithstanding the inability of many to see it? Did it not, during the tumultuous days of the civil rights movement two decades earlier, cast a penetrating beam upon American society, thus exposing the deep-rooted scourge of racism and finally forcing it into the dark corners of a discredited fringe?

Reasons for opening the priesthood to blacks

It is not immediately clear whether there were any pressures placed on the Church that might have 'encouraged' the 1978 revelation, as was the case with plural marriage. Some have maintained that in light of a growing number of lawsuits by the Internal Revenue Service against various discriminatory institutions (among which Bob Jones University was a primary target), the Church felt that it was in danger of losing its tax-exempt status. A more likely motivation might have been that a new Mormon temple had just been built in Saõ Paolo, Brazil, where a large portion of the population – including major donors – were of African descent. It would have been politically untenable to bar members who bore the 'mark of Cain' from entering the very temple they had helped to build, so the doctrine had to be changed to accommodate this new reality. All of this is conjecture, of course. However, it is clear from the following official description that regardless of any practical considerations, the decision to extend the priesthood to blacks was made neither lightly nor spontaneously:

> The question of extending the blessings of the priesthood to blacks had been on the minds of many of the Brethren over a period of years. It had repeatedly been brought up by Presidents of the Church. It had become a matter of particular concern to President Spencer W. Kimball.
>
> Over a considerable period of time he had prayed concerning this serious and difficult question. He had spent many hours in that upper room in the temple by himself in prayer and meditation. On this occasion he raised the question before his Brethren – his Counselors and the Apostles. Following this discussion we joined in prayer in the most sacred of circumstances. President Kimball himself was voice in that prayer. I do not recall the exact words that he spoke. But I do recall my own feelings and the nature of the expressions of my Brethren. There was a hallowed and sanctified atmosphere in the room. For me, it felt as if a conduit opened between the heavenly throne and the kneeling, pleading prophet of God who was joined by his Brethren. The Spirit of God was there. And by the power of the Holy Ghost there came to that prophet an assurance that the thing for which he prayed was right, that the time had come, and that now the wondrous blessings of the priesthood should be extended to worthy men everywhere regardless of lineage.[45]

Black Mormons' impressions

How did black Mormons feel about the decision to allow 'every faithful, worthy man' into the priesthood? The following reaction of a black member of the church, who incidentally was married to a white woman – 'after careful consideration of the difficulties they might face and after receiving counsel about the challenges of interracial marriage' – serves to illustrate the absolute trust the church leadership enjoys among many of its followers:

> By early June of 1978, Brother Stevenson had graduated from BYU, received a commission as an army officer, and moved with his wife to his post in Anniston, Alabama. On the morning of June 9, a Church leader called to tell him of the revelation making the priesthood available to all worthy male members. Brother Stevenson in turn called his wife home from work to share the news. They cried together and prayed in gratitude. They were sealed in the Salt Lake Temple on 21 April 1979.[46]

However, not all black Mormons were swept up in the same euphoria. It was particularly troubling to some that the First Presidency had made no attempt to comment on the 'Negro doctrine' set forth in its scriptures, let alone to disavow any part of it.[47] Furthermore, with the opening up of the priesthood to blacks in 1978, some vestiges of church-sanctioned discrimination remained. In the most recent (1979) revision of his seminal book *Mormon Doctrine*, Apostle Bruce R. McConkie maintains:

> Cain, Ham and the whole negro race have been cursed with a black skin, the mark of Cain, so they can be identified as a caste apart, a people with whom the other descendants of Adam should not intermarry.[48]

> . . . worthy males of all races can now receive the Melchizedek Priesthood, perform ordinances, and hold positions of presidency and responsibility. It means that members of all races may now be married in the temple, although interracial marriages are discouraged by the Brethren . . .[49]

McConkie may have drawn his conclusions about interracial marriage from the Book of Mormon, in which skin color is portrayed as a 'mark' or curse that is propagated through intercourse:

> And the skins of the Lamanites were dark . . . that their seed might be distinguished from the seed of their brethren, that thereby the Lord God might preserve his people, that they might not mix and believe in incorrect traditions which would prove their destruction . . . And again: I will set a mark upon him that mingleth his seed with thy brethren, that they may be cursed also.[50]

In addition, Church President Spencer W. Kimball, shortly after the 1978 revelation, advised Latter-day Saints not to 'cross racial lines in dating and marrying,' ostensibly as a way to promote greater compatibility in relationships.[51] By comparison, 'Abdu'l-Bahá nearly seventy years earlier declared:

> Praise be to God! As both races are under the protection of the All-Knowing God, therefore the lamps of unity must be lighted in such a manner in these meetings that no distinction be perceived between the white and colored . . . If it be possible, gather together these two races, black and white, into one Assembly, and put such love into their hearts that they shall not only unite but even intermarry. Be sure that the result of this will abolish differences and disputes between black and white.[52]

'Abdu'l-Bahá underscored this point by blessing the marriage of Louis Gregory to Louise Mathew in 1912.

In the United States today, despite advertising campaigns depicting ethnically diverse people, the LDS Church has so far been woefully unsuccessful in attracting African American members into its rank and file, not to mention its leadership. Although a number of black Americans have converted to the Mormon faith since 1978, many of them report that they did not know about the priesthood restriction at the time they joined. Embry's oral histories reveal that while most black Mormons she interviewed are glad they joined the Church, several expressed doubt that they would have made the same decision had they been aware of the former policy.[53]

Armand L. Mauss, a Mormon sociology professor and an expert on race issues within the LDS Church, believes that 'the residue of racialist teaching still found in LDS literature, whether glorifying some lineages or denigrating others, can only get in the way of bringing the world unto Christ.' He further suggests that the Church's discriminatory policy had a 'strictly human origin. An open admission of this realization may be the best way to start dealing with the black issue in Mormon history. There is no reason for even the most orthodox Mormon to be threatened by the realization that the prophets do not do everything by revelation and never have.'[54]

A spiritual shockwave

There is no denying that the Church of Jesus Christ of Latter-day Saints, like so many other Christian churches, has a racist past. Most of these churches either supported or tolerated slavery throughout the 19th century, and segregation through the first half of the 20th century, but the LDS Church turned out to be the 'Johnny-come-lately' of full integration. In recent years, however, it has strongly affirmed the oneness of humanity, and now condemns all forms of discrimination based on race or cultural background. The Mormon community as a whole has also become increasingly diverse, although the membership is still overwhelmingly white. The official LDS web site proclaims:

> The Church views all humankind as children of the same Heavenly Father, literally brothers and sisters. As stated by the Quorum of the Twelve Apostles in 1987: 'We repudiate efforts to deny to any person his or her inalienable dignity and rights on the abhorrent and tragic theory of the superiority of one race or color over another.'[55]

Such a significant change may have been compelled by outside pressures rather than from within. Like other churches, the Church of Jesus Christ of Latter-day Saints has been forced to move with the winds of time and adapt its doctrine, or be left behind. The Bahá'í Faith, on the other hand, has race and gender equality as the cornerstone of its Sacred Writings, and has upheld these principles in direct opposition to the prevailing thought of the time. Bahá'ís believe that the revelations of the Báb and Bahá'u'lláh have sent a spiritual shockwave throughout the entire planet, causing a radical but subconscious change in people's attitudes. This in turn has resulted in the gradual alignment of other religions with its principles.

In the words attributed to German philosopher Arthur Schopenhauer, 'All truth passes through three stages. First, it is ridiculed. Second, it is violently opposed. Third, it is accepted as being self-evident.'

Current Mormon attitudes about race

Today's LDS Church is not the same church it was as recently as twenty or thirty years ago. As concerns the issue of racism in our everyday encounters with Mormons, we must draw a clear line between the Church of the *past* and of the *present* on one hand, and between *church leadership* and the *individual believer* on the other. When church policy was discriminatory, there were always members who did not agree. Now that church policy is inclusive, there are a few members who still cling to the old way of thinking.

We cannot expect such a sudden change of direction by the Church's leadership to result in the immediate rooting out of all prejudice among its individual members. I was present at a church meeting during which a member of the high priesthood made a few inappropriate remarks concerning an African American neighbor. Perhaps more disturbing than the remarks themselves – which were ironically part of a well-intentioned, if botched, message of inclusion – were the scattered chuckles that ensued in the room. However, such insensitivities about race, inappropriate as they were especially in a religious setting, are probably less a product of Mormon doctrine than of the persistent stereotypes that continue to plague our society in general.

Yet there is good news, too. At a more recent meeting of the same group, the topic for discussion was the Church's 'doctrine of inclusion,' formally published in 2001. The consultation was open and frank, and yielded a number of opinions from individuals expressing a sincere desire to confront and reverse the culture of exclusionism to the extent it is still manifest in the Mormon community. One way to do this, it was suggested, is for Mormons to get out of their 'comfort zone' and seek out true friendships with people of other races and religions, without any expectations of converting them. Similar suggestions have been made by the church leadership itself. A June 2002 *Ensign* article titled 'Sharing the Gospel with Sensitivity' offers the following advice:

> Our motivation . . . should be a deep love for our friends and neighbors, indeed for every son and daughter of God. Our acquaintances must know that our friendship is not contingent upon their joining the Church. When they feel that we truly care about them, they will begin to recognize that what we are offering them is based upon our love for them, not just a desire to increase the membership of the Church.[56]

The LDS Church has made significant strides in distancing itself from its discriminatory past. On February 26, 2001, National Public Radio aired a news story about the now-defunct Freedman's Bank, which was established in 1865 by the United States government for former slaves and other black Americans. Bank records, long collecting dust in the National Archives, contained the names of nearly half a million people spanning four generations. Bringing to bear its vast genealogical expertise and resources, the Church of Jesus Christ of Latter-day Saints produced a CD-ROM disc of these names, thus making it possible for millions of black Americans to trace their family histories. The Church has received praise from the African American community for this work. It was also significant that this CD was released during Black History Month, and several members of the African American community who were interviewed expressed hope that this act would inspire other predominantly white institutions to honor black people as well.

Conclusion

Today's Latter-day Saints should not be held accountable for their church's past racial discrimination, and confronting them with it will only serve to alienate them needlessly and place them on the defensive. Conversely, if in private conversation with a Mormon we hear a racially insensitive remark, we can – according to the dictates of wisdom – help him to see the error of it, and not immediately blame it on his religion. While it may be difficult to imagine that people of African descent have only enjoyed equal opportunity within the LDS Church for just over three decades, today's average Latter-day Saint has the same attitude toward race as any other American, and most demonstrate a true appreciation of diversity and a commitment to race unity. The few Mormons who continue to harbor feelings of superiority, fear or suspicion toward other races are perhaps victims of their upbringing and their relative isolation in predominantly white communities. Without evoking hostility on the part of such souls, Bahá'ís could help them to see the beauty of the rose garden of humanity.

A powerful change appears to be taking shape within the LDS Church itself. For years it resisted the pressures of integration placed upon it from the outside. Now, the best teachers of Mormons are other Mormons, as committed individuals take it upon themselves to excise any remnants of prejudice from among their own ranks. As we associate with Latter-day Saints on a regular basis, we will meet these fellow soldiers in our fight against racism, and be able to form strong bonds with them.

APPENDIX 3

MORMONS AND RELIGIOUS TOLERANCE

Mormons are sometimes accused of isolating themselves within their religion and passing judgment on those not of their faith, especially if they do not follow the same strict behavioral guidelines as Mormons do – such as not drinking coffee and refraining from recreational activities on Sundays. Stories abound of LDS mothers quizzing their children's neighborhood playmates about what 'ward' they belong to; an incorrect answer (or mere puzzlement at the question) would then cause the mother to discourage further association between that boy or girl and her own children.

Latter-day Saints do in fact consider theirs to be the only true religion of Jesus Christ. The reference work *Mormon Doctrine* states:

> With the exception of the restored gospel, every system of religion in the world today is born of religious syncretism.[1]

> True religion, the religion of Jesus Christ, was instituted of God for the benefit of man, and it is found only in the Church of Jesus Christ of Latter-day Saints.[2]

However, notwithstanding the exclusiveness of these statements, they do not necessarily point to an intolerance of other religions or their adherents.

Joseph Smith preached religious tolerance

Joseph Smith, from what we can ascertain of his life and writings, was intensely curious about religion in all its manifestations, and quite open-minded. He actively participated in a number of other religious movements – Freemasonry in particular – both prior to and after establishing his own church, and apparently retained his respect for people of other faiths and cultures in the later years of his life. In March 1839, while imprisoned in Clay County, Missouri's Liberty Jail – a contradiction in terms if ever there was one – Smith wrote to

371

the members of his church:

> . . . we ought always to be aware of those prejudices which sometimes
> so strangely present themselves, and are so congenial to human nature,
> against our friends, neighbors, and brethren of the world, who choose to
> differ from us in opinion and in matters of faith. Our religion is between
> us and our God. Their religion is between them and their God.
>
> There is a love from God that should be exercised toward those of
> our faith, who walk uprightly, which is peculiar to itself, but it is without
> prejudice; it also gives scope to the mind, which enables us to conduct our-
> selves with greater liberality towards all that are not of our faith, than what
> they exercise towards one another. These principles approximate nearer to
> the mind of God, because it is like God, or Godlike.[3]

In an 1842 editorial for the *Times and Seasons* church monthly, Smith pointed
out the futility and transience of religious divisions:

> The Mussulman condemns the heathen, the Jew, and the Christian, and
> the whole world of mankind that reject his Koran, as infidels, and consigns
> the whole of them to perdition. The Jew believes that the whole world
> that rejects his faith and are not circumcised, are Gentile dogs, and will
> be damned. The heathen is equally as tenacious about his principles, and
> the Christian consigns all to perdition who cannot bow to his creed, and
> submit to his *ipse dixit*.
>
> But while one portion of the human race is judging and condemning the
> other without mercy, the Great Parent of the universe looks upon the whole
> of the human family with a fatherly care and paternal regard; He views them
> as His offspring, and without any of those contracted feelings that influence
> the children of men, causes 'His sun to rise on the evil and on the good, and
> sendeth rain on the just and on the unjust.' He holds the reins of judgment
> in His hands; He is a wise Lawgiver, and will judge all men, not according to
> the narrow, contracted notions of men, but 'according to the deeds done in
> the body whether they be good or evil,' or whether these deeds were done in
> England, America, Spain, Turkey, or India. He will judge them, 'not accord-
> ing to what they have not, but according to what they have,' those who have
> lived without law, will be judged without law, and those who have a law, will
> be judged by that law. We need not doubt the wisdom and intelligence of
> the great Jehovah; He will award judgment or mercy to all nations accord-
> ing to their several deserts, their means of obtaining intelligence, the laws
> by which they are governed, the facilities afforded them of obtaining correct

information, and His inscrutable designs in relation to the human family; and when the designs of God shall be made manifest, the curtain of futurity be withdrawn, we shall all of us eventually have to confess that the Judge of all the earth has done right.[4]

And in a letter dated February 13, 1844 he expressed the following sentiment:

. . . I never feel to force my doctrine upon any person; I rejoice to see prejudice give way to truth, and the traditions of men dispersed by the pure principles of the Gospel of Jesus Christ.[5]

This commitment to religious tolerance was by no means limited to words. On March 1, 1841, the City of Nauvoo, Illinois – whose theocratic government was wholly under the control of the LDS Church and its prophet, Joseph Smith – passed this 'Ordinance on Religious Liberty in Nauvoo':[6]

Be it ordained by the City Council of the City of Nauvoo, that the Catholics, Presbyterians, Methodists, Baptists, Latter-day Saints, Quakers, Episcopals, Universalists, Unitarians, Mohammedans, and all other religious sects and denominations whatever, shall have free toleration, and equal privileges, in this city; and should any person be guilty of ridiculing, and abusing or otherwise depreciating another in consequence of his religion, or of disturbing or interrupting any religious meeting within the limits of this city, he shall, on conviction thereof before the Mayor or Municipal Court, be considered a disturber of the public peace, and fined in any sum not exceeding five hundred dollars, or imprisoned not exceeding six months, or both, at the discretion of said Mayor or Court.[7]

Religious tolerance is also prescribed in the LDS scriptures themselves, and has even been adopted into the Articles of Faith:

Contend against no church, save it be the church of the devil.[8]

We claim the privilege of worshiping Almighty God according to the dictates of our own conscience, and allow all men the same privilege, let them worship how, where or what they may.[9]

Mormon scriptures suggest the validity of other religions

The Book of Mormon affirms that God has revealed Himself in different ways, in different parts of the world:

> Wherefore, I speak the same words unto one nation like unto another . . . For I command all men, both in the east and in the west, and in the north, and in the south, and in the islands of the sea, that they shall write the words which I speak unto them; for out of the books which shall be written I will judge the world, every man according to their works, according to that which is written.[10]

> For behold, the Lord doth grant unto all nations, of their own nation and tongue, to teach his word, yea, in wisdom, all that he seeth fit that they should have; therefore we see that the Lord doth counsel in wisdom, according to that which is just and true.[11]

Opening with the above quotation from Alma, an article in the LDS periodical *Ensign* on the subject of Zoroastrianism postulates:

> It appears that the Lord may have granted unto the ancient nation of Iran a portion of his word that he saw fit that they should have. The man to whom and through whom the word seems to have come to the people of Iran is commonly called in English *Zoroaster* . . . Anyone who knows the religion and philosophy of life of Judaism or of Christianity recognizes numerous similarities between them and the Zoroastrian religion; and anyone who knows the restored gospel of Jesus Christ sees even more concepts in common. Doubtless some of the similarities between the historic religious systems may be attributed to borrowings; on the other hand, is it not possible that there may be some ideas and concepts that are similar because they both have come from the revelations of God? . . . Through the perspective of the gospel, it is possible to see why revelations may have been sent to such men as Zoroaster and why some of his teachings would resemble those of our prophets. In fact, it may have been the Magi of Zoroastrianism who perceived by some manner of revelation from the heavens that a miracle child was born in Judea to be a king and who came to worship him.[12]

Similar acknowledgments have been made in articles about Islám and Buddhism.

History of persecution

Mormons are sensitive to the issue of religious tolerance in part because for most of their collective history they have been subjected to religious persecution themselves. Even today, Mormon missionaries are often the targets of derision, and in extreme cases, violence.

In earlier times, one way for Mormons to deal with their own persecution was to isolate themselves from the outside world. Nauvoo, Illinois had in the days of Joseph Smith become a Mormon epicenter, with its own theocratic government and a militia that rivaled the United States Army in size. Years later, Salt Lake City, Utah was established as a new Mormon homeland, again with a theocratic government and a completely self-sustaining economy. Salt Lake's strong isolationist attitude eventually gave way to economic interests when the transcontinental railroad cut a path directly through it.

Such prolonged insularity, combined with a history of persecution by other religious sects, may ironically have caused Mormons themselves to become somewhat ignorant and intolerant of other belief systems. Fortunately, this trend has seen a dramatic reversal in recent decades as Mormons have increasingly come in contact with the followers of a host of other religions.

Tolerance and diversity improving

The LDS Church and its membership are becoming increasingly accepting of other religions, as is reflected in the following statement by former Church President Gordon B. Hinckley:

> We recognize the good in all people. We recognize the good in all churches, in their efforts to improve mankind and to teach principles that lead to good, stable, productive living. To people everywhere we simply say, 'You bring with you all the good that you have, and let us add to it. That is the principle on which we work.'[13]

Indeed, in the wake of the September 11 tragedy Mormons were quick to come to the defense of Muslims and others (such as Sikhs) who, due to their appearance, had been the target of hate crimes.

There is further evidence of a sincere effort on the part of the LDS Church to inculcate in its membership a spirit of inclusion. In a November 2001 *Ensign* magazine article titled 'Doctrine of Inclusion', Elder M. Russell Ballard – a member of the Quorum of the Twelve Apostles and thus a general authority of the Church – remarked:

Perceptions and assumptions can be very dangerous and unfair. There are some of our members who may fail to reach out with friendly smiles, warm handshakes, and loving service to all of their neighbors. At the same time, there may be those who move into our neighborhoods who are not of our faith who come with negative preconceptions about the Church and its members. Surely good neighbors should put forth every effort to understand each other and to be kind to one another regardless of religion, nationality, race, or culture . . .

We must understand . . . that not everyone is going to accept our doctrine of the Restoration of the gospel of Jesus Christ. For the most part, our neighbors not of our faith are good, honorable people – every bit as good and honorable as we strive to be. They care about their families, just like we do. They want to make the world a better place, just like we do. They are kind and loving and generous and faithful, just like we seek to be.[14]

Referring to 'narrow-minded' LDS parents who don't allow their children to play with non-member children in the neighborhood, Elder Ballard added:

This kind of behavior is not in keeping with the teachings of the Lord Jesus Christ. I cannot comprehend why any member of our Church would allow these kinds of things to happen.[15]

Locally, Mormons have been quite active in the field of interfaith cooperation. The late Darl Andersen, a long-time Mormon bishop in the Phoenix area, was well known and respected as an interfaith activist, and knew many Bahá'ís in the region. One of Bishop Anderson's lasting legacies was his commitment to building religious tolerance through a 'Golden Rule' publicity campaign, in which the Bahá'í Writings were featured prominently. And whereas the Utah-based church leadership itself has traditionally remained aloof from such associations, this appears now to be changing. Elder Ballard reports:

Here in Utah, a group of concerned citizens formed the Alliance for Unity. This effort has been endorsed by our Church as well as other churches and organizations. One of its purposes is 'to seek to build a community where differing viewpoints are acknowledged and valued.' Perhaps there has never been a more important time for neighbors all around the world to stand together for the common good of one another.[16]

An effective way for the Church to promote its 'doctrine of inclusion' is to acquaint the faithful with the principles and practices of other religions, and to point out similarities to their own faith where they exist. In recent years, *Ensign* magazine has featured a number of articles about other religions, including a lengthy story on Islam, its history, traditions and basic beliefs, as well as a brief history of the life of the Prophet Muhammad. Adorned with beautiful photographs of Muslim holy sites, the article emphasized the commonalities between the Mormon and Muslim faiths, extolled the many virtues – particularly piety, charity and hospitality – of the followers of Muhammad, and called for increased understanding of and dialogue with Muslims. Its author shared the following convictions:

> I was grateful to state that we belong to a church that affirms the truths taught by Muhammad and other great teachers, reformers, and religious founders. We recognize the goodness reflected in the lives of those in other religious communities. While we do not compromise revealed eternal truths of the restored gospel, we never espouse an adversarial relationship with other faiths. Rather, in accordance with modern prophetic counsel, we seek to treasure up that which is virtuous and praiseworthy in other faiths and to cultivate an attitude of 'affirmative gratitude' toward them. As Latter-day Saints, we believe that it is vital to respect and benefit from the spiritual light found in other religions, while seeking humbly to share the additional measure of eternal truth provided by latter-day revelation.[17]

Modifying our vocabulary

In the previously referred to article on inclusion, M. Russell Ballard offered a suggestion that is of particular significance to Mormons and Bahá'ís alike:

> I believe it would be good if we eliminated a couple of phrases from our vocabulary: 'nonmember' and 'non-Mormon.' Such phrases can be demeaning and even belittling. Personally, I don't consider myself to be a 'non-Catholic' or a 'non-Jew.' I am a Christian. I am a member of The Church of Jesus Christ of Latter-day Saints. That is how I prefer to be identified – for who and what I am, as opposed to being identified for what I am not. Let us extend that same courtesy to those who live among us. If a collective description is needed, then 'neighbors' seems to work well in most cases.[18]

Like the LDS community, the Bahá'í community is also undergoing a change of culture of sorts in terms of its orientation toward the population at large.

Certainly the term *non-Bahá'í* is used throughout the literature of the Bahá'í Faith as a necessary means of distinguishing between individuals who have accepted the message and station of Bahá'u'lláh and those who have not. It is also quite proper to identify someone who has not declared himself a Bahá'í in the context of teaching activities – such as the percentage of non-Bahá'í participants in children's classes – much as it is for a person's ethnicity to be mentioned in a discussion about diversity. However, there is a danger of a person's 'non-Bahá'í-ness' becoming the predominant characteristic in the mind of the Bahá'í, which may create an invisible yet perceptible barrier to true fellowship. The first defense against such an attitude is to remember that, whether Bahá'í or non-Bahá'í, 'each person who is drawn to explore Bahá'u'lláh's teachings will need to find his own place in the never-ending continuum of spiritual search.'[19] The next step is to reach out to people of other faiths, invite them to join in our activities, and learn from them as they learn from us.

In the Bahá'í community, the enthusiastic adoption of such an 'outward-looking orientation' has resulted in a sizable group of people who are actively and passionately engaged in the Bahá'í core activities, but who have yet to officially declare their belief in Bahá'u'lláh. Many members of this 'community of interest' become Bahá'ís at some stage during their participation in these activities. In its December 2005 letter outlining the second Five Year Plan, the Universal House of Justice observed that

> desire and willingness to open certain aspects of community life to the wider public should be integrated into a pattern of behaviour that attracts souls and confirms them. Much has been achieved in this respect as the friends have adopted new ways of thinking and acting at a collective level. In welcoming large numbers into its embrace, the community is learning to see more readily the latent potentiality in people and to avoid setting artificial barriers for them based on preconceived notions. A nurturing environment is being cultivated in which each individual is encouraged to progress at his or her own pace without the pressure of unreasonable expectations. At the heart of such developments is a growing awareness of the implications of the universality and comprehensiveness of the Faith. Collective action is governed more and more by the principle that Bahá'u'lláh's message should be given liberally and unconditionally to humanity.[20]

In this light, Elder Ballard's exhortation, although directed at the Mormon faithful, could certainly be taken to apply to Bahá'ís as well.

Personal experiences

My personal experiences with Latter-day Saints have consistently been characterized by warmth, engagement and acceptance. While all know me to be a 'non-member' – and most know me to be a Bahá'í – I have never once been made to feel excluded on one hand, or pressured to join the Church on the other. After having attended Sunday school and priesthood meetings regularly for a number of years, I still feel warmly welcomed, and have always been able to freely express my thoughts in group discussions. These thoughts, when inspired by the Bahá'í Writings, often evoke very positive reactions from my fellow churchgoers. With a select few I am even able to discuss the Bahá'í Faith openly. In one instance, a church member who had some knowledge of the Bahá'í Faith confided in me that in his view, 'Mormons can learn a lot from the Bahá'ís.'

Several genuine friendships have developed out of my participation in these meetings. As a result of these friendships, I've come to see that a number of Latter-day Saints clearly recognize the oneness of the human family, and demonstrate a sincere interest in learning about other religions as a way to enrich their own spirituality. A few of them even lament, openly or privately, that some of their coreligionists still see the earnest study of other faiths as potentially dangerous, or are unwilling to acknowledge the truths that are enshrined in the teachings of every religion.

Conclusion

Taken as a whole, the Mormon attitude toward other religions is somewhat bifurcated. On one hand, the Church of Jesus Christ of Latter-day Saints claims to be the only valid religion on earth, with all other religions being based on 'syncretism,' or a fusion of different belief systems. On the other, it publicly recognizes the good that other religions have to offer and acknowledges that the founders of those religions may have received 'a portion' of God's Word.

In practice, when Mormons are approached in a spirit of acceptance, they will respond in kind.

APPENDIX 4

STORIES INVOLVING MORMONS AND THE BAHÁ'Í FAITH

At least two popular stories have circulated among a small number of Bahá'ís for many years, and these occasionally come up in Bahá'í conversations about Mormons. The origin of these stories is unknown, and no written record, official or unofficial, has ever been produced to substantiate them.

The temple incident

It is sometimes related that during their stay in Salt Lake City, Utah, 'Abdu'l-Bahá and His companions attempted to visit the Mormon temple, but were denied entrance. According to most versions of the story, 'Abdu'l-Bahá is then reported to have said something along the lines of 'This temple was built for My Father, did ye but know,' or 'They have built Me a temple but they won't let Me in.'

In a *World Order* magazine article referring to this alleged visit, William P. Collins concludes:

> There appears . . . to be no evidence to substantiate such an attempted visit, either in notes left by early believers in Salt Lake or in records of 'Abdu'l-Bahá's travels such as Mírzá Mahmúd's diary.[1]

However, an account of this event was given in a 1965 interview with Sachiro Fujita, an early believer who accompanied 'Abdu'l-Bahá on His visit to Salt Lake City.[2] Mr Fujita mentions that the company was in fact denied entrance to a Mormon church building (as opposed to the temple). Access to temples has always been restricted to church members in good standing, but Mormon churches are generally open to the public, at least during Sunday worship services. Given that 'Abdu'l-Bahá was accompanied by a considerable entourage, it is likely that church custodians were unprepared for such an official visit and, fearing a spectacle, turned Him away. If any conversation did occur between

'Abdu'l-Bahá and the Mormon church officials, it has not been recorded.

The mass conversion

According to another story, Shoghi Effendi is reported to have once made a statement in the presence of a group of Bahá'ís suggesting that the LDS Church would be one of the first Christian churches to convert *en masse* to the Bahá'í Faith.

If true, this would certainly be a startling claim. Presumably such a mass conversion would have to be precipitated by an official declaration from the president of the LDS Church, an unlikely proposition at best considering it would involve the public admission that every church president dating back to Brigham Young had been incorrect about the time and circumstances of the Return of Christ. Even then, it is difficult to imagine the entire body of Mormon believers simply acquiescing to such a spectacular disclosure, which would very likely spell the end of the LDS organization as it is known today. The thousands of Mormons who rebelled against the Church when it discontinued the practice of plural marriage are ample evidence that a sudden change of direction is not always accepted by the rank-and-file faithful.

Finally, the entire concept of mass conversion by fiat appears wholly at odds with the Bahá'í principle of independent investigation of truth. This is not to say that a mass conversion of the generality of mankind will never come about, or that it must necessarily be a protracted affair; on the contrary, we are promised that some day the entire planet will come to an acceptance of the Bahá'í Revelation. However, it would seem that regardless of the pace of such worldwide acceptance, it will remain essentially an organic process that comes down to individuals making their own independent determination about the truth of the Cause of Bahá'u'lláh. This would more likely result in a gradual draining away of people from their former religious organizations, as opposed to a church-by-church conversion to the Faith.

It is unknown where this story originated. However, as William P. Collins notes, 'There is no evidence to support it, nor does it seem from the Bahá'í texts that such a mass conversion of Mormons is envisioned or expected.'[3]

Attach no importance to stories

Notwithstanding the many connections shared between Mormons and Bahá'ís, we must exercise care not to put too much stock in this kind of hearsay. Strictly speaking, this includes pilgrims' notes, but it specifically refers to other, completely undocumented statements and actions attributed to Shoghi

Effendi and 'Abdu'l-Bahá. While these kinds of stories may be interesting to Bahá'ís, they serve no useful purpose in our dealings with our Mormon friends. What's more, they could be harmful to our efforts if allowed to masquerade as fact. The following warning was issued on behalf of Shoghi Effendi:

> He would also urge you to attach no importance to the stories told about 'Abdu'l-Bahá or to those attributed to Him by the friends. These should be regarded in the same light as the notes and impressions of visiting pilgrims. They need not be suppressed, but they should not also be given prominent or official recognition.[4]

BIBLIOGRAPHY

'Abdu'l-Bahá. *'Abdu'l-Bahá in London*. London: Bahá'í Publishing Trust, 1982.

— *Abdul Bahá on Divine Philosophy*. Comp. Isabel Fraser Chamberlain. Boston: The Tudor Press, 1916.

— *Foundations of World Unity*. Wilmette, Ill: Bahá'í Publishing Trust, 1945.

— *Memorials of the Faithful*. Trans. Marzieh Gail. Wilmette, Ill: Bahá'í Publishing Trust, 1971.

— *Paris Talks: Addresses given by 'Abdu'l-Bahá in 1911*. London: Bahá'í Publishing Trust, 12th ed. 1995.

— *The Promulgation of Universal Peace: Talks Delivered by 'Abdu'l-Bahá during His Visit to the United States and Canada in 1912*. Comp. Howard MacNutt. Wilmette, Ill.: Bahá'í Publishing Trust, 2nd ed. 1982.

— *The Secret of Divine Civilization*. Trans. Marzieh Gail. Wilmette, Ill: Bahá'í Publishing Trust, 1971.

— *Selections from the Writings of 'Abdu'l-Bahá*. Haifa: Bahá'í World Centre, 1978.

— *Some Answered Questions*. Wilmette, Ill: Bahá'í Publishing Trust, 2nd ed. 1994.

— *Tablets of Abdul-Baha Abbas*. 3 vols. New York: Bahai Publishing Society, 1909-1919.

— *Tablets of the Divine Plan*. Wilmette, Ill.: Bahá'í Publishing Trust, 1st pocket-size ed. 1993.

— *Will and Testament of 'Abdu'l-Bahá*. Wilmette, Ill: National Spiritual Assembly of the Bahá'ís of the United States and Canada, 1944.

Allen, James B.; Leonard, Glen M. *The Story of the Latter-day Saints*. 2nd rev.ed. Salt Lake City: Deseret Book Company, 1992.

Anderson, Richard L. 'Joseph Smith's Testimony of the First Vision', in *Ensign* (Apr. 1996), p. 10. Text available at http://www.lds.org, Gospel Library, Magazines, Ensign.

Anderson, Robert D. *Inside the Mind of Joseph Smith: Psychobiography and The Book of Mormon*. Salt Lake City: Signature Books, 1999.

Andrus, Hyrum L. *Doctrinal Commentary on the Pearl of Great Price*. Salt Lake City: Deseret Book Co., 1998. Digital copy available in *LDS Collector's Library 2005*, in author's possession.

Asay, Carlos E. 'Opposition to the Work of God', in *Ensign* (Nov. 1981), p. 67. Text available at http://www.lds.org, Gospel Library, Magazines, Ensign.

The Báb. *Selections from the Writings of the Báb*, Wilmette, Ill.: Bahá'í Publishing Trust, 1st pocket-size ed. 2006.

Bahá'í Canada. Magazine. Thornhill, Ont: National Spiritual Assembly of the Bahá'ís of Canada.

Bahá'í Education: A Compilation. Extracts from the Writings of Bahá'u'lláh, 'Abdu'l-Bahá, and Shoghi Effendi. Comp. Research Department of the Universal House of Justice. Wilmette, Ill: Bahá'í Publishing Trust, 1977. Available online at http://bahai-library.com/index.php5?file=compilation_baha_education.

Bahá'í International Community. *Suggestions and Proposals for International Women's Year: Statement to the 25th Session of the UN Commission on the Status of Women.* New York, 14 January–4 February 1974. Text available at http://statements.bahai.org/74-0098.htm.

— *The Right to Development: Exploring Its Social and Cultural Dimensions.* Submitted to the workgroup on Social and Cultural Dimensions of Development at the 33rd session of the Sub-Commission on the Prevention of Discrimination and Protection of Minorities, Geneva, Switzerland, 26 August 1980. Text available at http://www.bic-un.bahai.org/80-0250.htm.

— *The Family in a World Community.* Pamphlet distributed at the World NGO Forum Launching the United Nations International Year of the Family (IYF), Malta, November 1993. Text available at http://statements.bahai.org/93-1125.htm.

Bahá'í International Teaching Centre. *Reflections on Growth*. Periodical. Haifa: Bahá'í World Centre.

Bahá'í Marriage and Family Life: Selections from the Writings of the Bahá'í Faith. Thornhill, Ont.: Bahá'í Canada Publications, 1983.

Bahá'í Prayers: A Selection of Prayers Revealed by Bahá'u'lláh, The Báb, and 'Abdu'l-Bahá. Wilmette, Ill: Bahá'í Publishing Trust, 2002.

Bahá'í World Faith. Wilmette, Ill: Bahá'í Publishing Trust, 2nd ed. 1976.

Bahá'u'lláh. *Epistle to the Son of the Wolf.* Trans. Shoghi Effendi. Wilmette, Ill: Bahá'í Publishing Trust, 2nd ed. 1953.

— *Gleanings from the Writings of Bahá'u'lláh*. Trans. Shoghi Effendi. Wilmette, Ill.: Bahá'í Publishing Trust, 1976.

— *The Hidden Words of Bahá'u'lláh*. Trans. Shoghi Effendi. Wilmette, Ill: Bahá'í Publishing Trust, 1975.

— *The Kitáb-i-Aqdas: The Most Holy Book.* Haifa, Israel: Bahá'í World Centre, 1978; Wilmette, Ill: Bahá'í Publishing Trust, 1993.

— *The Kitáb-i-Íqán: The Book of Certitude.* Trans. Shoghi Effendi. Wilmette, Ill.: Bahá'í Publishing Trust, 2nd ed. 1994.

— *Lawḥ-i-Ṭibb* or *Tablet of Medicine*. Provisional translation, available online at http://bahai-library.com/index.php5?file=bahaullah_lawh_tibb_anonymous.

— *Prayers and Meditations by Bahá'u'lláh.* Trans. Shoghi Effendi. Wilmette, Ill: Bahá'í Publishing Trust, 1987.

— *The Proclamation of Bahá'u'lláh.* Haifa: Bahá'í World Centre, 1967.

— *The Seven Valleys and the Four Valleys.* Wilmette, Ill: Bahá'í Publishing Trust, 3rd ed. 1976.

— *The Summons of the Lord of Hosts.* Haifa: Bahá'í World Centre, 2002.

— *Tablets of Bahá'u'lláh Revealed After the Kitáb-i-Aqdas.* Haifa: Bahá'í World Centre, 1978.

Ballard, M. Russell. 'Doctrine of Inclusion', in *Ensign* (Nov. 2001), p. 35. Text available at http://www.lds.org, Gospel Library, Magazines, Ensign.

Benson, Ezra Taft. 'Prepare for the Days of Tribulation', in *Ensign* (Nov. 1980), p. 32. Text available at http://www.lds.org, Gospel Library, Magazines, Ensign.

Bible: *The Holy Bible.* King James Version. Oxford: Oxford University Press, various dates.

Bible Dictionary. Salt Lake City: The Church of Jesus Christ of Latter-day Saints, 1979.

The Book of Mormon. Salt Lake City: The Church of Jesus Christ of Latter-day Saints, 1981.

Burnett, M. Dallas. 'Lamanites and the Church', in *Ensign* (Jul. 1971), p. 11. Text available at http://www.lds.org, Gospel Library, Magazines, Ensign.

Burton, Theodore M. 'Kingdom of God', in *Ensign* (June 1971), p. 83. Text available at http://www.lds.org, Gospel Library, Magazines, Ensign.

Cannon, Donald Q.; Dahl, Larry E.; Welch, John W. 'The Restoration of Major Doctrines through Joseph Smith: The Godhead, Mankind, and the Creation', in *Ensign* (Jan. 1989), p. 27. Text available at http://www.lds.org, Gospel Library, Magazines, Ensign.

Carlyle, Thomas. *History of Friedrich II of Prussia, Called Frederick the Great.* Project Gutenberg. Text available at http://www.gutenberg.org.

Carmack, John K. 'Unity in Diversity', in *Tambuli* (Aug. 1992), p. 27. Text available at http://www.lds.org, Gospel Library, Magazines, Liahona.

Christiansen, ElRay L. 'Power Over Satan', in *Ensign* (Nov. 1974), p. 22. Text available at http://www.lds.org, Gospel Library, Magazines, Ensign.

— 'The Adversary', in *New Era* (Sept. 1975), p. 4. Text available at http://www.lds.org, Gospel Library, Magazines, New Era.

Clark, James R. (comp). *Messages of the First Presidency of The Church of Jesus Christ of Latter-day Saints.* 6 vols. Salt Lake City: Bookcraft, 1965–75.

Claybaugh, Jonn D. 'As Flaming Fire and a Ministering Angel', in *Ensign* (Oct. 1999), p. 54. Text available at http://www.lds.org, Gospel Library, Magazines, Ensign.

Collins, William P. 'The Bahá'í Faith and Mormonism: A Preliminary Survey', in *World Order*, vol. 15, no. 1/2 (Fall 1980/Winter 1981), pp. 33-45.

— 'The Bahá'í Faith and Mormonism: Further Reflections', in *World Order*, vol. 17, no. 3 (Spring 1983), pp. 25-33.

The Compilation of Compilations: Prepared by the Universal House of Justice 1963–1990. Maryborough: Bahá'í Publications Australia, 1991.

*Conference Report*s. April 4, 1915; April 6-9, 1922; October 3-5, 1926; April 6-9, 1939. Salt Lake City: The Church of Jesus Christ of Latter-day Saints, 1915–1939. Digital copy available in *LDS Collector's Library 2005*, in author's possession:

Conference Report. Sydney Australia Area Conference, 29 Feb. 1976.

Conkling, J. Christopher. *A Joseph Smith Chronology.* Salt Lake City: Deseret Book Co., 1979.

Cowan, Richard O. *The Church in the Twentieth Century.* Salt Lake City: Bookcraft, 1985.

Craig, G. Y. ; Jones, E. J. *A Geological Miscellany.* Princeton: Princeton University Press, 1982.

Developing Distinctive Bahá'í Communities: *Guidelines for Spiritual Assemblies.* Comp. Office of Assembly Development, National Spiritual Assembly of the Bahá'ís of the United States. Wilmette, Ill: Bahá'í Publishing Trust, rev. ed. 1998; 2008 (online edition).

The Doctrine and Covenants. Salt Lake City: The Church of Jesus Christ of Latter-day Saints, 1981.

Doctrine and Covenants and Church History Gospel Doctrine Teacher's Manual. Text available at http://www.lds.org, Gospel Library, Lessons, Sunday School.

Dunn, Paul H. '"Oh Beautiful for Patriot Dream"', in *Ensign* (Nov. 1975), p. 53. Text available at http://www.lds.org, Gospel Library, Magazines, Ensign.

'Editor's Table: Modern Revelation', in *Improvement Era*, vol. V (Aug. 1902), no. 10, pp. 805-7. Salt Lake City: The Church of Jesus Christ of Latter-day Saints, 1902. Digital copy available in *LDS Collector's Library 2005*, in author's possession.

Ehrman, Bart D. 'After the New Testament: The Writings of the Apostolic Fathers', *The Teaching Company Course No. 6537* (transcript). Chantilly, Virginia: The Teaching Company, 2005.

Embry, Jessie L. *Black Saints in a White Church: Contemporary African American Mormons.* Salt Lake City: Signature Books, 1994.

Encyclopedia of Latter-Day Saint History. Ed. Arnold K. Garr, Donald Q. Cannon, Richard O. Cowan. Salt Lake City: Deseret Book Co., 2000.

Eshrakhavari, 'Abdu'l-Hamid. *Páyam-i-Bahá'í*, vol. 272 (July 2000), p. 15.

Esslemont, J. E. *Bahá'u'lláh and the New Era.* Wilmette, Ill.: Bahá'í Publishing Trust, 5th ed.1998.

The First Presidency and Council of the Twelve Apostles of The Church of Jesus Christ of Latter-day Saints. 'The Family: A Proclamation to the World', in *Ensign* (Nov. 1995), p. 102. Text available at http://www.lds.org, Gospel Library, Magazines, Ensign.

'First Public Mentions of the Bahá'í Faith', UK Bahá'í Heritage Site, http://users. whsmithnet.co.uk/ispalin/heritage/firsts.htm; also at http://bahai-library.com/ essays/faith.in.west.html.

Frequently Asked Questions. Community of Christ (formerly the Reorganized Church of Jesus Christ of Latter Day Saints). Text available at http://www.cofchrist.org/ ourfaith/faq.asp.

Furútan, 'Alí-Akbar (comp.). *Stories of Bahá'u'lláh*. Oxford: George Ronald, 1997.

Gospel Principles. Salt Lake City: The Church of Jesus Christ of Latter-day Saints, 1997.

Greenwood, Val D. 'I Have a Question', in *Ensign* (Sept. 1987), p. 27. Text available at http://www.lds.org, Gospel Library, Magazines, Ensign.

Guide to the Scriptures: Joseph Smith Translation. Available online at http://scriptures. lds.org/en/gs/j/38.

Haight, David B. 'Remembering the Savior's Atonement', in *Ensign* (Apr. 1988), p. 7. Text available at http://www.lds.org, Gospel Library, Magazines, Ensign.

Hartley, William G.; Sessions, Gene A. *Church History c. 1878-1898, Late Pioneer Utah Period*. Available online at http://www.lightplanet.com/mormons/daily/ history/1878_1898/eom.htm.

Hinckley, Gordon B. 'Messages of Inspiration from President Hinckley', in *LDS Church News* (Nov. 2, 1996).

— 'Priesthood Restoration', in *Ensign* (Oct. 1988), p. 69. Text available at http:// www.lds.org, Gospel Library, Magazines, Ensign.

— *Teachings of Gordon B. Hinckley*. Salt Lake City: Deseret Book Co., 1997. Digital copy available in *LDS Collector's Library 2005*, in author's possession.

— 'What Are People Asking about Us?', in *Ensign* (Nov. 1998), p. 70. Text available at http://www.lds.org, Gospel Library, Magazines, Ensign.

— 'Words of the Living Prophet', in *Liahona* (Jun. 1997), p. 32. Text available at http://www.lds.org, Gospel Library, Magazines, Liahona.

Holland, Jeffrey R. 'A Promised Land', in *Ensign* (Jun. 1976), p. 23. Text available at http://www.lds.org, Gospel Library, Magazines, Ensign.

Honnold, Annamarie (ed.). *Vignettes from the Life of 'Abdu'l-Bahá*. Oxford: George Ronald, rev. ed. 1997.

Hunter, Howard W. 'Of the World or of the Kingdom?', in *Ensign* (Jan. 1974), p. 53. Text available at http://www.lds.org, Gospel Library, Magazines, Ensign.

Huqúqu'lláh: The Right of God. Comp. Research Department of the Universal House of Justice, with Dr. Allan Waters. Sydney: Bahá'í Publications Australia, 2000; Wilmette, Ill: Bahá'í Publishing Trust, new ed. 2007.

'I Have a Question', in *Ensign* (Apr. 1984), p. 21. Text available at http://www.lds.org, Gospel Library, Magazines, Ensign.

Ioas, Sylvia. *Interview of Sachiro Fujita by Sylvia Ioas, Mount Carmel, November 24th, 1965.* Available at http://bahai-library.com/pilgrims/fujita.html.

Jackson, Lisa Ann. 'News of the Church', in *Ensign* (Sept. 2003), p. 78. Text available at http://www.lds.org, Gospel Library, Magazines, Ensign.

'John Taylor: A Letter from Exile', in *Tambuli* (Nov. 1978), p. 31. Text available at http://www.lds.org, Gospel Library, Magazines, Liahona.

Journal of Discourses. L. Tom Perry Special Collections, Harold B. Lee Library, Brigham Young University. Digital facsimile available at http://contentdm.lib.byu.edu/u?/JournalOfDiscourses3. vol. 2. Liverpool: F.D. Richards, 1855; vol. 10. Liverpool: Daniel H. Wells, 1865; vol. 16. Liverpool: Joseph F. Smith, 1874; vol. 20. Liverpool: William Budge, 1880; vol. 21. Liverpool: Albert Carrington, 1881.

Kimball, Spencer W. 'Privileges and Responsibilities of Sisters', in *Ensign* (Nov. 1978), p. 101. Text available at http://www.lds.org, Gospel Library, Magazines, Ensign.

Kimball, Stanley B. 'The Mormon Battalion March, 1846–47', in *Ensign* (July 1979), p. 57. Text available at http://www.lds.org, Gospel Library, Magazines, Ensign.

The Latter-day Saint Woman: Basic Manual for Women. Salt Lake City: The Church of Jesus Christ of Latter-day Saints, 2000. Text available at http://www.lds.org, Gospel Library, Lessons, Relief Society.

Lee, F. David. 'Questions and Answers', in *Tambuli* (June 1984), p. 15. Text available at http://www.lds.org, Gospel Library, Magazines, Liahona.

Lee, Felicia R. '"Big Love": Real Polygamists Look at HBO Polygamists and Find Sex', in *New York Times* (Mar. 28, 2006) (http://www.nytimes.com/2006/03/28/arts/television/28poly.html).

Lee, Harold B. 'First Presidency message', in *Ensign* (Dec. 1972), p. 2. Text available at http://www.lds.org, Gospel Library, Magazines, Ensign.

Lights of Guidance: A Bahá'í Reference File. Comp. Helen H. Hornby. New Delhi: Bahá'í Publishing Trust, 3rd ed. 1994. Available online at http://bahai-library.com/index.php5?file=hornby_lights_guidance.

Lynn, Karen. 'Q&A: Questions and Answers', in *New Era* (Sept. 1975), p. 14. Text available at http://www.lds.org, Gospel Library, Magazines, New Era.

Marquardt, H. Michael. 'The Book of Abraham Revisited', 1997. Available at http://www.xmission.com/~research/about/abraham.htm.

— *The Joseph Smith Revelations: Text and Commentary.* Salt Lake City: Signature Books, 1999.

'Some Interesting Notes on Succession at Nauvoo in 1844'. Available at http://www.xmission.com/~research/about/successi.htm.

Matthews, Robert J. 'The Fulness of Times', in *Ensign* (Dec. 1989), p. 46. Text available at http://www.lds.org, Gospel Library, Magazines, Ensign.

McConkie, Bruce R. *Mormon Doctrine*. Salt Lake City: Bookcraft, 1958; 2nd rev.ed. 1979.

— *A New Witness for the Articles of Faith*. Salt Lake City: Deseret Book Co., 1985.

— *Sermons and Writings of Bruce R. McConkie*. Ed. & arr. Mark L. McConkie. Bookcraft, 1989. Digital copy available in *LDS Collector's Library 2005*, in author's possession.

— 'The Seven Deadly Heresies', a speech given at Brigham Young University on June 1, 1980. Transcript available at http://speeches.byu.edu/ ?act=viewitem&id=658&tid=2.

Merriam-Webster's Online Dictionary. Available at www.m-w.com.

Millennial Star. L. Tom Perry Special Collections, Harold B. Lee Library, Brigham Young University. Digital facsimile available at http://contentdm.lib.byu.edu/u?/ MStar,12150. Vol. 28. Liverpool: Brigham Young, 1866.

Millet, Robert L. 'The Man Adam', in *Liahona* (Feb. 1998), p. 14. Text available at http://www.lds.org, Gospel Library, Magazines, Liahona.

Moffett, Ruhaniyyih Ruth. *Pilgrim's Notes of Ruhaniyyih Ruth Moffett* (1954). National Spiritual Assembly of the Bahá'ís of the Hawaiian islands, 1978. Available online at http://bahai-library.com/pilgrims/.

Monson, Thomas S. 'Building Your Eternal Home',in *Liahona* (Oct. 1999), p. 3. Text available at http://www.lds.org, Gospel Library, Magazines, Liahona.

— 'Hallmarks of a Happy Home', in *Liahona*, Oct. 2001, p. 3. Text available at http://www.lds.org, Gospel Library, Magazines, Liahona.

Nabíl-i-A'zam (Muḥammad-i-Zarandí). *The Dawn-Breakers: Nabíl's Narrative of the Early Days of the Bahá'í Revelation*. Trans. and ed. Shoghi Effendi. Wilmette, Ill.: Bahá'í Publishing Trust, 2nd ed. 1996.

National Bahá'í Review. Periodical, 1968–1983. Wilmette, Ill: National Spiritual Assembly of the United States.

National Spiritual Assembly of the Bahá'ís of the United States. *Reflections on the Current Progress and Status of the United States Bahá'í Community during the Five-Year Plan* (Dec. 18, 2002) Wilmette, Ill.

Nibley, Hugh. 'Islam and Mormonism – A Comparison', in *Ensign* (Mar. 1972), p. 55. Text available at http://www.lds.org, Gospel Library, Magazines, Ensign.

Nelson, Russell M. 'Blessed Are the Peacemakers', in *Ensign* (Nov. 2002), p. 39. Text available at http://www.lds.org, Gospel Library, Magazines, Ensign.

'News of the Church', in *Ensign* (Jan. 2003), p. 78.

Nielsen, Kent. 'People on Other Worlds', in *New Era* (Apr. 1971), p. 12. Text available at http://www.lds.org, Gospel Library, Magazines, New Era.

Oaks, Dallin H. 'Apostasy and Restoration', in *Ensign* (May 1995), p. 84. Text available at http://www.lds.org, Gospel Library, Magazines, Ensign.

— 'Brother's Keeper', in *Ensign* (Nov. 1986), p. 20. Text available at http://www.lds.

org, Gospel Library, Magazines, Ensign.

— 'Teaching and Learning by the Spirit', in *Liahona* (May 1999), p. 15. Text available at http://www.lds.org, Gospel Library, Magazines, Liahona.

— 'Weightier Matters', in *Ensign* (Jan. 2001), p. 13. Text available at http://www.lds.org, Gospel Library, Magazines, Ensign.

'On Darwin's Setback', in *Church News* (Apr. 7, 1973), p. 16.

Ostling, Richard N.; Ostling, Joan K. *Mormon America: The Power and the Promise.* New York, NY: HarperCollins, 2000.

'Our Daily Bread', in *Liahona* (Apr. 1996), p. 25.

Our Heritage: A Brief History of the Church of Jesus Christ of Latter-Day Saints. Salt Lake City: The Church of Jesus Christ of Latter-day Saints, 1996. Digital copy available in *LDS Collector's Library 2005*, in author's possession.

Pace, Glenn L. 'Follow the Prophet', in *Ensign*, May 1989, p. 25. Text available at http://www.lds.org, Gospel Library, Magazines, Ensign.

Packer, Boyd K. 'The Law and the Light', a talk given at the Book of Mormon Symposium, Brigham Young University, 30 October 1988.

— 'Personal Revelation – Available To All', in *Friend* (June 1990), inside front cover. Text available at http://www.lds.org, Gospel Library, Magazines, Friend.

— 'The Shield of Faith', in *Ensign* (May 1995), p. 7. Text available at http://www.lds.org, Gospel Library, Magazines, Ensign.

Parkin, Max H. 'Missouri's Impact on the Church', in *Ensign* (Apr. 1979), p. 57. Text available at http://www.lds.org, Gospel Library, Magazines, Ensign.

The Pearl of Great Price. Salt Lake City: The Church of Jesus Christ of Latter-day Saints, 1981.

Peterson, Daniel C.; Ricks, Stephen D. 'Comparing LDS Beliefs with First-Century Christianity', in *Ensign* (Mar. 1988), p. 7. Text available at http://www.lds.org, Gospel Library, Magazines, Ensign.

Peterson, H. Burke. 'The Welfare Production–Distribution Department', in *Ensign* (Nov. 1975), p. 116. Text available at http://www.lds.org, Gospel Library, Magazines, Ensign.

The Plan of Salvation. Missionary booklet. Salt Lake City: The Church of Jesus Christ of Latter-day Saints, 2005.

Popov, Linda Kavelin, with Dan Popov and John Kavelin. *The Family Virtues Guide: Simple Ways to Bring Out the Best in Our Children and Ourselves.* New York: Penguin Plume, 1997.

The Holy Qur'an. Trans. Abdullah Yusuf Ali. Lahore, 1934; Tahrike Tarsile Quran, Inc., 1998.

Rabbani, Rúḥíyyih, *The Guardian of the Bahá'í Faith.* London: Bahá'í Publishing Trust, 1988.

Rasmussen, Ellis T. 'Zoroastrianism', in *Ensign* (Nov. 1971), p. 32. Text available at http://www.lds.org, Gospel Library, Magazines, Ensign.

Richards, L. *The Law of Tithing*. Pamphlet. 1983.

Rohlfing, Laurel. 'Sharing Time: Jesus Organized His Church', in *Tambuli* (Feb. 1991), p. 6. Text available at http://www.lds.org, Gospel Library, Magazines, Liahona.

— 'Sharing Time: Read the Scriptures Daily', in *Friend* (Mar. 1991), p. 12. Text available at http://www.lds.org, Gospel Library, Magazines, Friend.

Romney, Marion G. 'A Glorious Promise', in *Tambuli* (July 1981), p. 1. Text available at http://www.lds.org, Gospel Library, Magazines, Liahona.

'Saints and Indians', a radio documentary feature of the Worlds of Difference Project (www.homelands.org/worlds). Broadcast on National Public Radio's *Talk of the Nation* on January 23, 2005. Audio files in the possession of the author.

Scott, Richard G. 'The Power of a Strong Testimony', in *Ensign* (Nov. 2001), p. 87. Text available at http://www.lds.org, Gospel Library, Magazines, Ensign.

Searle, Don L. 'Four Who Serve', in *Ensign* (Feb. 1992), p. 38. Text available at http://www.lds.org, Gospel Library, Magazines, Ensign.

Sears, William. *Thief in the Night or The Strange Case of the Missing Millennium*. Oxford: George Ronald, 1961, 2002.

— *The Wine of Astonishment*. Oxford: George Ronald, rev. ed. 2008.

Seely, David Rolph 'The Joseph Smith Translation: "Plain and Precious Things" Restored', in *Ensign* (Aug. 1997), p. 9. Text available at http://www.lds.org, Gospel Library, Magazines, Ensign.

Semple, Ian. Address given on 26 July 1991 in the Reception Concourse of the Seat of the Universal House of Justice in connection with the Spiritual Enrichment Programme at the Bahá'í World Centre. Available online at http://bahai-library.com/talks/semple.obedience.html.

Shoghi Effendi. *The Advent of Divine Justice*. Wilmette, Ill: Bahá'í Publishing Trust, rev. ed. 1984.

— *Arohanui: Letters from Shoghi Effendi to New Zealand*. Suva, Fiji: Bahá'í Publishing Trust, 1982.

— *Bahá'í Administration: Selected Messages 1922–1932*. Wilmette, Ill: Bahá'í Publishing Committee, 1953.

— *Dawn of a New Day*. Bahá'í Publishing Trust of India, n.d. Text available at http://reference.bahai.org.

— *Directives from the Guardian*. Comp. G. Garrida. New Delhi : Bahá'í Publishing Trust for the National Spiritual Assembly of the Bahá'ís of the Hawaiian Islands, 1973.

— *God Passes By*. Wilmette, Ill: Bahá'í Publishing Trust, 3rd ed. 1974.

— *High Endeavors: Messages to Alaska.* Anchorage: National Spiritual Assembly of the Bahá'ís of Alsaka, 1976.

— *Messages to Canada.* National Spiritual Assembly of the Bahá'ís of Canada, 1965.

— *Messages to America, 1932–1946.* Wilmette, Ill: Bahá'í Publishing Committee, 1947.

— *Messages to the Bahá'í World: 1950–1957.* Wilmette, Ill.: Bahá'í Publishing Trust, 1971.

— *The Light of Divine Guidance,* 2 vols. Hofheim-Langenhain: Bahá'í-Verlag, 1985.

— *The Promised Day is Come.* Wilmette, Ill: Bahá'í Publishing Trust, rev. ed. 1980.

— *Unfolding Destiny. The Messages from the Guardian to the Bahá'ís of the British Isles.* London: Bahá'í Publishing Trust, 1981.

— *The World Order of Bahá'u'lláh.* Wilmette, Ill.: Bahá'í Publishing Trust, 1st pocket-sized ed. 1991.

Shumway, Eric B. 'Bridging Cultural Differences', in *Ensign* (July 1979), p. 67. Text available at http://www.lds.org, Gospel Library, Magazines, Ensign.

Skinner, Andrew C. 'Apostasy, Restoration, and Lessons in Faith', in *Ensign* (Dec. 1995), p. 25. Text available at http://www.lds.org, Gospel Library, Magazines, Ensign.

Smith, Joseph Jr. *History of the Church of Jesus Christ of Latter-day Saints.* 7 vols. Comp. with Introduction and Notes by B. H. Roberts. Salt Lake City: Deseret Book Co., 2nd rev.ed. 1949.

— *Pearl of Great Price: Selections from the Book of Moses, An extract from the translation of the Bible as revealed to Joseph Smith the Prophet, June 1830–February 1831.* Salt Lake City: The Church of Jesus Christ of Latter-day Saints.

— *Teachings of the Prophet Joseph Smith.* Section 4 (1839–1842). Selected and Arranged by Joseph Fielding Smith. Salt Lake City: Deseret Book Co., 1976. Digital copy available in *LDS Collector's Library 2005,* in author's possession.

Smith, Joseph Fielding. *Answers to Gospel Questions.* 5 vols. Vol. 5. Salt Lake City: Deseret Book Co., 1966. Digital copy available in *LDS Collector's Library 2005,* in author's possession.

— *Man . . . His Origin & Destiny.* Salt Lake City: Deseret Book Co., 1954. Digital copy available in *LDS Collector's Library 2005,* in author's possession.

— *Teachings of Presidents of the Church: Joseph F. Smith.* Salt Lake City: The Church of Jesus Christ of Latter-day Saints, 1998.

Smith, R. Lloyd. 'Sharing the Gospel with Sensitivity', in *Ensign* (June 2002), p. 53. Text available at http://www.lds.org, Gospel Library, Magazines, Ensign.

So Great an Honor: Becoming a Bahá'í. Brochure. Wilmette, Ill: National Spiritual Assembly of the Bahá'ís of the United States.

Star of the West. 8 vols. Chicago: Bahá'í News Service, 1910–1935. Oxford: George

Ronald, RP 1978 and 1984.

Stephens, Kenneth D. *So Great A Cause*. Happy Camp, Calif.: Naturegraph, 1988.

Stratton, Clifford J. 'Caffeine – The Subtle Addiction', in *Tambuli* (Mar. 1990), p. 25. Text available at http://www.lds.org, Gospel Library, Magazines, Liahona.

Taherzadeh, Adib. *The Covenant of Bahá'u'lláh*. Oxford: George Ronald, 1995.

'Talking with Your Children about Moral Purity', in *Ensign* (Dec 1986), p. 57. Text available at http://www.lds.org, Gospel Library, Magazines, Ensign.

Tanner, John S. 'Sin – On the Tips of Our Tongues', in *Ensign* (Feb. 1991), p. 30. Text available at http://www.lds.org, Gospel Library, Magazines, Ensign.

Tanner, N. Eldon. 'No Greater Honor: The Woman's Role', in *Ensign* (Jan. 1974), p. 7. Text available at http://www.lds.org, Gospel Library, Magazines, Ensign.

Taylor, John. *The Gospel Kingdom*. Selected by G. Homer Durham. Salt Lake City: Deseret Book Co., 1943.

— *The Government of God* (1852). Chapter 3 reprinted in 'The Government of God', in *Ensign* (Aug. 1971), pp. 18-19.

Times and Seasons. L. Tom Perry Special Collections, Harold B. Lee Library, Brigham Young University. Digital facsimile available at http://contentdm.lib.byu.edu/u?/NCMP1820-1846,8375. Vol. 5. John Taylor (ed.) Nauvoo, Ill.: 1844–45.

Topping, Gary. 'One Hundred Years at the Utah State Historical Society', excerpted from the official web site of the Utah State Historical Society, http://history.utah.gov/aboutus/toppingarticle.html (no longer available online).

Toronto, James A. 'A Latter-day Saint Perspective on Muhammad', in *Ensign* (Aug. 2000), p. 51. Text available at http://www.lds.org, Gospel Library, Magazines, Ensign.

The Universal House of Justice. *Individual Rights and Freedoms: A Statement of the Universal House of Justice*. Haifa: Bahá'í World Centre, 29 December 1988.

— *The Institution of the Counsellors*. A document prepared by the Universal House of Justice, 29 January 2001. Available online at http://bahai-library.com.

— *Messages from the Universal House of Justice 1963–1986: The Third Epoch of the Formative Age*. Comp. Geoffry W. Marks. Wilmette, Ill: Bahá'í Publishing Trust, 1996.

— *Messages from the Universal House of Justice 1968–1973*. Wilmette, Ill: Bahá'í Publishing Trust, 1976.

— *One Common Faith*. Haifa: Bahá'í World Centre, 2005.

— *Turning Point: Selected Messages of the Universal House of Justice and Supplementary Material, 1996–2006*. West Palm Beach, Fla.: Palabra Publications, 2006.

— *Wellspring of Guidance: Messages 1963-1968*. Wilmette: Bahá'í Publishing Trust, 1976.

White, Jean Bickmore. 'Women's Suffrage in Utah', in *Utah History Encyclopedia*.

Available online at http://www.media.utah.edu/UHE/w/WOMANSUFFERAGE. html.

Wilcox, Patricia. *Bahá'í Families: Perspectives, Principles, Pracitce.* Oxford: George Ronald, 1991.

Witherington, Ben III. *New Testament History: A Narrative Account.* Grand Rapids, Mich.: Baker Academic, 2001.

World Order. Periodical, 1966–. Wilmette, Ill: National Spiritual Assembly of the United States.

Women. Haifa: Bahá'í World Centre, 1986. Also in *Compilation of Compilations*, vol. 2, pp. 355-407. Available online at http://bahai-library.com/file. php5?file=compilation_women].

Woodruff, Wilford. *The Discourses of Wilford Woodruff.* Ed. G. Homer Durham. Salt Lake City: Bookcraft, 1946. Digital copy available in *LDS Collector's Library 2005*, in author's possession.

Young, Brigham. *Teachings of Presidents of the Church: Brigham Young.* Salt Lake City: The Church of Jesus Christ of Latter-day Saints, 1997.

WEB SITES

Adherents.com – http://www.adherents.com

Bahá'í World Statistics (August 2001) – http://users.whsmithnet.co.uk/ispalin/ statistics

Community of Christ (fka The Reorganized Church of Jesus Christ of Latter Day Saints) – http://www.cofchrist.org

Online newsroom of the Church of Jesus Christ of Latter-day Saints – http:// newsroom.lds.org

The Bahá'í Faith – http://www.bahai.org

Utah State Historical Society – http://history.utah.gov

Utah History Encyclopedia – http://www.media.utah.edu

REFERENCES

Bible references

Biblical references are rendered in their traditional style as *Book chapter:verse*. Books are abbreviated in the generally accepted style, e.g. '2 Cor.' refers to Paul's second epistle to the Corinthians.

LDS references

References to LDS scriptural and historical works follow the conventions outlined below:

- *1 Nephi, 2 Nephi, Jacob, Enos, Jarom, Omni, Words of Mormon, Mosiah, Alma, Helaman, 3 Nephi, 4 Nephi, Mormon, Ether* and *Moroni* refer to the identically named sections of the Book of Mormon, usually followed by a pair of numbers in the format *chapter:verse*.
- *D&C* refers to *The Doctrine and Covenants* and is usually followed by a pair of numbers in the format *section:verse*.
- *Moses* and *Abraham* refer to *The Book of Moses* and *The Book of Abraham*, respectively, as found in the compilation work *The Pearl of Great Price*. The book reference is usually followed by a pair of numbers in the format *chapter:verse*.
- *JS–M (Joseph Smith–Matthew)* refers to a retranslation by Joseph Smith of selected verses from the Gospel of St Matthew, and may be followed by a verse number.
- *JS–H (Joseph Smith–History)* is a reference to the canonized autobiographical account of Joseph Smith's early life, including his 'First Vision.' Both JS–M and JS–H are contained in the compilation *The Pearl of Great Price*.
- *History of the Church* refers to the seven-volume historical record of the Church of Jesus Christ of Latter-day Saints, largely in journal form, with introductions and notes by B. H. Roberts. Until the time of Joseph Smith's death, this history includes many personal notes by the Church's founder himself, as well as letters and newspaper articles he deemed worthy of inclusion in the record.
- *Journal of Discourses* is a collection of 26 volumes comprising various public

discourses by principal leaders of the Church of Jesus Christ of Latter-day Saints during its early history. Both the *History of the Church* and *Journal of Discourses* collections are official church publications.

Bahá'í references

Most references to the Bahá'í Writings are rendered in the standard *author, book, page* form, as these Sacred Texts were originally published as books without individually numbered verses. Some exceptions to this are the Hidden Words and the Kitáb-i-Aqdas, as well as recently translated Writings of Bahá'u'lláh which have verse numbers printed in the margin. Where sections or paragraphs are individually numbered, those references are provided in addition to the page number.

Preface
1. 'Abdu'l-Bahá, *Foundations of World Unity*, pp. 73-4.
2. D&C 9:8.
3. 'Abdu'l-Bahá, cited in Esslemont, *Bahá'u'lláh and the New Era*, p. 120.
4. 'Abdu'l-Bahá, in *Bahá'í Education*, no. 46, p. 18.
5. Bahá'u'lláh, *Gleanings*, CXI.
6. 'Abdu'l-Bahá, *Tablets of the Divine Plan*, p. 56.

Introduction
1. Bahá'u'lláh, Bishárát (Glad-Tidings), in *Tablets of Bahá'u'lláh*, p. 22.
2. 'Abdu'l-Bahá, *Selections*, no. 34, p. 69.
3. 'Abdu'l-Bahá, *Secret of Divine Civilization*, p. 36.
4. Matt. 27:52-53.
5. LDS Newsroom (http://newsroom.lds.org; accessed March 15, 2007).
6. The author is aware that the Reorganized Church of Jesus Christ of Latter Day Saints was in 2001 renamed the *Community of Christ*. However, since this church shares a major portion of its history, as well as most of its latter-day scriptures, with the LDS Church, it will be referred to by its old name here.
7. Sources: www.bahai.org, www.adherents.com.
8. Bahá'í World Statistics (http://users.whsmithnet.co.uk/ispalin/statistics), dated August 2001, which includes the following note: 'The statistics for Local Spiritual Assemblies and localities come primarily from the 2000 Annual Statistical Reports from National Spiritual Assemblies, which contain information as of May 2, 2000. Especially the latter figures should be taken as estimates since it is not always possible for National Spiritual Assemblies to provide exact counts.'
9. Ostling and Ostling, *Mormon America*, p. 378.
10. LDS Newsroom (http://newsroom.lds.org); Statistical Information, Worldwide Church Statistics, Membership (accessed March 15, 2007).
11. A 1999 report by the US National Teaching Committee points out that from 1960 to 1995, US Bahá'í membership increased by 1,400%, compared to LDS growth of 197% in the same period. And in a paper reflecting on the Five Year

Plan, the National Spiritual Assembly of the United States reported that during the 1990s, the Bahá'í Faith 'slightly exceeded' the Mormons' annual growth rate of 1.93% (December 18, 2002, p. 8).

12. Cowan, *The Church in the Twentieth Century*, pp. 298-9.
13. Bahá'u'lláh, *The Kitáb-i-Aqdas*, para. 30, p. 30.
14. Shoghi Effendi, letter of June 1945, in *Bahá'í News*, no. 175, p. 3; also in *Directives from the Guardian*, no. 133, p. 49.
15. Allen and Leonard, *The Story of the Latter-day Saints*, p. 225.
16. Ostling and Ostling, *Mormon America*, pp. 48, 240.
17. Shoghi Effendi, 'The Unfoldment of World Civilization', in *The World Order of Bahá'u'lláh*, pp. 180-81.
18. Bahá'u'lláh, Súriy-i-Mulúk (Súrih to the Kings), para. 105, in *Summons of the Lord of Hosts*, p. 230; also in *Gleanings from the Writings of Bahá'u'lláh*, CXIII, p. 230.
19. The Báb, Persian Bayán IV:18, in *Selections*, pp. 90-91.

Chapter 1

1. The official collection *History of the Church* identifies both Joseph Smith and his brother Hyrum as 'Master Masons' throughout their respective ministries as Prophet and Patriarch of the LDS Church (*History of the Church*, vol. 6, pp. 287, 603). The ultra-secretive temple endowments designed by Smith are reported to bear a striking resemblance to Masonic rituals.
2. Richard L. Anderson, 'Joseph Smith's Testimony of the First Vision', in *Ensign* (Apr. 1996), p. 10. Footnotes and scriptural references omitted.
3. JS-H 1:5-8 (*Pearl of Great Price*).
4. Jas. 1:5.
5. JS-H 1:16-17.
6. Bahá'u'lláh, Súriy-i-Haykal (Súrih of the Temple), paras. 6-7, in *Summons of the Lord of Hosts*, pp. 5-6.
7. JS-H 1:18-19. (*Pearl of Great Price*).
8. Bahá'u'lláh, *Kitáb-i-Íqán*, paras. 29-30, pp. 31-32.
9. 'Abdu'l-Bahá, talk at the Universalist Church, Washington, DC, 6 November 1912, in *Promulgation of Universal Peace*, p. 392; also in *Foundations of World Unity*, p. 81.
10. Carlyle, *History of Friedrich II of Prussia, Called Frederick the Great*, vol. 1, ch. 1 (Project Gutenberg: www.gutenberg.org).
11. Attributed to 'Abdu'l-Bahá, in *'Abdu'l-Bahá in London*, p. 125.
12. Nibley, 'Islam and Mormonism – A Comparison', in *Ensign* (Mar. 1972), p. 55.
13. Matthews, 'The Fulness of Times', in *Ensign* (Dec. 1989), p. 46.
14. JS-H 30-35, 42.
15. This warning has some significance, considering that one of Joseph Smith's occupations had been as a 'money-digger', in which he employed various divination techniques. Moroni's warning appears here to dissuade Smith from considering the golden plates of the Book of Mormon and other, presumably ancient artifacts, as buried treasure.
16. JS-H 54.

17. There are a number of additional details known about this process that, for the sake of brevity, will not be discussed here.
18. JS-H 73-74.
19. Cf. Alma 3:6; 3 Nephi 21:23.
20. Based on a passage in the Book of Mormon (3 Nephi 2:14-16), some Mormon missionaries in the time of Joseph Smith expected newly baptized American Indians to have their 'curse' lifted and become white.
21. http://eom.byu.edu/index.php/Lamanite_Mission_of_1830-1831.
22. D&C 88:63.
23. D&C 88:118; D&C 109:7.
24. D&C 45:10.
25. D&C 38:7.
26. Robert D. Anderson, *Inside the Mind of Joseph Smith*, pp. 4-5.
27. Joseph Smith Jr, February 12, 1843, in *History of the Church*, vol. 5, pp. 271-2. Emphasis in original.
28. Sears, *Thief in the Night*, pp. 188-9. Emphasis in original.
29. Joseph Smith Jr, November 13, 1833, in *History of the Church*, vol. 1, pp. 439-40.
30. Sections 87 and 130 of *The Doctrine and Covenants* establish that Joseph Smith associated such a war with the Return of Christ.
31. Joseph Smith Jr, March 10, 1843, in *History of the Church*, vol. 5, p. 301.
32. Joseph Smith Jr, March 19, 1843, in *History of the Church*, vol. 5, p. 308.
33. Joseph Smith Jr, March 23, 1843, in *History of the Church*, vol. 5, p. 310.
34. D&C 130:14-15.
35. 'I Have a Question', in *Ensign* (Apr. 1984), p. 21.
36. *History of the Church*, vol. 7, pp. 102-3.
37. ibid. vol. 6, pp. 549-50.
38. D&C 135:4-6.
39. Ostling and Ostling, *Mormon America*, p. 17.
40. Stephens, *So Great a Cause*, p. 72.
41. Cited in Marquardt, 'Some Interesting Notes on Succession at Nauvoo in 1844', http://www.xmission.com/~research/about/successi.htm.
42. Cited in Packer, 'The Shield of Faith', in *Ensign* (May 1995), p. 7 (Draft Declaration of the Twelve Apostles, reporting March 1844 meeting of Twelve, *Brigham Young Papers*, LDS Church Archives).
43. A biographical note lists the probable cause of death as a 'bilious fever' contracted after being chased through the woods by the same mob that killed Joseph and Hyrum Smith (*History of the Church*, vol. 7, pp. 111, 216-22). Some skeptics, noting the suspicious timing of Samuel's death and the effect it had on settling the issue of succession, have suggested that bilious fever was a common misdiagnosis for arsenic poisoning. However, no credible evidence of foul play has ever been produced.
44. *History of the Church*, vol. 7, p. 229.
45. *Times and Seasons*, vol. 5 (Jan. 1844–Jan. 1, 1845), no. 16 (Sept. 2, 1844). Whole No. 100, p. 632.
46. *History of the Church*, vol. 6, p. 223.
47. The first mention of Brigham Young as 'prophet' in official historical documents

occurs in an address by Heber C. Kimball dated September 19, 1852 (*Journal of Discourses*, vol. 2, p. 354).

48. 2 Nephi 3:6-8.
49. *Merriam-Webster Online Dictionary*. Available at www.m-w.com.
50. Pilgrims' notes are personal observations, reminiscences or quotations by individual believers who were in the presence of 'Abdu'l-Bahá or Shoghi Effendi. They are not part of Bahá'í scripture and should not be regarded as authentic, although they may capture the essence of what was said.
51. Pilgrim's notes of Ruhaniyyih Ruth Moffett.
52. Cf. Mosiah 8:15.
53. There is at least one example in the Mormon scriptures of Jesus being referred to as a prophet. In the Book of Mormon, Jesus is quoted as follows: 'Behold, I am he of whom Moses spake, saying: A prophet shall the Lord your God raise up unto you of your brethren, like unto me; him shall ye hear in all things whatsoever he shall say unto you. And it shall come to pass that every soul who will not hear that prophet shall be cut off from among the people' (3 Nephi 20:23).
54. From a letter dated February 7, 1977 written on behalf of the Universal House of Justice to an individual, in Hornby, *Reference File*, p. 320; cited in Collins, 'The Bahá'í Faith and Mormonism: Further Reflections', in *World Order*, vol. 17, no. 3 (Spring 1983), pp. 25-33.
55. Collins, 'The Bahá'í Faith and Mormonism: Further Reflections', in *World Order*, vol. 17, no. 3 (Spring 1983), pp. 25-33.
56. D&C 67:5.
57. D&C 93:47. For additional examples, see B. H. Roberts' introduction to *History of the Church*, vol. 5, pp. xxxvi-vii.
58. Frequently Asked Questions about the Community of Christ (fka Reorganized Church of Jesus Christ of Latter Day Saints), retrieved November 25, 2007, from *http://www.cofchrist.org/ourfaith/faq.asp*.
59. Collins, 'The Bahá'í Faith and Mormonism: Further Reflections', in *World Order*, vol. 17, no. 3 (Spring 1983), pp. 25-33.

Chapter 2

1. Ostling and Ostling, *Mormon America*, p. 261.
2. *The Book of Mormon*, title page.
3. Ostling and Ostling, *Mormon America*, p. 267.
4. Stephens, *So Great a Cause*, pp. 32-3 (emphasis in original).
5. ibid.
6. 3 Nephi 8:14.
7. Mormon 1:7.
8. Collins, 'The Bahá'í Faith and Mormonism: Further Reflections', in *World Order*, vol. 17, no. 3 (Spring 1983), pp. 25-33.
9. Joseph Smith, in *History of the Church*, vol. 4, p. 461.
10. Shoghi Effendi, *High Endeavors*, no. 97.
11. Collins, 'The Bahá'í Faith and Mormonism: A Preliminary Survey', in *World Order*, vol. 15, no. 1/2 (Fall 1980/Winter 1981), pp. 33-45.

12. Collins, 'The Bahá'í Faith and Mormonism: Further Reflections', in *World Order*, vol. 17, no. 3 (Spring 1983), pp. 25-33.

13. ibid.

14. 2 Nephi 4:16-35.

15. D&C, 'Explanatory Introduction'.

16. Marquardt, *The Joseph Smith Revelations*, p. 10.

17. ibid. pp. 3-19.

18. Gen. 1:16 (KJV).

19. Moses 2:16 (*Pearl of Great Price*); emphasis added.

20. Moses 2:26 (*Pearl of Great Price*); emphasis added.

21. The use of plural pronouns such as 'us' and 'our', when referring to God, is misconstrued by many Mormons to mean that multiple personages are addressed. In fact, it is a common language device used to convey the exalted position of a single person, such as a king.

22. Gen. 1:26.

23. Abraham, ch. 1, Summary (*Pearl of Great Price*).

24. Marquardt, 'The Book of Abraham Revisited,' 1997. Available online at http://www.xmission.com/~research/about/abraham.htm.

25. Abraham 3:22-28 (*Pearl of Great Price*).

26. Abraham 4:1-5 (*Pearl of Great Price*).

27. *Guide to the Scriptures: Joseph Smith Translation*. Available online at http://scriptures.lds.org/en/gs/j/38.

28. See Chapter 3, 'The Articles of Faith', the 8th Article of Faith.

Chapter 3

1. *Gospel Principles*, Unit Three: Communication between God and Man, 7: The Holy Ghost, p. 36. According to D&C 130:22, 'The Father has a body of flesh and bones as tangible as man's; the Son also; but the Holy Ghost has not a body of flesh and bones, but is a personage of Spirit.' The first two are rooted in the belief that Jesus was resurrected in the flesh, and that man was created in God's physical image. The third implies that 'spirit' is a form of matter subject to the limitations of time and space.

2. *Gospel Principles*, p. 36.

3. Peterson and Ricks, 'Comparing LDS Beliefs with First-Century Christianity', in *Ensign* (Mar. 1988), p. 7.

4. McConkie, *Mormon Doctrine*, 2nd ed., s.v. 'Plurality of Gods', p. 576.

5. Alma 11:28-29.

6. 3 Nephi 11:27.

7. 2 Nephi 31:21.

8. 'Abdu'l-Bahá, *Some Answered Questions*, ch. 27, pp. 113-15.

9. *Tablets of Abdu'l-Baha Abbas*, pp. 117-18.

10. 'Abdu'l-Bahá, *Some Answered Questions*, ch. 29, p. 120.

11. Bahá'u'lláh, Lawh-i-Maqsúd (Tablet of Maqsúd), in *Tablets of Bahá'u'lláh*, p. 164.

12. Bahá'u'lláh, *Hidden Words*, Arabic no. 31.

13. D&C 93:38.

14. Bahá'u'lláh, *Hidden Words*, Arabic no. 22.
15. Moroni 8:8-9.
16. 'Abdu'l-Bahá, *Some Answered Questions*, ch. 66, p. 240.
17. *Tablets of Abdu'l-Baha Abbas*, p. 543.
18. Bahá'u'lláh, *Gleanings*, XLV.
19. Bahá'u'lláh, *The Kitáb-i-Aqdas*, para. 4; also in Gleanings, CLV.
20. 'Abdu'l-Bahá, in *'Abdu'l-Bahá in London*, p. 56.
21. Bahá'u'lláh, *Gleanings*, LXVI, p. 130.
22. 'Abdu'l-Bahá, *Some Answered Questions*, ch. 19, p. 91.
23. Bahá'u'lláh, *The Kitáb-i-Aqdas*, para. 1; also in *Gleanings*, CLV.
24. Rohlfing, 'Sharing Time: Jesus Organized His Church', in *Tambuli* (Feb. 1991), p. 6.
25. Witherington, *New Testament History*, pp. 175-6.
26. Cf. Eph. 4:11.
27. Cf. Acts 13:1; also, Paul claims the gift of prophecy in 1 Cor. 13:2.
28. Ehrman, 'After the New Testament', p. 46.
29. Skinner, 'Apostasy, Restoration, and Lessons in Faith', in *Ensign* (Dec. 1995), p. 25.
30. According to the Gospels, Simon Peter was Jesus' first Apostle. Since Peter and Paul were the longest surviving of the apostles (both are believed to have been executed under Nero around 65 CE), the phrase 'following the deaths of Christ's early Apostles' refers to roughly the same time frame as 'after the passing of His First Apostle.'
31. Shoghi Effendi, 'The World Order of Bahá'u'lláh: Further Considerations', in *The World Order of Bahá'u'lláh*, p. 20.
32. 'Abdu'l-Bahá, *Some Answered Questions*, ch. 11, pp. 47-8.
33. Matt. 16:19.
34. Joseph Smith Jr., 'Try the Spirits', an editorial in *Times and Seasons* (Apr. 1842), in *History of the Church*, vol. 4, p. 574.
35. Oaks, 'Apostasy and Restoration', in *Ensign* (May 1995), p. 84.
36. Peterson and Ricks, 'Comparing LDS Beliefs with First-Century Christianity', in *Ensign* (Mar. 1988), p. 7.
37. Sears, *The Wine of Astonishment*, p. 99.
38. ibid. pp. 103-4 (emphasis in original).
39. Bahá'u'lláh, *Kitáb-i-Íqán*, para. 98, pp. 89-90.
40. 1 Nephi 13:26-29.
41. Matt. 13:13.
42. John 16:12;
43. John 16:25.
44. 1 Nephi 14:10.
45. Bahá'u'lláh, *Kitáb-i-Íqán*, para.93, pp. 86-87.
46. This term has its origin in the following two verses in the Bible: (a) 'And the LORD said unto Moses, *Gather unto me seventy men of the elders of Israel*, whom thou knowest to be the elders of the people, and officers over them; and bring them unto the tabernacle of the congregation, that they may stand there with thee' (Num. 11:16); and (b) 'AFTER these things the Lord appointed other *seventy*

also, and sent them two and two before his face into every city and place, whither he himself would come . . . And the *seventy* returned again with joy, saying, Lord, even the devils are subject unto us through thy name' (Luke 10:1-17).

47. The Universal House of Justice, in *The Institution of the Counsellors*.

48. *Bible Dictionary*, s.v. 'Revelation', p. 762.

49. Letter of November 1, 1940 on behalf of Shoghi Effendi to an individual believer, November 1, 1940; quoted in a memorandum from the Research Department of the UHJ to David Garcia, August 6, 1996 (http://bahai-library.com/uhj/sabeans.etc.ht ml).

50. Joseph Smith, in *History of the Church*, vol. 3, pp. 391-2.

51. Shoghi Effendi, in *Directives from the Guardian*, no. 32, p. 12.

52. To place this statement in context, it was in response to a question about Bahá'u'lláh's assertion that Abraham was commanded by God to sacrifice Ishmael, an event which is not related in the Old Testament but is described in the Qur'án. Shoghi Effendi explained that Bahá'u'lláh's specific mention of this event carries more weight than its omission from the Old Testament.

53. As was previously noted in the discussion of the Sixth Article of Faith, the Bahá'í Writings make it clear that the canonization or abridgment of the Bible would not have amounted to 'corruption of the text', and should never be used as a reason not to accept the Bible as the Word of God.

54. Seely, 'The Joseph Smith Translation: "Plain and Precious Things" Restored', in *Ensign* (Aug. 1997), p. 9.

55. Ostling and Ostling, *Mormon America*, p. 292.

56. Seely, 'The Joseph Smith Translation', in *Ensign* (Aug. 1997), p. 9.

57. ibid.

58. Matt. 6:10.

59. *Gospel Principles*, ch. 42.

60. 'Abdu'l-Bahá, *Some Answered Questions*, ch. 12, p. 65.

61. A number of Bahá'í sources claim that the Ottoman Empire signed an official Edict of Toleration on or around March 23, 1844. While there are references to evidence in existence to substantiate this claim, it is not widely recognized by historians. In any case, the immigration of a substantial number of Jews and the establishment of Jewish institutions in the Holy Land around that time is an undisputed fact.

62. 'Abdu'l-Bahá, *Some Answered Questions*, ch. 12, pp. 65-6.

63. *Gospel Principles*, ch. 42.

64. D&C 110:11.

65. Woodruff, *Discourses*, 51:801, pp. 188-9.

66. Taylor, in *The Gospel Kingdom*, p. 309.

67. Shoghi Effendi, *The Advent of Divine Justice*, p. 5.

68. Joseph Smith Jr., from a letter to the Church dated March 25, 1839, written from Liberty Jail in Clay County, Missouri (*History of the Church*, vol. 3, pp. 303-304).

69. Paul H. Dunn, 'Oh Beautiful for Patriot Dream', in *Ensign* (Nov 1975), p. 53.

70. 'Abdu'l-Bahá, *Tablets of the Divine Plan*, Tablet to the Bahá'ís of the Central States, para. 11, p. 79.

71. 'Abdu'l-Bahá, *The Promulgation of Universal Peace*, p. 104.

72. Holland, 'A Promised Land', in *Ensign* (Jun. 1976), p. 23.
73. Bahá'u'lláh, *Gleanings*, XIV, p. 27.
74. Bahá'u'lláh, *Gleanings*, XLIII, pp. 92-3.
75. 'Abdu'l-Bahá, *Selections*, no. 37, p. 78.
76. Taylor, *The Government of God* (1852), p. 20. Chapter 3 reprinted in 'The Government of God', in *Ensign* (Aug. 1971), pp. 18-19.
77. Shoghi Effendi, letter of May 4, 1953, in *Messages to the Bahá'í World*, p. 155.
78. The Universal House of Justice, letter dated July 7, 1976, at http://bahai-library.com/unpubl.articles/church.html.
79. D&C 134:4, 7, 9.
80. *Salt Lake City Tribune*, Oct. 3, 2005.
81. D&C 134:5.
82. Bahá'u'lláh, *Gleanings*, CII.
83. D&C 134:6.
84. Bahá'u'lláh, *The Kitáb-i-Aqdas*, paras. 123-4, p. 63.
85. 1 Cor. 13:4-7.
86. Bahá'u'lláh, Lawḥ-i-Ḥikmat, in *Tablets of Bahá'u'lláh*, pp. 138-9.

Chapter 4

1. Rev. 22:18.
2. Articles of Faith, 9.
3. 2 Nephi 29:8-10.
4. Bahá'u'lláh, *Gleanings*, CLIII, p. 324.
5. Jacob 4:8; 1 Thess. 5:20.
6. Mormon 9:7-19.
7. Bahá'u'lláh, Súriy-i-Haykal, in *Summons of the Lord of Hosts*, para. 241, p. 122.
8. Cf. Bahá'u'lláh, *Gleanings*, XIII, from the Kitáb-i-Íqán, para. 3 passim.
9. Packer, 'Personal Revelation – Available To All', in *Friend* (June 1990), inside front cover.
10. 'Editor's Table: Modern Revelation', in *Improvement Era*, vol. V (Aug. 1902), no. 10, pp. 805-7.
11. Ezra Taft Benson, *Korea Area Conference 1975*, p. 52. Cited in Lesson 37: 'We Thank Thee, O God, for a Prophet', *Doctrine and Covenants* and *Church History Gospel Doctrine Teacher's Manual*, p. 213.
12. Taherzadeh, *The Covenant of Bahá'u'lláh*, pp. 405-6.
13. 'Abdu'l-Bahá, cited in the introduction to *The Kitáb-i-Aqdas*, pp. 4-5.
14. D&C 101:32-34.
15. Matthews, 'The Fulness of Times', in *Ensign* (Dec. 1989), p. 46.
16. Romney, 'A Glorious Promise', in *Tambuli* (July 1981), p. 1.
17. Matthews, 'The Fulness of Times', in *Ensign* (Dec. 1989), p. 46.
18. Millet, 'The Man Adam', in *Liahona* (Feb. 1998), p. 14.
19. Matthews, 'The Fulness of Times', in *Ensign* (Dec. 1989), p. 46.
20. Joseph Smith Jr., in *Teachings of the Prophet Joseph Smith*, Section 4 (1839–1842), pp. 167-8.
21. Matthews, 'The Fulness of Times', in *Ensign* (Dec. 1989), p. 46.
22. Bahá'u'lláh, *Kitáb-i-Íqán*, para. 7, p. 7.

23. Collins, 'The Bahá'í Faith and Mormonism: Further Reflections', in *World Order*, vol. 17, no. 3 (Spring 1983), pp. 25-33; embedded footnotes removed. Emphasis in original.
24. 'Abdu'l-Bahá, *Some Answered Questions*, ch.11, p. 45.
25. Bahá'u'lláh, *Gleanings*, XXII, p. 55.
26. D&C 130:14-16.
27. Dan. 12:8-9.
28. Joseph F. Smith, *Teachings of Presidents of the Church: Joseph F. Smith*, p. 268.
29. From a letter written on behalf of Shoghi Effendi to an individual believer, January 25, 1943, in the compilation *Prayer, Meditation, and the Devotional Attitude*. Also in *Directives from the Guardian*, section 205, p. 77.
30. Shoghi Effendi, *Directives from the Guardian*, section 205, p. 77.
31. 'Abdu'l-Bahá, *Foundations of World Unity*, p. 87.
32. In Bahá'u'lláh, *The Kitab-i-Aqdas*, note 130, p. 221.
33. Joseph F. Smith, *Teachings of Presidents of the Church: Joseph F. Smith*, p. 266.
34. Gordon B. Hinckley, from an interview quoted in Ostling and Ostling, *Mormon America*, p. 149.
35. Mr Ian Semple, from an address given on July 26, 1991 in the Reception Concourse of the Seat of the Universal House of Justice in connection with the Spiritual Enrichment Programme at the Bahá'í World Centre. Available at http://bahai-library.com/talks/semple.obedience.html.
36. See Marquardt, *The Joseph Smith Revelations*.
37. This has not always been so. Shortly after Joseph Smith's death, the Quorum of the Twelve Apostles (headed by Brigham Young) were adamant that Joseph would remain their prophet in perpetuity, primarily to fend off attempts by Sidney Rigdon to claim for himself the title of Prophet or Guardian of the Church. In a speech given on August 8, 1844, Apostle Amasa M. Lyman suggested: 'There is no need of a President, we have a head here. What is that head? The Quorum of the Twelve Apostles are the head. We now see the necessity of the Apostleship' (HC 7:237).
38. From a discourse by Elder Orson Pratt, delivered on June 23, 1878 (*Journal of Discourses*, Vol. 20, pp. 8-9).
39. JS-H 1:74.
40. Alma 12:9-11.
41. Bahá'u'lláh, *Kitáb-i-Iqán*, paras. 283-6 passim., pp. 254-7.
42. Cf. Isa. 6:9.
43. Matt. 13:11-16.
44. *Bible Dictionary*, 1979 ed., s.v. 'Parables', pp. 740-741.
45. Bahá'u'lláh, *Kitáb-i-Iqán*, para. 53, p. 49.
46. Bahá'u'lláh, *Hidden Words*, Persian no. 16.
47. F. David Lee, 'Questions and Answers', in *Tambuli* (June 1984), p. 15.
48. Shoghi Effendi, *The Promised Day is Come*, p. 3.
49. Shoghi Effendi, *The World Order of Bahá'u'lláh*, p. 31.
50. Bahá'u'lláh, *Hidden Words*, Persian no. 12.
51. Jalál-ud-Dín Rúmí, *Mathnaví* (quoted in Bahá'u'lláh, *The Seven Valleys and the Four Valleys*, p. 52).

52. Monson, 'Hallmarks of a Happy Home', in *Liahona* (Oct. 2001), p. 3; 'Building Your Eternal Home', in *Liahona* (Oct. 1999), p. 3.

Chapter 5

1. Mosiah 3:19.
2. Joseph F. Smith, *Teachings of Presidents of the Church: Joseph F. Smith*, pp. 371-2.
3. Joseph Smith Jr., 'The King Follett Sermon', in *History of the Church*, vol. 6, pp. 302-17.
4. Holley, *Religion for Mankind*, p. 229, cited in Honnold, *Vignettes from the Life of 'Abdu'l-Bahá*, p. 10.
5. *Bahá'í World*, vol. XIII, p. 1187, cited in Honnold, *Vignettes from the Life of 'Abdu'l-Bahá*, p. 10.
6. 'Abdu'l-Bahá, in *Paris Talks*, ch. 18, p. 55.
7. Alma 37:25.
8. Bahá'u'lláh, *Hidden Words*, Persian no. 67.
9. Mosiah 3:25-27.
10. 2 Nephi 9:39.
11. 'Abdu'l-Bahá, *Selections*, no. 111, p. 136.
12. Bahá'u'lláh, *Epistle to the Son of the Wolf*, p. 132.
13. *Gospel Principles*, pp. 13-14.
14. Shoghi Effendi, *High Endeavors*, 98.
15. ibid. 96.
16. 'Abdu'l-Bahá, *Some Answered Questions*, ch. 50, pp. 196-7.
17. D&C 93:29.
18. *Gospel Principles*, p. 31.
19. 'Abdu'l-Bahá, *Some Answered Questions*, ch. 30, pp. 123-4.
20. *Gospel Principles*, p. 33.
21. 'Abdu'l-Bahá, *Some Answered Questions*, ch. 30, pp. 124-5.
22. *Gospel Principles*, p. 33.
23. 'Abdu'l-Bahá, *Some Answered Questions*, ch. 52, pp. 200-01.
24. 2 Nephi 2:27.
25. Bahá'u'lláh, *Gleanings*, LXXV, p. 143.
26. Bahá'u'lláh, *The Kitáb-i-Aqdas*, para. 157, p. 76.
27. Bahá'u'lláh, *Kitáb-i-Íqán*, para. 88, pp. 80-81.
28. Bahá'u'lláh, *Gleanings*, LXXXI, pp. 156-7.
29. Bahá'u'lláh, *Hidden Words*, Persian no. 41.
30. *Gospel Principles*, pp. 297-8; scriptural references removed.
31. *Bible Dictionary*, s.v. 'Degrees of Glory', p. 655.
32. Moses 1:37-38.
33. Statement attributed to 'Abdu'l-Bahá in a document titled 'Explanation of Spiritual Evolution as Taught from the Baha'i Teachings', by Lua Getsinger. Available online at http://bahai-library.com/visuals/evolution.txt.html.
34. *Gospel Principles*, p. 291.
35. Joseph Smith Jr., 'The King Follett Sermon', in *History of the Church*, Vol. 6, pp. 302-17.

36. This points to yet another difference between the Mormon and Bahá'í views of the afterlife. In *Some Answered Questions*, 'Abdu'l-Bahá indicates that the next world is 'sanctified from time and place' (p. 241), whereas Mormon doctrine refers to the necessity for spirits to wait either for the Resurrection or the passing of a thousand years.
37. *Gospel Principles*, p. 298; scriptural references removed.
38. Bahá'u'lláh, *Gleanings*, LXXXI, pp. 155-6.
39. *'Abdu'l-Bahá in London*, pp. 74-5.
40. *Gospel Principles*, p. 291.
41. Taherzadeh, *The Covenant of Bahá'u'lláh*, pp. 253-4.
42. Shoghi Effendi, in *Directives from the Guardian*, no. 45, pp. 16-17.
43. Taherzadeh, *The Covenant of Bahá'u'lláh*, p. 256.
44. Ostling and Ostling, *Mormon America*, pp. 351-71.
45. The Universal House of Justice, letter of May 27, 1966, in *Wellspring of Guidance*, pp. 87-8. Cited in *Compilation on Scholarship*, no. 60, p. 21.
46. The Universal House of Justice, *Individual Rights and Freedoms*, p. 15.
47. Asay, 'Opposition to the Work of God', in *Ensign* (Nov. 1981), p. 67.
48. ibid. (emphasis in original).
49. Shoghi Effendi, in *Directives from the Guardian*, no. 45, pp. 16-17.
50. 'Abdu'l-Bahá, *Tablets of the Divine Plan*, p. 56.
51. Shoghi Effendi, *Messages to the Bahá'í World, 1950–1957*, pp. 10-11.
52. Bahá'u'lláh, quoted by 'Abdu'l-Bahá in *Bahá'í World Faith*, pp. 435-6.
53. This name refers to those of the family of the Báb.
54. *Will and Testament of 'Abdu'l-Bahá*, para. 13, p. 10.
55. *Gospel Principles*, p. 290.
56. Bahá'u'lláh, *Gleanings*, LXXXI, p. 157.
57. 'Abdu'l-Bahá, *Memorials of the Faithful*, p. 12.
58. 2 Nephi 9:13.
59. Esslemont, *Bahá'u'lláh and the New Era*, p. 20-21.
60. 'Abdu'l-Bahá, *Some Answered Questions*, ch. 81, pp. 284-5.
61. ibid. ch. 66, pp. 239-40.
62. Cannon, Dahl and Welch, 'The Restoration of Major Doctrines through Joseph Smith', in *Ensign* (Jan. 1989), p. 27.
63. *Gospel Principles*, p. 9.
64. Bahá'u'lláh, *Hidden Words*, Arabic no 3.
65. 'Abdu'l-Bahá, in *The Promulgation of Universal Peace*, p. 70.
66. Joseph Smith Jr., 'The King Follett Sermon', in *History of the Church*, vol. 6, pp. 302-17.
67. Cannon, Dahl and Welch, 'The Restoration of Major Doctrines through Joseph Smith', in *Ensign* (Jan. 1989), p. 27.
68. *Gospel Principles*, pp. 289-90.
69. *'Abdu'l-Bahá in London*, p. 96.
70. *Gospel Principles*, p. 290.
71. D&C 130:18-19
72. Bahá'u'lláh, *Gleanings*, LXXXI, pp. 155-6.
73. 'Abdu'l-Bahá, *Some Answered Questions*, ch. 66, pp. 239-40.

74. *Gospel Principles*, p. 9.
75. ibid.
76. Joseph Smith Jr., 'The King Follett Sermon', in *History of the Church*, vol. 6, pp. 302-17.
77. Mormon 9:9.
78. Bahá'u'lláh, *Gleanings*, LXXIII, p. 141.
79. Bahá'u'lláh, *Gleanings*, LXXXII, p. 161.
80. Bahá'u'lláh, *Gleanings*, LXXXI, p. 156.
81. 'Abdu'l-Bahá, *Some Answered Questions*, ch. 63, p. 233.
82. Bahá'u'lláh, *Gleanings*, LXXXI, p. 156.
83. *Gospel Principles*, p. 257.
84. Attributed to 'Abdu'l-Bahá, quoted in Esslemont, *Bahá'u'lláh and the New Era*, p. 194.
85. Bahá'u'lláh, *Kitáb-i-Íqán*, para. 98, pp. 89-90.
86. Romney, 'A Glorious Promise', in *Tambuli* (July 1981), p. 1.
87. *Gospel Principles*, p. 232.
88. 'Abdu'l-Bahá, *Selections*, no. 86, p. 118.
89. *Tablets of Abdul-Baha Abbas*, pp. 605-6.
90. *'Abdu'l-Bahá in London*, p. 75.
91. Shoghi Effendi, *Dawn of a New Day*, p. 58.
92. The First Presidency and Council of the Twelve Apostles of The Church of Jesus Christ of Latter-day Saints, quoted in 'The Family: A Proclamation to the World', in *Ensign* (Nov. 1995), p. 102.
93. *Our Heritage*, 8: A Period of Trials and Testing, President John Taylor, 93.
94. Mark 12:18-25.
95. Acts 23:8.
96. Matt. 22:29-30.
97. Luke 20:34-36.
98. Letter on behalf of Shoghi Effendi to an individual believer, December 4, 1954; in *National Bahá'í Review*, no. 92 (Sept. 1975), p. 6; also in *Lights of Guidance*, no. 450.
99. D&C 132:16-17.
100. 'Abdu'l-Bahá, *Tablets of Abdul-Baha Abbas*, p. 206.
101. Bahá'u'lláh, *Gleanings*, LXXXVI.
102. Shoghi Effendi, *Directives from the Guardian*, no. 122.
103. Related in Furútan (comp.), *Stories of Bahá'u'lláh*, no. 72.
104. 'Abdu'l-Bahá, in *Bahá'í Prayers*, p. 64.
105. *Gospel Principles*, p. 291.
106. 'Abdu'l-Bahá, *Some Answered Questions*, ch. 62, p. 232.
107. Bahá'u'lláh, *Gleanings*, LXXXI, p. 157.
108. Bahá'u'lláh, *Gleanings*, LXXXII, p. 161.
109. 'Abdu'l-Bahá, *Memorials of the Faithful*, p. 12.

Chapter 6

1. In Bahá'u'lláh, *The Kitáb-i-Aqdas*, note 104, p. 212.
2. Use of the term *counsel* is deliberate here; although subsequent presidents of

the LDS Church have given his counsel the force of commandment, Joseph Smith specifically stated that this Word of Wisdom was to be 'sent greeting; not by commandment or constraint . . .' (D&C 89:2). In any case, it is clear from the historical record that Smith was not fanatical about his restrictions on alcohol. For example, as mayor of Nauvoo he passed an ordinance to allow the sale of liquor to visitors passing through, and he once advised the women's Relief Society not to become entangled in temperance societies.

3. D&C 89:5-9 & 17, 'Word of Wisdom'.
4. D&C 27:2.
5. Haight, 'Remembering the Savior's Atonement', in *Ensign* (Apr. 1988), p. 7 (emphasis in original).
6. *History of the Church*, vol. 7, p. 99.
7. 'Abdu'l-Bahá, quoted in Shoghi Effendi, *The Advent of Divine Justice*, p. 33.
8. Bahá'u'lláh, quoted in Shoghi Effendi, *The Advent of Divine Justice*, p. 33.
9. 'Abdu'l-Bahá, *Selections*, no. 129, paras. 6, 7, 9, pp. 147-8.
10. The Universal House of Justice, March 4, 1974, in *National Bahá'í Review* (Sept. 1986).
11. Ostling and Ostling, *Mormon America*, p. 177.
12. Oaks, 'Brother's Keeper', in *Ensign* (Nov. 1986), p. 20.
13. *History of the Church*, vol. 4 (July 12, 1841), p. 383.
14. *History of the Church*, vol. 6, p. 111 (emphasis in original).
15. In *History of the Church*, a log entry by Joseph Smith reads: '*Wednesday, 3 [May, 1843].* – Called at the office and drank a glass of wine with Sister Jenetta Richards, made by her mother in England, and reviewed a portion of the conference minutes.' (HC 5:380). Note that the wine was, in accordance with the Word of Wisdom, 'of your own make.'
16. Excerpt from a letter written on behalf of the Universal House of Justice to a National Spiritual Assembly, February 8, 1982 in *Developing Distinctive Bahá'í Communities*, p. 16.37.
17. Letter from the Universal House of Justice to the International Teaching Centre, January 15, 1976, enclosed with a letter written on its behalf to a National Spiritual Assembly, February 8, 1982, ibid. p. 16.36.
18. Written on behalf of Shoghi Effendi, October 2, 1935, enclosed with a letter written on behalf of the Universal House of Justice, February 8, 1982, ibid. p. 16.35.
19. Written on behalf of Shoghi Effendi, November 6, 1935, enclosed with a letter written on behalf of the Universal House of Justice to a National Spiritual Assembly, February 8, 1982, ibid.
20. Letter from the Universal House of Justice dated January 15, 1976, enclosed with a letter written on behalf of the Universal House of Justice, dated February 8, 1982, to a National Spiritual Assembly, ibid. p. 16.37.
21. 'Abdu'l-Bahá, *Selections*, no. 129, para. 10, pp. 148-9.
22. 'Abdu'l-Bahá, cited in Bahá'u'lláh, *The Kitáb-i-Aqdas*, note 170, p. 239.
23. *Gospel Principles*, p. 193.
24. 'Abdu'l-Bahá, *Selections*, no. 129, para. 12, pp. 149-50.
25. September 5, 1841, *History of the Church*, vol. 4, p. 414.

26. 'Abdu'l-Bahá, *Selections*, no. 133, para. 2, pp. 152-2.
27. Bahá'u'lláh, *The Kitáb-i-Aqdas*, para. 113, p. 60.
28. Bahá'u'lláh, *The Kitáb-i-Aqdas*, note 170, p. 239.
29. D&C 89:10-17, 'Word of Wisdom'.
30. D&C 88:124.
31. 'Abdu'l-Bahá, in *Extracts from The Writings Concerning Health, Healing, and Nutrition*, rev. 1990. Compiled by The Research Department of the Universal House of Justice, for inclusion with a letter dated 3 September 1984 to the Local Spiritual Assembly of Bisbee, Arizona. Also published in *Compilation of Compilations*, vol. I, pp. 459-88.
32. The Persian/Arabic text is published in Majmu'ih-yi Alváh-i-Mubarakih, pp. 222-6. See http://bahai-library.com/index.php5?file=bahaullah_lawh_tibb_anonymous.
33. Bahá'u'lláh, Lawḥ-i-Ṭibb, provisional translation available online at http://bahai-library.com/index.php5?file=bahaullah_lawh_tibb_anonymous.
34. D&C 89:7, 9.
35. Brigham Young, Discourses of Brigham Young, selected and arranged by John A. Widtsoe, p. 182; quoted in *Teachings of Presidents of the Church: Brigham Young*, ch. 29.
36. Eshrakhavari, in *Páyam-i-Bahá'í*, vol. 272 (July 2000), p. 15.
37. McConkie, *Mormon Doctrine*, p. 845.
38. *Priesthood Bulletin*, vol. 8, no. 1 (Feb. 1972); quoted in Clifford J. Stratton, 'Caffeine – The Subtle Addiction', in *Tambuli* (Mar. 1990), p. 25.
39. Heber J. Grant, in Conference Report (Apr.922), p. 165.
40. Kimball, 'Privileges and Responsibilities of Sisters', in *Ensign* (Nov. 1978), p. 105.
41. *Gospel Doctrine*, pp. 273-4.
42. Bahá'u'lláh, *Hidden Words*, Persian no. 35.
43. Shoghi Effendi, *The Advent of Divine Justice*, pp. 29-30.
44. ibid. p. 23.
45. D&C 42:40-41.
46. Bahá'u'lláh, Gleanings, CXXXVI., para. 5, p. 297.
47. D&C 88:74; cf. James 4:8.
48. Bahá'u'lláh, quoted in Shoghi Effendi, *The Advent of Divine Justice*, p. 31.
49. John S. Tanner, 'Sin – on the Tips of Our Tongues', in *Ensign* (February 1991), p. 30.
50. D&C 20:54.
51. Bahá'u'lláh, Kitáb-i-'Ahd (Book of the Covenant), in *Tablets of Bahá'u'lláh*, pp. 219-220.
52. Bahá'u'lláh, *Kitáb-i-Íqán*, paras. 213-14, pp. 193-4; also in *Gleanings*, CXXV, paras. 2-3, pp. 264-5.
53. Written on behalf of Shoghi Effendi to an individual believer, October 19, 1947. Available at http://bahai-library.com/guardian/easy.familiarity.html.
54. President Kimball, in Conference Report, Sydney Australia Area Conference, February 29, 1976, p. 55; quoted in 'Talking with Your Children about Moral Purity', in *Ensign* (Dec. 1986), p. 57.
55. Pilgrim's note recorded by Ann M. Boylan in 1912. With regard to this quotation,

a letter to an individual written on behalf of Shoghi Effendi (Oct. 19, 1947) reads: 'The Master's words . . . which you quoted, can certainly be taken as the true spirit of the teachings on the subject of sex. We must strive to achieve this exalted standard.' This letter is quoted by the Universal House of Justice in a letter to the National Spiritual Assembly of the United States, Feb.10, 1974, in National Bahá'í Review (1979), p. 5. Also available at http://bahai-library.com/guardian/easy.familiarity.html.

56. *Gospel Principles*, p. 248.
57. Kimball, 'Privileges and Responsibilities of Sisters', in *Ensign* (Nov. 1978), p. 105.
58. Letter on behalf of Shoghi Effendi to an individual believer, September 5, 1938. Quoted in *Messages from the Universal House of Justice 1968–1973*, pp. 107-8; also in *Bahá'í Marriage and Family Life*, no. 42, pp. 13-14.
59. Shoghi Effendi, *The Light of Divine Guidance*, vol. 2, p. 71.
60. *Gospel Principles*, p. 253.
61. Bahá'u'lláh, *Gleanings*, LIX, para. 6, p. 117.
62. *Gospel Principles*, p. 251.
63. Bahá'u'lláh, *The Kitáb-i-Aqdas*, para. 19, p. 26.
64. Bahá'u'lláh, *Gleanings*, LX, para. 3, p. 118.
65. Bahá'u'lláh, *Gleanings*, XLVI, para. 4, pp. 100-01.
66. *Gospel Principles*, p. 252.
67. Bahá'u'lláh, *The Kitáb-i-Aqdas*, para. 49, p. 37.
68. Letter on behalf of Shoghi Effendi to an individual believer, March 26, 1950, in *Lights of Guidance*, p. 365.

Chapter 7
1. The First Presidency and Council of the Twelve Apostles of The Church of Jesus Christ of Latter-day Saints, quoted in 'The Family: A Proclamation to the World', in *Ensign* (Nov. 1995), p. 102.
2. From a letter written on behalf of Shoghi Effendi to an individual believer, April 15, 1939, quoted in *Lights of Guidance*, no. 950, p. 283.
3. Bahá'í International Community, *The Family in a World Community*, a pamphlet first distributed at the World NGO Forum Launching the United Nations International Year of the Family (IYF), Malta, November 1993.
4. The First Presidency and Council of the Twelve Apostles of The Church of Jesus Christ of Latter-day Saints, quoted in 'The Family: A Proclamation to the World', in *Ensign* (Nov. 1995), p. 102.
5. *Gospel Principles*, p. 237.
6. The Universal House of Justice, letter to the National Spiritual Assembly of the Bahá'ís of New Zealand, December 28, 1980, in *Bahá'í Marriage and Family Life*, no. 183, p. 57; also in *Messages from the Universal House of Justice 1963–1986*, no. 272, paras. 2-4, pp. 470-71.
7. Bahá'u'lláh, in *Bahá'í Education*, p. 6.
8. The First Presidency and Council of the Twelve Apostles of The Church of Jesus Christ of Latter-day Saints, quoted in 'The Family: A Proclamation to the World', in *Ensign* (Nov. 1995), p. 102.

9. *Gospel Principles*, pp. 238-39.
10. 'Abdu'l-Bahá, in *Bahá'í Education*, p. 19.
11. 'Abdu'l-Bahá, in *The Bahá'í World*, vol. 9 (1940–1944), p. 543, quoted in *Bahá'í Education*, no. 145, p. 56.
12. *Gospel Principles*, pp. 236-37.
13. 'Abdu'l-Bahá, in *Bahá'í Marriage and Family Life*, no. 93, p. 30.
14. *Gospel Principles*, p. 237.
15. 'Abdu'l-Bahá, *Selections*, no. 108, p. 134.
16. 'Abdu'l-Bahá, talk on June 9, 1912, in *The Promulgation of Universal Peace*, pp. 180-181.
17. 'Abdu'l-Bahá, *Selections*, no. 95, p. 125.
18. *Gospel Principles*, p. 237.
19. From a letter written on behalf of Shoghi Effendi to an individual believer, July 9, 1939, in *Bahá'í Education*, no. 122.
20. 'Abdu'l-Bahá, in *Bahá'í Marriage and Family Life*, no. 154, p. 47.
21. The Universal House of Justice, letter to the National Spiritual Assembly of the Bahá'ís of New Zealand, December 28, 1980, in *Bahá'í Marriage and Family Life*, no. 183, p. 57; also in *Messages from the Universal House of Justice 1963–1986*, no. 272, para. 6, pp. 472; and quoted in *Bahá'í Law and Principle: Creating Legal and Institutional Structures for Gender Equality* (Bahá'í International Community).
22. *Gospel Principles*, p. 238.
23. The Universal House of Justice, letter to the National Spiritual Assembly of the Bahá'ís of New Zealand, December 28, 1980, in *Bahá'í Marriage and Family Life*, no. 183, p. 59; also in *Messages from the Universal House of Justice 1963–1986*, no. 272, para. 6, pp. 472; and quoted in *Bahá'í Law and Principle: Creating Legal and Institutional Structures for Gender Equality* (Bahá'í International Community).
24. *Gospel Principles*, p. 238.
25. Letter on behalf of the Universal House of Justice, August 9, 1984, in *Women*, no. 74.
26. *Gospel Principles*, p. 238.
27. 'Abdu'l-Bahá, *Selections*, no. 114, p. 139.
28. Letter on behalf of Shoghi Effendi, 16 November 1939, in *Bahá'í Education*, p. 56.
29 'Abdu'l-Bahá, *Selections*, no. 113, p. 138.
30. Letter on behalf of the Universal House of Justice, 16 June 1982, in *Women*, no. 73.
31. *Tablets of Abdul-Baha Abbas*, p. 606, quoted in *Bahá'í Education*, p. 50.
32. Bahá'í International Community, *Proposals for International Women's Year*, no. 5.
33. 'Abdu'l-Bahá, Tablet revealed on August 28, 1913, in *Paris Talks*, ch. 59, pp. 195-6.
34. White, 'Women's Suffrage in Utah', *Utah History Encyclopedia*.
35. *The Latter-day Saint Woman: Basic Manual for Women, Part B*, Lesson 14, 'Withstanding the Evils of the World', p. 110.
36. Bahá'í International Community, *The Family in a World Community*.
37. N. Eldon Tanner, 'No Greater Honor: The Woman's Role', in *Ensign* (Jan. 1974), p. 7.
38. 'Abdu'l-Bahá, talk on May 20, 1912, in *The Promulgation of Universal Peace*, p. 135; quoted in *Messages from the Universal House of Justice 1963–1986*, no. 272, para. 6b, p. 473.
39. *Gospel Principles*, pp. 239-40.

40. *Tablets of Abdul-Baha Abbas*, pp. 262-3, in *Bahá'í Marriage and Family Life*, no. 174, p. 55.
41. 'Abdu'l-Bahá, in *Bahá'í Marriage and Family Life*, no. 154, p. 47.
42. 'Abdu'l-Bahá, *Selections*, no. 102, p. 129.
43. Bahá'u'lláh, in *Bahá'í Prayers*, p. 103.

Chapter 8
1. Letter on behalf of Shoghi Effendi to the National Spiritual Assembly of the Bahá'ís of the British Isles, August 8, 1942, in *Bahá'í Education: A Compilation*, p. 68.
2. Cf. D&C 20:77, 79. Curiously, if even a minor mistake is made during the recital of the revealed sacrament prayer, the reader must immediately start over from the beginning, until the entire prayer has been read flawlessly.
3. Cf. D&C 109. Incidentally, one of the Bahá'í occasional prayers is dedicated to the 'Mother Temple of the West', a title bestowed by 'Abdu'l-Bahá on the Bahá'í House of Worship in Wilmette, Illinois.
4. *Gospel Principles*, ch. 25.
5. Bahá'u'lláh, *The Kitáb-i-Aqdas*, para. 16, p. 25.
6. ibid. para. 10, pp. 22-3.
7. *Gospel Principles*, ch. 25.
8. 'Abdu'l-Bahá, *Selections*, no. 35, pp. 69-70.
9. Bahá'u'lláh, *The Kitáb-i-Aqdas*, para. 149, pp. 73-4.
10. Shoghi Effendi, *Directives from the Guardian*, no.32, p. 12.
11. Bahá'u'lláh, *Gleanings*, CXXXVI, para. 2, p. 295.
12. Bahá'u'lláh, *The Kitáb-i-Aqdas*, note 165, p. 236.
13. See 'The Nineteen Day Feast', in *Compilation of Compilations*, vol. 1, nos. 983-989, p. 448.
14. Rohlfing, 'Sharing Time: Read the Scriptures Daily', in *Friend* (Mar. 1991), p. 12.
15. 'Our Daily Bread' (Visiting teaching message), in *Liahona* (Apr. 1996), p. 25.
16. Bahá'u'lláh, *Gleanings*, XCV, para. 3, p. 195.
17. Bahá'u'lláh, *Hidden Words*, Persian no. 33.
18. Bahá'u'lláh, *Gleanings*, XLIII, para. 9, p. 97.
19. Alma 32:27-43; Cf. Matt. 13:3-8.
20. *Tablets of Abdul-Baha Abbas*, vol.1, p. 149.
21. These are listed in the order in which they usually occur; however, some wards switch the Sunday School and Priesthood/Relief Society meetings to avoid scheduling conflicts with other wards sharing the same building.
22. Cf. D&C 20:65.
23. D&C 46:5-6.
24. Letter from the Universal House of Justice to an individual, August 12, 1981, in 'The Nineteen Day Feast', in *Compilation of Compilations*, vol. 1, p. 443.
25. The Universal House of Justice, quoted in a letter dated December 16, 2008 from the National Spiritual Assembly of the Bahá'ís of the United States.
26. Karen Lynn, 'Q&A: Questions and Answers', in *New Era* (Sept. 1975), p. 14.
27. D&C 119:4-5.
28. *Gospel Principles*, ch. 32.

29. Ostling and Ostling, *Mormon America*, p. 115.
30. Letter from the Universal House of Justice, 11 October 1982, in *Ḥuqúqu'lláh: The Right of God* (2000), pp. 37-8.
31. The Universal House of Justice, in Bahá'u'lláh, *The Kitáb-i-Aqdas*, note 125, p. 219.
32. Letter from the Universal House of Justice to an individual believer, 14 February 1993, in *Ḥuqúqu'lláh: The Right of God* (2007), no. 71.
33. Letter from the Universal House of Justice to an individual, 26 February 1973, ibid. no. 57.
34. Bahá'u'lláh, ibid. no. 2.
35. Bahá'u'lláh, from a previously untranslated tablet, ibid. no. 12.
36. *Gospel Principles*, ch. 32.
37. Bahá'u'lláh, from a previously untranslated tablet, in *Ḥuqúqu'lláh: The Right of God* (2007), no. 13.
38. Richards, *The Law of Tithing*, p. 8.
39. Bahá'u'lláh, from a previously untranslated tablet, in *Ḥuqúqu'lláh: The Right of God* (2007), no. 11.
40. *Gospel Principles*, ch. 32.
41. Letter from the Universal House of Justice to the National Spiritual Assembly of Iran, in *Ḥuqúqu'lláh: The Right of God* (2007), no. 55.

Chapter 9
1. D&C 88:81.
2. D&C 38:40.
3. *Gospel Principles*, ch. 33.
4. Bahá'u'lláh, quoted in Shoghi Effendi, *The Advent of Divine Justice*, p. 45.
5. Letter on behalf of Shoghi Effendi, July 1930, in *Directives from the Guardian*, no. 197.
6. The Universal House of Justice, 1996 Riḍván Message to Europe, in *Turning Point*, no. 6, para. 9, p. 50.
7. Shoghi Effendi, *The Advent of Divine Justice*, p. 51-2.
8. Gordon B. Hinckley, conference, Taiwan Taipei Mission, 24 May 1996. Quoted in 'Words of the Living Prophet', in *Liahona* (June 1997), p. 32.
9. The Universal House of Justice, Riḍván 2006 letter, in *Turning Point*, no. 38, para. 11, p. 220.
10. Letter from Shoghi Effendi, January 28, 1939, in *Messages to America*, p. 17.
11. Oaks, 'Teaching and Learning by the Spirit', in *Liahona* (May 1999), p. 15.
12. 'Abdu'l-Bahá, *Selections*, no. 208, p. 264.
13. ibid. no. 146, p. 175.
14. ibid. no. 209, pp. 264-5.
15. *Teachings of Presidents of the Church: Joseph F. Smith*, ch. 9: 'Our Missionary Duty', p. 82.
16. D&C 38:41.
17. 'Abdu'l-Bahá, *Selections*, no. 174, p. 203.
18. *Teachings of Presidents of the Church: Joseph F. Smith*, ch. 9: 'Our Missionary Duty', p. 82.

19. 'Abdu'l-Bahá, *Selections*, no. 217, p. 270.
20. Bahá'u'lláh, I<u>sh</u>ráqát, ninth I<u>sh</u>ráq, in *Tablets*, p. 129; also Bi<u>sh</u>árát, thirteenth Glad-Tidings, in *Tablets*, p. 27.
21. *Teachings of Presidents of the Church: Joseph F. Smith*, ch. 9: 'Our Missionary Duty', p. 83.
22. 'Abdu'l-Bahá, Tablet to the Bahá'ís of the United States and Canada, para. 20, in *Tablets of the Divine Plan*, p. 56.
23. Bahá'u'lláh, *Epistle to the Son of the Wolf*, para. 22, p. 15.
24. R. Lloyd Smith, Area Authority Seventy, 'Sharing the Gospel With Sensitivity', in *Ensign* (June 2002), p. 53.
25. Since Mormons understand Babylon to be a symbol for the worldly condition of sin, the directive to go 'out of Babylon' is a call to leave behind the things of this world.
26. D&C 133:7-8,10.
27. Matt. 24:14.
28. Sears, *Thief in the Night*, part 1, ch. 3.
29. 'Abdu'l-Bahá, Tablet to the Bahá'ís of the United States and Canada, paras. 9 & 14, in *Tablets of the Divine Plan*, pp. 53-4.
30. 'Abdu'l-Bahá, Tablet to the Bahá'ís of the United States and Canada, paras. 7-8, in *Tablets of the Divine Plan*, pp. 41-2.
31. 'Abdu'l-Bahá, Tablet to the Bahá'ís of the United States and Canada, para. 13, in *Tablets of the Divine Plan*, p. 54.
32. *Teachings of Presidents of the Church: Joseph F. Smith*, ch. 9: 'Our Missionary Duty', p. 78.
33. 'Abdu'l-Bahá, *Memorials of the Faithful*, p. 10.
34. *Merriam-Webster's Collegiate Dictionary*, online version.
35. Shoghi Effendi, *The Advent of Divine Justice*, p. 66.
36. The Universal House of Justice, letter of July 13, 1964, in *Wellspring of Guidance*, p. 32.
37. The Universal House of Justice, letter of 18 October 2007 to a Local Spiritual Assembly in California, in *Developing Distinctive Bahá'í Communities*, pp. 5.97-8.
38. Shoghi Effendi, *Bahá'í Administration*, p. 125.
39. *The Plan of Salvation* (a booklet handed out during missionary talks), p. 16.
40. Cf. Bahá'u'lláh, *Prayers and Meditations*, XL.
41. Shoghi Effendi, *The Advent of Divine Justice*, p. 52.

Chapter 10
1. 'Abdu'l-Bahá, *Some Answered Questions*, ch. 47, p. 181.
2. ibid. p. 183.
3. 'Abdu'l-Bahá, *Star of the West*, vol. 11, no. 19 (Mar. 2, 1921), p. 315.
4. 'Abdu'l-Bahá, *Some Answered Questions*, ch. 49, pp. 191-3.
5. ibid. ch. 47, p. 184.
6. ibid. ch. 51, p. 199.
7. 'Abdu'l-Bahá, talk on July 5, 1912, in *The Promulgation of Universal Peace*, p. 219.
8. Quoted from an April 16, 2003 radio broadcast of *The Diane Rehm Show* (http://

wamu.org/programs/dr/03/04/16.php).

9. 'Abdu'l-Bahá, *Some Answered Questions*, ch. 49, p. 192.

10. The terms 'entered' and 'receptacle' are used metaphorically here, as 'Abdu'l-Bahá has explained that 'the rational soul . . . does not descend into the body', rather 'the spirit is connected with the body, as this light is with this mirror' (*Some Answered Questions*, ch. 66, p. 239).

11. Craig and Jones, *A Geological Miscellany*.

12. D&C 77:6.

13. Claybaugh, 'As Flaming Fire and a Ministering Angel', in *Ensign* (Oct. 1999), p. 54.

14. Joseph Fielding Smith, *Answers to Gospel Questions*, vol. 5, p. 112.

15. 'On Darwin's Setback', in *Church News* (Apr. 7, 1973) p. 16 (editorial).

16. From a discourse by Elder Orson Pratt, November 22, 1873, in *Journal of Discourses*, vol. 16, pp. 315-17.

17. 'Abdu'l-Bahá, *Some Answered Questions*, ch. 47, p. 183.

18. ibid. p. 180.

19. From a discourse by Elder Orson Pratt, November 22, 1873, in *Journal of Discourses*, vol. 16, p. 316.

20. Joseph Fielding Smith, *Answers to Gospel Questions*, vol. 5, p. 116.

21. McConkie, Doctrinal New Testament Commentary 3:95-96, in *Mormon Doctrine*, 2nd ed., p. 681.

22. McConkie, *A New Witness for the Articles of Faith*, p. 647.

23. Isa. 65:25.

24. 'Abdu'l-Bahá, *The Promulgation of Universal Peace*, p. 107.

25. McConkie, 'The Seven Deadly Heresies', a speech given at Brigham Young University on June 1, 1980 (transcript available at *speeches.byu.org*).

26. Melvin A. Cook, Professor of Metallurgy, University of Utah, in his introduction to Joseph Fielding Smith's *Man . . . His Origin & Destiny*.

27. McConkie, *Sermons and Writings of Bruce R. McConkie*, p. 337.

28. Hunter, 'Of the World or of the Kingdom?', in *Ensign* (Jan. 1974), p. 53.

29. *Gospel Doctrine*, p. 38.

30. 'Abdu'l-Bahá, talk on October 25, 1912, in *The Promulgation of Universal Peace*, p. 374.

31. Letter on behalf of the Universal House of Justice to an individual believer, March 23, 1983, in *Compilation on Scholarship*, no. 64, in *Compilation of Compilations*.

32. Boyd K. Packer, 'The Law and the Light', Book of Mormon Symposium, BYU, October 30, 1988.

33. 'Abdu'l-Bahá, talk on April 19, 1912, in *The Promulgation of Universal Peace*, p. 31.

34. Lee, in *Ensign* (Dec. 1972), p. 2 (First Presidency Message).

35. Quoted in Greenwood, 'I Have a Question', in *Ensign* (Sept. 1987), p. 27.

36. McConkie, Doctrinal New Testament Commentary 3:95-96 in *Mormon Doctrine*, 2nd ed., p. 681.

37. D&C 101:32-34.

38. Num. 23:23.

39. Joseph Smith Jr., *History of the Church*, vol. 4, p. 184.

40. Dan. 12:4.

41. Joseph Fielding Smith, in *Conference Report*, October 4, 1926 (Second Day, Afternoon Session), p. 117.
42. William Sears, *Thief in the Night*, pp. 47-9.
43. Shoghi Effendi, 'The Unfoldment of World Civilization', in *The World Order of Bahá'u'lláh*, p. 203.
44. Bahá'u'lláh, *Epistle to the Son of the Wolf*, p. 32.
45. 'Abdu'l-Bahá, talk on May 25, 1912, in *The Promulgation of Universal Peace*, pp. 143-4.
46. Moses 1:31-35, 37-38 (*The Pearl of Great Price*).
47. Bahá'u'lláh, Súriy-i-Vafá, in *Tablets*, p. 188.
48. Bahá'u'lláh, *Gleanings*, LI, p. 104.
49. ibid. LXXXII, para. 11, p. 163.
50. 'Abdu'l-Bahá, talk on June 9, 1912, in *The Promulgation of Universal Peace*, p. 175.
51. Matt. 19:24; Mark 10:25.
52. 'Abdu'l-Bahá, *Some Answered Questions*, ch. 27, p. 113.
53. Letter on behalf of Shoghi Effendi, February 20, 1950, in *Bahá'í Canada*, Suppement 6; quoted by Mr Ian Semple in his talk dated September 6, 2001 at the Bahá'í House of Worship in Wilmette, Illinois.
54. 'Abdu'l-Bahá, *Some Answered Questions*, ch. 47, p. 182.
55. This letter was actually in response to a question about intelligent life on other planets, but its explanation is equally applicable to less well developed life forms.
56. From a letter dated 11 January 1982 written on behalf of the Universal House of Justice to an individual believer.
57. Kent Nielsen, 'People on Other Worlds', in *New Era* (Apr. 1971), p. 12.
58. Moses 1:33.

Chapter 11

1. This list is by no means complete, as the Bahá'í Writings suggest that a number of God's Messengers appeared in pre-historic times. Also missing from this list are the Founders of Native American, African, and other indigenous religions. While the names of most of these Founders have been lost, their teachings live on in the rich oral traditions of those cultures.
2. John 1:1-2.
3. 'Abdu'l-Bahá, talk on June 16, 1912, in *The Promulgation of Universal Peace*, pp. 197-8.
4. Bahá'u'lláh, *Gleanings*, XXXI, p. 74.
5. ibid. CXI, p. 114.
6. McConkie, *Mormon Doctrine*, pp. 628, 626, cited in Collins, 'The Bahá'í Faith and Mormonism: A Preliminary Survey', in *World Order*, vol. 15, no. 1/2 (Fall 1980/Winter 1981), pp. 33-45.
7. Moroni 7:12-13.
8. 2 Nephi 29:3-14.
9. Alma 29:8.
10. Bahá'u'lláh, *Gleanings*, LXXVI, para. 1, p. 145.
11. Jacob 2:21.

12. Bahá'u'lláh, *Hidden Words*, Arabic no. 68.
13. Alma 26:37.
14. 'Abdu'l-Bahá, in *Bahá'í Prayers*, 2002 ed., pp. 113-14; and in many Bahá'í prayer books.
15. 1 Nephi 26:33.
16. 'Abdu'l-Bahá, talk on April 23, 1912, in *The Promulgation of Univeral Peace*, p. 44.
17. Mosiah 18:21.
18. 3 Nephi 11:28-29.
19. Bahá'u'lláh, *Gleanings*, V, pp. 8-9.
20. Bahá'u'lláh, *Gleanings*, CXLVI, p. 315.
21. *Tablets of Abdul-Baha Abbas*, pp. 119-20.
22. 'Abdu'l-Bahá, *Selections*, no. 221, p. 280.
23. 'Abdu'l-Bahá, talk at Hull House, Chicago, on April 30, 1912, in *The Promulgation of Universal Peace*, pp. 68-9.
24. 'Abdu'l-Bahá, in *Bahá'í World Faith*, p. 359.
25. Romney, *Church News* (Feb. 10, 1973), p. 15, cited in Shumway, 'Bridging Cultural Differences', in *Ensign* (July 1979) pp. 67-71.
26. Carmack, 'Unity in Diversity', in *Tambuli* (Aug. 1992), p. 27 (emphasis in original).
27. Oaks, 'Weightier Matters', in *Ensign*, (Jan. 2001), p. 13.
28. These are subjective observations of this author. No statistical data is available to support these observations, as the Church of Jesus Christ of Latter-day Saints does not track the ethnicity of its members.
29. Letter on behalf of the Universal House of Justice, August 27, 1989, to the Followers of Bahá'u'lláh; quoted in *Developing Distinctive Bahá'í Communities* (2008), p. 13.4.
30. Bahá'í International Community, 'The Right to Development: Exploring Its Social and Cultural Dimensions'. Submitted to the working group on Social and Cultural Dimensions of Development at the 33rd Session of the Sub-Commission on the Prevention of Discrimination and Protection of Minorities, 26 August 1980.
31. Shumway, 'Bridging Cultural Differences', in *Ensign*, (July 1979), p. 67.
32. Burton, 'Kingdom of God', in *Ensign* (June 1971), p. 83.
33. 'Abdu'l-Bahá, talk on April 16, 1912, in *The Promulgation of Universal Peace*, pp. 18-19.
34. Taylor, *The Government of God* (1852). Chapter 3 reprinted in 'The Government of God', in *Ensign* (Aug 1971), pp. 18-19.
35. Bahá'u'lláh, *Epistle to the Son of the Wolf*, pp. 62-3.
36. Taylor, *The Government of God* (1852). Chapter 3 reprinted in 'The Government of God', in *Ensign* (Aug 1971), pp. 18-19.
37. 'Abdu'l-Bahá, *Divine Philosophy*, p. 42.
38. Shoghi Effendi, *The Promised Day is Come*, p. 105-7.
39. Shoghi Effendi, 'The Goal of a New World Order', in *The World Order of Bahá'u'lláh*, p. 46.
40. Ostling and Ostling, *Mormon America*, p. 92.
41. Nelson, 'Blessed Are the Peacemakers', in *Ensign* (Nov. 2002), p. 39.
42. *Teachings of Presidents of the Church: Brigham Young*, Ch. 36, p. 267.

43. Rabbani, *The Guardian of the Baháʼí Faith*, p. 189.

Chapter 12

1. From a letter dated 7 February 1977 written on behalf of the Universal House of Justice to an individual, in Hornby, *Reference File*, p. 320; cited in Collins, 'The Baháʼí Faith and Mormonism: Further Reflections', in *World Order*, vol. 17, no. 3 (Spring 1983), pp. 25-33.
2. Although the Báb was the Herald and Forerunner of Baháʼuʼlláh, both are considered Manifestations (Prophets) of God, and no real distinction is made between their respective missions or Writings. As Baháʼís believe it is the same Christ Spirit that appears in each Manifestation, Christ can be said to have returned twice in quick succession during the 19th century: first in 1844 with the Declaration of the Báb, and again in 1863 with the Declaration of Baháʼuʼlláh. Thus, Mormon (and more generally, Christian) references to the time of the Second Coming can be linked to major events relating to the lives of either the Báb or Baháʼuʼlláh.
3. Joseph Smith Jr, February 12, 1843, in *History of the Church*, vol. V, pp. 271-2. Emphasis in original.
4. D&C 130:12-13.
5. Baháʼuʼlláh, *Gleanings*, para. 18, XIV, p. 35.
6. Source: *www.americancivilwar.com*.
7. D&C 130:14-16.
8. HC 2:182.
9. Quoted in Nabíl, *The Dawn-Breakers*, pp. 582-3.
10. 'First Public Mentions of the Baháʼí Faith', UK Baháʼí Heritage Site, http://users.whsmithnet.co.uk/ispalin/heritage/firsts.htm; also at http://bahai-library.com/essays/faith.in.west.html.
11. Baháʼuʼláh, Tablet of Carmel, in *Tablets of Baháʼuʼlláh*, pp. 3-5.
12. *History of the Church*, vol. 1, p. 323.
13. D&C 85:7-8.
14. D&C 2.
15. D&C 35:4.
16. The Báb, Persian Bayán, VII:2, in *Selections*, p. 95.
17. From a letter on behalf of Shoghi Effendi, quoted in the introduction to the *Kitáb-i-Aqdas*, p. 8.
18. D&C 110. This reveals a possible confusion on the part of Joseph Smith, since the New Testament renders the name *Elijah* in its Greek form, *Elias*. Accordingly, *Elijah* and *Elias* refer to the same prophet.
19. D&C 128:18-19; see also Ephesians 1:10.
20. Shoghi Effendi, *God Passes By*, p. 100.
21. The Báb, quoted in Nabíl, *The Dawn-Breakers*, p. 94.
22. Joseph Smith Jr, 'Joseph Smith–Matthew: An extract from the translation of the Bible as revealed to Joseph Smith the Prophet in 1831: Matthew 23:39 and chapter 24', *Pearl of Great Price*, JS–Matthew 1:24-26; cf. Matt. 24:25-27.
23. Whitmer, *History of the Church*, ch. V, quoted in *History of the Church*, vol 1, p. 176 (2nd footnote).
24. ʼAbdu'l-Bahá, talk on April 17, 1912, New York, in *The Promulgation of Universal*

Peace, p. 23.
25. D&C 45:64.
26. Rev. 2:17.
27. The *Urim and Thummim* were first mentioned in the Old Testament. Joseph Smith has interpreted these names as collectively referring to a physical device to facilitate the process of revelation, otherwise known as the philosopher's stone. Smith claimed to have made use of such a device in translating the Book of Mormon, as well as in receiving revelation.
28. D&C 130:11.
29. 'Abdu'l-Bahá, in *'Abdu'l-Bahá in London*, pp. 93-4.
30. *Tablets of Abdul-Baha Abbas*, p. 521.
31. D&C 109:19.
32. 3 Nephi 20:43-45; Isa. 52:14-15.
33. 3 Nephi 21:9-10; cf. Acts 13:41.
34. 3 Nephi 21: 26-29; Isa. 52:12.
35. Isa. 52:14.
36. Translated as 'black pit', this Tehran dungeon had previously been used as an underground water reservoir, and was notorious for its complete lack of light, its damp coldness, its indescribably foul stench and its countless vermin. The 100-pound chains Bahá'u'lláh was made to carry were equally infamous. In *Epistle to the Son of the Wolf*, He wrote: 'Shouldst thou at some time happen to visit the dungeon of His Majesty the Sháh, ask the director and chief jailer to show thee those two chains, one of which is known as Qará-Guhar, and the other as Salásil. I swear by the Day-Star of Justice that for four months this Wronged One was tormented and chained by one or the other of them' (p. 77).
37. Bahá'u'lláh, Súriy-i-Mulúk, *The Summons of the Lord of Hosts*, para. 12, pp. 189-90; also in *Gleanings*, CXVIII, p. 252.
38. Bahá'u'lláh, Tablet to Pope Pius IX, in *Proclamation of Bahá'u'lláh*, p. 84.
39. D&C 38:21-22.
40. Mosiah 13:34.
41. Bahá'u'lláh, *Proclamation of Bahá'u'lláh*, pp. 27-8.
42. Bahá'u'lláh, *Gleanings*, XIX, para. 1, pp. 46-7.
43. 3 Nephi 29:2.
44. D&C 1:11-13.
45. D&C 6:1-4.
46. D&C 33:3.
47. D&C 33:17-18.
48. D&C 34:7.
49. D&C 34:12.
50. D&C 35:26-27.
51. D&C 39:21.
52. D&C 51:20.
53. D&C 54:10.
54. D&C 58:3-7.
55. D&C 88:126.
56. D&C 128:24.

57. Alma 34:31-32.
58. Quoted in *History of the Church*, vol. 4, p. 133. Emphasis in original. The first issue of the *Millennial Star* was published May 27, 1840.
59. The Báb, *Selections*, p. 7.
60. D&C 38:7-9.
61. Alma 39:16.
62. D&C 88:74; also see Jas. 4:8.
63. D&C 45:1-2, 6.
64. Bahá'u'lláh, *Gleanings*, CLIII, para. 4, p. 325.
65. Bahá'u'lláh, *Gleanings,*, LII, para.1, p. 105.
66. Bahá'u'lláh, *Kitáb-i-Íqán*, para. 23, p. 23.
67. 2 Nephi 28:16-27.
68. John 2:18-21.
69. Lit. 'God with us'. Isa. 7:14; Cf. Matt. 1:23.
70. Matt. 4:13-16.
71. From a discourse by Elder Orson Pratt delivered on June 23, 1878 (*Journal of Discourses*, vol. 20, pp. 8-9).
72. Isa. 29:11-12.
73. Dan. 7:9-10.
74. Those familiar with the New Testament may recall that the thrusting of hands in Jesus' side is the sign of a 'doubting Thomas.'
75. 3 Nephi 11:8, 15-17.
76. Mic. 7:12.
77. Dan. 7:13.
78. Matt. 24:30.
79. Matt. 26:64.
80. Mark 14:62.
81. Bahá'u'lláh, *Kitáb-i-Íqán*, paras. 79-81, pp. 71-74.
82. 4 Nephi 1:45.
83. D&C 88:63.
84. D&C 10:55.
85. Matt. 24:14.
86. *Gospel Principles*, p. 279.
87. 2 Pet. 1:16-18.
88. 1 Nephi 11:28.
89. D&C 93:11, 15-17.
90. Luke 1:32-33.
91. Bahá'u'lláh, *Gleanings*, XIX, para. 5, pp. 48-49.
92. *History of the Church*, e.g. vol. 4, pp. 128, 189, 415, 588. Although reports of 'bloody rain' are quite rare, several were recorded between 1819 and 1872. While some were dismissed as hoaxes, chemical analyses performed on actual samples of this rain revealed a combination of minerals that linked the rain to meteoric activity.
93. 1 Thess. 5:2; 2 Pet. 3:10; Cf. Matt. 24:43.
94. *Gospel Principles*, pp. 277, 280.
95. Luke 9:54-56.

96. Luke 17:20-21.
97. Shoghi Effendi, *The Promised Day is Come*, pp. 3-4.
98. While it is true that, especially in the Acts of the Apostles, the resurrection referred to can be interpreted either physically or spiritually, the spiritual meaning casts these Bible verses in new light. For example, most Christians believe that if we deny the bodily resurrection of Jesus, our faith is in vain because of this statement by Paul: 'But if there be no resurrection of the dead, then is Christ not risen: And if Christ be not risen, then is our preaching vain, and your faith is also vain' (1 Cor. 15:13-14). If interpreted physically, there is no apparent reason for this causality, and we are compelled to accept it on faith. Yet taken spiritually, the logic of this statement is abundantly clear, because without a resurrection *of the dead*, or afterlife, Jesus' spirit could not have ascended to heaven and our faith would indeed be in vain.
99. 1 Cor. 15:41-44.
100. John 11:24-26; emphasis added.
101. Alma 40:16-18.
102. Matt. 27:52-53; Helaman 14:25.
103. Alma 40:6, 19-21.
104. *Gospel Principles*, pp. 278-9.

Chapter 13
1. 'Abdu'l-Bahá, from a tablet translated from the Persian, *Compilation on Bahá'í Education*, no. 43; *Bahá'í Education*, p. 25.
2. Unlike its Bahá'í namesake, the LDS fireside is a large event with a prominent speaker and usually some form of entertainment.
3. Letter from the Universal House of Justice to the Continental Boards of Counsellors, December 27, 2005, in *Turning Point*, p. 199.
4. The International Teaching Centre, *Reflections on Growth*, no. 14 (Oct. 2006).
5. The Universal House of Justice, Message to the Bahá'ís of the world, January 17, 2003.
6. The Universal House of Justice, Riḍván Message to the Bahá'ís of the world, April 2002.
7. Benson, 'Prepare for the Days of Tribulation', in *Ensign* (Nov. 1980), p. 32.
8. H. Burke Peterson, 'The Welfare Production–Distribution Department', in *Ensign* (Nov. 1975), p. 116.
9. Bahá'u'lláh, *Kitáb-i-Aqdas*, para.33.
10. ibid.
11. Shoghi Effendi, *Directives from the Guardian*, no. 218, pp. 82-3; and in Bahá'u'lláh, *The Kitáb-i-Aqdas*, note 56, p. 192.
12. Letter from the Department of the Secretariat on behalf of the Universal House of Justice, to an individual, September 8, 1999, reprinted in the *Institution of the Huqúqu'lláh Newsletter*, no. 38 (Oct. 1999).
13. Universal House of Justice, Riḍván Message to the Bahá'ís of the world, April 2000.
14. National Spiritual Assembly of the Bahá'ís of the United States, in a letter to all Local Spiritual Assemblies, August 15, 2007.

15. 'Abdu'l-Bahá, *Paris Talks*, Ch. 18, para. 4, p. 56.
16. Shoghi Effendi, letter of July 18, 1957, in *Messages to Canada*, p. 67.
17. Shoghi Effendi, letter of July 28, 1939, in *Messages to America*, p. 28.
18. Bahá'u'lláh, *The Seven Valleys*, p. 9.
19. See Deut. 14:2 and 1 Pet. 2:9. Considering that Jews have traditionally been called 'the chosen people', it is interesting that Mormons consider themselves 'Israelites by . . . adoption' (*Gospel Principles*, ch. 42, p. 273).
20. Random House Webster's College Dictionary.
21. 'Abdu'l-Bahá, *Selections*, no. 35, pp. 70-71.
22. 3 Nephi 12:2.
23. Scott, 'The Power of a Strong Testimony', in *Ensign* (Nov. 2001), p. 87.
24. Bahá'u'lláh, *Hidden Words*, Persian no. 33.
25. Bahá'u'lláh, *Kitáb-i-Íqán*, para. 216, 195-6.
26. 'Abdu'l-Bahá, *Tablets of Abdul-Baha Abbas*, p. 706; also in *Bahá'í World Faith*, p. 369.
27. Bahá'u'lláh, Short Obligatory Prayer, in most Bahá'í prayer books.
28. Bahá'u'lláh, *Kitáb-i-Íqan*, para. 99, p. 91.
29. 'Abdu'l-Bahá, *Tablets of Abdul-Baha Abbas*, p. 194.
30. 'Abdu'l-Bahá, talk on 3 December 1912, in *The Promulgation of Universal Peace*, p. 461.
31. Bahá'u'lláh, in *Bahá'í Education*, p. 5.

Chapter 14
1. Letter dated 7 February 1977 on behalf of the Universal House of Justice to an individual, in *Lights of Guidance*, no. 1028, p. 380.
2. Collins, 'The Bahá'í Faith and Mormonism: Further Reflections', in *World Order*, vol. 17, no. 3 (Spring 1983), pp. 25-33.
3. 'Abdu'l-Bahá, *Selections*, no. 212, p. 268.
4. Bahá'u'lláh, Lawh-i-Hikmat (Tablet of Wisdom), in *Tablets of Bahá'u'lláh*, p. 142.
5. Bahá'u'lláh, *Gleanings*, IV, para. 1, p. 6.
6. Pace, 'Follow the Prophet', in *Ensign* (May 1989), p. 25.
7. Christiansen, 'Power Over Satan', in *Ensign* (Nov. 1974), p. 22.
8. Christiansen, 'The Adversary', in *New Era* (Sept. 1975), p. 4.
9. Quoted in Honnold, *Vignettes from the Life of 'Abdu'l-Bahá*, p. 10.
10. Christiansen, 'The Adversary', in *New Era* (Sept. 1975), p. 4.
11. Bahá'u'lláh, Lawh-i-Maqsúd (Tablet of Maqsúd), in *Tablets of Bahá'u'lláh*, p. 173.
12. Shoghi Effendi, *Arohanui*, no. 18.
13. Bahá'u'lláh, Tablet of Ishráqát (Splendours), Eighth Ishráq, in *Tablets of Bahá'u'lláh*, p. 128; also in Bahá'u'lláh, *The Kitáb-i-Aqdas*, pp. 91-2.
14. 'Abdu'l-Bahá, *Selections*, no. 15, p. 30.
15. Bahá'u'lláh, *Gleanings*, LXXXIX, para. 3, p. 176.
16. 'Abdu'l-Bahá, *Selections*, no. 34, p. 69.
17. 'Abdu'l-Bahá, *Selections*, no. 12, p. 27.
18. Letter on behalf of Shoghi Effendi to an individual, October 28, 1925, in *Unfolding Destiny*, p. 421.

19. Bahá'u'lláh, Ṭarázat (Ornaments), Second Ṭaráz, in *Tablets of Bahá'u'lláh*, pp. 35-6.

Appendix 1

1. Hinckley, 'What Are People Asking about Us?', in *Ensign* (Nov. 1998), p. 70.
2. Felicia R. Lee, ' "Big Love": Real Polygamists Look at HBO Polygamists and Find Sex', in *New York Times*, March 28, 2006 (http://www.nytimes.com/2006/03/28/arts/television/28poly.html).
3. D&C 132:61-63.
4. *Our Heritage: A Brief History of the Church of Jesus Christ of Latter-Day Saints*, p. 93.
5. Heber C. Kimball, in *Millennial Star*, vol. 28, no. 12, p. 190.
6. Stanley B. Kimball, 'The Mormon Battalion March, 1846–47', in *Ensign* (July 1979), p. 57.
7. Discourse by Elder Joseph F. Smith July 7, 1878, in *Journal of Discourses*, vol. 20, p. 28.
8. Discourse by President Brigham Young, August 31, 1873, in *Journal of Discourses*, vol. 16, p. 166.
9. *History of the Church*, vol. 5, p. xxx.
10. ibid. p. xxix.
11. D&C 132:54.
12. William Clayton, in a sworn statement before John T. Caine, a notary public in Salt Lake City, on February 16, 1874; cited in *History of the Church*, vol. 5, p. xxxii.
13. Joseph Smith Jr., October 5, 1843, in *History of the Church*, vol. 6, p. 46. Emphasis in original.
14. Frequently Asked Questions about the Community of Christ (fka Reorganized Church of Jesus Christ of Latter Day Saints), retrieved September 3, 2006, from http://www.cofchrist.org/seek/faq.asp.
15. Jacob 2:24-27.
16. D&C 132:1, 34-35.
17. D&C 132:38-39.
18. Matt. 1:6.
19. www.lds.org, Newsroom, 'Myth-Conceptions about the Church'.
20. 'John Taylor: A Letter from Exile', in *Tambuli* (Nov. 1978), p. 31.
21. Discourse by Elder Orson Pratt, October 6, 1879, in *Journal of Discourses*, vol. 20, p. 326.
22. Discourse by Elder George Q. Cannon, July 20, 1879, in *Journal of Discourses*, vol. 20, p. 326.
23. Hartley and Sessions, *Church History c. 1878-1898, Late Pioneer Utah Period*.
24. *Our Heritage*, p. 93.
25. ibid.
26. D&C Official Declaration 1, from the Cache Stake Conference, Logan, Utah, Sunday, November 1, 1891. Cited in Woodruff, *Discourses*, p. 215.
27. Wilford Woodruff, cited in Clark, *Messages of the First Presidency of The Church of Jesus Christ of Latter-day Saints*, vol. 5, p. 320.
28. Ostling and Ostling, *Mormon America*, pp. 76-9.

29. Topping, 'One Hundred Years at the Utah State Historical Society'.
30. *BYU 1983-84 Fireside and Devotional Speeches*, September 20, 1983, p. 11; cited in Hinckley, *Teachings of Gordon B. Hinckley*, pp. 35-6.
31. Bahá'u'lláh, *The Kitáb-i-Aqdas*, para. 63.
32. Bahá'u'lláh, *The Kitáb-i-Aqdas*, note 89.
33. Qur'án 4:3. (Yusuf Ali translation).
34. Qur'án 4:129 (Yusuf Ali translation).

Appendix 2
1. *Gospel Principles*, Unit Ten: Life After Death, ch. 46: The Last Judgment, Judgments of God, p. 294; scriptural references removed.
2. *Encyclopedia of Latter-Day Saint History*, s.v. 'Blacks'.
3. Conkling, *A Joseph Smith Chronology*, p. 87.
4. Embry, *Black Saints in a White Church*, p. 39.
5. 'News of the Church', in *Ensign* (Jan. 2003), p. 78.
6. Moses 7:8.
7. Moses 7:22.
8. Joseph Smith Jr, *History of the Church*, vol. 3, p. xxvi.
9. *Journal of Discourses*, vol. 10, p. 250.
10. Alma 3:6.
11. 3 Nephi 2:14-16.
12. 2 Nephi 30:6.
13. Ostling and Ostling, *Mormon America*, p. 99.
14. Jacob 3:9.
15. 2 Nephi 26:33.
16. B. H. Roberts, in Joseph Smith Jr, *History of the Church*, vol. 3, p. xxix.
17. 'Abdu'l-Bahá, Tablet addressed to the Bahá'ís of the United States and Canada, April 8, 1916, in *Tablets of the Divine Plan*, p. 33.
18. Burnett, 'Lamanites and the Church', in *Ensign* (July 1971), p. 11.
19. Interviews conducted as part of the radio documentary 'Saints and Indians', a feature of the Worlds of Difference Project (www.homelands.org/worlds). Broadcast on National Public Radio's *Talk of the Nation* on January 23, 2005.
20. Bahá'u'lláh, *Prayers and Meditations*, CXXXVII.
21. ibid. CLXXVIII.
22. Qur'án 3:104-107.
23. Embry, *Black Saints in a White Church*, pp. 9-10.
24. As of 1984, the RLDS Church has also allowed women to be ordained to the priesthood.
25. Ostling and Ostling, *Mormon America*, p. 344.
26. Embry, *Black Saints in a White Church*, p. 12.
27. The mention of Cincinnati is a specific reference to Elijah Abel, for whom Joseph Smith had a profound respect (*Black Saints*, p. 38).
28. Joseph Smith, January 1843, in *History of the Church*, vol. 5, pp. 217-18.
29. Joseph Smith, in *History of the Church*, vol. 3, p. 29 (May 8, 1838).
30. The introduction to D&C 134 reads, '*A declaration of belief regarding governments and laws in general, adopted by unanimous vote at a general assembly of the Church*

held at Kirtland, Ohio, August 17, 1835.' B.H. Roberts in *History of the Church* reports that Joseph himself 'was absent from Kirtland at the time of the general assembly of the priesthood which accepted it, on a visit to the Saints in Michigan' (vol. 5, p. xxxi), so we cannot be sure that Smith agreed with this opinion.

31. D&C 134:12.
32. Joseph Smith in *History of the Church*, vol. 2, p. 453.
33. B. H. Roberts, in Joseph Smith Jr, *History of the Church*, vol. 3, p. xxiii; emphasis in original.
34. ibid. p. xxiii.
35. *Journal of Discourses*, vol. 10, p. 190.
36. John Taylor, in *Journal of Discourses*, vol. 21, p. 16.
37. Elder Melvin J. Ballard, *Conference Report*, April 1915, Second Overflow Meeting, pp. 61-2.
38. Elder George F. Richards, *Conference Report*, April 1939, Second Day, Morning Meeting, pp. 58-9.
39. Statement of the First Presidency to President Ernest L. Wilkinson of the Brigham Young University, cited in Andrus, *Doctrinal Commentary on the Pearl of Great Price*, pp. 406-7; partially cited in Ostling and Ostling, *Mormon America*, p. 101. Note that Andrus dates this statement to August 17, 1951, while Ostling and Ostling use August 17, 1949.
40. Ostling and Ostling, *Mormon America*, p. 361.
41. www.lds.org, Newsroom, 'Myth-Conceptions about the Church' (http://lds.org/newsroom/page/0,15606,4038-1---16-168,00.html).
42. Merrill J. Bateman, cited in Jackson, 'News of the Church', in *Ensign* (Sept. 2003), p. 78.
43. McConkie, *Mormon Doctrine*, 1958 ed.
44. McConkie, 'All Are Alike unto God', an address to a Book of Mormon Symposium for Seminary and Institute Teachers, Brigham Young University, 18 August 1978; cited in Embry, *Black Saints in a White Church*, pp. 34-35.
45. Hinckley, 'Priesthood Restoration', in *Ensign* (Oct. 1988), p. 69.
46. Searle, 'Four Who Serve', in *Ensign* (Feb. 1992), p. 38.
47. Ostling and Ostling, *Mormon America*, pp. 103-4.
48. McConkie, *Mormon Doctrine*, 2nd ed. (rev. 1979), p. 114; also cited in Ostling and Ostling, *Mormon America*, p. 103.
49. ibid. p. 527.
50. Alma 3:6-15.
51. Ostling and Ostling, *Mormon America*, p. 99.
52. 'Abdu'l-Bahá, in *Bahá'í World Faith*, p. 359.
53. Embry, *Black Saints in a White Church*, p. 77.
54. Cited in Ostling and Ostling, *Mormon America*, p. 106.
55. www.lds.org, Newsroom, 'Myth-Conceptions about the Church' (http://lds.org/newsroom/page/0,15606,4038-1---16-168,00.html).
56. Elder R. Lloyd Smith, 'Sharing the Gospel with Sensitivity', in *Ensign* (Jun. 2002), p. 53.

Appendix 3

1. McConkie, *Mormon Doctrine*, 2nd ed., p. 628.
2. ibid. p. 626.
3. Joseph Smith Jr, from a letter to the Church dated March 25, 1839, written from Liberty Jail in Clay County, Missouri, cited in *History of the Church*, vol. 3, pp. 303-4.
4. Joseph Smith Jr, in *Times and Seasons* (Apr. 15, 1842), reproduced in *History of the Church*, vol. 4, pp. 595-6. Emphasis in original.
5. Joseph Smith Jr, in *History of the Church*, vol. 6, p. 213.
6. John C. Bennett, the mayor of Nauvoo who undersigned this ordinance, was appointed 'assistant president' to the First Presidency one month later on April 8, 1841 (*History of the Church*, vol. 4, pp. 340-41).
7. City Ordinances, in *Times and Seasons*, vol. 2, no. 9 (Mar. 1, 1841), p. 337.
8. D&C 18:20.
9. Articles of Faith, 11.
10. 2 Nephi 29:8, 11.
11. Alma 29:8.
12. Rasmussen, 'Zoroastrianism', in *Ensign* (Nov. 1971), p. 32. Emphasis in original.
13. Gordon B. Hinckley, from an interview with Philippines Television, 30 April 1996; cited in 'Messages of Inspiration from President Hinckley', in *LDS Church News* (Feb. 1996).
14. Ballard, 'Doctrine of Inclusion', in *Ensign* (Nov. 2001), pp. 36-7.
15. ibid.
16. ibid. p. 38.
17. Toronto, 'A Latter-day Saint Perspective on Muhammad', in *Ensign* (Aug. 2000), p. 51.
18. Ballard, 'Doctrine of Inclusion', in *Ensign* (Nov. 2001), p. 35.
19. The Universal House of Justice, *One Common Faith*, p. 52.
20. The Universal House of Justice, Letter to the Conference of the Continental Boards of Counsellors, December 27, 2005, in *Turning Point*, p. 200, para.15.

Appendix 4

1. Collins, 'The Bahá'í Faith and Mormonism: A Preliminary Survey', in *World Order*, vol. 15, no. 1/2 (Fall 1980/Winter 1981), pp. 33-45.
2. Interview of Sachiro Fujita by Sylvia Ioas, Mount Carmel, November 24, 1965 (http://bahai-library.com/pilgrims/fujita.html).
3. Collins, 'The Bahá'í Faith and Mormonism', op.cit.
4. Shoghi Effendi, in *Directives from the Guardian*, no. 1.

Index

427

Arabia 260, 353
Arizona 2, 6, 306, 333-4
armaments 281
arrogance 130-31
art(s) 153, 154, 170, 243, 303, 315
Articles of Faith 50-51, 52-92, 325, 352
  see also specific entries
asceticism 174, 306
Assemblies (Bahá'í) *see* Spiritual
  Assemblies
assistance, divine 212-13
Assyria 291
audacity 318
authority
  in Bahá'í Faith 73, 106-7, 130, 253
  civil 89-90
  in LDS Church 59-61, 65, 73
  see also priesthood authority
  responsibility of those in 313
Auxiliary Boards 73, 130
Aztecs 37

Báb 9, 101, 167, 249, 277-8, 286, 418
  Declaration of 23, 24, 27, 217, 241-2,
    418
  Dispensation of 274, 285
  prophecies of 11, 275, 285
  Resurrection, explanation of 11, 136
  Revelation, Writings of 32, 94, 195
  Shrine of 272
Bábís 9, 285
Babylon 216, 311, 414
backbiting 172
Bádí' 278
Bahá'í(s), Bahá'í Faith
  Administrative Order 7, 8, 73, 129,
    175, 189, 200-02, 265
  attitude to other religions 1, 59, 306,
    326, 328-31
  attitude to race 355-6, 362, 367, 368
    see also humanity; mankind, one-
    ness of
  community 130, 170, 179, 200-02,
    215-16, 253, 302, 307, 308-10,
    313-18, 323, 377-8
  conduct 170-71, 175-6, 302, 316-18,
    328-31

families *see* family
fundamentals of Faith 308-9
involvement in society 315-18
and Joseph Smith 31-4, 268, 324-5
and LDS missionaries 326-8
and LDS scriptures 40-41, 324-5
marriage *see* marriage
membership 4, 396-7
and non-members 200-02, 303, 377-8
new believers 309
pioneers 215-16, 219
principles 281, 302, 315-18, 322
  see also specific entries
responsibilities 73, 133-4, 160, 170,
  205-6, 210, 214, 254, 267, 271,
  302, 327
scholars, scholarship 237
training xiii, 180, 303
see also teaching
Bahá'í Councils, Regional 73
Bahá'í cycle, Era 10, 24, 82, 273, 275,
  280-81
Bahá'í Dispensation 268, 297
Bahá'í International Community 258-9
Bahá'í State, future 267
Bahá'í World Centre 5
Bahá'í World Commonwealth 87
Bahá'í Writings 41, 68, 76, 105, 195, 376
  see also specific entries
Bahá'u'lláh 23, 27, 249, 286
  Covenant of 65, 78, 97-8, 133, 253,
    265, 309, 318, 347
  Declaration of 23, 270, 285, 418
  Dispensation of 8, 84, 97, 268, 271,
    274, 275, 297
  and new name(s) 278
  Promised One 270
  Revelation of 32, 86, 94, 101-2, 242-
    5, 272, 275, 297, 355
  suffering of 11, 58, 129n, 280-81, 419
  Universal Manifestation 275
  vision in dungeon 14, 102
  Will and Testament of 253
  Writings of 194-5
    see also Bahá'í Writings
  see also Greatest Name, World Order
    of Bahá'u'lláh

CPSIA information can be obtained at www.ICGtesting.com
Printed in the USA
LVOW11s0812120615

442235LV00002B/2/P